revelation of Revelation

AN URGENT MESSAGE FOR THE CHURCH

VOLUME 1
INTRODUCTION TO REVELATION

The Naked Apostles
Phil and Colleen Livingston

Published by: The Naked Apostles

WAUCONDA, IL

Copyright © 2013, 2017, 2026 by The Naked Apostles, Phil and Colleen Livingston. Third edition 2026

All rights reserved. No part of this publication may be reproduced, distributed or transmitted in any form or by any means, including photocopying, recording, or other electronic or mechanical methods, without the prior written permission of the publisher, except in the case of brief quotations embodied in critical reviews and certain other noncommercial uses permitted by copyright law. For permission requests, write to the publisher, addressed "Attention: Permissions Coordinator," at the address below.

Phil and Colleen Livingston/The Naked Apostles
304 Barrington Road
Wauconda, IL 60084
www.nakedapostles.org
email: info@nakedapostles.org

Ordering Information:
Quantity sales. Special discounts are available on quantity purchases by corporations, associations, and others. For details, contact via email or the address above.

revelation of Revelation, *An Urgent Message for the Church* Volume 1: Introduction to Revelation/The Naked Apostles, Phil and Colleen Livingston.
ISBN 978-0-9960102-4-5

Table of Contents

Introduction 1
Chapter 1: The Seven Letters of Revelation 9
Chapter 2: The Vision of Revelation and the Four Narratives 25
Chapter 3: The Story of Judgment and Redemption 77
Chapter 4: Death, Salvation, and the Afterlife 89
Chapter 5: The Bride and the Woman who Rides the Beast 213
Chapter 6: What is Spiritual Union with Christ? 257
Glossary 343
Bibliography 383
About the Authors 385
Other Books by the Authors 391

Dedicated to those who through this book may become the Church Pure/the Bride of Christ

He who overcomes will inherit these things, and I will be his God and he will be My son.

— Revelation 21:7 New American Standard Bible

Volume 1
Introduction to Revelation

Volume 2
The Seven Letters of Revelation

Volume 3
The Seven Seals
The first narrative of the vision
6:1-11:19

Volume 4
The Main Characters
The second narrative of the vision
12:1-16:21

Volume 5
The Fall of Babylon and the *Church Corrupt*
The third narrative of the vision
17:1-21:8

Volume 6
The New Jerusalem
The fourth narrative of the vision
21:9-22:21

Introduction

There was a fellow from the big city. He was a bit lost in the country trying to get to his destination. He finally stopped and asked a local good ol' boy for directions. The local was friendly and polite as he greeted him with a big smile. The big city guy showed him a map and asked for directions. The good ol' boy looked at the map, gave it back and scratching his beard said, "You can't get there from here!"

revelation of Revelation is a six volume set. Volumes 2 through 6 are a line-by-line interpretation of the book of Revelation starting with the seven letters to the Church. It is not a fragmented interpretation where random verses are given meaning that sound good but invalidate other verses, as the majority of the teachings on Revelation do. revelation of Revelation is an interpretation that gives an understanding that causes every verse to seamlessly fit into every other verse without contradicting each other. Instead, the interpretation in these volumes goes on to fill in the blanks of the rest of scripture. This gives us more of a complete picture of them while clearing up any seeming contradictions in those books as well. In the end it is like the book of Revelation is a key that when understood in context to itself, unlocks all of the scriptures before it; just as the last chapter in a great mystery book finally allows its readers to understand the whole story.

AMP Rev 2:2-5 I know your industry and activities, laborious toil and trouble, and your patient endurance, and how you cannot tolerate wicked [men] and have tested and critically appraised those who call [themselves] apostles (special messengers of Christ) and yet are not, and have found them to be impostors and liars. I know you are enduring patiently and are bearing up for My name's sake, and you have not fainted or become exhausted or grown weary. <u>But I have this [one charge to make] against you: that you have left (abandoned) the love that you had at first [you have deserted Me,</u>

your first love]. Remember then from what heights you have fallen. Repent (change the inner man to meet God's will) and do the works you did previously [when first you knew the Lord], or else I will visit you and remove your lampstand from its place, unless you change your mind and repent.

When it comes to the majority of the contemporary teachings of the scriptures, including the understanding of our salvation, the saying of the good ol' boy is proven true, "You can't get there from here!" The way we understand our faith and the message of the Bible makes it impossible to understand the whole of it and unravel its mysteries. The Bible does not read like a step-by-step instruction manual. The reason being is because the way we understand the contents of the Bible frames it in a way that does not allow us to truly understand, or blinds us to a proper context that allows us to understand the whole of it. *Jesus* ran into this problem constantly from even the most educated among the keepers of the scriptures. For example, the learned Nicodemus could only think in terms of a physical rebirth. And as a result of his mindset, questioned *Jesus* wondering what that looks like because he could not think in terms of a spiritual rebirth—being reborn a spiritual creature—not born a second time as a physical creature (as in being reincarnated).

AMP Jn 3:4 Nicodemus said to Him, How can a man be born when he is old? Can he enter his mother's womb again and be born?

Even his apostles who learned from Him daily could not understand His meaning because of how they framed their understanding in a nonspiritual way. And again, to the Pharisees and to His disciples, *Jesus* says:

MSG Mt 16:5-12 On their way to the other side of the lake, the disciples discovered they had forgotten to bring along bread. In the meantime, Jesus said to them, "Keep a sharp eye out for Pharisee-Sadducee yeast." Thinking he was scolding them for forgetting bread, they discussed in whispers what to do. Jesus knew what they were doing and said, "Why all these worried whispers about forgetting the bread? Baby believers! Haven't you caught on yet? Don't you remember the five loaves of bread and the five thousand people, and how many baskets of fragments you picked up? Or the seven loaves that fed four thousand, and how many baskets of leftovers you collected? Haven't you realized yet that bread isn't the problem? The problem is yeast, Pharisee-Sadducee yeast." Then they got it: that he wasn't concerned about eating, but teaching—the Pharisee-Sadducee kind of teaching.

MSG Mt 15:12-20 Later his disciples came and told him, "Did you know how upset the Pharisees were when they heard what you said?" Jesus shrugged it off. "Every tree that wasn't planted by my Father in heaven will be pulled up by its roots. Forget them. They are blind men leading blind men. When a blind man leads a blind man, they both end up in the ditch." Peter said, "I don't get it. Put it in plain language."

Jesus replied, "You, too? Are you being willfully stupid? Don't you know that anything that is swallowed works its way through the intestines and is finally defecated? But what comes out of the mouth gets its start in the heart. It's from the heart that we vomit up evil arguments, murders, adulteries, fornications, thefts, lies, and cussing. That's what pollutes. Eating or not eating certain foods, washing or not washing your hands—that's neither here nor there."

MSG Mk 7:18 Jesus said, "Are you being willfully stupid? Don't you see that what you swallow can't contaminate you?

Without the wisdom of our understanding being framed in a spiritual sense, we may derive good life lessons from the Bible but never truly understand, even skew its true meaning.

Likewise, many of the messages in the Bible are fragments that we must glean together with the whole to understand. For example, the New Testament letters speak in a way that leave out much information for us to fully understand because there are parts that the writers assume their readers already know as foundational to their faith, because they themselves taught them in person.

AMP2Th 2:5 Do you not recollect that when I was still with you, I told you these things?

This fact, the cultural differences between their times and ours, coupled with language translations and the thousands of years that separated us from the circumstances that were addressed in their writings, makes it very difficult to have a proper and wholistic context of their meanings.

This is Volume 1, *Introduction to Revelation*. It focuses on explaining many foundational Biblical concepts in a unified context that does not invalidate the meaning of other areas of the scriptures, giving the impression that those areas contradict each other. Volume 1 is devoted to bringing a unifying understanding of the Bible before we set off on a line-by-line interpretation of the book of Revelation, which begins with Volume 2, *The Seven Letters of Revelation*. To understand the messages and the salvation of Christ in the unifying context that we outline in this Volume, makes it possible for us to, "get there from here." With these unifying foundational understandings that Volume 1 addresses, the book of Revelation becomes a key that unlocks our minds to see the true meaning of the Bible and all prophecy.

The book of Revelation and its seven letters are written to those who have given their lives to Christ. It is addressed to no one else. Once properly interpreted, Revelation is a clear description of what is going to happen in the *end times* as well as encapsulating history past and present, from the garden and original sin then the new beginning to the end. The new beginning is referring to post-flood history.

The *new beginning* was life on earth starting over with the eight people and the animals who were with them on the ark and had survived the flood. However, evil went right back to work in humans after the new beginning. Revelation speaks about the second and final time God decided to destroy all of humanity, only this time the earth and the entire natural universe. The *first judgment* saved a contingency of both humans and animals before a flood destroyed all other living things.

This *second judgment*, which we are under currently, will utterly destroy all flesh, the earth, and the universe it resides in. The first was of water and the second is of fire. Through Revelation we will see that this *second judgment* is already in process since a few generations after the new beginning (the flood).

God had made a promise to Noah at the new beginning.

NIV Ge 9:9-17 *"I now establish my covenant with you and with your descendants after you and with every living creature that was with you—the birds, the livestock and all the wild animals, all those that came out of the ark with you—every living creature on earth. I establish my covenant with you: <u>Never again will all life be cut off by the waters of a flood; never again will there be a flood to destroy the earth.</u>" And God said, "This is the sign of the covenant I am making between me and you and every living creature with you, a covenant for all generations to come: I have set my rainbow in the clouds, and it will be the sign of the covenant between me and the earth. Whenever I bring clouds over the earth and the rainbow appears in the clouds, I will remember my covenant between me and you and all living creatures of every kind.<u> Never again will the waters become a flood to destroy all life.</u> Whenever the rainbow appears in the clouds, I will see it and remember the everlasting covenant between God and all living creatures of every kind on the earth." So God said to Noah, "This is the sign of the covenant I have established between me and all life on the earth."*

It could be reasonable to believe that the Lord made this promise about water so we would not fear the rains which bring us life sustaining water. This is what was written about the *second judgment:*

AMP 2Pe 3:4-12 *. . . Where is the promise of His coming? For since the forefathers fell asleep, all things have continued exactly as they did from the beginning of creation. For they willfully overlook and forget this [fact], <u>that the heavens [came into] existence long ago by the word of God, and the earth also which was formed out of water and by means of water, Through which the world that then [existed] was deluged with water and perished. But by the same word the present heavens and earth have been stored up (reserved) for fire, being kept until the day of judgment and destruction of the ungodly people.</u> Nevertheless, do not let this one fact escape you, beloved, that with the Lord one day is as a thousand years and a thousand* *years as one day. The Lord does not delay and is not tardy or slow about what He promises, according to some people's conception of slowness, but He is long-suffering (extraordinarily patient) toward you, not desiring that any should perish, but that all should turn to repentance. <u>But the day of the Lord will come like a thief, and then the heavens will vanish (pass away) with a thunderous crash, and the [material] elements [of the universe] will be dissolved with fire, and the earth and the works that are upon it will be burned up.</u> Since all these things are thus in the process of being dissolved, what kind of person ought [each of] you to be [in the meanwhile] in consecrated and holy behavior and devout and godly qualities, While you wait and earnestly long for (expect and hasten) <u>the coming of the day of God by reason of which the flaming heavens will be dissolved, and the [material] elements [of the universe] will flare and melt with fire?</u>*

The *first judgment* was of water. We see God's promise kept by making the *final judgment* of fire. The *first judgment* of water left a new beginning for man. The final judgement of fire leaves no such opportunity. The physical human race will become extinct as well as the physical universe itself. However, within His judgment of humanity, God also executes a plan of *redemption*. It is not, however, for eight to start over, for natural humans to have a third chance to evolve without turning to evil, but instead for a number beyond counting to transcend the natural universe. If one believes in Noah and the flood, one then must believe in the *last day* to come and the *lake of fire* which will destroy every atom of the physical universe, as Peter pointed out.

AMP 2Pe 3:5-7 For they willfully overlook and forget this [fact], that the heavens [came into] existence long ago <u>by the word of God</u>, and the earth also which was formed out of water and by means of water, Through which the world that then [existed] was deluged with water and perished. <u>But by the same word</u> the present heavens and earth have been stored up (reserved) for fire, being kept until the day of judgment and destruction of the ungodly people.

Revelation shows us what brought us to this place of judgment. Likewise, how many squander its opportunity of a new beginning. Humanity has and is demonstrating, like a dog returning to his own vomit, that it desires to return to the pre-flood conditions which brought on that *first judgment*. Then Revelation shows us how the conduct of our ancestors has affected our future. It reveals clearly that from the new beginning to the end, which is approaching swiftly, man was and is bent on living by his own rules independent from God. The book of Revelation explains the harsh and sobering truth of the awful things God is allowing to happen as a part of His plan for redemption and judgment of the human race. It is important to realize that although God wills that all be saved, everyone will not be redeemed.

Chapter One

The Seven Letters of Revelation

The book of Revelation starts with a comprehensive letter of admonishment from *Jesus* to the whole Church, for all ages. In keeping with the privileges of being His own we are not blind-sighted and overtaken with life as it unfolds. We (us followers) do not have to live in a reactive way of facing life, but as proactive. It is not so much that we have control over our circumstances or how they unfold, but we can know what lies ahead given the choices we make and paths we travel. By the nature of our relationship with the Lord, we are not to be caught by surprise. Instead through Him we can have the needed insight to know how to navigate through our circumstances, and the wisdom to know the best path we should take. Not only for insider knowledge of how the world turns out, but in our everyday life. Call it, being prophetic, but it is one of the privileges and benefits we possess as the Lord's followers. Whether we tap into that advantage or not or offend His Spirit in a way that the Lord takes away that privilege, is another story. For those Christians who have offended the *Holy Spirit* by not serving Him but themselves, the Lord takes away this privilege of knowing; just as He states:

AMP Rev 3:1-3 AND TO the angel (messenger) of the assembly (church) in Sardis write: These are the words of Him Who has the seven Spirits of God [the sevenfold Holy Spirit] and the seven stars: I know your record and what you are doing; you are supposed to be alive, but [in reality] you are dead. Rouse yourselves and keep awake, and strengthen and invigorate what remains and is on the point of dying; for I have not found a thing that you have done [any work of yours] meeting the requirements of My God or perfect in His sight. So call to mind the lessons you received and heard; continually lay them to heart and obey them, and repent. In case you will not rouse yourselves and keep awake and watch, <u>I will come upon you like a thief, and you will not know or suspect at what hour I will come.</u>

With *Jesus* knowing the tendencies and errors to come, you can say His letters are the sevenness of His admonishment and encouragement to all of the Church for all time. Why is the number 7 used so many times and what does it signify? Letters of the Hebrew alphabet have deep spiritual meanings. Each letter has a numeric value as well. Unlike English where numbers have their own symbols apart from the letters of the alphabet, Hebrew letters double as numbers, each having a numeric value. There are 22 letters in their alphabet which have corresponding numeric values. Just as Hebrew letters have meaning, so do their corresponding numeric values have meaning. The seventh letter in the Hebrew alphabet is "Zayin," and it is also the number seven. The meaning of seven is divine perfection and completion. The number seven is used often in Revelation, in fact seven is a major theme of Revelation concerning all that it prophetically says will take place. What that then reflects is the "sevenness" of the subject, the divine perfection and completion of the subject spoken. Nothing is left undone, it is comprehensive and nothing needs to be added.

For example, in Revelation when the seventh and final seal opens up, its opening is the release of the *seven trumpets*, which are the release of seven different plagues. The sixth and seventh seals represent the seven years outpouring of God's judgment and wrath on the *Church Corrupt*, and on the world who persecute the people of God. The sixth seal has as its focus the judgment against, and redemption of the *Church Corrupt*. The seventh seal has as its focus God's wrath against the whole of the world who persecuted His elect. Both seals are opened at the same time because they are different aspects of the same seven-year time period. However, since God uses the evil in this world as a means to execute His judgment against the *Church Corrupt*, it says that when the seventh seal was opened, there was a half an hour of silence in Heaven. Since the sixth and seventh seals are opened simultaneously because they merely break down the same seven years of wrath, the half hour of silence is during the first 3½ years (when the Christians are being persecuted). This silence can also be interpreted as being still or inactive. One half of an hour represents a half-cycle of time. In this case, the cycle of time which is being referred to is a seven-year period, or a week of years.

NIV Rev 17:11-14 *The beast who once was, and now is not, is an eighth king. He belongs to the seven and is going to his destruction. "The ten horns you saw are ten kings who have not yet received a kingdom, but who <u>for one hour</u> will receive authority as kings along with the beast. They have one purpose and will give their power and authority to the beast. They will make war against the Lamb, but the Lamb will overcome them because he is Lord of lords and King of kings—and with him will be his called, chosen and faithful followers."*

In the book of Revelation, the seven years of God's wrath (the time of the beast) is referred to as "one hour." So when Revelation tells us about the *great tribulation* it refers to it as about a half an hour of silence/inactivity from Heaven which equates into 3½ years.

In other words, the seventh seal was in a refrain for 3½ years before the contents of the seventh seal could be implemented and loosed in the world. This is so the whole world would first finish its destiny of effecting judgment against the *Church Corrupt*. However, once that is accomplished, God's wrath will waste no time in punishing the world. The judgment of the *Church Corrupt* is carried out by the human forces of the world while the Heavens are silent—inactive, not answering the prayers of the saints or intervening to aid them, letting the world have the world. This state is biblically referred to as a *desolation*. It is a time period when the Lord turns His face away from any intervening help while giving the people over to their own devices. This is His way of resisting the proud or those who fall away to worship other gods.

NIV Da 9:26B *... The end will come like a flood: War will continue until the end, and <u>desolations have been decreed.</u>*

AMP Jas 4:5-8 *Or do you suppose that the Scripture is speaking to no purpose that says, The Spirit Whom He has caused to dwell in us yearns over us and He yearns for the Spirit [to be welcome] with a jealous love? But <u>He gives us more and more grace (power of the Holy Spirit, to meet this evil tendency and all others fully). That is why He says, God sets Himself against the proud and haughty, but gives grace [continually] to the lowly (those who are humble enough to receive it).</u> be subject to God. Resist the devil [stand firm against* *him], and he will flee from you. Come close to God and He will come close to you.*

AMP 2Ch 7:13-15 If I shut up heaven so no rain falls, or if I command locusts to devour the land, or if I send pestilence among My people (describing a desolation), *If My people, who are called by My name, shall humble themselves, pray, seek, crave, and require of necessity <u>My face and turn from their wicked ways, then will I hear from heaven, forgive their sin, and heal their land. Now My eyes will be open and My ears attentive to prayer offered in this place.</u>*

It is important to take note that throughout history, and especially when it comes to His "people," these time periods of *desolation* were regional ones meant to turn them back to Him. However, the *desolation* time period during the first 3½ years of His 7 years of wrath, is a *global desolation* and is likewise meant to turn the Church Corrupt back to Him.

NIV Rev 8:1-2 When he opened the seventh seal, there was silence in heaven for about half an hour (half of a week of years—3 ½ years). *And I saw the seven angels who stand before God, and to them were given seven trumpets.*

During that *desolation* time of silence or inactivity, the world kills every believer they can get their hands on. However, when it is over and time for the world to get its comeuppance during the final 3½ years, the *desolation* ends. God intervenes by putting a mark on each surviving believer that held fast to his belief. They cannot be killed or harmed just as the Israelites who had their doorpost marked with the blood of the lamb while wrath was poured out against Egypt. Then, His intervention continues with a variety of punishments carried out not by men, but by spiritual forces. Each being launched by the blast of a trumpet—*seven trumpets*.

When the *sixth seal* finishes its work in judgment against the saints, God turns His wrath against the world by sounding the *seven trumpets* releasing their corresponding plagues. In sounding the *seven trumpets* with their corresponding *seven bowls* of wrath, God is showing us that there is a sevenness to His wrath against the world. In other words, by framing His wrath in the *structure of sevens*, He is reflecting that His wrath against the world will be divinely perfect, and utterly comprehensive. No evil will go unaccounted for, will have opportunity to continue, or have the means to start again from its ashes.

With the release and completion of the *seventh seal*, God's plan for *judgment* and *redemption* is complete and perfect. The *seven trumpets* within the *seventh seal* is the perfect and complete execution of *judgment* against the world who hated His redeemed. This is something the saints can take confidence in; from its ashes, evil can never rise up again. Likewise, by God framing the execution of His plan for *judgment* and *redemption* (the *seven seals*) using the *structure of sevens* to frame it within, He is communicating that His plan is divinely perfect, and totally comprehensive, leaving no stone unturned. We know framing things within a sevenness is a true interpretation because just as the end of the world is framed within a sevenness, the creation of the world was also framed within the *structure of sevens*; the seven days of creation. The *structure of sevens* is the order and organization of God.

It is the same with the seven letters to the seven churches. Truly there were more than seven churches when *Jesus* wrote these letters. However, He used the *structure of sevens*. This means He broke things down, framing His emphasized points into seven categories—framed using a seven-point plan (as it were). What *Jesus* wrote, in its sevenness, is sufficient, perfectly covering everything the Church needs in order to avoid further error, in addition, the insight needed to recover from a falling away. *Jesus* does so showing us through these seven churches that their errors will be fatal if left unchecked.

These were not seven different letters just to the seven churches in Asia. They were not written as separate letters to be sent to only their corresponding churches. No! This was a single letter meant for and sent to all Christians and was a part of a bigger body of work which includes the rest of the book of Revelation. Each of the seven admonishments (letters) were addressed to a specific angel. However, during the time Revelation was written there were a great deal more than seven churches.

The following is in answer to those who would say the seven letters were written to the seven churches they were addressed to, and they are not prophetically speaking to the whole Church over all its ages.

NIV Rev 1:11-20 ... *"Write on a scroll what you see and send it to the seven churches: to Ephesus, Smyrna, Pergamum, Thyatira, Sardis, Philadelphia and Laodicea." I turned around to see the voice that was speaking to me. And when I turned I saw seven golden lampstands, and among the lampstands was someone "like a son of man," dressed in a robe reaching down to his feet and with a golden sash around his chest. His head and hair were white like wool, as white as snow, and his eyes were like blazing fire. His feet were like bronze glowing in a furnace, and his voice was like the sound of rushing waters. In his right hand he held seven stars, and out of his mouth came a sharp double-edged sword. His face was like the sun shining in all its brilliance. When I saw him, I fell at his feet as though dead. Then he placed his right hand on me and said: "Do not be afraid. I am the First and the Last. I am the Living One; I was dead, and behold I am alive for ever and ever! And I hold the keys of death and Hades.* <u>*"Write, therefore, what you have seen, what is now and what will take place later.*</u> *The mystery of the seven stars that you saw in my right hand and of the seven golden lampstands is this: The steven stars are the angels of the seven churches, and the seven lampstands are the seven churches.*

Note: The Lord says, *Write, therefore, what you have seen, what is now and what will take place later.* Showing that this single letter sent to the seven churches of Asia is prophetic, explaining to us a prophetic understanding of what is happening and what will unfold in the future. With these prophetic words framed within the *structure of sevens*, it tells us this single letter sent to the *seven churches* truly is a prophetic message spanning the entire history of the Church, now and until the end. Not only was all of what the Lord spoke to the individual sent to all seven churches addressed, but the entire book of Revelation was sent along with it as a single body of work. The balance of the Revelation letter gets into great detail about what the Lord spoke addressing the *seven churches* mentioned. To each one He addressed, *Jesus* ended with these words, "He who has an ear, let him hear what the Spirit says to the churches." By this statement *Jesus* is speaking to all His followers for all time. By saying in each occasion anyone who is willing, listen to what the Spirit is saying, He is not just talking to specific churches.

The book of Revelation starts out with *Jesus* walking among the *seven lampstands* with its seven angelic guardians over them in His hand. Those *seven lampstands* and their seven angelic guardians in Heaven before the throne of God most certainly are the sevenness of the whole Church over all its ages from the beginning to the end. That flame represents the *Holy Spirit* which is in the earth that burns within the hearts of all the individuals who comprise the Church from its beginning to its end. The fire in those lampstands is the *Spirit* of the *bride* already alive and ready to be received and embodied by those who would be redeemed. The living *Spirit* of life ultimately is not to be embodied by an inanimate object—a lampstand. No, the *Spirit* of the *bride* was perfected even before the creation of the world and has been waiting to be clothed and embodied with the living breathing *soul*s who would receive Him, His Church.

When the *Spirit* of the *bride* is finished being imparted to the full number of those who are to become His *bride* (born again of a new *spirit*) then there will be no need for the lampstands which house the *Spirit* of the *bride* in the meantime.

NIV Lk 14:16-23 *Jesus replied: "A certain man was preparing a great banquet and invited many guests. At the time of the banquet he sent his servant to tell those who had been invited, 'Come, for everything is now ready.' "But they all alike began to make excuses. The first said, 'I have just bought a field, and I must go and see it. Please excuse me.' "Another said, 'I have just bought five yoke of oxen, and I'm on my way to try them out. Please excuse me.' "Still another said, 'I just got married, so I can't come.' "The servant came back and reported this to his master. Then the owner of the house became angry and ordered his servant, 'Go out quickly into the streets and alleys of the town and bring in the poor, the crippled, the blind and the lame.' " 'Sir,' the servant said, 'what you ordered has been done, but there is still room.' "Then the master told his servant, 'Go out to the roads and country lanes and make them come in, so that my house will be full.*

The *delay* between the sixty-two sevens and the one-seven is the *Church Age*. This *delay* was created by God so that the *Spirit* of the *bride* would be appropriated by as many individuals who would receive it considering the Jews rejected their place as His *bride* (illustrated in the above verse). It is in the *Father*'s plans to have certain numbers who become *celestial* humans (the *bride* of *Christ*) and are saved from the destruction of humanity. This multitude beyond counting who will be saved in this *final judgment* infinitely surpasses the handful who survived the judgment of the flood.

For that *Spirit* within the lampstands will then finally burn within the *great multitude* and all those who are to become born again of a new Spirit. These living *soul*s are given *celestial* bodies (clean white robes) and will stand before Him embodying that *Spirit* of the *bride*, worshipping Him. The *Spirit* of the *bride* will then no longer be embodied in those *seven lampstands*. This was the plan of the *Father* and the promise of a *bride* to the *Son* from the beginning. The *Son* has known her and has been waiting since before creation for the *Spirit* of His *bride* to be made manifest in the *soul*s and persons of those who would love Him. In great expectation He has known the beauty of the *Spirit* of the *bride* long before the faces of His *bride* started to embody that *Spirit*.

Remember, sevenness is the theme and structure of Revelation. As such, it communicates utter inclusiveness, completeness, and perfection of what it tells. The *seven lampstands* in Heaven (the fullness of His *bride*, the *Church*) certainly is not merely seven of the Asian churches at the time this letter was written. When the vision shows us *Jesus* walking among the *seven lampstands*, inspecting them before speaking these letters to the *seven churches*, this is our clue that He is speaking to the whole *Church* over history future. As this is arguably the case, it would be better understood that those seven individual churches He addressed embodied the *spirit* and sevenness of everything which is correct and in error concerning the entire *Church* over all its existence, past, present, and future.

There are those who say that it is clear by His language that *Jesus* is addressing strictly those He specifically mentions, the *seven churches* only. Let us take a deeper look:

NIV Ge 3:16-19 *To the woman he said, "I will greatly increase your pains in childbearing; with pain you will give birth to children. Your desire will be for your husband, and he will rule over you." To Adam he said, "Because you listened to your wife and ate from the tree about which I commanded you, 'You must not eat of it,' "Cursed is the ground because of you; through painful toil you will eat of it all the days of your life. It will produce thorns and thistles for you, and you will eat the plants of the field. By the sweat of your brow you will eat your food until you return to the ground, since from it you were taken; for dust you are and to dust you will return."*

When the Lord spoke to Adam telling him the consequences of his sin, He told Him that it was by the sweat of his brow (hard labor) the ground would produce for him, and that his body would no longer live forever but will die and decompose back into the soil. You cannot say the Lord wasn't speaking in a prophetic way, and that His words were only for Adam and Eve since he used the pronouns "you" and "your" referring to only Adam and Eve. The Lord wasn't just talking to Adam about what Adam would experience because of his sin. No! Their sin introduced evil into all of humanity for all time, because his sin corrupted the human *spirit* for all. God was clearly speaking to Adam and Eve and all their offspring concerning everything that their sin affects, in a totally encompassing way.

Every individual born of Adam and Eve chooses between good and evil, however, the tendency and corrupt possibility is alive and living within them, desiring to have expression because of Adam's sin which necessitates a choice. Sin is a life-principle, it is a living *spirit*, it is the *spirit* of the *devil*, never at rest until it finds expression. Once it had been ingested into the human *spirit* and even into the *spirit* of the *Church*, it is not like a thorn stuck inside the flesh of the body, nor is it an unwelcome lifeless inanimate object inside of a host (human *spirit*). Rather it is a dormant but living *spirit* distorting our perception of life, looking and waiting to have expression. Once it enters in, like a common cold or a fever, it must run its course until it comes to its end. Those who have introduced sin into humanity and into the *Church* have done an abominable thing that has a festering and lasting ill effect on all humanity and on the *Church* until it has run its course by coming to the end of itself. That end (once it has run its course) is the death of it. Sin has no future. As Roman's tells us:

AMP Ro 6:21-23 But then what benefit (return) did you get from the things of which you are now ashamed? [None] for the end of those things is death. But now since you have been set free from sin and have become the slaves of God, you have your present reward in holiness and its end is eternal life. For the wages which sin pays is death, but the [bountiful] free gift of God is eternal life through (in union with) Jesus Christ our Lord.

As such, the consequences Adam's sin invoked were not just his but were imposed on all of humanity for all of history. All of humanity will die, and by sweat and toil will the ground produce food for them. The Lord was talking to all of mankind for all of history and what it would suffer as a result of the sin of Adam, when He was addressing Adam. Therefore, what He spoke to Adam was prophetic for all ages.

Likewise, it is the same for the errors or the sins of the Church. As *Jesus* pointed out to those *seven churches,* the evils introduced to the *Church* corrupted the entire Church for all time until it is purified through the *great tribulation.* As such, the introduction of those evils invoked and put into motion will play out through all the *Church* for all time. Based on what evil gets introduced into the *spirit* of the *Church, Jesus* predicted where the *Church* is going and what will happen as it grows like a bacteria and has expression over time. It is only when God intervenes and puts an end to evil in a way that destroys any and every means of expression it could have, will it cease to exist. The history of man, and the flood has shown God this. Even His beloved *Church* has proven this true as it does not heed His warnings in these *seven letters* becoming decidedly corrupt over time. He finally says of it, "I will spew you out of my mouth" (as told to us in these letters even thousands of years before it happened). How grievous it must have been for God to see sin enter into the previously pure human *spirit* of Adam and Eve, knowing how it will play itself out throughout all the history of mankind. Likewise, how grievous it must have been for *Jesus* to see sin enter into the hearts of those who possess the *Holy Spirit* (the *Spirit* of the *bride*) knowing how it will infect the *Church* future.

All Biblical prophecy speaks to the beginning and to the end of a matter. All Biblical prophecy has a *contemporary expression* and an *end times expression*. Likewise, all Biblical prophecy has a *regional/local manifestation* as well as a *global manifestation*. This is why *Jesus* said:

AMP Mt 5:18 *For truly I tell you, until the sky and earth pass away and perish, not one smallest letter nor one little hook [identifying certain Hebrew letters] will pass from the Law until all things [it foreshadows] are accomplished.*

The foreshadowing of a prophecy is not only the release of the words, but the local and contemporary manifestation of it. The accomplishment or fulfillment of the prophecy is the global and *end times* final manifestation of it. We may see the intervention of God in a matter and think of it as done and His people set free of their oppression. However, as long as even one minute factor remains incomplete, like an enemy not utterly defeated and not fully destroyed, the prophecy is not yet fulfilled to the letter.

When a factor of a prophecy remains incomplete, this means evil has not yet finished running its full course but has only been set back from its ultimate fulfillment. Likewise, the power of God has not yet brought it to its final end, leaving nothing to rise from its ashes. The Bible paints a picture of this kind of prophetic situation where evil against God's people has been defeated but not yet destroyed leaving it to rise up on another day. It refers to a stump of a tree which has been cut down, and a shoot grows up out of the stump. This guarantees that this enemy will someday resurface and once again become an issue. In the end, left to run its course, it will grow to a global scale. At which time the Lord will, according to His plans and timing, destroy the evil utterly, with nothing left to rise from the ashes, the stump pulled out of the earth and burned in the fire, forever. It is then that the sevenness of prophecy and of the law will be finished—fulfilled.

If the above is kept in mind, it is easier to understand prophecy. Without keeping the above in mind, it is difficult to separate out what has already happened in history from when, in a prophecy, it speaks about what will happen at the end. One would mistakenly believe the unfinished local and contemporary expression of a prophecy is the fulfillment of the prophecy. More accurately, it is the affirmation of what will take place on a global scale in the end and the foreshadowing of it. It is only when the Lord has caused evil to serve His plan for redemption on the proper scale and in the proper timing of it to serve His ultimate good, will He destroy it utterly. Thus, at that time fulfilling every letter of His prophetic words. Most often, the reason evil is left as a shoot to sprout up again is a matter of retarding its growth and maturity until it fulfills a global timing and its ultimate end.

The beginning and end of the matter is one in the eyes of the Lord, and when we read prophecy, this makes it hard for us who are one-dimensional to sort out the local and contemporary expression from the global and *end times* final expression.

Those *seven churches* the Lord addressed were practical examples (so to speak) embodying the sevenness of their errors/sins and His admonitions. Because the rest of the churches at that time and now are familiar with the struggles and reputations of those *seven churches*. For *Jesus* they were a perfect prophetic picture of the sevenness of what He wanted to communicate to His *Church* as a whole, over all time. Therefore, this makes these letters prophetic, showing the evils that infiltrate the *Church*. Then showing over history future, the results and consequences of the introduction of these evils as well as the remedies *Jesus* takes and the warnings He speaks concerning them.

To perceive and function according to the errors of the past may seem normal for the generations that follow. This is why *Jesus* says of them:

NIV Rev 2:4-5 Yet I hold this against you: You have forsaken your first love. Remember the height from which you have fallen! Repent and do the things you did at first. If you do not repent, I will come to you and remove your lampstand from its place.

However, we cannot say we are blind to them. That is because, He who walks among the lampstands studying the *Spirit* of His *bride* and how in the heart it fights against the sinful *spirit* of man, has told us through these *seven letters*. He has sufficiently admonished and warned us in advance (outlined the sevenness) concerning the effect over time that the introduction of these errors/sins has and will have upon us, His *Church*. Including the struggles we face in our *soul*s wrestling with giving priority and preference to and serving the new Spirit within, over the sinful *spirit* of man that we all possess. Until we die to this corrupt human body, we will have this cage match within and have to constantly choose which *spirit* within to serve. When we die to this body, we will not only be free from its corruptness, but we will be free from the sinful human *spirit* that animates it. To be free from the sinful human *spirit* is to be dead to the body it animates. It is only then that our *soul* will be clothed in a clean white robe, an uncorrupted *celestial* body, and the singular born again *spirit* that animates that (resurrected) body, will we be finally free from wrestling with our sin nature, which we will finally be dead to. Same *soul* (mind/personality), new incorruptible body, and new but pure *spirit* without the influence of our sinful human *spirit*. However, the Lord needs us to be His body in the earth moved by His *Spirit* in order to bring redemption to as many that will receive Him. So we must wrestle, patiently wait and serve the Lord until redemption has finished its work in us, finally freeing us utterly from our sin nature. This is why Paul says:

AMP 2Co 4:6-11 *For God Who said, Let light shine out of darkness, has shone in our hearts so as [to beam forth] the Light for the illumination of the knowledge of the majesty and glory of God [as it is manifest in the Person and is revealed] in the face of Jesus Christ (the Messiah). However, we possess this precious treasure [the divine Light of the Gospel] in [frail, human] vessels of earth, that the grandeur and exceeding greatness of the power may be shown to be from God and not from ourselves. We are hedged in (pressed) on every side [troubled and oppressed in every way], but not cramped or crushed; we suffer embarrassments and are perplexed and unable to find a way out, but not driven to despair; We are pursued (persecuted and hard driven), but not deserted [to stand alone]; we are struck down to the ground, but never struck out and destroyed; Always carrying about in the body the liability and exposure to the same putting to death that the Lord Jesus suffered, so that the [resurrection] life of Jesus also may be shown forth by and in our bodies. For we who live are constantly [experiencing] being handed over to death for Jesus' sake, that the [resurrection] life of Jesus also may be evidenced through our flesh which is liable to death.*

And again:

AMP Eph 1:10-14 [He planned] for the maturity of the times and the climax of the ages to unify all things and head them up and consummate them in Christ, [both] things in heaven and things on the earth. In Him we also were made [God's] heritage (portion) and we obtained an inheritance; for we had been foreordained (chosen and appointed beforehand) in accordance with His purpose, Who works out everything in agreement with the counsel and design of His [own] will, So that we who first hoped in Christ [who first put our confidence in Him have been destined and appointed to] live for the praise of His glory! In Him you also who have heard the Word of Truth, the glad tidings (Gospel) of your salvation, and have believed in and adhered to and relied on Him, were stamped with the seal of the long-promised Holy Spirit. That [Spirit] is the guarantee of our inheritance [the firstfruits, the pledge and foretaste, the down payment on our heritage], in anticipation of its full redemption and our acquiring [complete] possession of it—to the praise of His glory.

Revelation begins by showing real examples of the churches these evils have already infested. It also showed examples of the churches that have grown while maintaining the right heart and have not lost their first love. This Revelation letter contains specific words addressing the different hearts of His churches with the body of the letter showing us in detail how history will unfold. This body of work, Revelation, is to all the Christian Church over all time, warning, admonishing, encouraging, correcting and explaining everything so we are not ignorant, fearful, and discouraged over the profound events that must take place. The book of Revelation is a prophetic message that starts with an intimate and personal word to His *bride*. What follows is a graphically symbolic representation of what He tells His *bride*, the *Church,* and why history has to unfold this way. It was in this format that the letter (Revelation) was distributed to all of Christendom. Meaning, it is one piece of work meant for all the churches of all time to read and take to heart and not to specific churches.

As a final insight that speaks to the many who believe the first section was actually seven separate letters written only to the *seven churches* mentioned (in spite of the fact that they were not specifically addressed to them but to the angels over them). They argue that they do not see a prophetic style of communication about them, but more of a literal communication about the churches mentioned. This is a really short-sighted and a humanistic way of perceiving the words of *Jesus*. As pointed out, when *Jesus* views and speaks towards something, His wisdom and insight is not one-dimensional or flat as ours is. When He looks, He sees a thing as it is both in its essence, and what it looks like projected out into the future to its end. We, on the other hand, see things only as they are on the surface.

This is proven true when *Jesus* rebuked Peter by saying, "get behind me Satan." He was not simply name calling as we might name call because He was upset with what Peter suggested. It was because *Jesus*, in His normal way of perceiving, saw the *spirit* essence of the words which came out of Peter's mouth. When *Jesus* responded, He responded past the surface of who spoke and what was spoken, but He addressed the very essence of the *spirit* behind those words. He spoke directly to the *devil*, whose *spirit* and motivations those words were inspirited by. He spoke to the essence or the life-principle behind those words, and not to whom the mouth belonged which spoke them.

It is certain this may have confused and dismayed Peter, discouraged that *Jesus* was calling him Satan of all things. If it had, then Peter did not understand from what context and perception *Jesus* spoke from, any more than those who believe these letters are not prophetic and do not speak to the entire *Church* for all time. They erroneously assume *Jesus* thinks and perceives like them. That is why they are blind to a spiritual and prophetic perception, not believing these letters have a much larger scope than they assign them as having.

After these intimate words *Jesus* speaks directly to His *bride*, *Jesus* then prophetically tells His *bride* the story of sin, *redemption*, and *judgment* in its entire sevenness from beginning to end. That story sadly includes the fate of His *Church* who these errors/sins have entered into and have lost their first love of Him. Losing their first love, *Jesus*, does not mean they do not love Him anymore. It simply means they lost *Jesus* as being their first love, even their only love when it comes to preference, priority, and the "go to" choice when it comes to what they serve. When the honeymoon is over (so to speak) we all are guilty, in one degree or another, of going back to serving our own needs, desires and agendas first. We then start employing *Jesus* to fulfill our needs and plans as we prioritize them.

Concerning what follows after addressing *Church* issues, the book of Revelation outlines history, past and future, four times over. With each occasion there is a different subject, emphasis, and starting point. However, although they have different starting points, all four narratives end with the very end. Some give more or different details which by the end of the fourth narrative, there is a sevenness, a perfect and comprehensive understanding of what will take place and why. This tells us there is no special knowledge beyond this account that someone may claim to have. According to the *structure of sevens* there is no extra or special knowledge which is genuinely from God outside of what is contained on the pages of the book of Revelation. John affirms the sevenness of its content by saying at the end:

NAS Rev 22:18-19 *I testify to everyone who hears the words of the prophecy of this book: if anyone adds to them, God will add to him the plagues which are written in this book; and if anyone takes away from the words of the book of this prophecy, God will take away his part from the tree of life and from the holy city, which are written in this book.*

Chapter Two

The Vision of Revelation and the Four Narratives

After the seven letters are dictated there is a brief change of settings. John is called up to Heaven and the first of four narratives of the book of Revelation begins. Just as there are four gospels, there are four narratives of the Revelation. Again, numbers have important meanings. The number four means, God's creative works. Below is a description of the four different narratives of God's plan of redemption and judgment as told in Revelation:

The *first narrative* reveals the execution of God's plan for redemption and judgment, according to the *structure of sevens*. It starts at 6:1 and finishes with verse 11:18. This telling is accomplished through the vision of the breaking of the *seven seals* on the scroll. The scroll is a blueprint of the *Father*'s plan which has been kept secret. It is revealed only to the *Son* who will show Himself worthy by becoming the sacrificial Lamb that gives Himself up for the redemption of man. Then He is told by the *Father* to share its content with His servants, the prophets, so that the redeemed can also know and not be ignorant or surprised at what is to come and what it will accomplish.

As with all four narratives the first is a complete narrative letting us in on the "sevenness" of its scope. We see the main events through the breaking of the *seven seals*. Outlining a narrative of Revelation according to its sevenness is identical to the outline of the story of the seven days of creation. The seven days of creation revealed the entire scope of creation through its seven main or historically relevant and altering events making that narrative complete in its sevenness. We see the seven most influential happenings/events in the narrative of the *seven seals* which alter the natural course of the future, sealing the fate of humanity, the world, and the entire universe which it resides in. However, it is important to point out that the narrative of these seven "happenings" or "stages of events" are confined to revealing only the implementation of the intervening judgments and redemption of God. In this way, God gives His elect clarity, an unintrusive look specifically at the execution of sentence and clemency being imposed on humanity.

The narrative of the seven days of creation at the beginning of the Bible showed us the sevenness of God's power to design, create, and set into motion the universe we live in. The narrative of the *seven seals* at the end of the Bible shows us the sevenness of God's redemption in addition to His judgment, both of which have already been set in motion and are well along their way. This sevenness shows God's power to both bring to a screeching halt and destroy the entire universe that He set into motion at creation, as well as a power to save humans from the destruction despite themselves.

The first four seals were released simultaneously. They are referred to as the four horsemen, or as God calls them in the Old Testament, the four winds of His destruction. Contrary to the idea that everything in Revelation is futuristic, the four horsemen were released in the earth soon after the flood. At that time the world was judged for wanting the *antichrist* or the Assyrian, who is *Nimrod*, to be king over them. The world desired him to be king over them so they might be protected from God by this king of the world because they decided to no longer conform to the commands of God, but instead do as they will. Thus, *Nimrod* becomes the *antichrist*. It follows that the people decided to worship, as gods, the fallen angels who created the giants as well as the giants who were killed by the flood. They betrayed God and worshiped the very beings that God had saved them from. Could mankind slap the Almighty any more insultingly in the face?

After the flood and before the release of the four horsemen, their curses did not exist on mankind. These things were not a factor humanity had to contend with until a certain point in time. By all accounts, all the things that these four horsemen encompass and were loosed on the world were not prevalent until this judgement came along with the destruction of the Tower of Babel. At which time God spread mankind around the globe into 70 different nations assigning each a different language. Like a dog returning to its own vomit, we tried everything to rebuild the same conditions that prevailed before the flood. In 800AD Pope Leo III committed the same atrocity by revitalizing and reinstituting the fallen Roman Empire that had been destroyed. It then became the Holy Roman Empire.

Nimrod and the people at that time knew they were doing exactly what brought on the flood. We know this because one of the main purposes of the Tower of Babel they built was to protect themselves with higher ground in the case God brought down another flood, because of what they were indulging in.

It must be kept in mind that because of its sevenness, each narrative is a comprehensive telling of the subject it is covering. The fact that the four horsemen was released soon after the flood is telling us that the judgement of fire has been already set in motion as early as four generations after the flood. The Tower of Babel fell 339 years after Noah and his family disembarked the ark. Noah, his son Shem, and Abraham were alive when the tower fell. We are still under the curse of the four horsemen and will remain so until *Jesus* returns.

It seems unconscionable that after a demonstration of such destructive power that God released, that man, so bent on rebellion, would go right back to it so soon afterwards. However, through the agendas of Ham and his wife and one of their offspring, *Nimrod*, he incites the people to rebel against God. Those who were not willing, *Nimrod* forced through violence to worship the hierarchy of gods and *demigod*s he instated. Persecution of the God-fearing people to become apostates started back then as *Nimrod* constructed his empire.

Nimrod is born a giant through the interbreeding of the corrupted giant genes in the wife of Ham. This is a factor that the three sons of Noah did not have in their DNA. It is said in Genesis that Noah and his family were the only people whose genes had not been corrupted in the *preflood* days. However, this does not account for the wives of their sons. In particular, Ham's wife is responsible for bringing the giant gene on this side of the flood. *Nimrod*, being a giant himself is hateful of God for wiping off the face of the earth all the giants (*demigods*) through the flood. Likewise, he hated God for confining to the *Abyss* the fallen angelic *celestial* beings who coupled with physical human women, producing the giants. This intervention and act by the Almighty gave man a fresh start on the other side of the flood freeing them from the hell and dominating influence the gods and *demigods* heartlessly and mercilessly exerted over man. Humans, the crown of God's creation, became like soulless cattle or sheep to them. God was freeing man from their influence while taking back His rightful authority over humanity.

Giants were also biblically known as; *Nephilim*, men of renown, or *demigods* (according to mythologies). When, for example, a Roman emperor declared himself a god, they were declaring themselves to have, as a part of their nature, *celestial* origins or that they were the offspring of the gods who were the fathers of the *demigods*/giants. Thus, accrediting themselves to have an authority over, and supernatural powers above that of natural humans.

As a result of their massive size, strength, supernatural powers, and *celestial* nature, these *preflood* giants ruled mankind. They were hybrids of *celestial* beings and physical humans, as the Bible tells us. Their domination, cruelty and selfishness due to having no restraints, made living on earth an unspeakable horror. *Nimrod*, being a freak (in size and strength) among the other humans of his day, studied the *preflood* world and identified with the *Nephilim* as his ancestors. They were referred to as gods or *demigods* in mythology because of their partial *celestial* nature. *Nimrod* declared himself a god claiming to be 1/3 human and 2/3 *celestial*. However, the giants after the flood were (for a lack of a better word) a genetically watered-down version of a *Nephilim*. Through interbreeding to make the giant gene possessed by his mother dominant in her children, *Nimrod* became one. He was close to twice the size of a normal human; however, he was of inferior stature compared to the *preflood* giants. The original first generation *preflood* giants were monstrously big.

Studying and identifying with the *preflood* giants, *Nimrod* grew in resentment, rebellion, and hatred of God for having wiped out his ancestors, even confining to the *Abyss* the *celestial* beings that fathered them. Because of the agenda of his family, beginning with Ham and his wife, to have their clan superior over the repopulation of the world, coupled with his freakish size, strength and brashness, he dominated, persuaded, and forced the people to follow him. He swore to protect humanity against God so they may do as they will. He also persuaded the people to worship the bygone gods (fallen angels) imprisoned in the *Abyss* and the deceased *demigod*s (the *celestial* beings who mated with human women and their offspring) of the *preflood* era who ruled the earth. *Nimrod* is the originator of *astrology* and the creator of the worship of the mythological gods. The deceased *demigod*s were likewise confined in the *Abyss*. However, what differs them from their *celestial* fathers is that their human offspring, the *demigod*s, die to their physical bodies and go to the *Abyss* disembodied. This is supported in the Bible when it says in Revelation that the Beast (*Nimrod*) was, is not now and will come up out of the *Abyss* on his way to his destruction (the *lake of fire*). This proves *Nimrod* was a *demigod* possessing DNA from fallen angels because a normal physical human goes disembodied to one of two other locations in *Hades*. Here are the three destinations in *Hades*:

1) *Paradise* or *Abraham's bosom*, where the righteous disembodied *soul*s wait to receive a *celestial* body and have eternal life. This is where *Jesus* went after He died, as it says in Revelation:

NIV Rev 6:9-11 When he opened the fifth seal, I saw under the altar the souls of those who had been slain because of the word of God and the testimony they had maintained. They called out in a loud voice, "How long, Sovereign Lord, holy and true, until you judge the inhabitants of the earth and avenge our blood?" Then each of them was given a white robe, and they were told to wait a little longer, until the number of their fellow servants and brothers who were to be killed as they had been was completed.

As previously noted, the breaking of the 5th seal is a prophetic vision of when *Jesus* died on the cross. He went to *Hades* in the place of *paradise*. Exactly where, while He was hanging on the cross, He promised the thief He would meet him that very day. While there, *Jesus* told the *144,000* martyred, disembodied patriarchs He would avenge their death only after the full number of their brothers had been killed. That will be after the *great tribulation*. However, in the meantime, *Jesus* gave them a *celestial* body to once again clothe their *soul*s with and set them free from the confines of *paradise* in *Hades*. This is why it is said:

NIV Mt 16:17-18 Jesus replied, "Blessed are you, Simon son of Jonah, for this was not revealed to you by man, but by my Father in heaven. And I tell you that you are Peter, and on this rock I will build my church, and the gates of Hades will not overcome it.

AMP Eph 4:8-10 Therefore it is said, When He ascended on high, He led captivity captive [He led a train of vanquished foes] and He bestowed gifts on men. [But He ascended?] Now what can this, He ascended, mean but that He had previously descended from [the heights of] heaven into [the depths], the lower parts of the earth? He Who descended is the [very] same as He Who also has ascended high above all the heavens, that He [His presence] might fill all things (the whole universe, from the lowest to the highest).

AMP 1Pe 3:18-19A For Christ [the Messiah Himself] died for sins once for all, the Righteous for the unrighteous (the Just for the unjust, the Innocent for the guilty), that He might bring us to God. In His *human body He was put to death, but He was made alive in the spirit, In which He went and preached to the spirits in prison . . .*

Then 40 days after *Jesus* set them free from their disembodied confinement in *Hades*, He led them to Heaven in audience before the throne of the *Father*. They were as the train of His robe. They were the *first fruits* of His redeeming work. The first to be clothed in a *celestial* body and be in the presence of God in Heaven. Where did they go for 40 days awaiting *Jesus* to bring them to Heaven with Him if they were broken out of *Hades* possessing a *celestial* body?

AMP Mt 27:50-54 *And Jesus cried again with a loud voice and gave up His spirit. And at once the curtain of the sanctuary of the temple was torn in two from top to bottom; the earth shook and the rocks were split. The tombs were opened and many bodies of the saints who had fallen asleep in death were raised [to life]; And coming out of the tombs after His resurrection, they went into the holy city and appeared to many people. When the centurion and those who were with him keeping watch over Jesus observed the earthquake and all that was happening, they were terribly frightened and filled with awe, and said, Truly this was God's Son!*

2) *Gehenna*, (also referred to as *Hell*) the hellish place where the evil disembodied *soul*s of humans await judgment before continuing their punishment in the permanent *lake of fire*.

3) The *Abyss*, a hellish bottomless pit designed specifically for the evil fallen *celestial* beings (angels) and their human offspring (the giants) are held over until the day of judgment when they will continue their punishment eternally. This is the place that the *Nimrod*, the *beast*, and *antichrist* will be given leave to escape, preceding the return of Christ.

The purpose of *Hades* and its three locations, especially in the case of the *Abyss*, is to confine disembodied *soul*s and evil *celestial* beings from having an influence in the affairs of living humans until the day of judgment. At which time *Hades* will be emptied. All the disembodied *soul*s will receive a new *celestial* body, then all will be sorted out and assigned to their eternal residence by the Lord—Heaven with the Lord or the *lake of fire*.

Nimrod was the first king, the first to wear a crown, the first to conquer and enslave people of other lands, and the originator of *idol worship*, god and *demigod worship*, and the creator of *astrology*. This accounts for why the stars and planets of *astrology* are named after the gods and *demigod*s because they were tied to his deified structure of false gods, giving a point of contact to identify with them as *celestial* beings. *Nimrod* is the *post-flood* culprit that caused the people to rebel against God. He had built the Tower of Babel for several reasons:

1) As a temple to worship the gods and *demigod*s

2) As a shelter to avoid being wiped out in the case of another flood.

3) A tower that was to reach up to the Heavens so he could ascend, fight God, and kill Him.

All the population was lining up under *Nimrod*'s domination and rebellion. It is at this time God destroyed the tower he built, divided the people into 70 different peoples, giving 70 different languages, spreading them out around the globe, and because of the unanimous rebellion, released the curse of the *four horsemen*. God had promised Noah He would not destroy the world and humanity with a flood again. However, we gave Him every reason to do so in only a handful of *post-flood* generations.

As horrible as disease, starvation, war, violence, cruel enslavement and premature death are, these *four horsemen* curses are to be considered a huge mercy by God so that we might understand what the consequences of our heart choices have led to. Not to mention these curses, in large part, are the very things that plagued the *pre-flood* world because of these giants that God saved us from, through the flood. This is what *Nimrod* and his subjects were rebelling against God to return to. God is actually giving us a limited taste of what we are striving for to help us see what we are inviting back into our lives—it's a wake-up call to come out of our denial. The Lord is trying to help us see like an alcoholic who has detoxed and gotten sober, then later thinks he really enjoyed alcohol and misses it. Then, in denial of all of the horrible things alcohol brought into his life, decides to return to drinking believing he likes that life better.

Since the release of the winds of God's destruction (*the four horsemen*) there have been kingdoms who rule over men by and through violence, and enslavement to enrich themselves. Likewise, death by wars, famine, disease, natural disasters, and the hostility towards humans by animals. Death has been given leave by God to take the lives of an ongoing 25% of humanity born into the world. Finally, the disembodied or naked *souls* which are killed are to be confined to the realm of the dead, known as *Hades*, until the *last day* when all will rise being embodied once again and face the judgment of God.

Note: Even allowing 25% of humanity being taken by death through the curse of the four horsemen is to be considered a mercy, a restraint. In the pre-flood world, the giants had no restraint, and nothing was able to resist or conquer them. They killed humans as if they were cattle and even ate them, according to literatures of antiquity. However, the power of the four horsemen have a restraint imposed on them by God, 25%.

Ever since the four winds of God's destruction have been released into the world, man has been plagued with these curses. No! It is not something that is going to happen, but something that obviously has already happened and conditions or a state of affairs that we all must persevere under. Make an advance in farming to curb starvation, then disease breaks out to take lives. Make advances in medicine, then wars break out. Bring peace between nations, and natural disasters will make up the deficit, so death has its due—25%.

Ironically, it is the curse of man that we have need to comfort and aid each other in the futile struggle of survival against the *four horsemen*. We are under a curse, God's judgment, and He has given the *devil* and his *antichrist* the power of the *four horsemen* to lord over men. Why? Because men have chosen to make him (the *devil* and his *antichrist*) king over themselves. However, just as much as it is a curse and punishment, it is a blessing that forces us to band together, becoming unselfish, compassionate and helpful towards each other. This is one of the purposes God is trying to affect within the hearts of men.

Jesus once said to the crowds that they did not understand His miracles, but they followed Him because He fed them.

Here is the significance of the miracles He performed: They demonstrated that *Jesus* had a power and authority over that of the *devil* and the *four horsemen*. He possesses even a power over *Hades* and death itself, as He demonstrated on more than one occasion. He and He alone can save us from the power and authority of the four horsemen. We learn through the biblical prophets that when *Jesus* returns for His *1,000-year reign*, a man will be thought of as having been cursed if he doesn't live out his life to well over a hundred years old, and if he doesn't, it will be a rarity. There will no longer be children born dead. No war. No longer will there be the hostility of nature and the animal kingdom towards humans. The lion will lay with the lamb and they both will eat grass. The child will play with the cobra and will not be bitten or poisoned. The curses which humanity brought on their own heads and have been living under ever since judgment was put in motion, will be lifted by *Jesus* when He comes into His Kingdom here on earth. It is already a matter of record that He has the power to do so because of the miracles He performed.

The *5th seal* is the release of the redemption of God. *The 5th seal* is when *Jesus* died on the cross so that those who receive His Spirit and believe in Him can themselves be saved from death.

The *6th and 7th seals* will be released simultaneously. It is the end and fullness of His judgment against humanity. First it is against His elect, then against the world who hated and killed them. The *6th seal* primarily deals with the judgment against His elect who are seduced into the end time's apostasy, the great falling away when *Nimrod* is brought back to life. This is the time of the *great tribulation*. God's judgment against the elect is carried out by the hands of the world and its government that the worldly Christians gave themselves over to (just as Gomer, the wife of Hosea, had to her lovers who were in adultery with her). The 7th *seal* deals primarily with the judgment and punishment of the world. They will suffer their punishment from the hands of heavenly agents.

We know the 6th and 7th seals are released simultaneously because they affect the same thing, the 7 years judgment of God. In addition, when the 7th seal was opened, it is said there was a half hour of silence in Heaven. A half an hour is to be taken for a half of a cycle or a half of a seven-year period—3½ years. This silence or inactivity is to allow and give the time ordained for the *antichrist* to rule during the *great tribulation* (the 6th *seal*) when he will destroy the *Church Corrupt*. Revelation says that God has granted *Nimrod* this power and put it in his heart to destroy the church until God's purposes are fulfilled.

AMP Rev 17:15-18 And [the angel further] said to me, The waters that you observed, where the harlot (the Church Corrupt) *is seated, are races and multitudes and nations and dialects (languages). And the ten horns that you saw, they and the beast will [be the very ones to] hate the harlot (the idolatrous woman); they will make her cheerless (bereaved, desolate), and they will strip her and eat up her flesh and utterly consume her with fire. For God has put it into their hearts to carry out His own purpose by acting in harmony in surrendering their royal power and authority to the beast, until the prophetic words (intentions and promises) of God shall be fulfilled. And the woman that you saw is herself the great city* (the Vatican—the seat of the Holy Roman Empire, the Roman Catholic Church) *which dominates and controls the rulers and the leaders of the earth.*

That purpose is to create the same situation that He did for Gomer that persuaded her to come to the conclusion, "I was better off with my husband." He did so by turning her lovers against her and cutting off all the ways that they had enriched her. That is the main purpose for allowing the return of the *antichrist* and granting the *great tribulation*: What God put in the hearts of the lovers of Gomer, He put in the heart of the *antichrist* to hate and kill the Christians. So that those God left behind to endure the *great tribulation* and had decided to side with the Pope (the *false prophet*) to become an apostate, would return to their first love, realizing, like Gomer, they were better off with their first love, *Jesus*. The Lord then would be able to save even them after they would have a change of heart with that realization and change of heart posture.

When that silence or inactivity on Heaven's part ends, a half an hour later (3½ years), the agents of Heaven will once again become active in the world bringing an end to the *great tribulation*. Now the elect will be protected from further harm, and the world will be punished for their evil. This is in fulfillment of the promise of God at the breaking of the *5th Seal* when He also gave the 144,000 disembodied *souls under the Altar, celestial* bodies. He then, in answer to their question, said He would not punish the world until the full number of their brothers had been martyred. The full number will finally have been martyred when the last of the elect is killed during the *great tribulation*. When that has happened not one single person of the elect will be allowed to be harmed.

The question many have is where, according to Revelation, are we at currently? We are currently between the 5th and 6th seals, and at the back end of the second delay between the 62-weeks of years and the 1-week of years. This time period we call the *Church Age*. It is a time period that through the Gospel the Lord draws the Gentiles into His salvation, because the Jews had rejected Him. The first 5 seals have already been released, ending with *Jesus* dying on the cross. This is a sobering, and profound turn of events which affect all life on planet earth! The earth will not die its natural death. Likewise, the entire universe will not be allowed to live out and continue the course of the kinetic energy which moves it forward by the power God set it in motion with at its creation. The first of the four narratives is an overview of these life altering events decreed by God. They are described according to the *structure of sevens*. The story of this subject is told from the beginning to end. We will learn increasingly more particulars in the next 3 narratives.

The *second narrative* starts with verse 11:19 and ends with verse 16:21. This narrative begins with the moment Adam and Eve sinned.

NIV Rev 11:19 *Then God's temple in heaven was opened, and within his temple was seen the ark of his covenant. And there came flashes of lightning, rumblings, peals of thunder, an earthquake and a great hailstorm.*

The ark of His covenant seen in the temple of God was *Jesus*, His *Son*. We see the disturbance it caused when Adam and Eve sinned. God had to make a judgment and implement a new plan to save mankind from their sin, while at the same time punish evil. An ark is a vessel. Just as Paul refers to our body as an earthen (clay) vessel, which within possesses the *Holy Spirit, Jesus* is that vessel, that ark. It is through Him alone, the way, the truth and the life, by which we are saved from the fate altering sin that Adam, Eve, and the *devil* committed. Ark has a double meaning here. *Jesus* is the true ark/vessel and covenant, and it is in Him that we can transcend the destruction of the physical universe by becoming *celestial* humans, then live out eternity in the *celestial* realm. Likewise, the ark/vessel Noah built that saved those who entered into it, was a foreshadowing of the true and eternal salvation. It saved its eight passengers who repopulated the earth, but they still succumbed to death of the body.

The purpose of this *second narrative* is to introduce to us the main players of this turn of events we have need to be saved from. They are:

1) The temple of God; is God almighty. The temple is the embodiment of Almighty God in Heaven.
NIV Rev 21:22 *I did not see a temple in the city, because the Lord God Almighty and the Lamb are its temple.*

2) The ark of God's covenant, the vessel that delivers us to His promised salvation, is *Jesus*, His *Son*. Later, He is depicted as the child the woman gives birth to. It says the temple was opened; this is depicting that the ark comes from Him, from within God's own person. And like a spiritual sonagram the vision shows us inside the body of the *Father* to see His coming *Son*. Meaning that vessel the woman was to give birth to, was Him—God. Likewise, making the ark (*Jesus*) His *Son*, and Almighty God the *Father* of the child *Jesus*.

NIV Mt 1:20 *But after he had considered this, an angel of the Lord appeared to him in a dream and said, "Joseph son of David, do not be afraid to take Mary home as your wife, because what is conceived in her is from the Holy Spirit.*

3) **The *Woman clothed with the sun*.** This is Eve, the mother of all the living, and all her offspring that is created by the plan of God to bring us salvation before the eventual destruction of the universe, including physical man. In introducing her we are shown which of her offspring salvation comes through. Israel is the *12 stars* that are the crown of her legacy. They are a people set apart for God's purposes. Then the child she gives birth to is *Jesus*, the ark of God. More accurately, *Jesus* comes from her in the sense that it is her offspring, the set apart Israelites, that the birth of *Jesus* comes from. In essence, *Jesus* comes from Eve, the mother of all the living.

4) **The *red dragon*,** is the *devil* who is the deceiver, the architect and *spirit* of rebellion against God. He is the father of lies.

5) **The *beast out of the sea*** is the *antichrist* and *Nimrod*. It is through the eight that survive the flood he comes from. This is why it is depicted that he came out of the sea. He was the offspring or legacy of those who survived the flood to dry land.

6) **The *beast out of the earth*,** this is the *false prophet*, the Pope of the Roman Catholic Church who deceives and leads the whole earth (even the saints) into the *great apostasy*—the great falling away, and forces them to worship the beast, the risen *Nimrod*, who he created a body for and gave it the breath of life.

7) **The *Lamb and the 144,000*** are *Jesus* and the patriarchs of Israel who paved the way for Him to come but died.

NIV Rev 12:15-13:1 *Then from his mouth the serpent spewed water like a river, to overtake the woman and sweep her away with the torrent. But the earth helped the woman by opening its mouth and swallowing the river that the dragon had spewed out of his mouth. Then the dragon was enraged at the woman and went off to make war against the rest of her offspring—those who obey God's commandments and hold to the testimony of Jesus. And the dragon stood on the shore of the sea. And I saw a beast coming out of the sea.*

After introducing us to the main characters and their destinies, the *second narrative* now skips ahead to the flood. *Then from his mouth the serpent spewed water like a river, to overtake the woman and sweep her away with the torrent.* The *devil* wanted the righteous offspring of the woman to be wiped out because they are a threat to him just as Abel was. To the *devil*'s dismay, 8 are saved by the ark. However, that ark can only stay afloat for so long and they too will perish. *But the earth helped the woman by opening its mouth and swallowing the river that the dragon had spewed out of his mouth.* The land mass divides, the continents are formed, and separated. Mountains went from the highest being 12,000 feet high at the time of the flood, to the highest now being 29,000 feet high. Fossils of sea creatures are found at the top of the highest mountains. The ocean basins are formed, and the waters of the flood recede to create dry land. It is a new beginning for man through the 8 survivors. The *devil* is outraged about this. *And the dragon stood on the shore of the sea.* We are told he is already waiting on the shores of the dry land even before the ark rests on land. *And I saw a beast coming out of the sea.* The *devil* is plotting the rise of his offspring to dominate the repopulation of the earth through *Nimrod* who will come out of the flood waters from one of the couples on that ark, Ham and his wife.

After establishing the new beginning with the 8 on board the ark, the narrative has set some context to introduce us to the rest of the main characters. Then by way of the remaining introductions, the *second narrative* tells the rest of the story in sequential order, to its end.

Understanding visions given by the Lord

In the vision John sees in the heavens a *woman clothed with the sun*, with the moon under her feet and a crown of twelve stars and she is pregnant, in pain, about to give birth. We must understand that what John describes is like a three-dimensional picture of a four-dimensional prophetic view. The fourth dimension being time. This is the way God sees a matter, from outside of time. When God looks at a thing, He sees it from its essence to every outward expression it will have, from its beginning all the way to its end. When we consider a prophetic picture, it might be like a snapshot of something which freezes that image in time, but with the right eyes and understanding we can see within that picture the past, present, and future of it.

Here is a similar example, we see and live in a three-dimensional world. If we take a photograph, it will be a two-dimensional picture lacking depth. However, with the right eyes and understanding, within the picture we can get a sense of depth. In this picture, if we consider perspective and the comparative size of the objects within, we can get a sense of depth even though the picture is only two-dimensional. However, if we were to only have a two-dimensional understanding and view of life, we would be ignorant and blind to the depicted depth the photo shows in its two-dimensional way. We would be ignorant of it altogether. It's the same when looking with a three-dimensional understanding and eyes at a four-dimensional prophetic picture of a subject. Unless we have prophetic eyes and understanding we are blind to the fourth-dimensional aspect of a vision given by God.

This vision John describes is no different. The subject in this prophetic picture shows the beginning, the end, and the journey in between. The vision is of Eve, the mother of all the living (as is the meaning of her name which also discounts the idea that there are other humans, not born of Eve, on the earth). It shows the stature of Eve in her God given glory and position before sin, and at the same time, after sin, and how God will use her destiny to salvage mankind. This vision reflects the repentant heart of Eve, the forgiveness of God, and His resulting remedy to salvage man through her legacy. Through her (her legacy) the crowning children of salvation, the 12 tribes of Israel come. They are a people set apart for God to bring about His plan and establish His Word in the world. And out of those 12 tribes will come the Savior. Just as God had pronounced over her in the garden that, "In pain you shall bring forth children," it is with great labor and pain suffered by her legacy that the child, the Savior (Jesus) arises out of them to save mankind.

After the vision of Eve another vision enters that reveals the *devil* with his seven manifesting heads. You might say that this second vision is connected to the vision of Eve, or even one and the same vision. This is because both their fates and legacies, for the life of humanity on earth, are forever bound because of Eve's sin. However, as depicted in the vision of Eve, God is intervening to separate out as many of her legacy that can be from the curse and destruction that fateful union she created with the *devil* has doomed. Eve, the mother of all the living, will not see the entirety of her offspring over thousands of years plunged into sin, pain, misery, and ultimately destroyed because of her sin. This is a wonderful miracle and consolation for the repentant Eve.

These *seven heads* of the *devil* are the continuous seven different faces of his over the world starting with Babylon transitioning into the Assyrian Empire ending with the Roman Empire transitioning into the Holy Roman Empire—the Roman Catholic Church. This empirical rule begins with the *devil*'s human agent and first-head, the *antichrist* (*Nimrod*), transitioning to emperors who possess the spirit of the *antichrist*. Then, ending with the reappearance of the *antichrist,* so that both the Christ and *antichrist* can have the final battle to rule over the earth.

Why drag out this showdown over thousands of years? The answer is that God does not want to save just one family as He did with the flood or with the people of Sodom and Gomorrah and their surrounding towns. Why did God save only one family in these two occasions? Because the people involved in both these occasions of judgment unanimously decided to go along with the evil God was striking out against. God's heart is to save all, however, individual choice prohibits that from happening. Were things really that bad? Yes, indeed they were and are and will be in the end. Many think that God brings judgment upon all because of a general consensus of the people involved that would be in rebellion against Him. This is not true in any sense! Peter explains of the righteous who are doomed to be among and suffer the unrighteous, however, when judgement comes, God will save them:

NIV 2Pe 2:3-9 In their greed these teachers will exploit you with stories they have made up. Their condemnation has long been hanging over them, and their destruction has not been sleeping. For if God did not spare angels when they sinned, but sent them to hell (the Abyss)*, putting them into gloomy dungeons to be held for judgment; if he did not spare the ancient world when he brought the flood on its ungodly people, but protected Noah, a preacher of righteousness, and seven others; if he condemned the cities of Sodom and Gomorrah by burning them to ashes, and made them an example of what is going to happen to the ungodly; and if he rescued Lot, a righteous man, who was distressed by the filthy lives of lawless men (for that righteous man, living among them day after day, was tormented in his righteous soul by the lawless deeds he saw and heard)—if this is so, then the Lord knows how to rescue godly men from trials and to hold the unrighteous for the day of judgment, while continuing their punishment* (in the Abyss of *Hades*).

We must understand that *final judgment* against humanity has already occurred! Sentence has been decided and the gavel of God has come down. The earth, the universe it is within, and man is doomed to total and absolute destruction by fire. However, the mercy of God hesitates to carry it out so that more than a handful of individuals will be salvaged. He told us this in Daniel:

AMP Da 9:20-27 While I was speaking and praying, confessing my sin and the sin of my people Israel, and presenting my supplication

before the Lord my God for the holy hill of my God (Jerusalem)—
*Yes, while I was speaking in prayer, the man Gabriel, whom I had
seen in the former vision, being caused to fly swiftly, came near to
me and touched me about the time of the evening sacrifice. He
instructed me and made me understand; he talked with me and said,
O Daniel, I am now come forth to give you skill and wisdom and
understanding. At the beginning of your prayers, the word [giving an
answer] went forth, and I have come to tell you, for you are greatly
beloved. Therefore consider the matter and understand the vision.
Seventy weeks [of years, or 490 years] are decreed upon your people
and upon your holy city [Jerusalem], to finish and put an end to
transgression, to seal up and make full the measure of sin, to purge
away and make expiation and reconciliation for sin, to bring in
everlasting righteousness (permanent moral and spiritual rectitude
in every area and relation) to seal up vision and prophecy and
prophet, and to anoint a Holy of Holies* (Jesus). *Know therefore and
understand that from the going forth of the commandment to restore
and to build Jerusalem until [the coming of] the Anointed One, a
Prince* (Jesus), *shall be seven weeks [of years] and sixty-two weeks
[of years]; it shall be built again with [city] square and moat, but in
troublous times. And after the sixty-two weeks [of years] shall the
Anointed One be cut off or killed and shall have nothing [and no
one] belonging to [and defending] Him* (Jesus the Christ). *And the
people* (the Roman Empire [sixth head of the beast]) *of the [other]
prince* (the antichrist) *who will come will destroy the city and the
sanctuary* (in 70 AD). *Its end shall come with a flood; and even to
the end there shall be war, and desolations are decreed. And he* (the
seventh head of the beast, the pope of the Roman Catholic Church)
*shall enter into a strong and firm covenant with the many for one
week [seven years]. And in the midst of the week he shall cause the
sacrifice and offering to cease [for the remaining three and one-half
years]; and upon the wing or pinnacle* (or climax) *of abominations
[shall come] one who makes desolate* (an offense so heinous and
appalling that God turns His face away from the world, withdraws

His *Holy Spirit*, giving the world over to itself for 3½ years), *until the full determined end is poured out on the desolator.*

Note: This abomination that is so appalling to God is when the Pope creates a body made of sacrificed humans for *Nimrod*, the *antichrist*, to come back to life from the *Abyss*.

AMP Isa 14:19 But you are cast away from your tomb like a loathed growth or premature birth or an abominable branch [of the family] and like the raiment of the slain; and you are clothed with the slain, those thrust through with the sword, who go down to the stones of the pit [into which carcasses are thrown], like a dead body trodden underfoot.

NIV Rev 17:8 The inhabitants of the earth whose names have not been written in the book of life from the creation of the world will be astonished when they see the beast, because he once was, now is not, and yet will come.

It is not a random or arbitrary decree of seventy years that God is imposing. There is a reason God has decreed this time period. Final and absolute judgment is coming on man and earth. These seventy sevens are a delay of that *final judgment*. The purpose of this delay of seventy sevens (weeks of years or seven-year time periods) before bringing down the hammer of judgment is as the Lord stated above:

"Seventy weeks [of years, or 490 years] are decreed upon your people and upon your holy city [Jerusalem], to finish and put an end to transgression, to seal up and make full the measure of sin, to purge away and make expiation and reconciliation for sin, to bring in everlasting righteousness (permanent moral and spiritual rectitude in every area and relation) to seal up vision and prophecy and prophet, and to anoint a Holy of Holies."

It is to bring forth a Savior so as to save as many that would receive Him and to show those given over to sin as unquestionably against God from this final destruction. Multitudes beyond counting, we are told in Revelation, are not just a handful. In addition to these 490 years, there are two pauses of time creating more delay to ensure more of humanity is spared. The 490 years of delay is broken into three segments. They would not be broken into three segments if there was no time between them. Otherwise, it would be simply 490 consecutive years before final destruction. In other words, there are delays within the delays which reflect the desire on the Lord's part to save as many humans as possible. This also accounts for why it is said in Revelation:

NIV Rev 10:5-6 Then the angel I had seen standing on the sea and on the land raised his right hand to heaven. And he swore by him who lives for ever and ever, who created the heavens and all that is in them, the earth and all that is in it, and the sea and all that is in it, and said, "There will be no more delay!

These two delays create thousands of years of a stay of execution. The first delay (between 487BC and 401BC) between the 7-7's and the 62-7's was 86 years. The second delay between the 62-7's (ending with the day that Christ was crucified) and the final 7-year time period we are in the midst of.

Think of it! There is no time to waste. Judgment is looming over us and is only a seven-year time period away, this we know. What we have little clue of is how much longer this delay will last before the last seven years begins. So far it has been about 2,000 years. The 490 years is a delay time given as a warning and the space for God's holy and set apart people (Israel) to get right with Him before it's too late. To date, the 2,000 years second pause is a delay time given as a warning and the space for the enemies of God, and of His set apart people, to likewise reconcile with God through His sent Savior. This gives all the time, space, and opportunity to be pardoned from the coming destruction.

If wondering how much longer this delay of the *Church Age* will last (which so far is about 2,000 years), before the last seven years comes and therefore brings the end; the verse below tells us how long it is supposed to last. It is easy to recognize that the Gospel has for the most part spread to all of the nations, so the time is obviously short.

NIV Mt 24:14 *And this gospel of the kingdom will be preached in the whole world as a testimony to all nations, and then the end will come.*

We should not believe we have plenty of time or that God will give more opportunity than the 70-7-year period, because it says:

AMP Rev 6:9-11 *When the Lamb broke open the fifth seal, I saw at the foot of the altar the souls of those whose lives had been sacrificed for [adhering to] the Word of God and for the testimony they had borne. They cried in a loud voice, O [Sovereign] Lord, holy and true, how long now before You will sit in judgment and avenge our blood upon those who dwell on the earth? Then they were each given a long and flowing and festive white robe and told to rest and wait patiently a little while longer, until the number should be complete of their fellow servants and their brethren who were to be killed* (ending with and including the dead from the great tribulation) *as they themselves had been.*

NIV Da 12:6-7 *One of them* (angels) *said to the man clothed in linen, who was above the waters of the river, "How long will it be before these astonishing things are fulfilled?" The man clothed in linen, who was above the waters of the river, lifted his right hand and his left hand toward heaven, and I heard him swear by him who lives forever, saying, "It will be for a time, times and half a time. When the power of the holy people* (Christians) *has been finally broken* (making reference to the 3½ years of the great tribulation), *all these things will be completed."*

It will be after 3½ years of the *great tribulation* against His people that the Lord will not only punish and crush the world and its *antichrist* movement (to have acceptance without conformity [to God's will and order], the *Religion of Cain*) that is in rebellion against God, but will also return and subdue the world, making it His Kingdom.

And again:

AMP Rev 10:1-7 *THEN I saw another mighty angel coming down from heaven, robed in a cloud, with a [halo like a] rainbow over his head; his face was like the sun, and his feet (legs) were like columns of fire. He had a little book (scroll) open in his hand. He set his right foot on the sea and his left foot on the land, And he shouted with a loud voice like the roaring of a lion; and when he had shouted, the seven thunders gave voice and uttered their message in distinct words. And when the seven thunders had spoken (sounded), I was going to write [it down], but I heard a voice from heaven saying, Seal up what the seven thunders have said! Do not write it down! Then the [mighty] angel whom I had seen stationed on sea and land raised his right hand to heaven (the sky), And swore in the name of (by) Him Who lives forever and ever, Who created the heavens (sky) and all they contain, and the earth and all that it contains, and the sea and all that it contains. [He swore] that no more time should intervene and there should be no more waiting or delay, But that when the days come when the trumpet call of the seventh angel is about to be sounded, then God's mystery (His secret design, His hidden purpose), as He had announced the glad tidings to His servants the prophets, should be fulfilled (accomplished, completed).*

The *devil*, Satan, who seduced Eve, are together complicit in their sin and rebellion against God, binding them in an unholy union. But because of the repentative and remorseful heart of Eve, the *devil* is also Eve's nemesis. It is a cage match within the soul of not only Eve, but all of her offspring. Because Eve (the mother of all the living) ingested the spirit of the devil, she had corrupted the human spirit for all time, making the devil the (spirit) father and god of her offspring, giving themselves over to his spirit; his worldview and understanding. As a part of what God decrees in the garden is not only His judgment, but also His plan for redemption.

The Lord's first objective is to polarize Eve's offspring into two different lines. Since both lines have a sin nature due to a corruption of the human spirit, those different lines are 1) those who fight to be independent from God, and 2) those who desire to be obedient and reconciled with God conforming to His will. The former operates out of the spirit and worldview of the devil making him the spiritual father of them, and the latter who operate out of the Spirit of God conforming to His will making them the children of God. This created distinction is the very foundation of God's plan for salvation. This is the most important prerequisite of God's plan for salvation. For all of history climaxing at the end, God has unfolded history in a way that puts a polarizing hatred between the two different camps. 1) Haters of God and His people, wanting to do their own will. And 2) lovers of God who desire to conform to God's will. This is reflected in the story of two brothers, Cain and Abel. However, since Abel was killed by Cain, Abel's line is continued through Seth.

Likewise, God's plan of polarization is also reflected in the end. We see this when we look at the world (Babylon) in opposition to the Church. This polarization (enmity) is meant to make a clear distinction between the righteous and the unrighteous. However, the spirit of Babylon has infiltrated the Church making it hard to make that distinction, as Jesus warns us with the parable of the wheat and the weeds.

NIV Mt 13:24-30 Jesus told them another parable: "The kingdom of heaven is like a man who sowed good seed in his field. But while everyone was sleeping, his enemy came and sowed weeds among the wheat, and went away. When the wheat sprouted and formed heads, then the weeds also appeared. "The owner's servants came to him and said, 'Sir, didn't you sow good seed in your field? Where then did the weeds come from?' "'An enemy did this,' he replied. "The servants asked him, 'Do you want us to go and pull them up?' "'No,' he answered, 'because while you are pulling the weeds, you may root up the wheat with them. Let both grow together until the harvest. At that time I will tell the harvesters: <u>First collect the weeds and tie them in bundles to be burned; then gather the wheat and bring it into my barn.</u>"'

The weeds are the worldly Christians who become apostates, *to be burned,* meaning they will endure the *great tribulation.* The wheat represents the saints who are *raptured, bring into my barn*, and avoid enduring the *great tribulation*. It also necessitates the *great tribulation* to remake this distinction between the two lines of offsprings crystal clear after the lines have become blurred through the Church becoming corrupt. As Jesus looks forward He gives us foreknowledge about this.

NIV Rev 3:15-22 I know your deeds, that you are neither cold nor hot. I wish you were either one or the other! So, because you are lukewarm—neither hot nor cold—I am about to spit you out of my mouth. You say, 'I am rich; I have acquired wealth and do not need a thing.' But you do not realize that you are wretched, pitiful, poor, blind and naked. I counsel you to buy from me gold refined in the fire, so you can become rich; and white clothes to wear, so you can cover your shameful nakedness; and salve to put on your eyes, so you can see. Those whom I love I rebuke and discipline. So be earnest, and repent. Here I am! I stand at the door and knock. If anyone hears my voice and opens the door, I will come in and eat with him, and he with me. To him who overcomes, I will give the right to sit with me on my throne, just as I overcame and sat down with my Father on his throne. He who has an ear, let him hear what the Spirit says to the churches."

The narrative references the judgment and salvation through the polarization God made in the garden (Gen 3:13-16) concerning the devil and Eve:

NIV Ge 3:15 And I will put enmity between you and the woman, and between your offspring and hers; he will crush your head, and you will strike his heel."

NAS Rev 12:4 And his tail swept away a third of the stars of heaven and threw them to the earth. And the dragon stood before the woman who was about to give birth, so that when she gave birth he might devour her child.

The stars of Heaven the devil will sweep down to the earth (the grave) are those the *antichrist* and the *false prophet* kill during the

3½ years of the *great tribulation*. This furthers the chasm between the lovers and haters of God, which, in turn, forces people in one camp or the other. Again, it separates the wheat from the chaff.

After He pronounces the curses she brought upon her head, God ordains that Eve will also have a line of offspring through whom the Redeemer, the Christ, will come. That offspring will be the children of God, and He will be their Father. That line of offspring will lead to the birth of Abraham resulting in the twelve tribes of Israel, which is represented in the vision of her by the crown of twelve stars on her head. Through Israel, the Redeemer comes who is depicted above as the son Eve gives birth to. When the Redeemer comes, He will crush the devil and the offspring of Eve's who possess the devil's spirit.

Then the narrative jumps ahead from the garden of Eden to the new beginning. The new beginning is the aftermath of the flood when the human agent of the devil, the *antichrist* (the antithesis of Christ), is born and creates his kingdom, Babylon, for the whole world to follow. The title "*antichrist*" does not solely mean that he is the opposite of Christ, in so much that he stops people from being saved. The *antichrist* is still a savior. However, he is a savior insomuch that he saves people from Almighty God and protects them from God's wrath so they may do as they will. Whereas the Christ is the Savior who saves people from their sin and out from under the bondage of the devil, reconciling them back to Almighty God while saving them from the eternal destruction the devil and his antichrist are doomed to. Understanding the title *antichrist* this way makes recorded history and the Bible, beyond a shadow of a doubt, point to *Nimrod* as that human agent of the devil—the *antichrist*.

It is at this point in the narrative that the whole world makes *Nimrod*, the *antichrist*, king over them that occasions the world to be judged for a second time. Astonishingly, it is just a handful of generations after the flood. This *second judgment*, however, is with fire and not with water as before. It is at the time that the *second judgment* was imposed that the four horsemen are released and thus the judgment of fire begins. Disease, natural disasters, both the plant life of earth, and its animals become hostile towards man. Famines and plagues befall men, wars and kingdoms which enslave and dominate men are granted power and loosed on the earth. By this, God is simply giving the people of the world over to their own devices—their desire to rebel against God, do their own will, and put themselves under an authority that will protect them from God's wrath.

Finally, as a part of the four horsemen curse, death is given leave to prematurely take an ongoing ¼ of the world's population before their time by the above-mentioned means. Then death confines their naked or disembodied souls in *Hades*, the realm of the dead. It is there that the disembodied souls will await the last day when all will rise and once again be clothed with a body in order to face the judgment of God. God calls the four horsemen throughout scripture, *the four winds of His destruction*. By cursing mankind with the four horsemen, in addition to giving man over to their own desires and devices, God is demonstrating through real life experience that He is Almighty over all. That He has absolute power over both the devil and his agent, the *antichrist*. In other words, they cannot protect the people from God whatsoever, it is an exercise in futility to attempt to do so.

God spoke in the garden that He would put (exploit) enmity, a hatred between these two lines of offspring from Eve. These two different lines of offspring and their fates are represented in the *second narrative* by the visions of the woman and the dragon.

NIV Ge 3:15 *And I will put enmity between you and the woman, and between your offspring and hers; he will crush your head, and you will strike his heel."*

NIV Mt 10:32-37 *"Whoever acknowledges me before men, I will also acknowledge him before my Father in heaven. But whoever disowns me before men, I will disown him before my Father in heaven. "Do not suppose that I have come to bring peace to the earth. I did not come to bring peace, but a sword. For I have come to turn "'a man against his father, a daughter against her mother, a daughter-in-law* against her mother-in-law—a man's enemies will be the members of his own household.' "Anyone who loves his father or mother more than me is not worthy of me; anyone who loves his son or daughter more than me is not worthy of me

NIV Gal 5:17 For the sinful nature desires what is contrary to the Spirit, and the Spirit what is contrary to the sinful nature. They are in conflict with each other . . .

AMP Jas 4:4 You [are like] unfaithful wives [having illicit love affairs with the world and breaking your marriage vow to God]! Do you not know that being the world's friend is being God's enemy? So whoever chooses to be a friend of the world takes his stand as an enemy of God.

AMP Mt 6:24 No one can serve two masters; for either he will hate the one and love the other, or he will stand by and be devoted to the one and despise and be against the other . . .

These two lines of offspring from the same mother and father are divided against each other. This division is a product of what Eve's sin has caused in the human heart combined with what necessitates God's redemption to be successful. In order for the salvation of God to work, there needs to be a clear line of demarcation with no grey area between, in order to distinguish those who would look to God to be saved from the bondage of sin, and those who would desire to be independent and freed from God and His authority over them. The *woman clothed with the sun* is the mother of all the living and her sin of dividing from God had brought about this inherent independence and opposition towards God in her offspring—all of her offspring! However, the Lord promises another line of offspring or a branch of it who, although having the same corrupt human spirit, have a heart to be reconciled with God. Before the destruction of all things, which is held off until after the redeeming work of Jesus, those who have a heart which desires to be reconciled with God can freely possess the gift of God's own Spirit. Thereby being set free from the corrupt human spirit which originally made them the offspring of the devil and under his bondage of sin, possessing his rebellious spirit.

NIV Eze11:19-21 *I will give them an undivided heart and put a new spirit in them; I will remove from them their heart of stone and give them a heart of flesh. Then they will follow my decrees and be careful to keep my laws. They will be my people, and I will be their God. But as for those whose hearts are devoted to their vile images and detestable idols, I will bring down on their own heads what they have done, declares the Sovereign LORD."*

Again, this naturally puts the two lines of offspring at odds. Their paradigms and spirit perspectives, even their heart purposes, both desire and serve something different from each other. Although both have a sin nature, one desires to reconcile with God, conforming to His will, the other desires to be independent and free from conformity to God and to do as they will—this is the heart of the devil.

AMP Mt 6:24A *No one can serve two masters; for either he will hate the one and love the other, or he will stand by and be devoted to the one and despise and be against the other.*

We see the first evidence of this enmity (hatred) when Cain kills his righteous brother Abel out of jealousy of his brother's standing with God. Cain with his corrupt, independent, and defiant spirit is the personification of the hearts of all Eve's offspring because she had ingested the spirit of the devil. In him we can see the effects the spirit of sin has had on the human spirit. All humankind would have the heart and ways of Cain had it not been for God's plan of redemption, including making a clear distinction between the two hearts of sinful people.

Sin causes division both from relationship with God and human relationships. It is not as the world thinks; it is not Biblical values and the laws of God that creates enmity and hatred and violence between the righteous and the unrighteous, it is the division caused by sin and independence from God!

The Lord promises Eve a line of offspring which will be His and will be redeemed. Again, to be clear, because of what Eve ingested (the spirit of the devil) all of humanity, all her offspring, were doomed to have the heart and motives of Cain. Eve's shame was not simply the bringing about of her own destruction and death. She is the mother of all the living and has done something which destroys all of humanity future. She had ingested something which corrupted the human spirit in a way which makes all her offspring, in their very essence, in opposition and in defiance towards the Lord of all creation.

Eve had doomed all of humanity future! Now this is a burden too great to carry for anyone with a conscience, especially for a mother who has doomed her children and all future generations. However, the Lord in His judgment decrees that through Eve, He would create a line of offspring which would save a huge contingency of fallen mankind. Through the Redeemer, the Child promised to Eve, that contingency of Eve's offspring are to become reborn from having the spirit of the devil, to instead having God's own Spirit! In this way, they are no longer the offspring of the devil possessing his spirit, but God's own children, reborn of His Spirit.

This prospect and promise is the hope and redemption from the eternal burden and shame of Eve. Facing the Lord in the garden and the sober reality of the consequences she had set in motion, it is in this other line of offspring that rest all of her esteem and consolation. This hope, this line of offspring was to propagate out of Abel. Abel, just as his brother, was born with the corrupt spirit of the devil, however, within him was a desire to conform to the will of God and be reconciled with Him. We see this inherent desire to reconcile reflected through his sacrifice which pleased the Lord. This is in contrast to his brother Cain, who sought only to appease the Lord and please himself with his sacrifice.

Abel, with his heart to be reconciled and conformed to God, was the hope and redemption of Eve's whole existence and legacy. Whereas, in Cain, who defiantly wanted to be accepted for who he was and what he willed, was the constant reminder of her sin. He personified the evil she brought upon the human race. Cain was the identified patient and represented her shame. Abel was her hope and represented her redemption.

It surely was not an isolated incident in which Abel's sacrifice was acceptable, and Cain's was not. Their whole lives Abel with his heart was loved and accepted, whereas Cain with his heart was a disappointment and not accepted. Herein lies the difference between the two lines of offspring the Lord spoke of in the garden. The incident recorded in the Bible had to have been the last straw of how the heart of Cain had left him on the outside rejected and wounded. However, knowing his heart posture the Lord warned Cain:

NIV Ge 4:3-7 In the course of time Cain brought some of the fruits of the soil as an offering to the LORD. But Abel brought fat portions from some of the firstborn of his flock. The LORD looked with favor on Abel and his offering, but on Cain and his offering he did not look with favor. So Cain was very angry, and his face was downcast. Then the LORD said to Cain, "Why are you angry? Why is your face downcast? If you do what is right, will you not be accepted? But if you do not do what is right, sin is crouching at your door; it desires to have you, but you must master it."

Cain had had it! He was unwilling to compromise himself by conforming to God. It was not an option for him. With that premise at heart, the only solution he saw was to eliminate the competition— a division from God, his brother, and parents that his sinful independent heart created. He killed the benchmark the whole of his life he was weighed against, he killed his brother Abel.

NIV Ge 4:8-12 Now Cain said to his brother Abel, "Let's go out to the field." And while they were in the field, Cain attacked his brother Abel and killed him. Then the LORD said to Cain, "Where is your brother Abel?" "I don't know," he replied. "Am I my brother's keeper?" The LORD said, "What have you done? Listen! Your brother's blood cries out to me from the ground. Now you are under a curse and driven from the ground, which opened its mouth to receive your brother's blood from your hand. When you work the ground, it will no longer yield its crops for you. You will be a restless wanderer on the earth."

When faced with the consequences of his deed it is still not within the realm of consideration for Cain to conform. He sees his circumstances as something God is doing to him, not circumstances of his own making. Why would Abel's family embrace him after that? Could a man expect a mother and father to embrace him after killing one of their beloved sons, even if he is also one of their sons?

Could anyone but hate and be angry at Cain for what he had done? Of course he was driven from their presence, he was an evil reminder of their loss. Rightfully so, there were those who would have him killed for his crime. It says even the ground cursed him and would not produce for him. For Eve, this is a double devastation, a loss of all hope. Not only was her beloved son killed, but he was also the first human to die causing unspeakable grief. Even worse, all her hope of redemption from her shame died with her son Abel. For it was through him the line of offspring and salvation of the human race was to come, remedying the horrific turn of events she had set in motion.

Cain did not view all that had turned against him as the natural consequences of his deed, but as a punishment imposed against him which was too great to bear. Neither was he willing to, nor did he believe he should have to conform to the will of his Creator, but that his Creator and his family were wrong for not accepting him for doing as he willed—what pleased him—just as in contemporary times the godless and independent, in their sin, blame the righteous and Biblical values on the division and violence in the world. Their solution now is as it was with Cain, to have acceptance without conformity to God, uniting against God (Author and Creator of Life) and the laws He set in motion. Sin creates division and violence!

NIV Ge 4:13-17 Cain said to the LORD, "My punishment is more than I can bear. Today you are driving me from the land, and I will be hidden from your presence; I will be a restless wanderer on the earth, and whoever finds me will kill me." But the LORD said to him, "Not so; if anyone kills Cain, he will suffer vengeance seven times over." Then the LORD put a mark on Cain so that no one who found him would kill him. So Cain went out from the LORD'S presence and lived in the land of Nod, east of Eden. Cain lay with his wife, and she became pregnant and gave birth to Enoch. Cain was then building a city, and he named it after his son Enoch*

The devil, and Cain, believed he had eliminated the other line of offspring. The devil and his dominance over the human race would now be preserved. His line of offspring are the survivors after the death of Abel and there was no longer a line of offspring to contend with. However, God gives Eve another child, Seth. Seth was not just a child to take the place of one she lost. For it says that Adam and Eve had other children besides Cain, Abel, and Seth (Gen 5:4). Seth was to be given the lost destiny of his brother Abel. That which was once to come out of Abel, the line of offspring which brings redemption to mankind, would now come out of Seth. As it says, at that time and through the offspring of Seth, *men began to call on the name of the Lord*. God would not have His promise go unfulfilled and His plan of redemption thwarted!

NIV Ge 4:25-26 Adam lay with his wife again, and she gave birth to a son and named him Seth, saying, "God has granted me another child in place of Abel, since Cain killed him." Seth also had a son, and he named him Enosh. At that time (and through Seth) men began to call on the name of the LORD.

Eve must suffer the pains of labor and be a part of this process of judgment and redemption from the beginning to its resolution. Let us take a closer look at God's judgment in the garden:

NIV Ge 3:13-16 Then the LORD God said to the woman, "What is this you have done?" The woman said, "The serpent deceived me, and I ate." So the LORD God said to the serpent, "Because you have done this, "Cursed are you above all the livestock and all the wild animals! You will crawl on your belly and you will eat dust all the days of your life. And I will put enmity between you and the woman, and between your offspring and hers; he will crush your head, and you will strike his heel." To the woman he said, "I will greatly increase your pains in childbearing; with pain you will give birth to children. Your desire will be for your husband, and he will rule over you."

Now let us look at what Revelation says:

NIV Rev 12:1 *A great and wondrous sign appeared in heaven: a woman clothed with the sun, with the moon under her feet and a crown of twelve stars on her head.*

Revelation (above) introduces Eve

NIV Rev 12:2 *She was pregnant and cried out in pain as she was about to give birth.*

Her child is born, she gives birth just as the Lord judged, with increased pain.

NIV Rev 12:3 *Then another sign appeared in heaven: an enormous red dragon with seven heads and ten horns and seven crowns on his heads.*

Above, enters her nemesis, the serpent, and we see the authority he has and gives to his offspring.

NIV Rev 12:4B *... The dragon stood in front of the woman who was about to give birth, so that he might devour her child the moment it was born.*

The enmity between her and the serpent now extends to include her offspring and his.

NIV Rev 12:5A *She gave birth to a son, a male child, who will rule all the nations with an iron scepter...*

By the decree of God, her righteous offspring is destined to crush the head of the serpent and his offspring, including the *antichrist*. He will take away all power from them to rule the world.

John's vision of the *woman* and the *dragon* in the *second narrative* tells us of the struggles between the *woman* and the *dragon*. Then after the birth of Christ (the baby she gives birth to) the enmity continues between the *devil* and his child the *antichrist*, and Eve and her Child—the Christ, including all of the people in the world who align with one camp or the other. At this stage, the story of John's vision comes to its end after having described the *great tribulation*, *Jesus'* return and His subjugation of the entire earth under His authority in the aftermath of the *battle of Armageddon* at Rev 12:14.

The *second narrative*:

The *second narrative* starts at Rev 12:15. The timeline of this narrative goes backwards starting with the time of the flood. The purpose is to introduce us to the *beast*, the *antichrist*, the next major player in the story of humanity. His story starts with the reason why God granted the flood to wipe out all the hybrid humans, the *Nephilim*—the giants. It is here that the story (prophecy) of the *second narrative* starts: the beginnings of the *antichrist*, his birth and his kingdom Babylon.

NLT Ge 6:1-4 When the human population began to grow rapidly on the earth, the sons of God saw the beautiful women of the human race and took any they wanted as their wives. Then the LORD said, "My Spirit will not put up with humans for such a long time, for they are only mortal flesh. In the future, they will live no more than 120 years." In those days, and even afterward, Nephilim (giants) lived on the earth, for whenever the sons of God (celestial beings-angels) *had intercourse with human women, they gave birth to children . . . these were the mighty men who were of old, men of renown (AMP).*

This (above) was the reason for the flood, to wipe out the giants who had no natural restraint, doing whatever they pleased making life on earth a living hell. Likewise, to wipe out all of man whose DNA had been corrupted by this happening. That is except for the DNA of Noah, his wife and sons. Thus, God is creating a new beginning for man from the hell they existed under. However, Noah's son Ham had as a wife, a person whose DNA was corrupted by these giant genes. This explains why it says above, "In those days, and even afterward, *Nephilim* (giants) lived on the earth." This explains why in John's vision this part starts with the flood.

NIV Rev 12:15-13:2 *Then from his mouth the serpent spewed water like a river, to overtake the woman and sweep her away with the torrent. But the earth helped the woman by opening its mouth and swallowing the river that the dragon had spewed out of his mouth* (the ocean basins are formed, the waters recede, and dry land makes for a new beginning). *Then the dragon was enraged at the woman and went off to make war against the rest of her offspring—those who obey God's commandments and hold to the testimony of Jesus. And the dragon stood on the shore of the sea. And I saw a beast coming out of the sea. He had ten horns and seven heads, with ten crowns on his horns, and on each head a blasphemous name. The beast I saw resembled a leopard, but had feet like those of a bear and a mouth like that of a lion. The dragon gave the beast his power and his throne and great authority.*

The *devil* saw his opportunity to once again dominate humanity on this side of the flood. It was in the DNA of Ham's wife. The devil waited on the shore for that ark to rest on dry land, because on it was the means to bring forth his human agent the *antichrist*, which is the beast coming out of one of the soul survivors of the flood—Ham's wife. Thus, through this vision, we are introduced and told the origins of the *beast* and *antichrist* and the authority he is given. It is a replica, a false copy and nemesis, of what God did through the child the woman gives birth to. It is He who God gives all His power, authority and throne over to, in order to further save mankind from the certain destruction and death the *devil* is leading humanity towards. The plan the *devil* has is carried out through his false savior and opponent of the real Savior, the Christ. The polarization of the righteous and unrighteous continues and takes new form from the very start of the *new beginning*.

However, not just the seed of the *antichrist* was on that ark, but through Noah's son, Shem, the seed of the Christ, the promised child that the *woman clothed with the sun* was pregnant with through her offspring, was also on that ark. These two opposing lines of offspring were present and represented on the other side of the flood at the *new beginning*. These two lines of offspring that God put enmity between also affirms that Eve was repentative after she understood the full weight of what her disobedience had set in motion. Although God did impose the consequences of the sin of Adam, Eve, and the *devil*, He honored her repentance by creating a plan for the redemption of her children. You could say the brothers Shem and Ham were as Seth and Cain and as were Cain and Abel fulfilling their respective roles and destinies in God's plan of salvation.

Question: If God picked the last family who had uncorrupted DNA (Noah's) saving only 8 out of the entire human race, why then would He allow Ham's wife who had corrupted DNA on board the ark? Although this may seem counterproductive on the surface, however, every member on that ark still had a sin nature even if they were pursuing God in their hearts. As such, when the world repopulates, and for God to carry out His plan, He needed to continue polarizing the righteous from the unrighteous in order to save only those sinners who have a heart's desire to be reconciled with God.

These roles and destinies continue to grow in scope through the formation of the 12 tribes of Israel (the twelve stars of the crown on Eve's head) and the formation of the Babylonian Empire (currently is the Holy Roman Empire [the Roman Catholic Church]) of the *beast, Nimrod*. It is through these two kingdoms that the enmity between the two offspring kicks into high gear. After establishing these two opposing people's redemption enters in with the liberation of Israel (the woman) from the bondage of slavery. Furthermore, with the Lord's presence being established among them through the law given to Moses, Israel is pulled out from under the power and authority of the *antichrist* (represented through Egypt at that time) then she is put under the power and authority of God. This narrative ends with the total annihilation of Babylon and its *antichrist* (the very thing God liberated His people from in the beginning). This *second narrative* concludes with the return of the conquering Christ establishing His Kingdom here on earth. This story is the full story of God's redeeming work in the earth from beginning to end which started as a promise to Eve in the garden.

In this *second narrative*, God identifies all the major players who have a leading role in man's fall and the story of God's plan for redemption and judgment. God shows us what the release of both His redemption and judgment looks like here on earth, and through whom it comes. This narrative also gives a background of each of those who play an important role in God's plan. The backgrounds of those involved, like the rest of Revelation, are wonderfully concise, but incredibly comprehensive.

Here is something noteworthy: It is not always easy to tell when the background of one subject ends and the beginning of the next one starts. As a result, the narrative has the appearance of not recording things in linear or sequential order. This is not the case, the comprehensive background of one figure can, in its timeline, overlap the background of the next. This gives the appearance of the vision sometimes going backwards in time if you do not recognize that the narrative or one of its subjects has switched from one figure to the next. In fact, if while reading Revelation, you notice it going back in time, breaking away from a linear narrative, it should be taken as a clue that the subject has changed and not that it is skipping back and forth in time.

A good example of this in the *second narrative* begins with verse 11:19. The subject of this narrative is the woman and the dragon, and the beginning of God's redemption. After making reference to Eve and the fall which facilitated the hatred between the *devil* and her and their respective offspring, it moves on to the birth of Christ. This subject ends with the time of God's wrath against the world after the *great tribulation*, the *devil* being thrown down to the earth, and his pursuit of the Israelites (the woman) and how they will be protected by God in the desert. Then verse 12:15 goes backwards to the flood and the *new beginning* of life on earth. This seemingly breaks free from the sequential order of the story of the *woman clothed with the sun* by going backwards from beyond the *great tribulation* to the flood.

This backtracking can be confusing and seems like a huge departure from the timeline that the vision was outlining, making it difficult at best to connect the dots. That confusion makes it all but impossible to interpret with this sudden shift of the timeline. Another factor that contributes to this dilemma is the fact that at the time this was written there was no use of paragraph division or punctuation, making it difficult to distinguish when one thought begins and ends as well as when a different subject begins. The interpreters needed to divide sentences and paragraphs up for us and they didn't always get it right even though they interpreted the words well.

However, the Spirit led eye will take note that there was a change of subjects at verse 12:15 and it is not a random going back and forth in time. This is not unlike recognizing when a movie suddenly jumps to a flashback in time. If you don't recognize it as a flashback, then you may be left confused about what is going on, thinking that this next scene is a continuation of the current storyline, making no sense at all. It leaves the reader of Revelation with the same effect, thinking that this break of going back in time is instead the next thing in succession to the previous. That being the case when it goes from the time of God's wrath to a flood, one would never logically interpret it as the flood of the past but a metaphor for a flood of something that is overwhelming.

In the case of John's vision, the beginning of the new subject overlaps the timeline of the former. The proper way to interpret, starting with verse 12:15 is to recognize the sudden backwards jump in the timeline. Catching this as a signal that it has completed one subject and is moving on to the next. Verse 12:15 starts to give background about the *antichrist* (*the beast out of the sea*). Unlike the *woman clothed with the sun*, and the clans of Israel which has its origin in the garden, the story of the *antichrist* and his Babylon (the world) has its origin at the new beginning, after the flood. The beast is the seed of the evil Ham and his wife who was one of the eight who survived the flood and repopulated the earth. The *devil* waiting on the shore of the sea (13:1) is him waiting for Noah's ark to rest on dry land so he can once again corrupt the human race starting with Ham and his bloodline.

Recognizing where one subject ends and the other begins also applies to the four different narratives. It is plain to distinguish between them when the story seemingly goes backwards or covers the same material it just spoke about. Here's a good example of that: The 3rd narrative ends with the New Jerusalem at 21:1. John says:

NIV Rev 21:1-2 Then I saw a new heaven and a new earth, for the first heaven and the first earth had passed away, and there was no longer any sea. I saw the Holy City, the new Jerusalem, coming down out of heaven from God, prepared as a bride beautifully dressed for her husband.

However, something strange happens. In the same chapter just 7 verses later, starting with verse 9, it starts speaking of the New Jerusalem from the beginning having the appearance of being redundant and covering the same ground twice just a few lines later. Only this time he starts the story differently.

NIV Rev 21:9-10 One of the seven angels who had the seven bowls full of the seven last plagues came and said to me, "Come, I will show you the bride, the wife of the Lamb." And he carried me away in the Spirit to a mountain great and high, and showed me the Holy City, Jerusalem, coming down out of heaven from God.

John is not deficient in his writing skills, nor is he being redundant or bouncing back and forth on his timeline. Rather he is beginning a new narrative. The 3rd one ends at 21:8 and the 4th one begins at verse 21:9. The 4th narrative begins with and has as its subject where the 3rd narrative ended, which is the *New Jerusalem*. It's a new story overlapping the previous story with its timeline! However, the other narratives do not just pick up where the previous ones ended as this one does. The next narrative may have as the beginning of its subject something that may bring it back almost to the beginning of the previous narrative, unlike the example above of the third and fourth narratives.

In giving background information on the important players of the story of humanity in the 2nd narrative, it contributes towards understanding details of how God's plan comes together, as well as how the story of humanity makes sense, flows, and helps us appreciate the struggles it takes to bring redemption to those who would choose it in a fallen world. It goes on to enlighten us of the final fate of these opposing forces or lines of the offspring of Eve through whom God's redemption and judgment is loosed on the earth. They are the Israelites, the *144,000*, *Jesus*, the *Church Pure*, the *Church Corrupt*, the *devil*, the *antichrist*, the *false prophet*, Babylon (the kingdom of the *antichrist*), and of course the Lord and His Kingdom.

The *third narrative*:

The *third narrative* begins with verse 17:1 and ends with verse 21:8.

AMP Mt 5:17-20 Do not think that I have come to do away with or undo the Law or the Prophets; I have come not to do away with or undo but to complete and fulfill them. For truly I tell you, until the sky and earth pass away and perish, not one smallest letter nor one little hook [identifying certain Hebrew letters] will pass from the Law until all things [it foreshadows] are accomplished. Whoever then breaks or does away with or relaxes one of the least [important] of these commandments and teaches men so shall be called least [important] in the kingdom of heaven, but he who practices them and teaches others to do so shall be called great in the kingdom of heaven. For I tell you, unless your righteousness (your uprightness and your right standing with God) is more than that of the scribes and Pharisees, you will never enter the kingdom of heaven.

When *Jesus* said these words, He was not just speaking about His purpose and actions while He was on the earth up until His *crucifixion*. He was talking about His role in God's plan all the way until its ultimate completion. This *third narrative* illustrates the fulfillment of all Biblical prophecy which speaks towards the total and permanent annihilation of Babylon, the *devil* and His human agent the *antichrist*, including all the power and authority they were granted through the release of the *four horsemen*. In other words, from the sin of Eve on to its end. Then it covers the establishment of the *Millennial Kingdom* of the *Lord* here on earth. Because the *New Jerusalem* is made of celestial matter (as the beginning of the *fourth narrative* informs us) and not physical matter, the Lord's Kingdom passes from its location on the earth to continue for all of eternity in the spiritual realm as the corrupted natural universe is disposed of in the *lake of fire* along with those who had chosen against God.

The *third narrative* begins with and has as its subject the discipline of the *Church Corrupt* who had empowered herself with Babylon, having had brought the spirit power of the *antichrist* into the Church. This is a shocking development! Although the *Church Pure* is *raptured* during the punishment of the *Church Corrupt* (the *great tribulation*); And those who hold tight to their testimony during the *great tribulation* are saved as the multitude beyond counting, the Church is utterly destroyed in the earth. It's fate on earth is never to rise up out of its ashes. Even during the *Millennium Reign* of Christ, according to the Bible, the Church and its Christian forms of worship are not there. During that time period the form of worship practiced will be the temple practices of the Israelites; this is according to Ezekiel and Revelation as a couple of examples. Let us look at how the Bible describes the fate and discipline of the Church:

NIV Rev 17:16-17 Then the angel said to me, "The waters you saw, where the prostitute sits, are peoples, multitudes, nations and languages. The beast and the ten horns you saw will hate the prostitute. They will bring her to ruin and leave her naked; they will eat her flesh and burn her with fire. For God has put it into their hearts to accomplish his purpose by agreeing to give the beast their power to rule, until God's words are fulfilled.

To leave her naked is to disembody her. The people of the Church will be "naked," disembodied *souls* finally bringing the numbers of the martyred to their fullness, triggering the judgment against the world.

NIV Rev 6:9-11 When he opened the fifth seal, I saw under the altar the souls of those who had been slain because of the word of God and the testimony they had maintained. They called out in a loud voice, "How long, Sovereign Lord, holy and true, until you judge the inhabitants of the earth and avenge our blood?" Then each of them was given a white robe, and they were told to wait a little longer, until the number of their fellow servants and brothers who were to be killed as they had been was completed.

Note: When the Lord tells them they will have to wait for the world to be judged until the number of their fellow servants and brothers who were to be killed as they had been was completed, the Bible informs us that He is talking to the *144,000*. In the verses that follow, the Bible lists each of the 12 tribes that comprised the *144,000*, who are the *firstfruits*, which ends at verse 8 of chapter 7. The very next verse, 7:9, describes and introduces John to the *great multitude* in their *celestial* bodies. One of the Heavenly elders brings them to John's attention and makes certain he knows who they are.

NIV Rev 7:13-15 Then one of the elders asked me, "These in white robes—who are they, and where did they come from?" I answered, "Sir, you know." <u>And he said, "These are they who have come out of the great tribulation; they have washed their robes and made them white in the blood of the Lamb.</u> Therefore, "they are before the throne of God.

By this we are being told that those who are the *144,000*, are made to wait until their brothers are killed as they were. Their brothers are the Christians who are killed in the *great tribulation*. We know this because as soon as that number is reached, not a single Christian can be killed. It says at that point, God gives them a mark on their foreheads that protects them. In addition, when that happens, immediately God's wrath starts to carry out the punishment of the inhabitants of the earth who killed them, as He promised the *144,000*.

Later it says:

AMP Rev 19:3 And again they shouted, Hallelujah (praise the Lord)! The smoke of her [burning] shall continue to ascend forever and ever (through the eternities of the eternities).

This is the end of the Church as we know it on the earth, but those believers who die during the *great tribulation* and are true to their testimony will not be destroyed but given clean white robes as the *144,000* were, which are *celestial* bodies. The *first resurrection* is for them, and they are the *great multitude* beyond counting.

NIV Rev 12:11-12 They overcame him by the blood of the Lamb and by the word of their testimony; they did not love their lives so much as to shrink from death. Therefore rejoice, you heavens and you who dwell in them! But woe to the earth and the sea, because the devil has gone down to you! He is filled with fury, because he knows that his time is short."

The saints who survived and possess the mark of God will rise in the sky to meet *Jesus* and those who had been *raptured*, along with all the dead who were killed in the *great tribulation*. Then, together, along with all the saints who have already received their *celestial* bodies, will return to the earth with Christ as *celestial* humans with the *New Jerusalem* when the time comes. They will rule as *celestial* beings over the natural humans with Christ for 1,000 years. Indeed, they will not be destroyed but cleansed through the loss of their natural bodies and the destruction in the earth of their Christian community. However, and again, there will be no Church/Christian practices during the 1,000 years, but only the temple worship of the Israelites. The Church would have already served its purpose—to give Christ a bride of *celestial* humans who would rule with Him during the *Millenium Reign* after the Jews had rejected that place. After all, in the Lord's absence they were His body in the earth carrying out His will. This tells us that we will continue to be the expression of Christ as co-leaders with Him and ministers to Him during the *Millenium Reign* as celestial humans; thereby never leaving His side, or losing our position of authority, for eternity. At this point all Christians are accounted for, making the Church in the physical realm irrelevant and obsolete—a bygone era. This is unlike the Israelites who must continue their ways during the *Millennial Reign* until the words and purposes of the Lord are fulfilled on the physical earth, also making Jesus' words true, *many who are first will be last, and many who are last will be first.* Mt 19:30

NIV Rev 12:17 Then the dragon was enraged at the woman and went off to make war against the rest of her offspring—those who obey God's commandments and hold to the testimony of Jesus.

The *second narrative* ends with this verse above (12:17). Those who hold to the *testimony of Jesus* are the ones who are in covenant with *Jesus*, the Christians. The Israelites are referred to as *the woman who gave birth to the male child* and *those who obey God's commandments (the law).* Together they are spoken of as being "the offspring" of the *woman clothed with the sun.* Even though the Israelites failed to give up their lives in the body so as to be in union with Christ, letting His Spirit live through them, the Bible refers to them as "the elect" of God. Those who are in union with Christ are His body in the earth and are referred to as "her child" who she gave birth to and were snatch up (*raptured*)—the *Church Pure.* They are in covenant relationship with Christ and are one flesh with Him in a spiritual, marital covenant, He in them, and them in Him.

NIV Ge 2:23-24 The man said, "This is now bone of my bones and flesh of my flesh; she shall be called 'woman,' for she was taken out of man." For this reason a man will leave his father and mother and be united to his wife, and they will become one flesh.

The Christians are the Lord's bride, His body in the earth.

NIV Rev 12:5 She gave birth to a son, a male child, who will rule all the nations with an iron scepter. And her child was snatched up to God and to his throne.

Jesus said after the last supper that they are one, His Spirit is theirs and their body is His—together they are one. It says of these that "her child is snatched up to God and to His throne." When it says her child, it includes those who actually are His body in the earth! This snatching up is referring to the *pretribulation rapture*. They will be *raptured* before the *end times global desolation* known as the *great tribulation*. Why? Because of the nature of a desolation. Jesus' Spirit will not be active in the earth, therefore His body, the *Church Pure* cannot be active in the earth—they are one. By what He spoke, Jesus promised that they will not be present during the horrors of the *great tribulation* as the *Church Corrupt* and the Israelites will.

AMP Jn 14:15-21 If you [really] love Me, you will keep (obey) My commands. And I will ask the Father, and He will give you another Comforter (Counselor, Helper, Intercessor, Advocate, Strengthener, and Standby), <u>that He may remain with you forever—The Spirit of Truth</u>, Whom the world cannot receive (welcome, take to its heart), because it does not see Him or know and recognize Him. But you know and recognize Him, for He lives with you [constantly] and will be in you. <u>I will not leave you as orphans [comfortless, desolate, bereaved, forlorn, helpless]</u>; I will come [back] to you. Just a little while now, and the world will not see Me any more, but you will see Me; because I live, you will live also. At that time [when that day comes] you will know [for yourselves] that I am in My Father, and you [are] in Me, and I [am] in you. The person who has My commands and keeps them is the one who [really] loves Me; and whoever [really] loves Me will be loved by My Father, and I [too] will love him and will show (reveal, manifest) Myself to him. [I will let Myself be clearly seen by him and make Myself real to him.]

Jesus says, *Just a little while now, and the world will not see Me any more, but you will see Me* and: *I will not leave you as orphans [comfortless, desolate, bereaved, forlorn, helpless]; I will come [back] to you.* This time period, Jesus is talking about, where He will leave them for a little while and will come back to them, is the time period from when He dies on the cross, to the day of Pentecost. That is when He returns to the earth, only this time He has changed earthly bodies. He now is embodied in His believers—He is one whole person with them, and not in the previous earthly body of Jesus. Therefore, this is the reason why Jesus said, *"the world will not see Me any more, but you will see Me.*" The world will not recognize Jesus in the body of those they are acquainted with and think are mere men. In those verses above Jesus stated as a promise, *"I will not leave you as orphans [comfortless, <u>DESOLATE,</u> bereaved, forlorn, helpless]."* So, if the world is to endure a *global desolation* for 3½ years, a time when He is silent and inactive in the earth, then to keep the above promise, He must take His bride, His body, whom He is one with, where He is. Understanding the relationship between Christians and their Lord is so important here because together their bodies being moved by His Spirit through obedience makes them one whole person with the Lord. Couple that understanding with Jesus' promise to never leave them, and the definition of a desolation (meaning an absence of God in the earth) is proof positive that there is a *pretribulation rapture*, a snatching up.

Note: It is important to realize that there are two raptures: there is a *pretribulation rapture* that Jesus describes when He talks about two men working in a field:

NIV Mt 24:37-42 As it was in the days of Noah, so it will be at the coming of the Son of Man. For in the days before the flood, people were eating and drinking, marrying and giving in marriage, up to the day Noah entered the ark; and they knew nothing about what would happen until the flood came and took them all away. That is how it will be at the coming of the Son of Man. Two men will be in the field; one will be taken and the other left. Two women will be grinding with a hand mill; one will be taken and the other left. "Therefore keep watch, because you do not know on what day your Lord will come.

We know Jesus is referring to a pretribulation rapture because He says it will be like in the days of Noah BEFORE the flood. In other words, some will be raptured before the great tribulation begins. Secondly, there will be an additional *rapture* after the seven years of God's wrath is complete, joining Him in the sky, immediately before His return to the earth for His *Millennial Reign*. The second rapture is what Paul is referring to in Thessalonians.

The *Church Corrupt,* on the other hand, the Lord has spewed out of His mouth because they have become apostates and have turned against Him.

AMP Rev 3:15-17 I know your [record of] works and what you are doing; you are neither cold nor hot. Would that you were cold or hot! So, because you are lukewarm and neither cold nor hot, I will spew you out of My mouth! For you say, I am rich; I have prospered and grown wealthy, and I am in need of nothing; and you do not realize and understand that you are wretched, pitiable, poor, blind, and naked.

NIV Mt 25:20-30 The man who had received the five talents (a measure of the Lord's own Spirit) *brought the other five. 'Master,' he said, 'you entrusted me with five talents. See, I have gained five more.' "His master replied, 'Well done, good and faithful servant! You have been faithful with a few things; I will put you in charge of many things. Come and share your master's happiness!' "The man with the two talents also came. 'Master,' he said, 'you entrusted me with two talents; see, I have gained two more.' "His master replied, 'Well done, good and faithful servant! You have been faithful with a few things; I will put you in charge of many things. Come and share your master's happiness!' "Then the man who had received the one talent came. 'Master,' he said, 'I knew that you are a hard man, harvesting where you have not sown and gathering where you have not scattered seed. So I was afraid and went out and hid your talent in the ground. See, here is what belongs to you.' "His master replied, 'You wicked, lazy servant! So you knew that I harvest where I have not sown and gather where I have not scattered seed? Well then, you* *should have put my money on deposit with the bankers, so that when I returned I would have received it back with interest. " <u>'Take the talent from him</u>* (the Lord takes back His Spirit from them, spewing them out of His mouth, in essence spiritually divorcing them because of their adultery with the world) <u>*and give it to the one who has the ten talents. For everyone who has will be given more, and he will have an abundance. Whoever does not have, even what he has will be taken from him. And throw that worthless servant outside, into the darkness, where there will be weeping and gnashing of teeth*</u> (the great tribulation).'

They must endure the *great tribulation* in order to be purified and return to bride status, becoming *celestial* humans as a result of their faithfulness while enduring this *global desolation*. It is for this reason alone that the Lord grants power to the beast (*antichrist*) and puts it in his heart to hate and kill the *Church Corrupt*. It is to save them as He did to Gomer, Hosea's wayward wife. Hosea's instruction to marry an unfaithful woman was a prophetic story meant to show how the Lord will save us, even after we have strayed, before He punishes the whole world.

AMP Rev 3:15-22 *I know your deeds, that you are neither cold nor hot. I wish you were either one or the other! So, because you are lukewarm—neither hot nor cold—I am about to spit you out of my mouth.* (meaning they will no longer be in Him and therefore left behind) *You say, 'I am rich; I have acquired wealth and do not need a thing.' But you do not realize that you are wretched, pitiful, poor, blind and naked. I counsel you to buy from me gold refined in the fire* (refined through the fires of the *great tribulation*), *so you can become rich; and white clothes to wear* (celestial bodies to clothe their souls with), *so you can cover your shameful nakedness* (of being a disembodied soul); *and salve to put on your eyes, so you can see* (the truth of your spiritual condition). *Those whom I love I rebuke and discipline. So be earnest, and repent. Here I am! I stand at the door and knock. If anyone hears my voice and opens the door, I will come in and eat with him, and he with me. To him who overcomes, I will give the right to sit with me on my throne, just as I overcame and sat down with my Father on his throne. He who has an ear, let him hear what the Spirit says to the churches."*

The Israelites had forfeited their place as the bride. As such, they remain natural humans until the *last day* after the *Millennium Reign* of Christ. This *Millennium Reign* is actually for the Israelites and God's promises being kept towards them. Should they all become *celestial* humans and if they all died off during the *great tribulation* becoming disembodied souls in *Hades*, there would be no natural Israelites to participate in the promised Kingdom of the Lord on the earth. That is why, for the second time, the Lord gives them a place to hide in the desert as opposed to snatching them up like those who are in union with Him. All three groups are protected and become what they are destined to be.

The *third narrative*:

The *third narrative* basically covers, in great detail, what happens during the 6th and 7th seals, and beyond, to the end. The narrative begins with the corruption of the Church. It shows how the *Church Corrupt* is redeemed in spite of themselves and made pure through their martyrdom while holding fast to their testimony, not worshipping the *beast*, or taking his mark. This time period is called, by Jesus, the time of darkness when "no one can work," or the *great tribulation*. After it covers how Babylon in the *Church Corrupt* is made pure through its destruction, it then covers how the world is punished, paid back for its misdeeds, then brought into submission to Christ and the government of His Kingdom. In telling us about the end, this narrative brings us further with more vivid detail than the two before it. It covers the *1,000-Year Reign* of Christ, the *last day of judgment*, and life beyond in the new heavens and new earth. It ends with some closing words and promises from the Father.

NIV Rev 21:1-8 *Then I saw a new heaven and a new earth, for the first heaven and the first earth had passed away, and there was no longer any sea. I saw the Holy City, the new Jerusalem, coming down out of heaven from God, prepared as a bride beautifully dressed for her husband. And I heard a loud voice from the throne saying, "Now the dwelling of God is with men, and he will live with them. They will be his people, and God himself will be with them and be their God. He will wipe every tear from their eyes. There will be no more death or mourning or crying or pain, for the old order of things has passed away." He who was seated on the throne said, "I am making everything new!" Then he said, "Write this down, for these words are trustworthy and true." He said to me: "It is done. I am the Alpha and the Omega, the Beginning and the End. To him who is thirsty I will give to drink without cost from the spring of the water of life. He who overcomes will inherit all this, and I will be his God and he will be my son. But the cowardly, the unbelieving, the vile, the murderers, the sexually immoral, those who practice magic arts, the idolaters and all liars—their place will be in the fiery lake of burning sulfur. This is the second death."*

The *fourth and final narrative* begins with verse 21:9 and goes to the end of the book (verse 22:21). It is the shortest of the four narratives. It concerns itself with life and where we will live it after all is said and done. It finishes with a few closing words first from Jesus, and then from John who this vision was revealed to. The last narrative begins with the *New Jerusalem* (exactly where the previous one ended). Included is insight into the *1,000-Year Reign* of Christ. Also covering how Jesus, His Father, angels, and celestial humans living in the *New Jerusalem* will interact with and rule over the natural humans on the earth. It reveals the favor and kept promises given to natural Israel which will cause the rest of the natural world to serve them right on up to the *last day* when the natural universe and all its elements will be destroyed. Then, it ends with the promise which awaits us afterwards, the new heavens and the new earth in the spiritual realm (the only surviving domain). It is to be occupied by the *New Jerusalem, celestial* humans, His angels, the Lord and His God and Father, and finally those who are declared sheep (redeemed) on the *last day* will be added to their numbers. They too, the sheep, will be celestial humans who are to be citizens in the world to come, at which time the bride of Christ will continue to govern with Him in the new heavens and the new earth.

These are the four narratives which comprise the vision and the book of Revelation. This was a short outline of them. Greater detail will be given in volumes three through six where line by line interpretation of the book of Revelation will be given. It is the purpose of volume one to be a basic outline and introduction to help frame all that will be revealed during volumes three through six in order to interpret it properly.

CHAPTER THREE

The Story of Judgment and Redemption

The entire natural universe, including the human race, has been judged and is being held over for utter destruction. The gavel has gone down, the world has been found guilty, the sentence has already been executed and is in process of completion. We are living on borrowed time; we are on a sinking ship. Peter tells us of the completion and last day of this judgment:

AMP 2Pe 3:10-12 *But the day of the Lord will come like a thief, and then the heavens will vanish (pass away) with a thunderous crash, and the [material] elements [of the universe] will be dissolved with fire, and the earth and the works that are upon it will be burned up. Since all these things are thus in the process of being dissolved, what kind of person ought [each of] you to be [in the meanwhile] in consecrated and holy behavior and devout and godly qualities, While you wait and earnestly long for (expect and hasten) the coming of the day of God by reason of which the flaming heavens will be dissolved, and the [material] elements [of the universe] will flare and melt with fire?*

And again, in Isaiah:

AMP Isa 34:1-4 *COME NEAR, you nations, to hear; and hearken, you peoples! Let the earth hear, and all that is in it; the world, and all things that come forth from it. For the Lord is indignant against all nations, and His wrath is against all their host. He has utterly doomed them, He has given them over to slaughter. Their slain also shall be cast out, and the stench of their dead bodies shall rise, and the mountains shall flow with their blood. All the host of the heavens shall be dissolved and crumble away, and the skies shall be rolled together like a scroll; and all their host [the stars and the planets]* shall drop like a faded leaf from the vine, and like a withered fig from the fig tree.*

Then that fire, which will dissolve every single atom in the physical universe will remain forever, and confined within it will be the souls of the dead who are not to live forever with the Lord.

These souls will have then endured a second death by being thrown alive into the *lake of fire* after having been resurrected to life. Humanity itself (natural humans clothed with flesh) has been condemned. This is the sentence the entire natural universe is under, no exceptions. All human flesh will be destroyed. Meaning anyone and everyone possessing human flesh will lose their embodiment of flesh becoming disembodied—dead—no exceptions. This sobering reality cannot be overstated!

AMP 2Pe 2:22-3:9 *There has befallen them the thing spoken of in the true proverb, The dog turns back to his own vomit, and, The sow is washed only to wallow again in the mire. BELOVED, I am now writing you this second letter. In [both of] them I have stirred up your unsullied (not spoiled or made impure) (sincere) mind by way of remembrance, That you should recall the predictions of the holy (consecrated, dedicated) prophets and the commandment of the Lord and Savior [given] through your apostles (His special messengers). To begin with, you must know and understand this, that scoffers (mockers) will come in the last days with scoffing, [people who] walk after their own fleshly desires And say, Where is the promise of His coming? For since the forefathers fell asleep, all things have continued exactly as they did from the beginning of creation. For they willfully overlook and forget this [fact], that the heavens [came into] existence long ago by the word of God, and the earth also which was formed out of water and by means of water, Through which the world that then [existed] was deluged with water and perished. But by the same word the present heavens and earth have been stored up (reserved) for fire, being kept until the day of judgment and destruction of the ungodly people. Nevertheless, do not let this one fact escape you, beloved, that with the Lord one day is as a thousand years and a thousand years as one day. The Lord does not delay and is not tardy or slow about what He promises, according to some people's conception of slowness, but He is long-suffering (extraordinarily patient) toward you, not desiring that any should perish, but that all should turn to repentance.*

Redemption is a gift from God. If anyone is to receive it, it is by the grace of God. However, as stated, all flesh will perish. All humans have souls that are immortal, and are not comprised of natural matter, and as such they will not melt in the fire of the last day but will be tormented by it while disembodied. The soul is the real man; it is the mind and personality. As such and given the soul is not comprised of natural matter, it will survive the destruction of the natural universe and that of its own flesh. However, it will become disembodied. It will be temporarily held in the realm of the dead (*Hades*), then given a new supernatural body so as to face the day of the Lord—the day of judgement. At which time if found unworthy, this second but spiritual body the soul now resides in, will experience what Peter calls, the second death. The first death of our physical body is a result of the sin of Adam and Eve. Our second death is a result of our own sin, how we conducted ourselves while alive in the body. Those who experience the second death will have as an ultimate residence, the *lake of fire* which is not a temporary place like *Hades*, but is eternal.

AMP Jude 1:10-16 But these men revile (scoff and sneer at) anything they do not happen to be acquainted with and do not understand; and whatever they do understand physically [that which they know by mere instinct], like irrational beasts—by these they corrupt themselves and are destroyed (perish). Woe to them! For they have run riotously in the way of Cain, and have abandoned themselves for the sake of gain [it offers them, following] the error of Balaam, and have perished in rebellion [like that] of Korah! These are hidden reefs (elements of danger) in your love feasts, where they boldly feast sumptuously [carousing together in your midst], without scruples providing for themselves [alone]. They are clouds without water, swept along by the winds; trees, without fruit at the late autumn gathering time—twice (doubly) dead, [lifeless and] plucked up by the roots; Wild waves of the sea, flinging up the foam of their own shame and disgrace; wandering stars, for whom the gloom of eternal darkness has been reserved forever. It was of these people, moreover, that Enoch in the seventh [generation] from Adam prophesied when he said, Behold, the Lord comes with His myriads of holy ones (ten thousands of His saints) To execute judgment upon all and to convict all the impious (unholy ones) of all their ungodly deeds which they have committed [in such an] ungodly [way], and of all the severe (abusive, jarring) things which ungodly sinners have spoken against Him. These are inveterate (having a particular habit, activity, or interest that is long-established and unlikely to change) *murmurers* (grumblers) *who complain [of their lot in life], going after their own desires [controlled by their passions]; their talk is boastful and arrogant, [and they claim to] admire men's persons and pay people flattering compliments to gain advantage.*

The question then is: How can anyone be redeemed if death to the body is the fate of all flesh without exception? An understandable way of characterizing redemption would be to escape disembodiment (death) and confinement in the *lake of fire* by means of a spiritual rebirth of the soul and of its attainment of a celestial embodiment. That is, to be born again. This time, however, it is with a celestial embodiment as the soul's clothing. The celestial or spiritual realm will remain for eternity and not be destroyed as the natural realm is doomed to. To survive in that environment, one needs to have an embodiment made up of spiritual matter and no longer of natural matter. This is why Jesus said we must be born again of a different species of humans—celestial humans,to enter into the Kingdom of God.

AMP Jn 3:3-7 Jesus answered him, I assure you, most solemnly I tell you, that unless a person is born again (anew, from above), he cannot ever see (know, be acquainted with, and experience) the kingdom of God. Nicodemus said to Him, How can a man be born when he is old? Can he enter his mother's womb again and be born? Jesus answered, I assure you, most solemnly I tell you, unless a man is born of water and [even] the Spirit, he cannot [ever] enter the kingdom of God. What is born of [from] the flesh is flesh [of the physical is physical]; and what is born of the Spirit is spirit (including an embodiment that is spiritual not physical). *Marvel not [do not be surprised, astonished] at My telling you, You must all be born anew (from above).*

Reborn as a spiritual or celestial creature, both in spirit and in body. That is, while the soul (mind and personality) remains but is convicted by the new spirit causing it to obey God.

AMP Heb 4:12 *For the Word that God speaks is alive and full of power [making it active, operative, energizing, and effective]; it is sharper than any two-edged sword, penetrating to the dividing line of the breath of life (soul) and [the immortal] spirit* (surgically separating, our soul from our corrupt human spirit) *and of joints and marrow* (surgically separating, our soul from our physical body) *[of the deepest parts of our nature], exposing and sifting and analyzing and judging the very thoughts and purposes of the heart* (convicting our soul, mind and personality to be in right standing with God).

The soul, therefore, will live on as a different kind of human creature than those who possess a natural embodiment of flesh. These humans who escape eternal disembodiment we refer to as, "celestial humans." This is God's plan of redemption.

AMP 1Co 15:44-47 *It is sown a natural (physical) body; it is raised a supernatural (a spiritual) body. [As surely as] there is a physical body, there is also a spiritual body. Thus it is written, The first man Adam became a living being (an individual personality); the last Adam (Christ) became a life-giving Spirit [restoring the dead to life]. But it is not the spiritual life which came first, but the physical and then the spiritual. The first man [was] from out of earth, made of dust (earthly-minded); the second Man [is] the Lord from out of heaven.*

By Paul calling Jesus the second or last Adam, he is communicating to us that Jesus is like Adam in that they both were the first and from them came an entire species of humans. The first Adam is a natural man embodied with physical flesh comprised from the elements of the natural universe (the dust). He was the first-born and from him came forth a species of natural humans also clothed in flesh. Jesus, the second Adam, is not embodied by the elements of the natural universe (except during His time in the earthly body of Jesus), but whose nature and domain is that of the spiritual realm. He too is the first-born and from Him comes a species of humans who are by nature celestial humans, and are clothed, as He, with a spiritual embodiment made of the elements of the spiritual realm. Paul started these verses off by saying, as sure as there are physical bodies made of the elements of the natural universe (of which we presently possess), there are also spiritual bodies made of the elements of the spiritual realm, or the spiritual dimension. Which the redeemed will possess as soon as they lay down their physical body without experiencing death (disembodiment).

The biblical name Adam comes from the Hebrew word Adamah, meaning "ground" or "earth" and also carries the meaning of "man" or "mankind." The name has a dual meaning: It is the proper name of the first man created by God from the elements (dust) of the earth. This is a wordplay of the original Hebrew text between Adam and ground.

Through the one Adam, the first-born of many, came a species of natural humans. Through the other Adam, also the first-born of many, came a species of celestial humans who formerly had a natural body, as Jesus did. Although there are only two species of humans and Paul refers to the first-born of each as an Adam, he doesn't rightfully call Jesus "the second Adam." Instead, he calls Him "the last Adam." This is because there is not and will not be any more species of humans.

Jesus says:

NIV Jn 14:6 *Jesus answered, "I am the way and the truth and the life. No one comes to the Father except through me.*

NIV Jn 11:25 *Jesus said to her, "I am the resurrection and the life. He who believes in me will live, even though he dies*

Much of the population cannot accept that it is only through Jesus one can be redeemed or saved. They believe there are many ways to seek out God and to find Him. According to the old humanistic proverb that states, there are many paths up the mountain, and they all lead to the same place, the top. They simply cannot come to terms with the idea that a loving God would only make one way to Him.

However, these same people do not grasp their true situation or that of humanity. They do not see how their independence is an affront to God, and how humanity is already under a death sentence. They have a premise of thought that all have access allowing them to approach God at their own leave. Not only that, but they don't understand that it is not by their choice if they want to relate to God, as if God has no say in the matter, or that He has no objections concerning humanity. Most importantly, they do not realize that the entire human race stands condemned, and it is only by becoming a different species of humans that they will be salvaged.

Jesus is the first-born and the source of that different kind of human species that will survive the destruction of the natural universe. It is only through union with Him that we can become a celestial human and become a part of that different species. It is not a simple matter of becoming a part of that different species. It is not a matter of climbing to the top of the mountain and having a knowledge of God, but a matter of becoming a different species of humans in order to survive the judgment of natural humans. In other words, going up the mountain won't help, but through the way, the truth, and the life we can metamorphosize into a new species of humans, just as the worm metamorphizes into a butterfly.

Just as through one man, God started and created the entire human race, so is it that He creates another species of humans through one man. The only difference being the first species produced humans through the birth of a new soul. Whereas the second species of humans are produced by the rebirth of an existing soul.

Humans are the most uniquely created beings in either the spiritual or natural realm. They are the only created beings with three natures, a spirit, soul, and body. They have a corresponding nature that is in line with the three natures of God, the Creator. The Spirit of God correlates with the human spirit. The Father, who is the will and mind of God, correlates with the soul or mind of man. And finally, the Word of God, which embodies God and His Spirit, and is the outward manifestation of God, which correlates to the body of man.

Both God and man are each one being with three distinct natures. You wouldn't address the man's body and see him as three distinct persons, but a being that is one person with three distinct natures. When you look at God seeing His embodiment, you see Him as one being.

All this being the case, man can relate to God in a way that no other created being can. No other created being, angelic or animal, has this unique makeup. All other created beings, celestial or natural, are biune beings. Their natures are two: spirit and body. The angelic creatures of the spirit realm are spirit, and celestial bodies. The animal creatures of the natural realm are spirit and natural bodies of flesh.

The second species of humans, known as celestial humans, are to be the last created species of beings who are triune beings having three natures; spirit, soul, and body and can, as a result, relate to every corresponding nature of God. They will live forever in direct fellowship with God and in the spiritual realm (the natural habitat of their newly received celestial bodies). Their numbers will remain the same forever. They do not die, and they do not propagate, but were selected and reborn from (or evolved out of) natural humans who already were living souls.

AMP Mt 22:29-32 *But Jesus replied to them, You are wrong because you know neither the Scriptures nor God's power. For in the resurrected state neither do [men] marry nor are [women] given in marriage, but they are like the angels in heaven. But as to the resurrection of the dead—have you never read what was said to you by God, I am the God of Abraham, and the God of Isaac, and the God of Jacob? He is not the God of the dead but of the living!*

After natural humans became corrupt and doomed under judgment, God did not make from scratch a new species of humans whose habitat would be in the spiritual realm while discarding all natural humans. He instead takes from among the corrupt. Then, He purifies the souls with the convicting power of the new Spirt. By granting a rebirth which attains a new Spirit and a new body. Then, when the process is complete, the purified natural human soul becomes a celestial human. Their natural habitat is no longer the physical earth, but the spiritual realm.

The natural humans whose habitat is the natural universe, do propagate. Their souls were created by God and He blew into the nostrils of Adam the life-giving spirit, the breath of life. However, because the human spirit became corrupted, death entered in. Not only in death, but both the natural species of humans and his natural habitat (the physical universe) is judged, doomed to an end and will be destroyed. Thus, the only survivors of the human race will be the celestial humans whose souls are not created new by God, but are salvaged souls chosen from among the condemned. They are souls taken from among natural humans who undergo a rebirth which changes both their spirit, body and habitat. Same soul, new creature, adapted to a new environment. These celestial humans will not be like the preverbal "fish out of water" in the spiritual dimension. They will be more like a fish keeping its personality and without dying receiving a body transplant which would allow it to live normally on dry land. Fully adapted to do so, and as a result no longer adapted to life in the ocean, from once it came.

In addition, after the destruction of both natural humans and the natural universe, only one realm will remain. That is the spiritual realm, which is the natural habitat of God, the angelic beings, and the celestial humans taken from among the natural humans, who are hence destroyed. Again, there will be a natural, or physical universe no more. By this plan of redemption and judgment, God has found a way. He has created a new species of humans born from the souls/personalities He has taken from among the condemned, who as a result of their new birth will transcend their destruction as a natural human. As such, there is only one way to survive the destruction of the natural universe and it is not a "path" we take, but a rebirth that makes us a different species of humans that we attain exclusively from the last Adam. As with the entire natural human race there was only one source, Adam. Likewise, it is through one source, the second Adam, that the entire celestial human race will be born out of.

AMP 1Co 15:48-57 Now those who are made of the dust are like him who was first made of the dust (earthly-minded); and as is [the Man] from heaven, so also [are those] who are of heaven (heavenly-minded). And just as we have borne the image [of the man] of dust, so shall we and so let us also bear the image [of the Man] of heaven. But I tell you this, brethren, flesh and blood cannot [become partakers of eternal salvation and] inherit or share in the kingdom of God; nor does the perishable (that which is decaying) inherit or share in the imperishable (the immortal). Take notice! I tell you a mystery (a secret truth, an event decreed by the hidden purpose or counsel of God). We shall not all fall asleep [in death], but we shall all be changed (transformed) In a moment, in the twinkling of an eye, at the [sound of the] last trumpet call. For a trumpet will sound, and the dead [in Christ] will be raised imperishable (free and immune from decay), and we shall be changed (transformed). For this perishable [part of us] must put on the imperishable [nature], and this mortal [part of us, this nature that is capable of dying] must put on immortality (freedom from death). And when this perishable puts on the imperishable and this that was capable of dying puts on freedom from death, then shall be fulfilled the Scripture that says, Death is swallowed up (utterly vanquished forever) in and unto victory. O death, where is your victory? O death, where is your sting? Now sin is the sting of death, and sin exercises its power [upon the soul] through [the abuse of] the Law. But thanks be to God, Who gives us the victory [making us conquerors] through our Lord Jesus Christ.

Even in God's condemnation and destruction of humanity, He, in His grace, has made a way for humans to transcend the natural world and their natural embodiment. God did so because all flesh will be destroyed leaving the immortal soul who is embodied by it, naked—unclothed—disembodied.

As a side note: This is proof that there is no life in the universe other than on earth, and that the cosmos is there as a wonder for humans to know there is a God and how big of a God He is. Otherwise, why would God destroy all of the universe and all life in it because of a problem on an isolated planet, earth.

In review, the one and only way out for the living soul is to be reborn again of a new spirit, becoming spiritual and not having a natural nature. Then, in turn, for the soul (the mind and personality) of the individual to undergo a rebirth, clothing him with a celestial body—no longer with natural flesh. Having a celestial body is the only way for an individual to circumvent the fate of all flesh, which is to be destroyed.

It is also important to note that references about "spirits" (of the spiritual realm) is a term referring to a particular life-principle (power and awareness) possessing a certain quality, however, it is without an embodiment. Spirit power and consciousness animates and gives substance to its embodiment. A spirit is no more embodied in the spirit realm than it would be in the natural realm. It is an invisible but living force, just as electricity is a powerful force, yet is invisible and has no form. There are spirit forces that we fight against which seek out expression of its motives and conscious energy through us. However, these spirit forces are only embodied when they motivate and move an embodied creature, such as an angel or a human being, for example. The spirit of jealousy is a conscious living power which will motivate and move a creature with a murderous anger, causing him to perceive what he sees in an envious and covetous way. It is then that the spirit of jealousy motivates, inspires and dictates in what light an individual perceives a matter, if that individual embodies the spirit of jealousy—or the spirit of jealousy is embodied by him.

CHAPTER FOUR

Death, Salvation, and the Afterlife

(Correcting the Errors Taught by the Contemporary Church)

If you were being evangelized by the contemporary church, they would ask, if you died today, where would you go, to Heaven or to *Hell*? If answered with uncertainty, they will convince you how important it is for you to make certain you do know. Next, they would tell you how one becomes saved/redeemed. The contemporary church would recite the following verse:

NIV Eph 2:8-9 For it is by grace you have been saved, through faith— and this not from yourselves, it is the gift of God—not by works, so that no one can boast.

How does one acquire this grace? The contemporary church would next recite the following verse:

NIV Ro 10:9-10 That if you confess with your mouth, "Jesus is Lord," and believe in your heart that God raised him from the dead, you will be saved. For it is with your heart that you believe and are justified, and it is with your mouth that you confess and are saved.

Here are a couple more foundational questions a new believer might have. When will we get our resurrected (*celestial*) body? The contemporary church will answer: After the resurrection of the dead. Where do we go when we die and before we become resurrected? The contemporary church will answer: your disembodied soul will be in a sleep-like state in a heavenly place until you are resurrected.

Death, salvation and the afterlife, these are some of the most important subjects which are skewed and misunderstood by the contemporary Christian church. Yes, these things are foundational to the faith, and yes, it might seem unreasonable to state this, however, it is the case. In general, the Church, pastors, and scholars alike understand death in a completely skewed context. Likewise, they think in terms of when you die you will either go to Heaven or to Hell. In general, the Church's understanding of the afterlife is one-dimensional. As such, they try to squeeze scriptures which speak about different subjects into one event, and in doing so understandably twist the meaning of what is said. Here is an excellent example:

It is a school of thought that when a Christian dies, he will remain in a state of sleep. Then, at the resurrection, that is, on the resurrection that occurs on the day of judgement, he will get his celestial body after a time of having been asleep. One has to ask the question, what is the difference between being dead and asleep while being disembodied? How are the redeemed to be distinguished from the condemned after their body dies until the day of resurrection? And why would they need to be asleep in a heavenly place if they are not conscious (aware), or dead in a state of sleep? This thought really doesn't make any sense.

Herein lies a perfect example of trying to make everything fit into one event resulting in a skewed understanding of it. Most Christians and their teachers do not recognize that the Bible tells us that there are two resurrections, two raptures, and two deaths. Believing that there is only one of each of these events causes us to have an utter misunderstanding of scriptures. Below we will address each of these subjects.

In regard to the Christian (or all souls that are dead, for that matter) being in a state of sleep, or unconsciousness, is based on both Jesus and Paul referring to the dead as being "asleep," or "asleep in Christ." As such, it is interpreted to mean the dead are in a state of sleep, unconsciousness—in a state of suspended animation. This is a skewed understanding of how they used the term "asleep" to describe the dead. Jesus and Paul did not mean dead Christians were in a state of unconsciousness—oblivious—such as the living would

revelation of Revelation • 91

be when they are asleep, and their bodies are not moving while asleep.

The Sadducees were one of the most powerful sects of the Jews at the time when Jesus was here in the body. They taught that there was no resurrection of the dead. Additionally, they believed that once you died, you ceased to exist—when you are dead, you are dead. This was a greatly debated doctrine at that time. The Pharisees who also were one of the most powerful sects of the Jews, believed that the soul lived on after the body dies. Also, that there was a resurrection of the dead on the last day at which time people would be judged. Jesus taught that the soul lives on and there is a resurrection of the dead. This is why He had more than a few followers who were the Pharisees. In fact, for this reason the Pharisees defended the teachings of Jesus against the teachings of the Sadducees. The Pharisees, Sadducees, Rabbis, and scribes were the keepers and interpreters of the word of God. If they misunderstood the scriptures, hotly debating them while creating divisions and sects, it should not be a big surprise that the contemporary church can do the same. Accordingly, we should expect the same result, that Christianity would also divide into sects, or denominations due to these misinterpretations.

Jesus once spoke to the Sadducees concerning this subject in the verses below. They had tried to test Him to determine if His teachings were true and could be trusted. Why this subject? Because it was one of the most foundational and hottest debated subjects during that time which divided them. What they interpreted from scripture proved (in their minds) that there was no life after death. They would deduce and prove their thinking by adding up different verses ending with, $2+2 = 5$.

Applying their logic to the law, when a man marries, the two become one. If the man dies, the wife is free to marry another, which the law allows. So, what if the woman has survived several husbands or what about couples that divorce having had multiple marriages? Continuing their logic, there obviously can be no afterlife. Their reasoning is, if they are one flesh, which wife would be with which husband in the afterlife? Therefore, God's perfect law would not allow for this impossible situation that cannot be resolved. Thus, there can be no afterlife and as a result, no resurrection of the dead.

NIV Mt 22:29-33 Jesus replied, "You are in error because you do not know (understand and interpret) *the Scriptures or the power of God. At the resurrection people will neither marry nor be given in marriage; they will be like the angels in heaven. But about the resurrection of the dead—have you not read what God said to you, 'I am the God of Abraham, the God of Isaac, and the God of Jacob'? He is not the God of the dead but of the living." When the crowds heard this, they were astonished at his teaching.*

By saying this, Jesus is telling us first; that our celestial bodies will not be sexually oriented but like the celestial bodies of angels. Furthermore, celestial humans will not give birth to new celestial humans (as physical humans do) increasing the population of Heaven. The fact is, the Bible tells us that celestial humans will never die, and they are not created but are gleaned from physical humans (souls) who are redeemed. After the conclusion of the day of judgment, the population of celestial humans will remain the same for all of eternity.

This skewed type of intellectual logic is repeated over and over again, including leaders in the Church, over the centuries.

AMP 1Co 2:12-14 Now we have not received the spirit [that belongs to] the world, but the [Holy] Spirit Who is from God, [given to us] that we might realize and comprehend and appreciate the gifts [of divine favor and blessing so freely and lavishly] bestowed on us by God. And we are setting these truths forth in words not <u>taught by human wisdom but taught by the [Holy] Spirit, combining and interpreting spiritual truths with spiritual language [to those who possess the Holy Spirit]</u>. But the natural, nonspiritual man does not accept or welcome or admit into his heart the gifts and teachings and revelations of the Spirit of God, for they are folly (meaningless nonsense) to him; and he is incapable of knowing them [of *progressively recognizing, understanding, and becoming better acquainted with them] because they are spiritually discerned and estimated and appreciated.*

AMP 1Co 2:16-3 For who has known or understood the mind (the counsels and purposes) of the Lord so as to guide and instruct Him and give Him knowledge? But we have the mind of Christ (the Messiah) and do hold the thoughts (feelings and purposes) of His heart. HOWEVER, BRETHREN, I could not talk to you as to spiritual [men], but as to nonspiritual [men of the flesh, in whom the carnal nature predominates], as to mere infants [in the new life] in Christ [unable to talk yet!] I fed you with milk, not solid food, for you were not yet strong enough [to be ready for it]; but even yet you are not strong enough [to be ready for it], For you are still [unspiritual, having the nature] of the flesh [under the control of ordinary impulses]. For as long as [there are] envying and jealousy and wrangling and factions among you, are you not unspiritual and of the flesh, behaving yourselves after a human standard and like mere (unchanged) men?

Note: We will show scripturally how these misunderstandings are true as we go along in this series.

Abraham, Isaac, and Jacob may be disembodied, but they are living souls. The proper context to understand why Jesus, at times, referred to the disembodied souls (the dead) as asleep; He was trying to express that when someone is dead to his body, he no more ceases to exist as a living soul (mind) than a person whose body lays still and is unconscious while he is in a state of sleep. When someone is in a state of sleep, it is the body which is unconscious, not the soul or mind of the man. Likewise concerning the dead, it is the body which is dead having no consciousness, not the living soul (the mind and personality). The body dying has no effect on the soul/mind other than to leave it naked, unclothed, disembodied and unable to give expression to itself or experience his environment through a body.

Being people that are by nature, superficial in their perception, we tend to perceive a person who has died as the end of that person. As such, Jesus was trying to find a superficial term to describe a state of being that is spiritual. This is true especially considering the fact that in the superficial perception of the people He was talking to, they believed that when someone was dead to the body they ceased to exist. Thus, He used the term, asleep to convey they were still living beings.

Twice in the book of Revelation and in other books of the Bible, the term "souls" was used to refer to those who were disembodied but living humans. Although all the living have souls and are referred to as persons, it becomes most accurate to refer to those who no longer have a body as souls. This is simply because they no longer have a body with which we can relate to in this physical realm. It's like thinking the clothes a person wears are the person. Obviously, this is not the case. When the person changes clothes he is the same person he was in the previous outfit. Our physical body is clothing for our soul or mind to interact in and experience the physical realm. Just as an astronaut needs to wear a space suit in order to interact in space. When he comes back to earth, he takes his space suit off and wears something more suitable on earth.

On one occasion John wrote in Revelation (6:9-11) about the souls or the disembodied of those who were martyred/killed for their faith. By what is described in those verses they obviously were aware of passing time, even what was happening on earth. They were termed as, "the souls that were at the foot of the altar." The altar, would be a specific place in *paradise* that those who sacrificed their lives for their faith in God, resided. *Paradise* is a place in the realm of the dead, *Hades*. Being in the confinement that only the dead reside in, coupled with them having been killed for their faith and therefore bodiless, explains why they are referred to as (living) souls.

These living and bodiless souls are spoken of as having witnessed the world crucify Jesus. As a result, they pleaded with the Father for justice against those who killed them, and the Lord. These disembodied souls were anything but unconscious in a state of sleep. Not only were they aware but they were upset, even appalled, and interacting with God over what just happened. They had been patiently waiting to receive their resurrected bodies and no longer be unclothed or disembodied souls confined in *Hades*—even if it was paradisiacal. They have been patiently waiting for those who hated God and killed them to be punished. Their patience had just gone beyond their threshold because they just witnessed the world kill the Lord who wanted to save them. It was like an "enough is enough" moment. What more proof do you need, Lord, they pleaded. They did not understand why God would continue to wait after seeing they are beyond redemption and worthy of being destroyed for how they rejected and killed us and now you?

NIV Rev 6:9-11 *When the Lamb broke open the fifth seal* (representing the time of His crucifixion), *I saw at the foot of the altar the souls of those whose lives had been sacrificed for [adhering to] the Word of God and for the testimony they had borne.* <u>*They cried in a loud voice, O [Sovereign] Lord, holy and true, how long now before You will sit in judgment and avenge our blood*</u> (Jesus now being among their ranks) *upon those who dwell on the earth? Then they were each given a long and flowing and festive white robe* (a celestial body to clothe their souls with) *and told to rest and wait patiently a little while longer, until the number should be complete of their fellow servants and their brethren who were to be killed as they themselves had been.* (Those who would be killed during the great tribulation.)

Note: The only way that they were able to, at this moment in time, receive a clean white robe (a *celestial* or resurrected body) was because Jesus had just died on the cross paying for our sin. This act finally reconciled us with God, allowing us to be redeemed while becoming a celestial human and in the presence of God, where He resides, as His children.

Again, it says in 1st Peter that when Jesus died to His physical body and was in *Hades* (the realm of the disembodied souls—the dead) He preached to the dead giving them a chance at salvation.

NIV 1Pe 3:19 through whom also <u>he went and preached to the spirits</u> (the dead) <u>in prison</u> (in Hades).

NIV 1Pe 4:5-6 But they will have to give account to him who is ready to judge the living and the dead. <u>For this is the reason the gospel was preached even to those who are now dead, so that they might be judged according to men in regard to the body, but live according to God in regard to the spirit.</u>

How could He preach to them if they are in a state of sleep, and for that matter how could He preach if He was like them, dead (even if it were for only 3 days)? The truth is, it is the body and not the living soul which is no longer conscious.

No richer description was made about the realm of the dead, *Hades*, than that of the story of Lazarus and the rich man. One might say, "but that is a parable." That is an assumption. There is a good case to believe it is a real-life example and not a parable. Whenever Jesus spoke in parables, He did not use proper names for the people in His parable. He always says something to the effect of, *there was a man*, or *there was a farmer* (for example). In using a named person, Jesus most likely was using a real example of a beggar and a rich man in that town who both had recently died that everyone knew of. Either way, Jesus gave a reliable picture of *Hades* or as the Hebrews call it, *Sheol*.

NAS LK 16:22-26 "Now the poor man died and was <u>carried away by the angels to Abraham's bosom</u> (the paradisiacal place in Hades); and the rich man also died and was buried. "<u>In Hades</u> he lifted up his eyes, being in torment, and saw Abraham far away and Lazarus in his bosom. "And he cried out and said, 'Father Abraham, have mercy on me, and send Lazarus so that he may dip the tip of his finger in water and cool off my tongue, for I am in agony in this flame.' "But Abraham said, 'Child, remember that during your life you received your good things, and likewise Lazarus bad things; but now <u>he is being comforted here, and you are in agony.</u> 'And besides all this, between us and you there is a great chasm fixed, so that *those who wish to come over from here to you will not be able, and that none may cross over from there to us.'*

You have to ignore these prominent verses in order to maintain that the soul sleeps when death of the body occurs. Neither Abraham in the paradisiacal place of *Hades*, or the rich man in the hellish place of *Hades* were asleep but were very much aware, even interactive. You cannot experience comfort or torment if you are unconscious, unaware of passing time. Otherwise, there would be no need for anesthesia when surgery is performed on us. Nor can you have conversation and interact, consciously aware, as all three examples revealed. Likewise, what would be the point for the realm of the dead, *Hades*, to have a paradisiacal place of confinement and a hellish place of torment, if when we die, we are in a sleep-like state of unconsciousness? Again, whether in sleep or in death, it is the body which is unconscious and is inactive, not the living soul it clothes.

Regarding the thought that Christians await the resurrection on the day of judgment to finally receive their celestial body while believing there is only one resurrection.

This idea is based on the fact that in the Gospels, Jesus spoke of a resurrection connected with judgement and salvation, a raising of people from the dead. In part, this misunderstanding can be accredited to the thought that there is only one resurrection. Let's look at what it says in the book of Revelation:

NIV Rev 20:4-6 I saw thrones on which were seated those who had been given authority to judge. And I saw the souls of those who had been beheaded because of their testimony for Jesus and because of the word of God. They had not worshiped the beast or his image and had not received his mark on their foreheads or their hands. They came to life and reigned with Christ a thousand years. (The rest of the dead did not come to life until the thousand years were ended.) This is the first resurrection. Blessed and holy are those who have part in the first resurrection. The second death (suffering the *lake of fire) has no power over them, but they will be priests of God and of Christ and will reign with him for a thousand years.*

The above verses not only indicate that there is more than one resurrection of the dead, but that those who are a part of the *first resurrection* will not be judged at the second, as many mistakenly believe. *The second death has no power over them,* indicating that they will not be up for judgement at the second resurrection, but on thrones serving as judges for those who are.

AMP Jn 5:24 <u>I assure you, most solemnly I tell you, the person whose ears are open to My words [who listens to My message] and believes and trusts in and clings to and relies on Him Who sent Me has (possesses now) eternal life. And he does not come into judgment [does not incur sentence of judgment, will not come under condemnation], but he has already passed over out of death into life.</u>

They will already have been forgiven and given their celestial bodies. *I saw thrones on which were seated those who had been given authority to judge.*

The participants of the *first resurrection* will be present and reign over the people of the earth during the Lord's *1,000-year reign*. In addition to ruling over the physical humans during the 1,000-year earthly reign, they will likewise sit as judges with the Lord for those raised at the second resurrection on the *last day*! This is the gift and privilege of being born again, having had been persecuted, and having as a first love, Jesus—being His tried-and-true bride. They will be co-rulers and judges over the world that persecuted them!

For this to happen is the whole point of the *1,000-year reign* of Christ when He defeats the world and makes it subject to Himself, the physical Israelites (who He gathers back to Zion to reform the nation with all twelve tribes represented), and the celestial Christians that return to the earth with Jesus at His second coming to co-rule as celestial humans.

The celestial humans co-ruling with Christ for a thousand years on earth over physical humans then extends eternally in the spiritual realm, happens so that the Lord's promise to Abraham and his descendants is kept. If it is not so, then it is pointless to have a 1,000-year reign on the physical earth and humanity would instead proceed straight to the last day and be judged. Jesus is the promised Messiah made to the patriarchs of old and is the hope of everyone born of Israeli decent. Under absolutely no circumstances can the earth be destroyed, deserving or not, before this promise to the forefathers of the Israelites be broken. To think the faithful go into a state of sleep until everything is over and done, robs the promised Israelites and the faithful from being exempt and treated differently than the unfaithful and rebellious. Think about it, to think in those terms of being in a state of sleep until it's all over, steals away the whole reason and reward of being the Lord's persecuted and faithful.

In addition, Jesus stated about the last day in Mt 25:31-46 (below), when there are no more physical humans because the entire universe has been destroyed, all the remaining disembodied souls will be resurrected from their disembodied state, given a new body in order to face the Lord and judgment. In fact, it says:

NIV Rev 20:11-15 *Then I saw a great white throne and him who was seated on it. Earth and sky fled from his presence, and there was no place for them* (in other words, no need for the earth and sky because there are no living physical humans, they are either disembodied *souls* in *Hades* or have already become *celestial* humans embodied with their resurrected body). *And I saw the dead, great and small, standing before the throne, and books were opened. Another book was opened, which is the book of life. The dead were judged according to what they had done as recorded in the books. The sea gave up the dead that were in it, and death and Hades gave up the dead that were in them, and each person was judged according to what he had done. Then death and Hades were thrown into the lake of fire. The lake of fire is the second death. If anyone's name was not found written in the book of life, he was thrown into the lake of fire.*

Hades will be emptied of all its occupants and just as the physical universe, it will be burned, melted and destroyed in the *lake of fire*.

Why? Because we are told by scriptures, there will no longer be need for this holding tank of dead and disembodied souls.

AMP 2Pe 3:10 But the day of the Lord will come like a thief, and then the heavens (the cosmos, outer space, the material universe) will vanish (pass away) with a thunderous crash, and the [material] elements [of the universe] will be dissolved with fire, and the earth and the works that are upon it will be burned up

NIV Mt 25:31-46 "When the Son of Man comes in his glory, and all the angels with him, he will sit on his throne in heavenly glory. All the nations will be gathered before him, and he will separate the people one from another as a shepherd separates the sheep from the goats. He will put the sheep on his right and the goats on his left. "Then the King will say to those on his right, 'Come, you who are blessed by my Father; take your inheritance, the kingdom prepared for you since the creation of the world. For I was hungry and you gave me something to eat, I was thirsty and you gave me something to drink, I was a stranger and you invited me in, I needed clothes and you clothed me, I was sick and you looked after me, I was in prison and you came to visit me.' "Then the righteous will answer him, 'Lord, when did we see you hungry and feed you, or thirsty and give you something to drink? When did we see you a stranger and invite you in, or needing clothes and clothe you? When did we see you sick or in prison and go to visit you?' "The King will reply, 'I tell you the truth, whatever you did for one of the least of these brothers of mine, you did for me.' "Then he will say to those on his left, 'Depart from me, you who are cursed, into the eternal fire prepared for the devil and his angels. For I was hungry and you gave me nothing to eat, I was thirsty and you gave me nothing to drink, I was a stranger and you did not invite me in, I needed clothes and you did not clothe me, I was sick and in prison and you did not look after me.' "They also will answer, 'Lord, when did we see you hungry or thirsty or a stranger or needing clothes or sick or in prison, and did not help you?' "He will reply, 'I tell you the truth, whatever you did not do for one of the least of these, you did not do for me.' "Then they will go away to eternal punishment, but the righteous to eternal life."

Again, much of the Church believes that all Christians will die and will be in a state of sleep, a state of unconsciousness, unaware of anything including passing time, then raised to life so they may share in His spiritual Kingdom in Heaven after the day of judgment. Even further, some understand and teach the above verses to say that in the *first resurrection* spoken of in Revelation (20:4-6) is when the sheep will be resurrected and those considered goats will be resurrected later when it speaks of it in Matthew (25:31-46) and will be sentenced to the *lake of fire* (the second death). In other words, the *first resurrection* is for the good guys (the sheep), and the resurrection on the *last day* is for the bad guys (the goats).

There is so much wrong with this interpretation. All you have to do is read what the verses say at face value to know how skewed these interpretations are. The verses in Matthew are describing the last day when judgment will occur. *"When the Son of Man comes in his glory, and all the angels with him, he will sit on his throne in heavenly glory. All the nations will be gathered before him, and he will separate the people one from another as a shepherd separates the sheep from the goats. He will put the sheep on his right and the goats on his left."* Clearly the Lord is sorting out the righteous from the wicked, assigning some to the *lake of fire* for eternity and others to spend eternity with Him.

The *first resurrection* happens at the advent of the *1,000-year reign* of Christ so that the celestial humans that participate in that resurrection can co-rule with Him during that time. The sole purpose of this resurrection is so the participants can co-rule with Christ as celestial humans over the physical humans. The second resurrection of the dead happens after the *1,000-year reign* of Christ because at this time every single element that comprises natural matter will melt and be destroyed bringing an end to humanity in the physical realm. Then, it is left only for all the dead throughout history to be assigned to their eternal place of residence.

It is utterly amazing how skewed the understanding of the Bible is with the contemporary church! Their knowledge and interpretations are based on shards or fragments of individual verses that support their thinking but are not, however, based on or in context to the whole of what the Bible says. It is as the old saying goes, a little bit of knowledge is dangerous. There are different circumstances by which one can be saved (meaning to gain a celestial body and escape judgment) all of which are listed in the Bible.

Most do not understand what death is or do not even think about it. Some think that we already have a body that is celestial in nature and when we die to our physical body, we simply live on in that spiritual body, in the spiritual realm. This would mean we have two bodies at the same time while we have a living physical body. This is not unlike the metaphysical believers would say, we have an astro-body or some such thing. And just live in it when we die.

All creatures, celestial (angelic) and physical, have only one body, and not multiple bodies in different dimensions. Created celestial creatures, like angels, have bodies made of celestial matter. Physical creatures like animals and humans have physical bodies. As outlined previously, all created creatures are biune beings, meaning they have two natures that comprise their being. That would be spirit and body. Spirit is the life, consciousness, and power that animates the body, whether celestial or physical. The body is the expression of that life and outward manifestation of the spirit that others can relate to.

The only exception to the above is the human being. Man was created as a triune being just as God is, having in addition to the spirit and body, a soul or mind. Like the body that the spirit of the man gives life and animation to, the spirit of the man gives life and consciousness to the soul. As the spirit and body do, the soul (mind) has multiple faculties that comprise its nature. The soul (mind) of the man is the personality, the seat of decision and rational, and the conscience. Unlike the spirit, the soul thinks and expresses itself with words. However, the spirit and soul of the man are, for all intents and purposes, invisible natures of the man. They have no embodiment of their own that they can interact with their environment through or a point of contact that other living beings can relate to and see them; otherwise, they would be three individual persons.

The relationship of the three different aspects of a human is like a lamp you can see that expresses light and heat. But the life and power of that lamp is electricity. Without the power of electricity, the lamp cannot function, it becomes just an inanimate or lifeless object. However, the electricity that makes it alive with heat and light is utterly invisible. There is no quality about it that we can see or even know that it exists. Without the physical object (the lamp) it has no medium or visible expression. However, electricity can also empower many different lamps or different kinds of objects; objects that are without electricity are inanimate. Although we cannot see electricity it is a force, a source of power and animation. It is not until it empowers an object that we can know that force.

It is the same for spirit and soul. Without a body either in the celestial or the physical realm they are still power, life-principle, having awareness, and animation having no embodiment to manifest, and neither express or interact as a living creature. For the spirit and soul of the man to have no body is not a pleasant or desirable but frustrating state. Not only can you not express yourself but due to a lack of a body, you become frustrated that you cannot gratify your desires, no matter how powerful they are within. Similar to what a drug addict experiences when he cannot have access to the drug he is in bondage to. This is the sting of death that Paul referred to:

NIV 1Co 15:53-55 For the perishable must clothe itself with the imperishable, and the mortal with immortality. When the perishable has been clothed with the imperishable, and the mortal with immortality, then the saying that is written will come true: "Death has been swallowed up in victory." "Where, O death, is your victory? Where, O death, is your sting?"

Death is merely the loss of the body, the disembodiment of a soul (the mind and individual personality of a man). When you have a limb amputated, you still are no less alive in your mind/soul than you were when you had it. Nor does the mind function any less. No! You are just handicapped in your body, not in your mind, even though it might be a stress or source of depression to the mind. This is exactly why the Bible refers to the body as clothing (for the soul/personality) and the state of being disembodied as being naked. This makes it understandable why we refer to the dead as souls, in spite of the fact that while in the body the man still possessed a soul, however, now he lives without a body.

NIV Rev 16:15 *"Behold, I come like a thief! Blessed is he who stays awake and keeps his clothes* (his body) *with him, so that he may not go naked* (become dead) *and be shamefully exposed."*

And referring to the dead as souls at the foot of the altar (in the paradisiacal place of *Hades*):

NIV Rev 6:11 *Then each of them was given a white robe*

There is no astro body for the soul. All created beings are given one body that is comprised of and can interact with the environment it resides in. Lose that, and you are bodiless.

To those with physical bodies in the natural/physical realm that die, that is what death is. The body has been severed from the life-principle that animated it, and it becomes lifeless, then decays. This, again, is similar to a lamp that no longer has electricity to power it. However, it does not mean the electricity is any less than what it was before the lamp, other than its power has no object to manifest through. That is unless it is granted a new object to manifest its power through. This makes the giving of a new or second body that is celestial by nature, to our indestructible soul, truly a gift from our Creator—at least for those who do not suffer the second death. After having been given a second but celestial body, that individual can escape the confinement of *Hades* and be present in the Heavenly or celestial realm that God lives in; then alive in His blissful realm, knowing Him face-to-face.

AMP 1Co 13:12 *For now we are looking in a mirror that gives only a dim (blurred) reflection [of reality as in a riddle or enigma], but then [when perfection comes* (when we finally have an uncorruptible celestial body)*] we shall see in reality and face to face! Now I know in part (imperfectly), but then I shall know and understand fully and clearly, even in the same manner as I have been fully and clearly known and understood [by God].*

Next, there is the skewed understanding of what happens when we die and who goes where.

The problem, as stated previously, is that without real understanding of what was just outlined, they try to make all the verses in the Bible which speak about these subjects make sense as being one event, or a one or the other destinations, and one qualification or condition of salvation. In order to make all the verses speak of one situation, one event, and one qualification, they must ignore some of what these verses say at face value.

In the example we chose, we stated that some believe that when a Christian dies, he is held over in a state of sleep and then given his celestial body on the last day or the day of judgment because it says all will have to face God and be judged. Or that the *first resurrection* is for the good guys and the bad guys will have to wait for the last day and be sent to the *lake of fire*. Let us first address this thought that everyone will be judged and face God on the last day.

Yes, everybody, from the first person to walk the face of the earth to the very last will face God and be judged. However, there are exceptions to this certainty. For example, those who repent and reconcile with God before the last day and before they die are exempt from facing judgment on the last day, according to the words of Jesus. Let's look at what Jesus taught concerning this understanding:

AMP Mt 5:21-26 You have heard that it was said to the men of old, You shall not kill, and whoever kills shall be liable to and unable to escape the punishment imposed by the court. But I say to you that everyone who continues to be angry with his brother or harbors malice (enmity of heart) against him shall be liable to and unable to escape the punishment imposed by the court; and whoever speaks contemptuously and insultingly to his brother shall be liable to and unable to escape the punishment imposed by the Sanhedrin, and whoever says, You cursed fool! [You empty-headed idiot!] shall be liable to and unable to escape the hell (Gehenna) of fire. So if when you are offering your gift at the altar you there remember that your brother has any [grievance] against you, Leave your gift at the altar and go. First make peace with your brother, and then come back and present your gift. Come to terms quickly with your accuser while you are on the way traveling with him, lest your accuser hand you over to the judge, and the judge to the guard, and you be put in prison. Truly I say to you, you will not be released until you have paid the last fraction of a penny.

Jesus is not just talking about petty grievances between people, but also what is at stake eternally. These same people that have grievances will be witnesses against you on the last day. It is a mistake to believe that just because time has passed our sins are no longer an issue. With God, even if millenniums have passed, the Lord does not forget and will balance the books simply because He is a just God.

The main point Jesus is making by these words is that even though we are people of sin, we can be released from their consequences if we face them and come to terms and reconcile them, because we have a forgiving God. Otherwise, Jesus says we will eternally have to pay the price of our sins. Those who reconcile with Him through His convicting Spirit within them by repentance after examining themselves, then constantly act on their repentative heart, have no need to face judgment on the last day. They have already judged themselves and were forgiven by the Lord—reconciled. They have circumvented the need for the last day of judgment, rendering it unnecessary. They have done what the day of judgement is purposed for before it has become too late, *on their way to court.*

AMP Jn 5:24-25 I assure you, most solemnly I tell you, the person whose ears are open to My words [who listens to My message] and believes and trusts in and clings to and relies on Him Who sent Me has (possesses now) eternal life. And he does not come into judgment [does not incur sentence of judgment, will not come under condemnation], but he has already passed over out of death into life. Believe Me when I assure you, most solemnly I tell you, the time is coming and is here now when the dead shall hear the voice of the Son of God and those who hear it shall live (eternally).

AMP Jn 8:51 I assure you, most solemnly I tell you, if anyone observes My teaching [lives in accordance with My message, keeps My word], <u>he will by no means ever see and experience death.</u>

Now that we have an understanding of what death is in the eyes of God, we can finally make sense of what Jesus has declared and therefore understand what happens after death to His believers. Death is the disembodiment of the soul leaving it unclothed without a body or naked and is not the ceasing of their existence. Given that understanding, when Jesus emphatically says, *he will by no means ever see and experience death,* we can take that to mean, us believers will never experience the disembodiment of our soul. How can that possibly happen when we die to our body, the last day has not occurred and will not for at least 1,000 years minimum? One answer is to ignore what Jesus said (above), then deduce that we are bodiless in a soul sleep until the last day of judgment. No! Considering scriptures, this cannot be!

The real and ONLY understanding that makes sense is that before our head hits the ground in death, we change bodies, receiving our celestial body while not even for a fraction of a second experience disembodiment. Think about it, even before our heart stops beating and our brain is dead, we change clothes and transform into possessing a celestial body. Paul tells us that this process happens in the twinkling of an eye—before one can blink. It even means there is a moment during this exchange of bodies that we are alive in both, that is if we are not to experience death whatsoever.

This is the privilege and gift of the followers of Jesus the Christ! And to teach we go into a soul sleep until the last day steals away our hope and reason to follow Jesus, putting us in the same boat as every other person that lived and will face judgment. Likewise, we do not go to the paradisical place in *Hades* which is a temporary destination for the disembodied, but to the residence of the Father and His Son, Jesus, long before the last day. It even says we come back with Him to the earth for His millennial reign and co-rule the physical humans, only not as physical humans with physical bodies but as celestial humans with celestial bodies like that of the angels and of Jesus. Again, the soul sleep concept robs us of knowing the rewards of believing.

The next issue is, how come that did not happen to the saints and forefathers of the Israelites?

Because of the giving of white robes (celestial bodies) to the *144,000* as the *firstfruits* of Jesus' redeeming work is the very reason why we know that the *fifth seal* is the sacrificial death of Jesus on the cross. Until Jesus had completed His redeeming work, no one could experience anything but suffer the fourth horsemen curse (death and confinement in Hades) and that of Adam and Eve. The curse of Adam and Eve is to die the first death, that is to become a disembodied soul. The physical body was never meant to die. There is an old saying that nothing is certain but death and taxes.

This death is temporal and is a result of the folly of Adam and Eve having corrupted the human spirit. However, there is a second death. That death happens when at the last day each individual has been raised and given a celestial or resurrected body and are judged by their own merit, how they conducted themselves while in the (physical) body. Those judged as deserving, due to their own folly will die the second death, which is permanent, eternal. They will not be confined in the temporal region of *Hades* but sent to be confined in the eternal *lake of fire*. *Hades*, like the earth, the physical universe, and all the people that have ever lived will see its end on the last day, after the *1,000-year reign* of Christ on the earth.

There are two lives or worlds to live in, the physical and the celestial, which are like the two locations for physical beings to live in; under the sea and above the sea, each creature having a body suitable for their environment.

There are two bodies, the physical and, when the time comes by the plan of salvation of God, the celestial. There are two deaths, the physical and the celestial.

NIV 1Co 15:35-58 But someone may ask, "How are the dead raised? With what kind of body will they come?" How foolish! What you sow does not come to life unless it dies. When you sow, you do not plant the body that will be, but just a seed, perhaps of wheat or of something else. But God gives it a body as he has determined, and to each kind of seed he gives its own body. All flesh is not the same: Men have one kind of flesh, animals have another, birds another and fish another. There are also heavenly bodies and there are earthly bodies; but the splendor of the heavenly bodies is one kind, and the splendor of the earthly bodies is another. The sun has one kind of splendor, the moon another and the stars another; and star differs from star in splendor. So will it be with the resurrection of the dead. The body that is sown is perishable, it is raised imperishable; it is sown in dishonor, it is raised in glory; it is sown in weakness, it is raised in power; it is sown a natural body, it is raised a spiritual body. If there is a natural body, there is also a spiritual body. So it is written: "The first man Adam became a living being"; the last Adam, a life-giving spirit. The spiritual did not come first, but the natural, and after that the spiritual. The first man was of the dust of the earth, the second man from heaven. As was the earthly man, so are those who are of the earth; and as is the man from heaven, so also are those who are of heaven. And just as we have borne the likeness of the earthly man, so shall we bear the likeness of the man from heaven. I declare to you, brothers, that flesh and blood cannot inherit the kingdom of God, nor does the perishable inherit the imperishable. <u>Listen, I tell you a mystery: We will not all sleep, but we will all be changed—in a flash, in the twinkling of an eye, at the</u>

last trumpet. For the trumpet will sound, the dead will be raised imperishable, and we will be changed. For the perishable must clothe itself with the imperishable, and the mortal with immortality. When the perishable has been clothed with the imperishable, and the mortal with immortality, then the saying that is written will come true: "Death has been swallowed up in victory." "Where, O death, is your victory? Where, O death, is your sting?" The sting of death is sin, and the power of sin is the law. But thanks be to God! He gives us the victory through our Lord Jesus Christ. Therefore, my dear brothers, stand firm. Let nothing move you. Always give yourselves fully to the work of the Lord, because you know that your labor in the Lord is not in vain.*

There are two confinements for the dead, the temporal, *Hades* and the *lake of fire*, the eternal.

There are two *raptures* (catching up of the living to heaven), one for those believers who do not become apostates when the Pope turns to oppose God and brings the *antichrist* back from the dead. And one for the living but fallen believers who become apostates but return to their first love (Jesus) and survive the *great tribulation* receiving a mark of God on their forehead when that time period comes. That catching up will happen at the return of Christ to the earth so they may be part of His Kingdom on the earth. The *second rapture* is what Paul was referring to in the above underlined verses.

There are two resurrections of the dead. One for the apostates that during the *great tribulation* repent for their falling away and are killed for holding fast to their conviction. At the onset of the return of Christ to the earth they will rise back to life. Then subsequently rise up to the sky along with the living believers who likewise repented but survived and received a mark of God protecting them from being killed. This happening is so that both can descend with Christ back to the earth to co-rule with Him over the physical beings on earth as a part of the Kingdom of the Lord. The second resurrection happens after the 1,000-year reign of Christ on the last day, the day of judgment. This is when all physical humans that have ever lived and died are given a celestial body, totally emptying out *Hades*, to face judgment. This includes all the remaining living physical humans alive on earth who die as a result of the entire physical universe being destroyed by fire. They cannot be given a second physical body because the judgement of fire has destroyed all physical matter down to the last atom. All that exists is the celestial—the spiritual. And because the soul and spirit of the man is not physical, those attributes of the man will survive the loss of their physical body.

AMP 2Pe 3:1-18 *BELOVED, I am now writing you this second letter. In [both of] them I have stirred up your unsullied (sincere) mind by way of remembrance, That you should recall the predictions of the holy (consecrated, dedicated) prophets and the commandment of the Lord and Savior [given] through your apostles (His special messengers). To begin with, you must know and understand this, that scoffers (mockers) will come in the last days with scoffing, [people who] walk after their own fleshly desires And say, Where is the promise of His coming? For since the forefathers fell asleep, all things have continued exactly as they did from the beginning of creation. For they willfully overlook and forget this [fact], that the heavens (the cosmos) [came into] existence long ago by the word of God, and the earth also which was formed out of water and by means of water, Through which the world that then [existed] was deluged with water and perished. But by the same word the present heavens and earth have been stored up (reserved) for fire, being kept until the day of judgment and destruction of the ungodly people. Nevertheless, do not let this one fact escape you, beloved, that with the Lord one day is as a thousand years and a thousand years as one day. The Lord does not delay and is not tardy or slow about what He promises, according to some people's conception of slowness, but He is long-suffering (extraordinarily patient) toward you, not desiring that any should perish, but that all should turn to repentance. But the day of the Lord will come like a thief, and then the heavens will vanish (pass away) with a thunderous crash, and the [material] elements [of the universe] will be dissolved with fire, and the earth and the works that are upon it will be burned up. Since all these things are thus in the process of being dissolved, what kind of person ought [each of] you to be [in the meanwhile] in consecrated and holy behavior and devout and godly qualities, While you wait and earnestly long for (expect and hasten) the coming of the day of God by reason of which the flaming heavens will be dissolved, and the [material] elements [of the universe] will flare and melt with fire? But we look for new heavens and a new earth according to His promise, in which righteousness (uprightness, freedom from sin, and right standing with God) is to abide. So, beloved, since you are expecting these things, be eager to be found by Him [at His coming] without spot or blemish and at peace [in serene confidence, free from fears and agitating passions and moral conflicts]. And consider that the long-suffering of our Lord [His slowness in avenging wrongs and judging the world] is salvation (that which is conducive to the soul's safety), even as our beloved brother Paul also wrote to you according to the spiritual insight given him, Speaking of this as he does in all of his letters. There are some things in those [epistles of Paul] that are difficult to understand, which the ignorant and unstable twist and misconstrue to their own utter destruction, just as [they distort and misinterpret] the rest of the Scriptures. Let me warn you therefore, beloved, that knowing these things beforehand, you should be on your guard, lest you be carried away by the error of lawless and wicked [persons and] fall from your own [present] firm condition [your own steadfastness of mind]. But grow in grace (undeserved favor, spiritual strength) and recognition and knowledge and understanding of our Lord and Savior Jesus Christ (the Messiah). To Him [be] glory (honor, majesty, and splendor) both now and to the day of eternity. Amen (so be it)!*

Since the death of Jesus, we have an option that no other person in the history of the world since and including Adam have had or even will have until the end of the human race. We can avoid experiencing death, but instead change the world we live in and the body we clothe our soul with and be with the Lord forever. We can become no longer physical humans but celestial humans even before our heads hit the ground in death. There is, likewise, the possibility of becoming celestial humans for even those who have and will be disembodied (suffer death) and were confined in *Hades*. That is to be deemed righteous on the last day, winning the approval of the Lord and by His grace become a child of God—a celestial human; something that was never a possibility or even a necessity before sin corrupted causing the fall of man.

This option is part of the redemption of God. Let's look deeper into that plan of redemption God had made; Jesus became a physical human that was sinless and therefore undeservingly suffered the first death, but then as a result deservingly became the first-born celestial human. Then according to God's plan, all those who become in a spiritual marital covenant relationship with Jesus, becoming one flesh with Him according to the declaration of God, will also become celestial humans as His bride. This makes the scriptures true when it says, He (Jesus) is the first born (celestial human) of many brothers. This makes Jesus the ark of the covenant that came from God who saves numbers of humans who are beyond counting, from the beginning of the fall to the end of the world. This differs from the ark Noah made, which saved only eight physical humans that were still subject to the death of the body. Jesus is truly the ONLY way, truth, and is the life that will safely transport our lives, rescuing us from the inevitable doom of this physical world and all the bodies of the people in it.

The next concern about death is to ask if the interpretation we say above is true, why then do the Christians who are killed during the *great tribulation* need to be risen from the dead to receive their celestial body, then rise up to the sky to meet Jesus along with the living Christians upon His return? Secondly, what about those who are declared sheep on the last day, why don't they have their celestial body already?

From the time Jesus died to the time the *great tribulation* begins, every Christian that is acceptable in their relationship with Jesus does not experience death. During the *great tribulation* it says that Heaven is silent (inactive) for about a half an hour (3½ years). When the tribulation begins and the Spirit of God withdraws from the earth leaving it in a global desolation, He takes with Him in a *rapture* or a catching up) the *two witnesses* who are first resurrected, and all the Christians who are firmly in relationship with the *Holy Spirit* and have not become a part of the apostasy, the great falling away. Their bodies do not even fall dead but they rise up to Heaven as their body transforms from physical to celestial. If their hearts are firmly connected to the *Holy Spirit*, it is impossible for those individuals to be separated from the Spirit and left behind when He withdraws from the earth for those 3½ years.

However, concerning the Christians who become a part of the great falling away, Jesus does what He warned us He would do in Revelation; He abandons them in the earth for 3½ years giving them over to their decision to be an apostate:

AMP Rev 3:15-16 *I know your [record of] works and what you are doing; you are neither cold nor hot. (I wish) Would that you were cold or hot! So, because you are lukewarm and neither cold nor hot, I will spew you out of My mouth!*

The *two witnesses*, the return of the *antichrist* facilitated by the pope of the Roman Catholic Church, and the *great tribulation* is the Lord's plan to save those He has first brought to a crossroad of decision to show them as either hot or cold—for Him or against Him. Then spew the cold out of His heart (divorce them) for becoming an apostate. Finally, He abandons those He divorced for 3½ years after putting it into the heart of the *antichrist* and the *false prophet* (the Pope) to hate them and kill them so as (like Gomer) turn their hearts back to their first love, the Lord, so He can finally save them as *hot* for relationship with Him.

After the 3½ years of the *global desolation*, the Holy Spirit and the forces of Heaven will become active in the earth again. Those who endure the *great tribulation* and turn from their apostasy, holding fast to their testimony even unto death, and do not worship the beast or take his mark, will be saved and back in the Lord's grace. The Lord will mark the survivors on their forehead and not one single Christian with this mark will be harmed or killed, ever. It says about this time of desolation, or silence/inactivity:

NIV Rev 13:4-10 Men worshiped the dragon because he had given authority to the beast, and they also worshiped the beast and asked, "Who is like the beast? Who can make war against him?" The beast was given a mouth to utter proud words and blasphemies and to exercise his authority for forty-two months (3½ years). *He opened his mouth to blaspheme God, and to slander his name and his dwelling place and those who live in heaven. He was given power to make war against the saints and to conquer them. And he was given authority over every tribe, people, language and nation. All inhabitants of the earth will worship the beast—all whose names have not been written in the book of life belonging to the Lamb that was slain from the creation of the world. He who has an ear, let him hear. If anyone is to go into captivity, into captivity he will go. If anyone is to be killed with the sword, with the sword he will be killed. This calls for patient endurance and faithfulness on the part of the saints.*

The ones who have been killed during this time of nonintervention on the part of the Lord, will not be transformed into a celestial body before their heads hit the ground in death. Why? Because they have been spewed out of the mouth of the Lord and as a result no longer have (for the next 3 ½ years the Holy Spirit within, because they had rejected Him becoming an apostate in opposition to God. It is the Holy Spirit within who rescues us to life before death can have us and *Hades* can contain our disembodied souls.

AMP Rev 6:7-8 When the Lamb broke open the fourth seal, I heard the fourth living creature call out, Come! So I looked, and behold, <u>an ashy pale horse [black and blue as if made so by bruising], and its rider's name was Death, and Hades (the realm of the dead) followed him closely.</u> And they were given authority and power over a fourth *part of the earth to kill with the sword and with famine and with plague (pestilence, disease) and with wild beasts of the earth.*

Even though they repented of their apostasy and were killed because of their faith, they must wait until the 7 years of the wrath of God is finished being poured out first for 3½ years on the saints who fell away, then on the world who persecuted them. Why? Because it will be too late. At this point the Holy Spirit has left the world for 3½ years and when He did, they had decided to oppose God and chose against Him because of the testimony of the *two witnesses*—a mutually agreed divorce. The apostates commit spiritual adultery dividing against the Lord and He, as a result, releases them by spiritual divorce (vomits them out of His mouth). However, secretly He has planned to win their hearts back to Him through the *great tribulation* just as He had turned Gomer's heart back to her husband, Hosea. The record of Hosea's marriage in the Bible was meant to give us a prophetic representation of how the Lord will use the *great tribulation* to win back the unfaithful.

Then, during the second half (the second 3½ years of His 7 years of wrath) the world who persecuted them will be punished by celestial creatures and acts of God.

When the second 3½ years are finished completing the 7 years of wrath, it is time for Jesus to return to the earth. The seventh trumpet is sounded. When that is about to happen Paul describes it in 1st and 2nd Thessalonians:

AMP 2Th 2:3-5 Let no one deceive or beguile you in any way, for that day will not come except the apostasy comes first [unless the predicted great falling away of those who have professed to be Christians has come], and the man of lawlessness (sin) is revealed, who is the son of doom (of perdition), Who opposes and exalts himself so proudly and insolently against and over all that is called God or that is worshiped, [even to his actually] taking his seat in the temple of God, proclaiming that he himself is God. Do you not recollect that when I was still with you, I told you these things?

AMP 1Th 4:13-18 *Now also we would not have you ignorant, brethren, about those who fall asleep [in death], that you may not grieve [for them] as the rest do who have no hope [beyond the grave]. For since we believe that Jesus died and rose again, even so God will also bring with Him through Jesus those who have fallen asleep [in death]. For this we declare to you by the Lord's [own] word, that we who are alive and remain until the coming of the Lord shall in no way precede [into His presence] or have any advantage at all over those who have previously fallen asleep [in Him in death]. For the Lord Himself will descend from heaven with a loud cry of summons, with the shout of an archangel, and with the blast of the trumpet of God. And those who have departed this life in Christ will rise first. Then we, the living ones who remain [on the earth], shall simultaneously be caught up along with [the resurrected dead] in the clouds to meet the Lord in the air; and so always (through the eternity of the eternities) we shall be with the Lord! Therefore comfort and encourage one another with these words.*

Here is further support from other prophecies in the scriptures.

NIV Rev 20:4 *<u>I saw thrones on which were seated those who had been given authority to judge.</u> And <u>I saw the souls of those who had been beheaded because of their testimony for Jesus and because of the word of God.</u> They had not worshiped the beast or his image and had not received his mark on their foreheads or their hands. They came to life and reigned with Christ a thousand years. (The rest of the dead did not come to life until the thousand years were ended.) This is the first resurrection.*

Reading the above verses at face value we can see that John mentions two groups of people.

I saw thrones on which were seated those who had been given authority to judge. John saw people seated on thrones. These are not disembodied souls as he distinguished the next group to be. These in the first group are those who already have their celestial bodies (white robes) and are already functioning as Heavenly beings. They are given authority to not only judge but to reign as coleaders with Christ over the physical humans of the earth. This group has already become celestial humans even before the last day!

And I saw the souls of those who had been beheaded The use of "And" here implies "in addition to" the group John had just talked about, meaning this is a separate and distinct group from the ones just mentioned. Describing them as, "the souls of those who had been beheaded," John is calling them dead—disembodied but living souls. This is verified by the fact that in the next line it says of them that they came back to life—they were disembodied, then resurrected meaning: to once again be clothed with a body. John witnessed this event of them becoming once again embodied in this vision. In order to be resurrected, one has to be a living but bodiless person because resurrection means to once again be given a body to clothe the naked living soul.

Furthermore, John says it is those who because of their faith in Christ that were martyred (beheaded) are the ones to be raised to life at the *first resurrection*. It is not all in the history of the world who have been martyred that will participate, but only those who die during the *great tribulation* while hanging on to their testimony. We have described above why this is the case. Again, this is one of the privileges of being in a covenant marital relationship with Jesus, the Lord, even if one did fall away but came back to their senses through the *great tribulation*. This is something the Jews denied by rejecting Jesus and as a result, it was offered to the Gentiles. This resurrection is exclusively for those repentant apostates who had the courage, even while facing death, to not deny their testimony of Christ, not worship the beast, and not take his mark during the *great tribulation*. It says of the rest of humanity that they will have to wait until the last day before they will be resurrected.

Next, regarding those who are redeemed on the last day and are declared sheep:

Those who are declared sheep on the last day at the judgement are the dead who have been judged to have eternal life from the first man to die, to the very last man to die. What Mt 25:31-46 really tells us, if we read at face value, when it comes to the last day is after all flesh has died and when all will be resurrected to face judgment, that the redeemed will be separated from those who will suffer a second death by being thrown alive into the *lake of fire*. That means that the resurrection on the last day will not be exclusively for the evil who will go to the *lake of fire*. Instead that resurrection is for all, both the good and the evil to be judged as worthy of either eternity with God or of a second but eternal death in the *lake of fire*. This negates the notion that the *first resurrection* is for the good guys and the second resurrection is for the bad guys who go to the *lake of fire*.

NIV Mt 25:31-33 "*When the Son of Man comes in his glory, and all the angels with him, he will sit on his throne in heavenly glory. All the nations will be gathered before him, and <u>he will separate the people one from another as a shepherd separates the sheep from the goats. He will put the sheep on his right and the goats on his left.</u>*

By these verses above, it is incorrect to believe that the resurrection on the last day will be only for the evil who will be sent to the *lake of fire*. On the last day all people who are still alive will die in a moment because their bodies will melt in the heat making them a disembodied soul. Then along with every soul in *Hades* from the beginning of time until then will also be resurrected to life (given a celestial body) in order to face the judgment seat of God.

Note: in *Hades* holds the souls of those who will be deemed sheep on the last day of judgement. When Jesus died on the cross, He went to *Hades* and set free those who had been martyred for His name's sake before the cross. The paradisiacal place (*Abraham's bosom*) was not emptied of the souls of those who would be declared sheep on the last day, and from that point on, the paradisiacal place will continue to receive the souls of those who will be declared sheep on the last day. However, from the time of the cross forward only those who die in *spiritual union* with Christ will circumvent that process and receive their celestial bodies before their heads hit the ground in death, as Jesus promised. Again, this is one of the privileges for those in spiritual, marital covenant relationship with the Lord.

The balance of humans who will be judged as acceptable to enjoy eternal life but are not in union with Christ will remain in the paradisiacal place of *Hades* awaiting the last day to receive their celestial bodies and live on with Christ for eternity. We need to keep in mind that Jesus told us in the Bible that there are more than one criteria by which an individual may be judged worthy (in His eyes) of eternal life with Him. Later it will be explained through scripture these different criteria of which an individual can be saved and receive eternal life with Christ while not having been in *spiritual union* with Him.

Hades will be completely emptied of every disembodied *soul* on the last day, which includes both the good and the evil—those being held in the paradisiacal place of *Hades*, those in the hellish place of *Hades*, and those in the *Abyss* of *Hades*. This will be a time to separate those who will go to the *lake of fire* suffering a second death, from those who after attaining a celestial body will live forever with God as celestial humans.

The next challenge of contemporary understanding concerns the qualifications needed to be counted among the redeemed.

It is held that it is not by any works but purely a gift from God so no man can boast. However, we see by those who are redeemed in both resurrections and are given by God the gift of redemption, becoming celestial humans, that indeed there are qualifying factors which made them eligible for one or the other resurrections. In spite of this, it is always a gift of God to attain redemption.

AMP Eph 2:3-10 Among these we as well as you once lived and conducted ourselves in the passions of our flesh [our behavior governed by our corrupt and sensual nature], obeying the impulses of the flesh and the thoughts of the mind [our cravings dictated by our senses and our dark imaginings]. We were then by nature children of [God's] wrath and heirs of [His] indignation, like the rest of mankind. But

God—so rich is He in His mercy! Because of and in order to satisfy the great and wonderful and intense love with which He loved us, Even when we were dead (slain) by [our own] shortcomings and trespasses, <u>He made us alive together in fellowship and in union with Christ;</u> [He gave us the very life of Christ Himself, the same new life with which He quickened Him, <u>for] it is by grace (His favor and mercy which you did not deserve) that you are saved (delivered from judgment and made partakers of Christ's salvation).</u> And He raised us up together with Him and made us sit down together [giving us joint seating with Him] in the heavenly sphere [by virtue of our being] in Christ Jesus (the Messiah, the Anointed One). He did this that He might clearly demonstrate through the ages to come the immeasurable (limitless, surpassing) riches of His free grace (His unmerited favor) in [His] kindness and goodness of heart toward us in Christ Jesus. <u>For it is by free grace (God's unmerited favor) that you are saved (delivered from judgment and made partakers of Christ's salvation) through [your] faith. And this [salvation] is not of yourselves [of your own doing, it came not through your own striving], but it is the gift of God; Not because of works [not the fulfillment of the Law's demands], lest any man should boast. [It is not the result of what anyone can possibly do, so no one can pride himself in it or take glory to himself.]</u> For we are God's [own] handiwork (His workmanship), recreated in Christ Jesus, [born anew] that we may do those good works which God predestined (planned beforehand) for us [taking paths which He prepared ahead of time], that we should walk in them [living the good life which He prearranged and made ready for us to live].

Whereas it is plainly true in the verses above and by man's own history that salvation through union with Jesus is purely a gift from God and not something we have a right to or can attain like climbing to a mountain top. However, the question is, do we really understand the context of this truth? Although it is not earned by the works we accomplish, but is something granted by Him who is the Judge and Creator and whose house and world it is. Likewise, nor is it granted by some fulfilled requirement of His that we must meet to qualify, but strictly by His love and compassion towards us, does He grant it. However, we still have a role in receiving it. It would be naive and ignorant to think otherwise. It is a covenant spiritual, marital relationship with the Lord that saves us.

When it comes to a physical, marital relationship, the man is not entitled to have a wife, even if he loves her and does everything to woo her. It is a gift that she gives herself to the man. It is in good faith, out of love, and a desire for oneness with him, that she freely does so. However, although she gives herself freely and wholly, it is not without expectations that she does. In fact, in order to have the marital oneness when the two are "one flesh," it is not without a role that must be fulfilled by the one who she gives herself to. The man cannot continue as a bachelor, seeing other women, not coming home but hanging out with his old friends as if nothing has changed. She may be one with him, but he is not one with her—he is breaking covenant. It is the same with the woman towards her husband. It is the same with our covenant relationship with Jesus. Jesus once said:

AMP Mt 10:35-40 For I have come to part asunder a man from his father, and a daughter from her mother, and a newly married wife from her mother-in-law—And a man's foes will be they of his own household. <u>He who loves [and takes more pleasure in] father or mother more than [in] Me is not worthy of Me; and he who loves [and takes more pleasure in] son or daughter more than [in] Me is not worthy of Me; And he who does not take up his cross and follow Me [cleave steadfastly to Me, conforming wholly to My example in living and, if need be, in dying also] is not worthy of Me.</u> Whoever finds his [lower] life will lose it [the higher life], and whoever loses his [lower] life on My account will find it [the higher life]. He who receives and welcomes and accepts you receives and welcomes and accepts Me, and he who receives and welcomes and accepts Me receives and welcomes and accepts Him Who sent Me.

For the *first resurrection* is a very exclusive event. The qualification or circumstances to be included in it is by proving your profession of faith as resolute in the face of death and rejection by the entire hostile world, not worshipping the beast, or taking his mark. Then to be killed for your faith during that 3 ½-year time period of the *great tribulation*. It is only those killed during the *great tribulation* who were faithful unto death, who will participate in this event. Then afterwards, they will be among the participants who meet Jesus in the sky in order to descend back to the earth with Him and co-rule the physical humans during His *1,000-year reign* at the second catching up (*rapture*).

The individuals who were formerly counted as His bride, having turned against the Lord, becoming apostates and thus His enemies, results in Him abandoning them in the midst of the *global desolation*. This happens when His Spirit is withdrawn from the earth creating a desolation and from the hearts of the apostates (spewed out of His mouth). As it was said by Jesus, I am going to spew you out of my mouth. Jesus gives them one last chance to prove themselves as faithful under the most dire circumstances that He created for the very purpose of a last chance (read the book of Hosea and you will fully understand why the Lord has granted and planned the *great tribulation*). Although the apostates were essentially divorced by the Lord for their unfaithfulness and doomed to suffer the *great tribulation*, given they prove themselves faithful, He will not begin His reign without them at His side as celestial humans. This too is an exclusive privilege of being in spiritual covenant relationship with Jesus. Not only will they co-rule for 1,000 years the world that killed them, but they will not face judgment on the last day but instead serve as judges over those being judged on that fateful day. This is the twist of fate that the Lord promised through the prophets.

In addition to the risen dead that died during the *great tribulation*, those who actually survive the *great tribulation* while also holding fast to their profession of faith without coming off their testimony of Christ, and did not worship the beast, or take his mark will, along with those who were just resurrected, raise up to the sky to join Jesus as they receive their celestial bodies without dying (becoming disembodied). Together, those dead and alive, at this resurrection following the *great tribulation* are called, "the *great multitude*" which are beyond counting (according to John).

AMP Isa 49:5-8 And now, says the Lord—Who formed me from the womb to be His servant to bring Jacob back to Him and that Israel might be gathered to Him and not be swept away, for I am honorable in the eyes of the Lord and my God has become my strength—<u>He says, It is too light a thing that you should be My servant to raise up the tribes of Jacob and to restore the survivors [of the judgments] of Israel; I will also give you for a light to the nations, that My salvation may extend to the end of the earth.</u> Thus says the Lord, the Redeemer of Israel, Israel's Holy One, to him whom man rejects and despises, to him whom the nations abhor, to the servant of rulers: Kings shall see you and arise; princes, and they shall prostrate themselves, because of the Lord, Who is faithful, the Holy One of Israel, Who has chosen you. Thus says the Lord, In an acceptable and favorable time I have heard and answered you, and in a day of salvation I have helped you; and I will preserve you and give you for a covenant to the people, to raise up and establish the land [from its present state of ruin] and to apportion and cause them to inherit the desolate [moral wastes of heathenism, their] heritages

This is the end of the Church on earth. Every Christian has been redeemed and accounted for and has received their reward leading up to the *1,000-year reign* of Christ. As far as the believers in Christ, everything is complete and there is no more Church or its ways of following Christ even during the *1,000-year reign*. As far as those that remained apostates during that time, they will be judged on the last day with the rest of the world and had lost their place as a believer. From then on, during the *1,000-year reign*, the only form of worshiping God will be the way of the Israelites and their temple worship. The delayed time between the 62-7's and the last 7 weeks of years known as the *Church Age* is over, complete and has served its purpose—everything is said and done for those who were saved through the *Church Age*!

NIV Mt 20:16 *"So the last will be first, and the first will be last."*

It is as Jesus said: What qualifies you to be a part of this group Paul affirms when he teaches about the *first resurrection*.

NIV 1Co 15:51-53 *Listen, I tell you a mystery: We will not all sleep* (die), *but we will <u>all</u>* (the living and the dead who held fast to their profession during the great tribulation) *be changed—in a flash, in the twinkling of an eye, at the last trumpet. For the trumpet will sound, the dead will be raised imperishable, and we* (who are alive) *will be changed. For the perishable must clothe itself with the imperishable, and the mortal with immortality.*

Next is the salvation and promises that needs fulfilling to the physical children of Abraham—the Israelites. The ensuing *1,000-year reign* after the return of Christ was created exclusively for them, to fulfill the promises the Lord made to their forefathers. During the *end times, global desolation,* the seven years of God's wrath that precedes His return, the Jews and the rest of those who have Israeli heritage are hidden away as we are told:

AMP Rev 12:3-6 *Then another ominous sign (wonder) was seen in heaven: Behold, a huge, fiery-red dragon, with seven heads and ten horns, and seven kingly crowns (diadems) upon his heads. His tail swept [across the sky] and dragged down a third of the stars and flung them to the earth. And the dragon stationed himself in front of the woman who was about to be delivered, so that he might devour her child as soon as she brought it forth. And she brought forth a male Child, One Who is destined to shepherd (rule) all the nations with an iron staff (scepter), and her Child was caught up to God and to His throne. And the woman [herself] fled into the desert (wilderness), where she has a retreat prepared [for her] by God, in which she is to be fed and kept safe for 1,260 days (42 months; three and one-half years).*

These verses are talking about the return of the *antichrist* and the ensuing *great tribulation*. The third of the stars the dragon flung to the earth is talking about the killing of the saints during the *great tribulation*. Imagine the *devil* and his *antichrist* manage to kill a third of the Christians left behind. There are close to 3 billion Christians on earth, which would mean that in a 3½ year time period they kill around 1 billion believers. It has to be factory assembly line killings for those numbers to be attained. The male child the woman brought forth is not only *Jesus* but those who are one with Him in *spiritual union*. The child being caught up to save them from this horror about to occur are those believers who are the body of Christ, are therefore one with Him and do not become apostates. They are *raptured* and given a *celestial* body. They sit this out just as Peter tells us:

NIV 2Pe 2:1-10A But there were also false prophets among the people, just as there will be false teachers among you. They will secretly introduce destructive heresies, even denying the sovereign Lord who bought them—bringing swift destruction on themselves. Many will follow their shameful ways and will bring the way of truth into disrepute. In their greed these teachers will exploit you with stories they have made up. Their condemnation has long been hanging over them, and their destruction has not been sleeping. For if God did not spare angels when they sinned, but sent them to hell, putting them into gloomy dungeons to be held for judgment; if he did not spare the ancient world when he brought the flood on its ungodly people, but protected Noah, a preacher of righteousness, and seven others; if he condemned the cities of Sodom and Gomorrah by burning them to ashes, and made them an example of what is going to happen to the ungodly; and if he rescued Lot, a righteous man, who was distressed by the filthy lives of lawless men (for that righteous man, living among them day after day, was tormented in his righteous soul by the lawless deeds he saw and heard)—if this is so, then the Lord knows how to rescue godly men from trials and to hold the unrighteous for the day of judgment, while continuing their punishment. This is especially true of those who follow the corrupt desire of the sinful nature and despise authority.

This is the same event Jesus teaches about:

AMP Mt 24:15-22 *So when you see the appalling sacrilege [the abomination that astonishes and makes desolate], spoken of by the prophet Daniel, standing in the Holy Place—let the reader take notice and ponder and consider and heed [this]—Then let those who are in Judea flee to the mountains; Let him who is on the housetop not come down and go into the house to take anything; And let him who is in the field not turn back to get his overcoat. And alas for the women who are pregnant and for those who have nursing babies in those days! Pray that your flight may not be in winter or on a Sabbath. For then there will be great tribulation (affliction, distress, and oppression) such as has not been from the beginning of the world until now—no, and never will be [again]. And if those days had not been shortened, no human being would endure and survive, but for the sake of the elect (God's chosen ones) those days will be shortened.*

When Jesus mentions, *And the woman [herself] fled into the desert (wilderness), where she has a retreat prepared [for her] by God, in which she is to be fed and kept safe for 1,260 days (42 months; three and one-half years)*, the woman (Eve) is the twelve tribes of Israel who gave birth to the child who is the Lord and all He gave spiritual birth to. He is talking about the Jews alive in Jerusalem and what they should do to be safe during the *great tribulation*. The natural questions are, if the Christians who are faithful are *raptured* during the *great tribulation*, why aren't the chosen people? Likewise, if the Christians who are left behind are not provided a place to be safe from the killings during the *great tribulation*, why are the Jews who are left behind given a place to be kept safe?

The *great tribulation* is an event specifically made to purify the believers in Christ, who will, one way or another, die and become celestial humans that will return with Christ to co-rule the earth. This is a position that the Israelites gave up when they turned on Christ and had Him killed. However, undeserving or not, the Lord is faithful to His promises made to their faithful forefathers. The promises the Lord made stipulates for the Israelites to have their Messiah conquer the entire world who hated and persecuted them. Then to gather all 12 tribes to their nation, Israel, under His rule. Then make the world subordinate to and serve the Israelites for 1,000 years, and then continue His reign forever, in the celestial realm.

NIVAMP 9:11-15 *"In that day I will restore David's fallen tent. I will repair its broken places, restore its ruins, and build it as it used to be, so that they may possess the remnant of Edom and all the nations that bear my name," declares the LORD, who will do these things. "The days are coming," declares the LORD, "when the reaper will be overtaken by the plowman and the planter by the one treading grapes. New wine will drip from the mountains and flow from all the hills. I will bring back my exiled people Israel; they will rebuild the ruined cities and live in them. They will plant vineyards and drink their wine; they will make gardens and eat their fruit. I will plant Israel in their own land, never again to be uprooted from the land I have given them," says the Lord their God.*

For the above to come true, it obviously requires that the Jews, including the rest of the twelve tribes who are spread out and hidden in plain sight throughout the world, to be alive. The *1,000-year reign* of Christ was decreed for their sake. If they too are killed off or transformed into celestial humans, entirely wiping out all of them from the face of the earth as the Christians are, how then will the Lord be able to keep His promises to their forefathers? Here is what this group of people here on earth will experience: Favor with the Lord who is present as their King; they will see retribution against their enemy and oppressors from all of history; they will be vindicated as physical humans on earth, elevated above all the nations which will be made to serve them; they will once again become a nation with all 12 tribes represented; they will live in paradisiacal bliss where the lion will lay with the lamb, the children will play with the cobra, out from the temple a river of living water will flow out to the Dead Sea making it team with life able to bring healing to all who drink of it; within their borders sickness and premature death (the power of the four horse horseman) will become nonexistent; they will have no need of a military or worries to defend their borders; then when the 1,000 years of the Lord's reign is finished and the earth is destroyed, they will go on to live for eternity as celestial humans in Heaven with the Lord. To be a participant in these promises requires that you are of Israeli decent and survive the 7 years of God's wrath. In addition to those with Israeli decent, are the ones who not only help the Israelites return to their homeland but also convert and live among them.

AMP Isa 66:20-23 And they shall bring all your brethren from all the nations as an offering to the Lord—upon horses and in chariots and in litters and upon mules and upon camels—to My holy mountain Jerusalem, says the Lord, just as the children of Israel bring their cereal offering in a clean vessel to the house of the Lord. And I will also take some of them for priests and for Levites, says the Lord. For as the new heavens and the new earth which I make shall remain before Me, says the Lord, so shall your offspring and your name remain. And it shall be that from one New Moon to another New Moon and from one Sabbath to another Sabbath, all flesh shall come to worship before Me, says the Lord.

NIV Eze 47:21-23 "You are to distribute this land among yourselves according to the tribes of Israel. <u>You are to allot it as an inheritance for yourselves and for the aliens who have settled among you and who have children. You are to consider them as native-born Israelites; along with you they are to be allotted an inheritance among the tribes of Israel.</u> In whatever tribe the alien settles, there you are to give him his inheritance," declares the Sovereign LORD.

Next is the resurrection of the dead on the last day—the day of judgment

As for the resurrection which occurs on the last day, it includes all humans who ever lived and have not yet become celestial humans. The qualifying factor or how you will be judged and counted as a sheep (not a goat) and go onto live in Heaven (not the *lake of fire*) will be by your motives and by your deeds while you were alive in the body. With the minimum qualification being that you gave, at the very least, a glass of cold water to one of the elect of the Lord's when they were in need. This is decidedly the lowest bar of qualification in which a man can escape the second or eternal death and become a celestial human. That is to have given comfort to one of God's own while they were still in the world.

AMP Rev 20:11-15 *Then I saw a great white throne and the One Who was seated upon it, from Whose presence and from the sight of Whose face earth and sky fled away, and no place was found for them* (they melted and were burned up in the lake of fire). *I [also] saw the dead, great and small; they stood before the throne, and books were opened. Then another book was opened, which is [the Book] of Life.* <u>*And the dead were judged (sentenced) by what they had done [their whole way of feeling and acting, their aims and endeavors] in accordance with what was recorded in the books.*</u> *And the sea delivered up the dead who were in it, death and Hades (the state of death or disembodied existence) surrendered the dead in them,* <u>*and all were tried and their cases determined by what they had done*</u> *[according to their motives, aims, and works]. Then death and Hades (the state of death or disembodied existence) were thrown into the lake of fire. This is the second death, the lake of fire. And if anyone's [name] was not found recorded in the Book of Life, he was hurled into the lake of fire.*

Jesus' teachings in the gospels regarding the last day resurrection agrees with what was said in Revelation (above), that they were judged by their deeds and the motives behind them.

NIV Mt 10:40-42 "*He who receives you receives me, and he who receives me receives the one who sent me. Anyone who receives a prophet because he is a prophet will receive a prophet's reward, and anyone who receives a righteous man because he is a righteous man will receive a righteous man's reward.* <u>*And if anyone gives even a cup of cold water to one of these little ones because he is my disciple, I tell you the truth, he will certainly not lose his reward.*</u>"

NIV Mt 25:31-46 "*When the Son of Man comes in his glory, and all the angels with him, he will sit on his throne in heavenly glory. All the nations will be gathered before him, and he will separate the people one from another as a shepherd separates the sheep from the goats. He will put the sheep on his right and the goats on his left.* <u>"*Then the King will say to those on his right, 'Come, you who are blessed by my Father; take your inheritance, the kingdom prepared for you since the creation of the world. For I was hungry and you gave me something to eat, I was thirsty and you gave me something to drink, I was a stranger and you invited me in, I needed clothes and you clothed me, I was sick and you looked after me, I was in prison and you came to visit me.'*</u> "*Then the righteous will answer him, 'Lord, when did we see you hungry and feed you, or thirsty and give you something to drink? When did we see you a stranger and invite you in, or needing clothes and clothe you? When did we see you sick or in prison and go to visit you?'* "*The King will reply,* <u>'*I tell you the truth, whatever you did for one of the least of these brothers of mine, you did for me.'*</u> "*Then he will say to those on his left, 'Depart from me, you who are cursed, into the eternal fire prepared for the devil and his angels. For I was hungry and you gave me nothing to eat, I was thirsty and you gave me nothing to drink, I was a stranger and you did not invite me in, I needed clothes and you did not clothe me, I was sick and in prison and you did not look after me.'* "*They also will answer, 'Lord, when did we see you hungry or thirsty or a stranger or needing clothes or sick or in prison, and did not help you?'* "*He will reply,* <u>'*I tell you the truth, whatever you did not do for one of the least of these, you did not do for me.'*</u> "*Then they will go away to eternal punishment, but the righteous to eternal life.*"

According to the verses above it is clear that at the last day those who are judged have the lowest bar of qualification by which to be saved and receive a celestial body. That qualification is by deeds and the motives one had while alive in the body. Even as little as giving aid and comfort to the Lord's elect, motivated by the fact that they were the Lord's elect. As it is said, any friend of my brother is a friend of Mine.

As an illustration, there was a movie called, *The Lilies of the Field*. It took place in an impoverished South American city. This man was compelled to build a church for these nuns. One local restaurant owner was assisting him both with his labor and his finances. However, this individual never went to church. So, the one fellow asked him, "Why do you not go to church?" He answered saying he did not believe in God. His follow up question naturally was, "Why then do you help these nuns in the building of this church?" He responded with one word, "Insurance." "What?" He went on to explain, "If I am wrong and there is a God, this is my insurance that I will be allowed to go to Heaven."

Here is where many in the contemporary church will take issue. They will say, "how is this possible because it is written, 'For it is by grace you have been saved, through faith—and this is not from yourselves, it is the gift of God—not by works, so that no one can boast." They would add that the qualifications pointed out above are not in line with these verses in the book of Ephesians. However, even they would have to agree that there is a qualifying factor that is required in order to take advantage of this gift. In fact, the most used scripture according to their way of thinking demands a qualification.

NIV Ro 10:9 <u>*That if you confess with your mouth, "Jesus is Lord," and believe in your heart that God raised him from the dead, you will be saved.*</u> *For it is with your heart that you believe and are justified, and it is with your mouth that you confess and are saved.*

Here is a better context to understand these verses from Ephesians stating that it is a gift of God so that no one can boast. Let's say for example, there is an underprivileged poor person oppressed in the ghetto having no hope or means to receive a higher education. However, a wealthy individual gives a gift of a scholarship which allows him to have that higher education. Without that gift there is no hope of having a higher education and even though he received that scholarship and attained a higher education, he cannot boast that it was by his own means that he received it. Without the gift of a scholarship, it was not possible.

However, this does not mean that there were no qualifying factors in receiving the gift of a scholarship. Indeed, he had to show determination and a desire to want a higher education. In addition, he had to qualify under some kind of criteria to receive it. For example, a talent for certain sports, or an academic achievement. Even though the person may have qualified to meet the criteria and qualifications of the scholarship fund, it still was a gift and it was up to the scholarship fund whether or not they would give it to him. The person having qualifying attributes meeting their criteria never and in no way at any time obligated the fund to give him that gift. It is their choice to give that grace if they choose.

Here is another misconception the majority of the Church is teaching the fate of sinners. Once we were watching on TV a prominent televangelist who once ran for president of our country, as well as founded a Christian university. It slips the mind what occasioned his words, but he was talking about a sinner who died, and he said of him on national TV that because of his sins he went to the *lake of fire* the moment he died.

According to his understanding, the temporary hellish place in *Hades* and the *lake of fire* were one and the same location, or to him *Hades* does not exist. This is unscriptural. The place where a living soul goes when he dies becoming disembodied is a temporary confinement called *Hades* or *Sheol*. *Hades* has within it, several compartments. One of which is a place of torment for those being held over for the *lake of fire*. Sometimes this place is called *Hell*, however, *Hell* is used mostly as a term for the *lake of fire*. Currently there are no beings in the *lake of fire*. It is a completely separate place from the hellish place in *Hades*. We will explain in more detail later, however, when you suffer death/disembodiment of your natural body of flesh, your living soul goes to *Hades* being reserved for judgment.

AMP Rev 6:8 *So I looked, and behold, an ashy pale horse [black and blue as if made so by bruising], and its rider's name was <u>Death, and Hades (the realm of the dead) followed him closely.</u> And they were* *given authority and power over a fourth part of the earth to kill with the sword and with famine and with plague (pestilence, disease) and with wild beasts of the earth.*

We see by the highlighted part of verse 8 (above) that there are two distinct events: death kills the body and *Hades* scoops up and confines the living but disembodied soul. However, their power is not absolute, their power ends there. Death and *Hades* are not the end for the living soul, for all souls, good and evil will be given a body once again. Then on the last day, all the souls in the history of humanity (except those who already have attained celestial bodies) will be resurrected back to life and set free from *Hades*, meaning, clothed in a body once again. Then each individual will be judged. If you are found wanting before the Lord, you will suffer a second death and be cast alive into the *lake of fire*. The first death will land you in *Hades*, if you then suffer a second death after being risen back to life, it is then to the *lake of fire*. No soul will be thrown into the *lake of fire* unless it is to die a second death. Therefore, no one will enter the *lake of fire* if it is the first time he has died.

The only exception are two souls who will be cast into the *lake of fire* 1,000 years before the last day of judgment. They are the beast (the *antichrist/Nimrod*) and his *false prophet* (the Pope). In the case of *Nimrod*, he died and is currently held over in the *Abyss* of *Hades*. When He rises from the dead to rule the globe it says of him:

AMP Rev 17:8 **The beast that you saw [once] was, but [now] is no more, <u>and he is going to come up out of the Abyss (the bottomless pit) and proceed to go to perdition</u> (the lake of fire). And the inhabitants of the earth whose names have not been recorded in the Book of Life from the foundation of the world will be astonished when they look at the beast, because he [once] was, but [now] is no more, and he is [yet] to come.**

After having come out of the *Abyss* back to life, and when his allotted time is finished he will not return to it, but prematurely endure their second death by being hurled alive into the *lake of fire* even before the last day. The *false prophet* (the Pope), who manufactured a body from the slain and call *Nimrod* back from out of *Hades* to occupy it, will accompany him into the *lake of fire*. Perhaps he circumvents the day of judgment by going directly to the *lake of fire* because he has done such an abominable thing and receives the same punishment as the soul he drew out of the *Abyss*. However, they will be the only two in the *lake of fire* until the last day of judgment comes. As it stands currently, until the day comes when they will be cast into the *lake of fire* suffering their second death, the *lake of fire* is empty.

The day they enter it will be the day the *battle of Armageddon* is fought in the future. When that happens, they will occupy the *lake of fire* alone until the last day comes 1,000-years later, after the reign of Christ on earth. That being the case, that prominent Christian leader is in error for having said that man who died went to the *lake of fire*. Although it may possibly be his destination some 1,000 plus years from now, for the time being, his death resulted in him becoming a disembodied soul and he is currently held over (confined) in *Hades*—the place of the dead—awaiting resurrection and judgment.

Note: One may ask at this point, what's the purpose of having a temporary place of *Hell* when at the last day God already knows how He is going to judge you and it is already decided you are going to be sent to a permanent place of torment?

As stated previously, through these verses we see that *Hades* has more than one compartment. One is *paradise* or *Abraham's bosom*, as Jesus called it. It is the place where people go who will be resurrected to life and are confined as a disembodied soul until that day. The other is *Hell*, where the rich man went. This is the place in *Hades* that people who will be resurrected and suffer a second death are held. There is a third place called the *Abyss*. The *Abyss* is also translated as the bottomless pit and used as a term for the unmeasurable depth of the ocean. This compartment of *Hades* is where the vilest and most evil are held. The *Abyss* is meant particularly for demons, the fallen angels who propagated with natural women giving up their supernatural status, as well as for the abortions of nature they created, including giants (*Nephilim*) and the hybrid animals that were mutated from their God given DNA, which necessitated the flood.

We find out in the book of Revelation, God releases those created creatures who are held captive in the *Abyss* as a means of executing His wrath on the people of the earth when that time comes after the *great tribulation*. It is a giving of the world under Nimrod over to their own creations they desire to go back to.

AMP *Rev 9:1-4* *THEN THE fifth angel blew [his] trumpet, and I saw a star that had fallen from the sky to the earth; and to the angel was given the key of the shaft of the Abyss (the bottomless pit). He opened the long shaft of the Abyss (the bottomless pit), and smoke like the smoke of a huge furnace puffed out of the long shaft, so that the sun and the atmosphere were darkened by the smoke from the long shaft. Then out of the smoke locusts came forth on the earth, and such power was granted them as the power the earth's scorpions have. They were told not to injure the herbage of the earth nor any green thing nor any tree, but only [to attack] such human beings as do not have the seal (mark) of God on their foreheads.*

The beast is called up out of the *Abyss* by the *false prophet* with the mind that he will save the people of the world from the *two witnesses* and from God so the people can do as they please without fear of retribution from God. The fact that it is out of the *Abyss* in *Hades*, and not out of *Hell* in *Hades*, that the beast ascends from, verifies that the *beast/antichrist* was a giant, a *Nephilim* or *demigod*—he has mixed DNA from, a hybrid of both the natural and supernatural).

Note: *Hades*, *Sheol*, *Hell*, and the *Abyss*, all have shifted meanings and usage throughout history. For example, the *Abyss* first meant the depths of the sea. The *Abyss* was also used on occasion as a word to mean the entire realm of the dead (*Hades*). *Sheol* has been used as a term for both *Hades* (the realm for the disembodied soul) and the *grave* (where the dead physical body is buried in the ground), however, it is meant to term the place that the disembodied soul is held over in, *Hades*, not the place of burial for the dead body of that soul. *Hell/Gehenna* are used to describe the *lake of fire*, however, *Hell* is also used as a term for the hellish compartment of torment in *Hades* (the realm of the dead) for those souls who are being held over to be resurrected, judged on the last day, and thrown alive into the *lake of fire* to endure a permanent but second death. To use the term *hell* to name the *lake of fire* leaves the hellish place in *Hades*, where the rich man went in Jesus' story, without a name. The majority of the time that hellish place in *Hades* is referred to simply as *Hades*. That is to not distinguish the different destinations within *Hades* and infer there is only one destination in *Hades*, the hellish place. So, *Hell* is a good term to name the destination in *Hades*, differing it from the other destinations. Then calling the permanent destination of the judged, *the lake of fire,* gives them both their own name.

After all the disembodied souls are resurrected on the last day (given bodies to stand and be judged), and the realm of the dead (*Hades/Sheol*) and its three compartments are emptied, the realm of the dead will also be thrown into the *lake of fire*. There will be no more death after that and as such, no need for this temporal place. This is the same fate as the physical universe. It too will be thrown into the *lake of fire* because there will no longer be any natural humans of flesh. The *lake of fire* is the permanent cosmic dump site for everything that is not pure and in harmony with the Heavens, including the physical universe, they will be extinct after the last day! The only survivors will be the new species of humans, those who become celestial in nature, who were not created starting life as a new born physical infant but have been transformed and taken from among physical humans in order to escape the extinction of the physical universe.

Let's look at these destinations in *Hades* in more detail:

The *grave*: The burial place in the ground for the dead body.

Hades/Sheol: The temporary confinement for the disembodied or naked souls—the realm of the dead. Of which there are three distinct destinations.

Paradise/Abraham's Bosom **and** ***under the Altar***: The paradisiacal compartment within *Hades* used to hold the disembodied souls of those who will eventually be redeemed and therefore recipients of a celestial body.

Being *under the Altar* is a specific or a sacred place or stature within the paradisiacal place of *Hades*. *Under the Altar* is a term for those disembodied souls whose lives were taken as a sacrifice so that Jesus could be born of human flesh and walk the earth or were killed because of their faith. To be killed for the cause of redemption is to be sacrificed on the altar of God in Heaven for the redemption of men. These hold a special place in the heart of God. To be *under the Altar* is to be a martyred (killed before their time) disembodied soul in the paradisiacal place of *Hades,* waiting for a celestial body so that it can live and walk in the Heavenly realm with the Lord.

Hell: The compartment within *Hades* is the place of torment for the guilty who will continue their torment in the *lake of fire*, after judgment day.

AMP Jude 1:12 *These men are blemishes at your love feasts, eating with you without the slightest qualm—shepherds who feed only themselves.* <u>*They are clouds without rain, blown along by the wind; autumn trees, without fruit and uprooted—twice dead.*</u> *They are wild waves of the sea, foaming up their shame; wandering stars,* <u>*for whom blackest darkness has been reserved forever.*</u>

AMP 2Pe 2:2 *And many will follow their immoral ways and lascivious doings; because of them the true Way will be maligned and defamed. And in their covetousness (lust, greed) they will exploit you with false (cunning) arguments.* <u>*From of old the sentence [of condemnation] for them has not been idle; their destruction (eternal misery) has not been asleep.*</u> *For God did not [even] spare angels* *that sinned, <u>but cast them into hell, delivering them to be kept there in pits of gloom</u> (the Abyss) <u>till the judgment and their doom.</u>*

The *Abyss*, the bottomless pit:

AMP 2Pe 2:4 For God did not [even] spare angels that sinned, but cast them into hell (the hellish place of Hades), delivering them to be kept there in pits (the Abyss, bottomless pit) of gloom till the judgment and their doom.

NIV Lk 8:30-31 Jesus asked him, "What is your name?" "Legion," he replied, because many demons had gone into him. And they <u>begged him repeatedly not to order them to go into the Abyss.</u>

NIV Rev 9:1-4 The fifth angel sounded his trumpet, and I saw a star that had fallen from the sky to the earth. <u>The star was given the key to the shaft of the Abyss. When he opened the Abyss, smoke rose from it like the smoke from a gigantic furnace. The sun and sky were darkened by the smoke from the Abyss. And out of the smoke locusts came down upon the earth and were given power like that of scorpions of the earth.</u> They were told not to harm the grass of the earth or any plant or tree, but only those people who did not have the seal of God on their foreheads.

NIV Rev 17:8 <u>The beast, which you saw, once was, now is not, and will come up out of the Abyss and go to his destruction.</u> The inhabitants of the earth whose names have not been written in the book of life from the creation of the world will be astonished when they see the beast, because he once was, now is not, and yet will come.

NIV Rev 20:1-3 And I saw an angel coming down out of heaven, <u>having the key to the Abyss and holding in his hand a great chain. He seized the dragon, that ancient serpent, who is the devil, or Satan, and bound him for a thousand years. He threw him into the Abyss, and locked and sealed it over him, to keep him from deceiving the nations anymore until the thousand years were ended.</u> After that, he must be set free for a short time.

The third compartment of *Hades* was made to confine the *devil*, fallen angels, hybrids of humans and angels, and demons. We see by the verses above that the *Abyss* is for celestial beings who have celestial bodies unlike the other two compartments of *Hades* reserved for disembodied souls. It is only those who possess physical bodies that experience death to the body. We also see that the *Abyss* is the destination for those with physical bodies that die but have been conceived with celestial DNA due to the mixing of DNA between spiritual and natural beings (*Nephilim*/giants), for example, *Nimrod*, Goliath and Lahmi his brother. This is interesting because although the *Nephilim* are part celestial, they have physical bodies making them mortal, not celestial, and God chooses to confine them in the *Abyss* along with celestial beings.

AMP Ge 6:1-7 WHEN MEN *began to multiply on the face of the land and daughters were born to them, The sons of God* (celestial beings) *saw that the daughters of men were fair, and they took wives of all they desired and chose. Then the Lord said, My Spirit shall not forever dwell and strive with man, <u>for he also is flesh</u>; but his days shall yet be 120 years. There were giants on the earth in those days—and also afterward—when the sons of God lived with the daughters of men, and they bore children to them. These were the <u>mighty men</u> who were of old, men of renown. The Lord saw that the wickedness of man was great in the earth, and that every imagination and intention of all human thinking was only evil continually. And the Lord regretted that He had made man on the earth, and He was grieved at heart. So the Lord said, I will destroy, blot out, and wipe away mankind, whom I have created from the face of the ground—<u>not only man, [but] the beasts and the creeping things and the birds of the air</u>—for it grieves Me and makes Me regretful that I have made them.*

These half celestial beings who were giants among the people, the Lord says of them that they are just men with mortal bodies, and He will not let them live forever like the celestial beings who fathered them. They will go to the *Abyss* as disembodied souls, unlike the rest of the beings there who retain their celestial bodies. We can see how this is true about the giants that had human bodies that died, because *Nimrod* is one of them and when he rises to life, it states that he comes up from out of the *Abyss*. It continues to say, "on his way to his destruction." That place of destruction will be the eternal *lake of fire*. Jude tells us that the *Abyss* can also be the destination for the worst of the worst humans. It is a special place of confinement that is temporal. A holding place until the day of judgment.

When the Lord says, *not only man, [but] the beasts and the creeping things and the birds of the air,* this is alluding to acknowledgment that the animals had their DNA corrupted too. This is the origin of dinosaurs who were destroyed in the flood along with the half-human, half-animal creatures spoken about in the mythologies of the world, for example: mermaids, minotaurs, centaurs, Enkidu, the companion of *Nimrod*, and the *demigod* Dagon who was half-fish, half-man worshiped by the Philistines and in the lands of Mesopotamia, Syria, and Canaan. These were not lifeless idols but *demigod*s (children of the fallen angels), mixed with humans and animals with celestial DNA. We can see how this is true because of what God lets loose out of the *Abyss* in order to punish the world who killed His saints. It says: *When he opened the Abyss, smoke rose from it like the smoke from a gigantic furnace. The sun and sky were darkened by the smoke from the Abyss. And out of the smoke locusts came down upon the earth and were given power like that of scorpions of the earth.*

NIV Rev 9:6-11 During those days men will seek death, but will not find it; they will long to die, but death will elude them. The locusts looked like horses prepared for battle. On their heads they wore something like crowns of gold, and their faces resembled human faces. Their hair was like women's hair, and their teeth were like lions' teeth. They had breastplates like breastplates of iron, and the sound of their wings was like the thundering of many horses and chariots rushing into battle. They had tails and stings like scorpions, and in their tails they had power to torment people for five months. They had as king over them the angel of the Abyss, whose name in Hebrew is Abaddon, and in Greek, Apollyon.

NIV Rev 9:15-21 And the four angels who had been kept ready for this very hour and day and month and year were released to kill a third of mankind. The number of the mounted troops was two hundred million. I heard their number. The horses and riders I saw in my vision looked like this: Their breastplates were fiery red, dark blue, and yellow as sulfur. The heads of the horses resembled the heads of lions, and out of their mouths came fire, smoke and sulfur. A third of mankind was killed by the three plagues of fire, smoke and sulfur that came out of their mouths. The power of the horses was in their mouths and in their tails; for their tails were like snakes, having heads with which they inflict injury. The rest of mankind that were not killed by these plagues still did not repent of the work of their hands; they did not stop worshiping demons (including the confined creatures who were evil hybrids between celestial, humans, and animals who came from the Abyss, described above), *and idols of gold, silver, bronze, stone and wood—idols that cannot see or hear or walk. Nor did they repent of their murders, their magic arts, their sexual immorality or their thefts.*

These creatures that are loosed out of the *Abyss* are creatures that were being held for the *lake of fire* after the day of judgement. Since they were captured and held in the *Abyss* means they were creatures that existed before the flood. They were not something God had created, but hybrids of animals and humans mixed with each other and with celestial DNA. They truly were monstrous creatures created not by God but the evilest forces that ruled the earth in the days leading up to the flood. The reason they were contained in the *Abyss* when the flood occurred was that God was protecting men on the earth from these monstrous supernatural creatures for a new beginning starting with Noah. However, since the flood, starting with *Nimrod* and all throughout history, men have been bent on seeking supernatural power by calling down these creatures and worshiping them. God obviously punishes us by giving us over to the very evils we seek out. Bringing *Nimrod* back from the dead to protect us from God so we can do as we will, will be the last straw.

KJV Ge 6:11-12 *The earth also was corrupt before God, and the earth was filled with violence. And God looked upon the earth, and, behold, it was corrupt; <u>for all flesh</u> (humans and animals alike) <u>had corrupted his way upon the earth</u>.*

This corruption of all flesh included the human and animal gene pool. At the time of the flood there were very few humans and animals left whose DNA had not been corrupted. This is why God did not leave it up to Noah to collect the animals to be saved on the ark but brought the ones He selected to the ark. As far as humans who populated the earth and did not have corrupted DNA, you could count on one hand, according to Genesis. In fact, out of the eight humans He saved on the ark, the Bible tells us according to their genealogy that only Noah, his wife, and their three sons had uncorrupted human DNA as God had created humans. However, this does not account for the wives of their three sons. We know through the genealogy of *Nimrod* whose mother was Ham's wife, although she herself was not a giant, she obviously possessed corrupt human DNA. And because of intentional incestual breeding through Ham's clan, *Nimrod*, and other giants, came to be in the post-flood era.

NIV Ge 6:4 *The Nephilim were on the earth in those days* (before the flood)—*<u>and also afterward</u>—when the sons of God went to the daughters of men and had children by them. They were the heroes of old, men of renown.*

It obviously was no temperamental or frivolous thing that led God to destroy all creatures and start again with both humans and animals. As for what will be released out of the *Abyss*, they too are truly abortions of nature. The Lord punishes us by giving us a dose of our own medicine, as it were, by releasing them out of the *Abyss* during the seven years of wrath before the return of Christ. Why? Because of our constant pursuit to endow ourselves with the power of these *demigod*s including; the sin of Sodom and Gomorrah whose cities were unanimously bent on making a giant of their own, using the manifest celestial angels who visited them; and in the future the predicted efforts by the Pope and the unanimous support of the world to bring back the giant, *Nimrod*, from out of the *Abyss* to rid themselves of God's *two witnesses*.

Note: The pursuit of Ham and his wife to interbreed bringing out the giant gene she possessed was an attempt to make their clan superior on the earth, just as Hitler attempted with the Aryan race. The difference between the clan of Ham and Sodom and Gomorrah was that the population of Sodom and Gomorrah attempted to make giants as done in *preflood* days, mixing the immortal with the mortal. They intended to use the angels that visited their cities and Lot. Whereas the clan of Ham was only trying to interbreed to make the giant gene dominant. This would produce a watered down or deluded version, so to speak, producing giants not nearly as monstrous as the *preflood Nephilim*. Although this was definitely an evil in the eyes of God, and the proverbial dog returning to its own vomit, it was in no way as abominable as mixing celestial beings with mortal beings again.

God destroyed Sodom and Gomorrah with burning sulfur because He was not willing to allow what had taken place and required the flood destroying all flesh in order to correct it. Likewise, raining down fire on Sodom and Gomorrah was a warning of how the second judgement will be of fire should we continue to call down supernatural evil on the earth. As it is and because of the stubborn pursuits of man, the judgement of fire that will destroy the entire universe has already been decreed and is in process.

NIV 2Pe 2:4-10 For if God did not spare angels when they sinned, but sent them to hell (the Abyss) *, putting them into gloomy dungeons to be held for judgment; if he did not spare the ancient world when he brought the flood on its ungodly people, but protected Noah, a preacher of righteousness, and seven others<u>; if he condemned the cities of Sodom and Gomorrah by burning them to ashes, and made them an example of what is going to happen to the ungodly</u>; and if he* *rescued Lot, a righteous man, who was distressed by the filthy lives of lawless men (for that righteous man, living among them day after day, was tormented in his righteous soul by the lawless deeds he saw and heard)—if this is so, then the Lord knows how to rescue godly men from trials <u>and to hold the unrighteous for the day of judgment, while continuing their punishment. This is especially true of those who follow the corrupt desire of the sinful nature and despise authority.</u> Bold and arrogant, these men are not afraid to slander celestial beings*

This is especially true of those who follow the corrupt desire of the sinful nature and despise authority. Nimrod's decree to the people was, "do as you will, and I will protect you from Yahweh." Since then, ungodly humans have despised the authority of their Creator desiring to do as they please and have boldly looked to the supernatural, the gods and *demigod*s/giants to protect and empower them from God; so they can freely fulfill every corrupt notion they desire to carry out. As stated before, in Nimrod's hatred of God and wanting to be the messiah of the world (making him the *antichrist*) it was him who designed the worship of the *preflood* fallen angels, and the *demigod*s they fathered to break the people free from subordination to God. However, these same powerful gods and *demigod*s, for the most part, were, at the advent of the flood, imprisoned and confined by God in the *Abyss*. Likewise, it was *Nimrod* who began the study of *astronomy* and developed *astrology* and developed the system of *idol worship*.

We hear in the world's mythologies of many creatures that are half-animal and half-human, even supernatural in nature. This is affirmation that they did exist. However, the Lord has been holding them in the *Abyss* since the flood so they can no longer interfere with human affairs. Just as will be the reason for confining the devil in the *Abyss* for 1,000 years, *He threw him into the Abyss, and locked and sealed it over him, to keep him from deceiving the nations anymore until the thousand years were ended.*

The Lord has been graciously protecting us from the fallen angels and the creatures created before the flood by confining them in the *Abyss*. However, even before the ark touched down on dry land until the coming end, men have been bent on returning to these times chasing after power, domination, and immortality. It will be the last straw when the Pope brings back from the dead, from the *Abyss*, a giant. The Pope will do this by having a body made out of parts of sacrificed men (AMP Isaiah 14:19). Jesus calls this thing; *the abomination that causes desolation*. Meaning, in modern terms; that tears it! That is the last straw! I am out of here (leaving the earth for 3 ½ years) and I will give them over to what they are bent on! They will see that I was actually protecting them from themselves but like the opening of Pandora's Box, they ignorantly insist on continually repeating this evil and they will see and experience what they seek after; because nothing else will deter them.

Note: Again, Sodom and Gomorrah having a place in the Bible was a warning. Fire consumed those cities not because of homosexuality but because they wanted to create their own giant by mixing DNA with these two angels that were manifest in human form. They wanted to have sexual relations with angels not homosexual sex with male humans! They knew Lot was entertaining angels. It is actually a ridiculous notion and huge misinterpretation of scriptures which negates the blatant warning from God to not dabble in this area ever again! It was a serious thing for Him to wipe out all humans and animals with the flood except the 8 and the animals on board the ark. The *first judgment* concerning this was a global flood and the *second judgment* is by fire. We are supposed to get that from what happened to Sodom and Gomorrah! But no, here we are again, seeking after the same things we have been repeatedly saved from.

The Lord's warning totally escapes us in our deception of thinking the issue in Sodom and Gomorrah that brought on their destruction was homosexuality. Here we are in these times doing the same—the dismantling of the Creator's natural laws which hold His creation together. We ignorantly do this by blurring the lines between genders even identifying with animals, cloning hybrids of animals and humans, and blurring the boundaries between the natural and the supernatural. This will climax when the Pope of the Catholic Church successfully brings *Nimrod* back from the supernatural realm in the *Abyss* to the natural realm in an effort to help us defy and defend against our Creator.

Note: A treasured verse in the Bible is:

AMP Ps 23:6 Surely goodness and love will follow me all the days of my life, and I will dwell in the house of the LORD forever.

A more accurate translation of the word *follow* as used by David in this verse, would be to hunt you down and overtake you as with a vengeance. The use of the word follow is like one who came into a small town, robbed the bank that the community kept their savings in, killed a favored citizen in the process, and fled. The town alarm would go off, the citizens would form a posse, and with a vengeance, relentlessly hunt that individual down until they catch him and bring him back to justice. In our ignorance, even the people of God run, whether we believe it is towards or away from Him, in His kindness and mercy, He relentlessly hunts us down and overtakes us as if with a vengeance, overwhelming us with His goodness and love to save us from ourselves.

The *lake of fire*: The eternal destination of everything which will not survive the last day of judgment becoming extinct forever: the earth, the universe, and all its physical elements (matter), the bodies of natural humans, *Hades*, fallen angels, demons, fallen humans (the souls of those who are condemned), even death itself. The *lake of fire* is the instrument of the *second death*.

The *first death* we suffer is because through the sin of Adam and Eve death entered into the world. As Paul says, the end of sin is death. Physical embodiment has since been doomed to death and decay including plants and animals—all of nature, including all the elements. However, in the fairness of God we all, meaning our disembodied souls, will rise from the dead given a celestial body, that is not subject to the destruction of the physical. However, as soon as we attain this new body, we will face judgement for how we conducted ourselves in the physical body to deem if we are worthy to live on for eternity. If not, we will suffer a second death by eternally being confined in the *lake of fire*. The first death is because corruption entered into the world through sin. Adam and Eve opened Pandora's Box and sin bringing death could not be stuffed back in the box. The second death is due to our own sin while in the body. This is the plan of God to save all who would be saved and is why there are two bodies and temporary places for the dead and there are two lives and deaths. What can be more fair from our Creator?

Heaven/**the spiritual realm:** Is the natural habitat of God, celestial humans, and angelic creatures. It is not made of natural matter as the physical universe is. It is comprised of spiritual matter. It is the future realm of the new heavens, the new earth, and the new Jerusalem. That is because these places are comprised of spiritual matter, and not of physical elements. *Heaven*, the spiritual or celestial realm, will be the sole surviving domain after the entire universe is destroyed by being thrown into the *lake of fire*. At the same time all the corruption in the spiritual realm coupled with all the corrupt angels and humans who have just received spiritual bodies, will be purged and confined for eternity in the *lake of fire* and evil will have been squashed for all time.

Redemption:

NIV Eph 2:8-9 *For it is by grace you have been saved, through faith—and this not from yourselves, it is the gift of God—not by works, so that no one can boast.*

Ro 10:9-10 *That if you confess with your mouth, "Jesus is Lord," and believe in your heart that God raised him from the dead, you will be saved. For it is with your heart that you believe and are justified, and it is with your mouth that you confess and are saved.*

Ephesians 2:8-9 and Romans 10:10 (above) are the verses which sparked the much-needed Reformation of the Church into a blazing flame. To this day the power and weight of these verses divide and define the Christian faith. How you embrace these two verses determines the authenticity of your faith in the minds of the majority of the Church. Before we look deeper at them, we will first outline the foundation of God's plan for redemption, then look at other verses to help us understand this great gift and opportunity to be redeemed.

Before death took its first life, the Lord made a plan that was fair for everyone. Death entered into the world, not only for man, but for his entire habitat including animals because the first man, Adam and his wife, sinned by corrupting the human spirit and its wisdom values. This made it impossible for all who are born with the human spirit to reconcile with God. Because of the corrupted human spirit, the human race is hopelessly condemned! By the nature of the human spirit and its wisdom values (our whole worldview) we are divided from God! From the moment of birth every person born sees themselves in relation to God, their world, and the people in it in a false to the truth skewed and twisted way. Because of the results of our skewed perception (wisdom values) and the selfish and self-centered deeds it inspires, the whole human race must die for this corruption to be extinguished.

AMP Jas 3:13-18 Who is there among you who is wise and intelligent? Then let him by his noble living show forth his [good] works with the [unobtrusive] humility [which is the proper attribute] of true wisdom. <u>But if you have bitter jealousy (envy) and contention (rivalry, selfish ambition) in your hearts, do not pride yourselves on it and thus be in defiance of and false to the Truth. This [superficial] wisdom is not such as comes down from above, but is earthly, unspiritual (animal), even devilish (demoniacal).</u> For wherever there is jealousy (envy) and contention (rivalry and selfish ambition), there will also be confusion (unrest, disharmony, rebellion) and all sorts of evil and vile practices. <u>But the wisdom from above is first of all pure (undefiled); then it is peace-loving, courteous (considerate, gentle). [It is willing to] yield to reason, full of compassion and good fruits; it is wholehearted and straightforward, impartial and</u>

unfeigned (free from doubts, wavering, and insincerity). And the harvest of righteousness (of conformity to God's will in thought and deed) is [the fruit of the seed] sown in peace by those who work for and make peace [in themselves and in others, that peace which means concord, agreement, and harmony between individuals, with undisturbedness, in a peaceful mind free from fears and agitating passions and moral conflicts].

As stated previously, it is the mercy and fairness of God that all should not lose their life because of the sin of the first man, even though his sin hopelessly corrupted the human spirit for all men. The first step of the remedy of God was to create a temporary place to hold those disembodied but living souls whose bodies of flesh died. On the last day when all flesh becomes extinct by having died a first death, all disembodied souls will be in *Hades*.

AMP Rev 6:8 So I looked, and behold, an ashy pale horse [black and blue as if made so by bruising], and its rider's name was <u>Death, and Hades (the realm of the dead) followed him closely</u>.

When it is all said and done on the last day at the end of time, it is then God will raise every disembodied soul back to life and they will once again be clothed with a body. Only it will be a celestial body, not a physical body, because every element and atom of the physical universe will be no more, and will be burned up, melted in the heat of the *lake of fire*. At that time all will be judged individually according to how they conducted their lives in the body and by the motives that inspired them. All who are found lacking by their own merit will suffer a *second death* by being thrown alive into the *lake of fire*. All who are approved will be celestial humans and they will spend all of eternity in fellowship with God. Again, because the human spirit is corrupt and because this was accomplished by the first man, death entered into the human experience for all. The *first death* we suffer is a result of that, but the *second* and *permanent death* is solely based on our own conduct.

However, getting a Heavenly body does not by itself correct the problem. That is because it is a spirit problem. The human spirit and its wisdom values are hopelessly corrupted. It is beyond redemption.

AMP Jer 17:9-10 The heart is deceitful above all things, and it is exceedingly perverse and corrupt and severely, mortally sick! Who can know it [perceive, understand, be acquainted with his own heart and mind]? (NAS Who really knows how bad it is?) I the Lord search the mind, I try the heart, even to give to every man according to his ways, according to the fruit of his doings . . .

Considering that the human spirit is beyond redemption and sees everything in a false to the truth way, the next part of God's remedy is to give us a new and uncorrupted spirit—the Holy Spirit.

In order to save us, the Lord surgically removes us from our instrument of sin, our body. Then gives us a new but celestial body that is not corrupted by the expression of sin. Then He surgically removes from us, our corrupt human spirit, giving us a new spirit. In this case, the Lord gives us His Spirit. The human spirit cannot be saved. Otherwise, the Lord would not have had to come and die in order to release His Spirit through His death, so that through union with Him we may be born again.

This is the first step in His salvation plan. However, salvation is not complete. This is because the Holy Spirit within us is meant to animate our new uncorrupted celestial body. In the meantime, it is meant to influence and sanctify our hearts until we receive our celestial body.

Here, however, is a small glitch; what keeps our human body animated (alive) is our human spirit. What this means is that until we die to our physical body, our corrupt human spirit is still active and a part of our nature. Once we die, we can be free from not only the corrupt body but the corrupt human spirit. Anything short of retaining our corrupt human spirit will cause our body to die. So, until we die, and even though we have the Holy Spirit within waiting to animate our new celestial body, we will have to contend with our human spirit and physical body. While on this earth, and after we have received the Holy Spirit, we will have to decide, decision by decision, what spirit perception and response we will choose to perceive and act out of—the Holy Spirit within or the corrupt human spirit that gives life to our body.

Knowing this is what makes true what Jesus spoke to us, *if you really love me, you will obey me.* To be in union with Jesus is to perceive and act out of His Spirit, not our sin nature thus being one with Him. The more we are moved by His Spirit, the more we are showing a faithful love of being in union with Him. To be moved out of our sin nature is a spiritual adultery. We can show no more love to Him who we are in union with than to perceive and be moved in our hearts by His Spirit in us. To obey Him is to truly love Him!

The real man is our soul, our mind, which is our personality and the seat of reason and decision. It cannot be replaced, otherwise we would cease being us and therefore truly be dead. Our soul the Lord cannot replace even though it has been corrupted by the spirit perception or wisdom values of our human spirit and the desires of our flesh. Our soul needs to be cleansed with truth, resulting in a new worldview, requiring a desire to see and respond to life according to truth and the wisdom that comes down from *Heaven*.

AMP Jas 3:17-18 But the wisdom (that is the perception of the Holy Spirit) from above is first of all pure (undefiled); then it is peace-loving, courteous (considerate, gentle). [It is willing to] yield to reason, full of compassion and good fruits; it is wholehearted and straightforward, impartial and unfeigned (free from doubts, wavering, and insincerity). And the harvest of righteousness (of conformity to God's will in thought and deed) is [the fruit of the seed] sown in peace by those who work for and make peace [in themselves and in others, that peace which means concord, agreement, and harmony between individuals, with undisturbedness, in a peaceful mind free from fears and agitating passions and moral conflicts].

The finishing step of our salvation is when we receive our celestial body finding ourselves before the Lord and His Father in the celestial realm. It is then that the Holy Spirit in our hearts will finally animate our new celestial body, leaving our human spirit useless and as dead to us as our physical body, freeing our minds from their corrupted influence. In the meanwhile, the Holy Spirit within us is the guarantee that we will have a celestial body that will be in fellowship with the Lord. Why? Simply because it is the life and consciousness that is given to us to animate our celestial body when we translate into it. Likewise, it is a spirit that is not in rebellion or discord towards Him, but in harmony with the Lord given that it is His very Spirit we possess as a matter of our marital covenant relationship with Him.

AMP Eph 1:13-14 In Him you also who have heard the Word of Truth, the glad tidings (Gospel) of your salvation, and have believed in and adhered to and relied on Him, were stamped with the seal of the long-promised Holy Spirit. That [Spirit] is the guarantee of our inheritance [the firstfruits, the pledge and foretaste, the down payment on our heritage], <u>in anticipation of its full redemption and our acquiring [complete] possession of it</u>—to the praise of His glory.

NIV 2Co 1:21-22 Now it is God who makes both us and you stand firm in Christ. He anointed us, set his seal of ownership on us, <u>and put his Spirit in our hearts as a deposit, guaranteeing what is to come.</u>

AMP 2Co 5:1-6 FOR WE know that if the tent which is our earthly home (body) is destroyed (dissolved), we have from God a building, a house (a body) not made with hands, eternal in the heavens. Here indeed, in this [present abode, body], we sigh and groan inwardly, because we yearn to be clothed over [we yearn to put on our celestial body like a garment, to be fitted out] with our heavenly dwelling, So that by putting it on we may not be found naked (without a body). For while we are still in this tent, we groan under the burden and sigh deeply (weighed down, depressed, oppressed)— not that we want to put off the body (the clothing of the spirit), but rather that we would be further clothed, so that what is mortal (our dying body) may be swallowed up by life. Now He Who has fashioned us [preparing and making us fit] for this very thing (by the convicting power of the Holy Spirit in us) *is God, <u>Who also has given us the [Holy] Spirit as a guarantee [of the fulfillment of His promise].</u> So then, we are always full of good and hopeful and confident courage; we know that while we are at home in the body, we are abroad from the home with the Lord [that is promised us].*

Having the Holy Spirit in our hearts while we are still in the physical body does not lay dormant while waiting for us to finally receive our celestial body it is meant to animate. That spirit is also at work exposing the truth and enlightening our minds resulting in a shift of our perception—our worldview—which convicts the thoughts and purposes of our mind. This renews our mind (soul) and cleanses it of impurities (false perceptions and worldviews) and sin, making us fit for eternal life in Heaven with the Lord. Only we must search out and give both preference and priority to the conviction of the Holy Spirit within so as to operate out of our new "born-again" spirit instead of our (what Paul calls) sin nature—our corrupt human spirit. To live for our corrupt human spirit is to despise and reject the Holy Spirit in us thereby putting us in spiritual adultery.

NIV Mt 6:24a "No one can serve two masters. Either he will hate the one and love the other, or he will be devoted to the one and despise the other. . ."

AMP Mt 6:19-31 ***Do not gather and heap up and store up for yourselves treasures on earth, where moth and rust and worm consume and destroy, and where thieves break through and steal. But gather and heap up and store for yourselves treasures in heaven, where neither moth nor rust nor worm consume and destroy, and where thieves do not break through and steal; <u>For where your treasure is, there will your heart be also.</u> The eye is the lamp of the body. So if your eye is sound, your entire body will be full of light. But if your eye is unsound, your whole body will be full of darkness. If then the very light in you [your conscience] is darkened, how dense is that darkness! <u>No one can serve two masters; for either he will hate the</u>***

one and love the other, or he will stand by and be devoted to the one and despise and be against the other. You cannot serve God and mammon (deceitful riches, money, possessions, or whatever is trusted in). Therefore I tell you, stop being perpetually uneasy (anxious and worried) about your life, what you shall eat or what you shall drink; or about your body, what you shall put on. Is not life greater [in quality] than food, and the body [far above and more excellent] than clothing? Look at the birds of the air; they neither sow nor reap nor gather into barns, and yet your heavenly Father keeps feeding them. Are you not worth much more than they? And who of you by worrying and being anxious can add one unit of measure (cubit) to his stature or to the span of his life? And why should you be anxious about clothes? Consider the lilies of the field and learn thoroughly how they grow; they neither toil nor spin. Yet I tell you, even Solomon in all his magnificence (excellence, dignity, and grace) was not arrayed like one of these. But if God so clothes the grass of the field, which today is alive and green and tomorrow is tossed into the furnace, will He not much more surely clothe you, O you of little faith? Therefore do not worry and be anxious, saying, What are we going to have to eat? or, What are we going to have to drink? or, What are we going to have to wear?*

Living out the rest of our physical life, choosing to perceive through and be moved by the born-again spirit in us, not only helps us connect with our new body and spirit in the world to come but guarantees our salvation and makes us faithful to the one who we are in marital covenant relationship with.

Few realize it but in the following verses, the process of salvation is described:

AMP Heb 4:11-13 *Let us therefore be zealous and exert ourselves and strive diligently to enter that rest [of God, to know and experience it for ourselves], that no one may fall or perish by the same kind of unbelief and disobedience [into which those in the wilderness fell]. For the Word that God speaks is alive and full of power [making it active, operative, energizing, and effective]; it is sharper than any two-edged sword, penetrating to the dividing line of the breath of life (soul) and [the immortal] spirit* (the dividing or separating or removal of the human spirit from our soul), *and of joints and marrow [of the deepest parts of our nature]* (surgically removing our soul from our physical body down to the marrow which receives life from the spirit and produces the blood that keeps us alive), *exposing and sifting and analyzing and judging the very thoughts and purposes of the heart* (not replacing, but purifying our soul//mind with truth). *And not a creature exists that is concealed from His sight, but all things are open and exposed, naked and defenseless to the eyes of Him with Whom we have to do.*

There is rabbinical literature which is not cannon that supports the above verses that this was the plan of God even before the first man died. However, we must add up different verses in scriptures to see how this holds true throughout the Bible. We learn in scriptures that even before Jesus was born and during His life in a human body, the Jews were divided on this very subject. There were two main opposing sects which were divided over this issue. They were the Sadducees and the Pharisees.

The Sadducees believed once you are dead, you are dead, soul and all. They did not believe that God would resurrect all humanity giving them a body by which to be judged for their own deeds. Nor that as a result of that judgment would either live forever or endure a second death. They believed they should make the most of this life because when it is finished your life-giving spirit returns to God and your soul and body cease to exist. This is the prominent belief of the Jews today.

The Pharisees, on the other hand, correctly understood from scriptures before Jesus was born that there would be a last day which would include a resurrection of the dead, a coming back to life, and then a judgment which will result in either life everlasting, or a second death and eternal torment of the surviving soul. They understood each human would have to give an account of themselves to God.

These two ruling parties often tested and judged Jesus by where He stood on this issue—the very issue which divided them. Below is one of the occasions this happened, the Sadducees presented this scenario as a supposedly unsolvable riddle in order to prove that there was no resurrection of the dead or life after death. That is why Jesus ended His answer to the Sadducees with, *He is not the God of the dead but of the living!* Meaning that the dead are merely disembodied living souls who live forever. By verse 34 we can tell this pleased and supported the belief of the Pharisees.

AMP Mt 22:23-34 The same day some Sadducees, who say that there is no resurrection [of the dead], came to Him and they asked Him a question, Saying, Teacher, Moses said, If a man dies, leaving no children, his brother shall marry the widow and raise up a family for his brother. Now there were seven brothers among us; the first married and died, and, having no children, left his wife to his brother. The second also died childless, and the third, down to the seventh. Last of all, the woman died also. Now, in the resurrection, to which of the seven will she be wife? For they all had her. <u>*But Jesus replied to them, You are wrong because you know neither the Scriptures nor God's power. For in the resurrected state neither do [men] marry nor are [women] given in marriage, but they are like the angels in heaven.*</u> *But as to the resurrection of the dead—have you never read what was said to you by God, I am the God of Abraham, and the God of Isaac, and the God of Jacob?* <u>*He is not the God of the dead but of the living!*</u> *And when the throng heard it, they were astonished and filled with [glad] amazement at His teaching.* <u>*Now when the Pharisees heard that He had silenced (muzzled) the Sadducees, they gathered together.*</u>

In the Babylonian writings of *Nimrod* who was born in the 3rd generation after the flood, his biggest quest was to seek after immortality. In one of his adventures seeking immortality, he traveled to *Hades*. In those times legend held that entering *Hades* was thought of as having to cross a river from the living to the realm of the dead. There was a ferryman there to transport you across the river from the living to the dead. And he must be paid, again, according to legend. This is how the custom of putting coins over the dead person's eyes developed. The coins were to pay the ferryman. Other customs hold that you do not have to pay but simply prove to the ferryman that you were dead.

In *Nimrod*'s case, according to *The Epic of Gilgamesh*, he bribed the ferryman to visit the other side to seek from the immortal celestial beings their counsel and power to become immortal (most likely in the realm of the *Abyss* where the fallen angels that he made gods of, and caused the people to worship are held until judgment). These celestial *preflood* prisoners are still embodied in their confinement unlike the naked souls of the deceased humans in *Hades*. They laughed at him, telling him it was not possible. But at his insistence they gave him a test, to show him how weak he was as a mortal human. They challenged him to stay awake without falling asleep for 7 days. Of course, he failed and was made to return to the living.

Note: God used *Nimrod's* obsession to become immortal and not die by granting him the ability to come back to life on his way to his destruction in the *lake of fire*. This is in order to carry out God's plan of salvation to win back the apostates, making them once again His bride.

NIV Rev 17:11-18 *The beast who once was, and now is not, is an eighth king. He belongs to the seven and is going to his destruction. "The ten horns you saw are ten kings who have not yet received a kingdom, but who for one hour* (seven years) *will receive authority as kings along with the beast. They have one purpose and will give their power and authority to the beast. They will make war against the Lamb, but the Lamb will overcome them because he is Lord of lords and King of kings—and with him will be his called, chosen and faithful followers." Then the angel said to me, "The waters you saw, where the prostitute* (the Church Corrupt [the Roman Catholic Church]) *sits, are peoples, multitudes, nations and languages. The beast and the ten horns you saw will hate the prostitute. They will bring her to ruin and leave her naked; they will eat her flesh and* *burn her with fire. <u>For God has put it into their hearts to accomplish his purpose by agreeing to give the beast their power to rule, until God's words are fulfilled.</u> The woman you saw is the great city* (at this point in time, it is the Vatican) *that rules over the kings of the earth."*

What elements of truth there are to this story in *The Epic of Gilgamesh* can seem dubious, however, all of mythology is rooted in fact, but distorted to bring undue glory to the gods and *demigod*s. However, it is a matter of record that *Nimrod*, as an obsession, chased after immortality. Furthermore, we know by the Bible that some kind of deal was made that God is allowing him to rise back to life for a short time on his way from the *Abyss* to the permanent *lake of fire*. However, the reason for using this story is to show that people from the third generation after the flood had knowledge of *Hades*.

What we can glean from this is that knowledge of *Hades*, confining the living but disembodied souls, the resurrection, and judgment on the last day is from antiquity (predating Jesus), and it was God's plan from the beginning. In addition, Jesus not only affirmed it as true but gave a much more authoritative and accurate understanding of the fate of man (concerning the first death, resurrection, and second death). Again, this plan is the fairness of God and creates the foundational way that humans will, on their own merit, be responsible for their own eternal fate and have a way to escape eternal death.

Here are, before the times of Jesus, a couple of verses in the Old Testament spoken by the prophets which affirm this was always the plan of God so that the individual man did not suffer eternal death because of the one man—the first man.

NAS ISA 26:19-21 <u>*Your dead will live; Their corpses will rise. You who lie in the dust, awake and shout for joy,*</u> *For your dew is as the dew of the dawn, And <u>the earth will give birth to the departed spirits</u>* (<u>they will rise from the dead).</u> *Come, my people, enter into your rooms*

And close your doors behind you; Hide for a little while Until indignation runs its course (the seven years of God's wrath starting with the great tribulation). *For behold, the LORD is about to come out from His place To punish the inhabitants of the earth for their iniquity; And the earth will reveal her bloodshed And will no longer cover her slain.*

Next it says in Daniel:

NIV Da 12:2 Multitudes who sleep in the dust of the earth will awake: some to everlasting life, others to shame and everlasting contempt (referring to the last day).

Death:

To God the real man is not the body but the mind or soul. For us, when someone's body dies, we see them no more. However, with God, He sees the living soul of the man disembodied, or naked (unclothed). When it says in the Bible, that they were wearing or given "white robes" it is referring to the naked soul being clothed with a celestial body.

NIV Rev 6:9-11 When he opened the fifth seal, I saw under the altar the souls of those who had been slain because of the word of God and the testimony they had maintained. They called out in a loud voice, "How long, Sovereign Lord, holy and true, until you judge the inhabitants of the earth and avenge our blood?" Then each of them was given a white robe...

This group of people *under the Altar* were called souls who had been slain or killed. They are called *souls* because they are living beings who are disembodied. Verse 11 says they are given a white robe. If they were disembodied souls, and if the robes given them were robes of fabric, it would be a cruel joke, given they had no body to wear the robe with. It would be like giving a man a pair of shoes to quiet him because he was still angry at the loss of his legs below his knees. The white robe each are given is a celestial body to clothe their soul with, and then as a result, they are no longer dead, disembodied, or naked. Why white? White, meaning pure or holy and not corrupt as the human body of flesh became because of the sins carried out in the body.

Salvation by good deeds and clean motives:

As we have previously gone over, because of the sin of Adam the first man, death entered into the world. And because of the corrupting of the human spirit, all men are doomed to die, becoming disembodied. The first and fair plan of God was to create *Hades* as a temporary confinement for the disembodied souls when they die. When every human soul had lived and died it will be the last day. Then all humans will be resurrected, once again clothed with a body. They will then face God and be judged. Those whose deeds while in the body were found acceptable by God, now having a celestial body, will live in fellowship with God forever. Those who will not be found acceptable will be thrown alive into the *lake of fire* and suffer death again, or what is called the second death. In this way one's eternal fate is not based on what Adam did. Our first death is because of Adam, or second death is because of us. Our death because of Adam is temporary, our death because of our motives and deeds while in the body, is eternal.

NIV Rev 20:11-15 Then I saw a great white throne and him who was seated on it. Earth and sky fled from his presence, and there was no place for them. And I saw the dead, great and small, standing before the throne, and books were opened. Another book was opened, which is the book of life. <u>The dead were judged according to what they had done as recorded in the books.</u> The sea gave up the dead that were in it, and death and Hades gave up the dead that were in them, and <u>each person was judged according to what he had done</u>. Then death and Hades were thrown into the lake of fire. The lake of fire is the second death. If anyone's name was not found written in the book of life, he was thrown into the lake of fire.

Jesus affirms that the last day when all the dead rise to life, will be judged by their deeds:

AMP Jn 5:28-29 *Do not be surprised and wonder at this, for the time is coming when all those who are in the tombs shall hear His voice, And they shall come out—<u>those who have practiced doing good</u> [will come out] to the resurrection of [new] life, and <u>those who have done evil</u> will be raised for judgment [raised to meet their sentence].*

The salvation of Jesus:

You could say that God's mercy has no bounds. *The last day*, or *the day of the Lord*, or *the day of judgment* are all different names for the same event. That day will provide a fair and equitable opportunity for every person ever born to go from being a natural human of flesh to a celestial human based on their own deeds. Man was never meant to die or be anything other than a physical human being. So, for humanity to sin and fall from His grace and for God to remedy this by giving us a raise in stature is extremely generous. It's like we are getting rewarded after having done wrong and given forgiveness having seen the errors of our ways. But that is not the whole of God's mercy! God provides another way of salvation. A way of salvation in which one never has to experience death at all!

NIV Jn 11:21-26 *"Lord," Martha said to Jesus, "if you had been here, my brother would not have died. But I know that even now God will give you whatever you ask." Jesus said to her, "Your brother will rise again." Martha answered, "I know he will rise again in the resurrection at the last day.<u> Jesus said to her, "I am the resurrection and the life. He who believes in me will live, even though he dies; and whoever lives and believes in me will never die. Do you believe this?"</u>*

When Jesus says, *He who believes in me will live, even though he dies*, He is talking about the resurrection of the dead. Because of the redeeming work Jesus did through His death on the cross, an additionally planned resurrection was established which will happen 1,000 years before the resurrection on the last day. Revelation calls this added resurrection of the dead, *the first resurrection*" (Rev 20:5). It is called the first not because it was the first one which was established and decreed by God, the last day resurrection was decreed and established first. The reason it is called the first is because it will be the first of two different resurrections to occur. The first one is a greater mercy and gift from God for those who would be the bride of Christ. These individuals hold a different status than those who become celestial humans on the last day. They will be celestial humans living in the New Jerusalem with Jesus and His Father and rule the earth and the natural humans who inhabit it for 1,000 years before the last day. The bride of Christ who becomes celestial humans before the last day will not have to wait in Hades, disembodied until the last day resurrection of the dead. They will instead have the opportunity to be with Jesus when He brings His Kingdom to the earth.

In addition, to the *first resurrection* and because of the redeeming work of Jesus, there already was a resurrection of some of the patriarchs of the Israelites. It was more than 2,000 years (and counting) before the *first resurrection* is scheduled to happen in the future. The resurrection for some of the patriarchs of the Israelites happened as soon as Jesus gave up His Spirit and died when He was crucified.

It says the gates of Hades (the realm of the dead—the prison of the disembodied) could not prevail against Him. Although Jesus died and went to Hades, the gates which would hold Him captive and disembodied; unable to escape as it does for all others in Hades, could not hold Him prisoner nor disembodied. Not only that but He set others held imprisoned free. He led the prisoners free and took them with Him out of Hades (resurrected and embodied again). There were *144,000* of them He set free that day 12,000 from every tribe of Israel. They were Israelites who were martyred as He was.

These *144,000* were pure in both their hearts of worship towards God, and in their genealogy as God's chosen people. It was through the obedience of these chosen people of God who also kept their DNA pure that the Word of God was able to come and be born in human flesh as Jesus. As such, they hold a special place in the heart of Jesus.

The Bible calls these *144,000* the *first fruits* of His redeeming work. This implies that they were the first of the dead to be given a new body, a celestial body, escape confinement in the realm of the dead, and to live and have fellowship with the Lord in *Heaven*. Although they were disembodied souls in the paradisiacal place of *Hades* (*under the altar*), they were the first to receive a celestial body and have fellowship before the throne of God and His Son, Jesus. This is why they are called the first fruits of His redeeming work. They are the ones of whom it was said they were given white robes (celestial bodies) but would have to wait for the full number of those who would be martyred before justice was poured out on those who killed them. This is what the scripture says about the *144,000*:

144,000 Sealed

NIV Rev 7:3-8 *"Do not harm the land or the sea or the trees <u>until we put a seal on the foreheads of the servants of our God.</u>" Then I heard the number of those who were sealed: 144,000 from all the tribes of Israel. From the tribe of Judah 12,000 were sealed, from the tribe of Reuben 12,000, from the tribe of Gad 12,000, from the tribe of Asher 12,000, from the tribe of Naphtali 12,000, from the tribe of Manasseh 12,000, from the tribe of Simeon 12,000, from the tribe of Levi 12,000, from the tribe of Issachar 12,000, from the tribe of Zebulun 12,000, from the tribe of Joseph 12,000, from the tribe of Benjamin 12,000.*

Most believe that this verse is talking about the future when the Lord's 7 years of wrath is released. Revelation does not just tell us of the future, the *end times*. It actually speaks about all of history from original sin to the very end. When it says, *Do not harm the land or the sea or the trees until we put a seal on the foreheads of the servants of our God.* It is talking about marking His faithful servants before the release of the four horsemen, so that they would be able to accomplish their destiny in God's plan of salvation.

The Fifth Seal

NIV Rev 6:9-11 *When he opened the fifth seal, I saw under the altar the souls of those who had been slain because of the word of God and the testimony they had maintained. They called out in a loud voice, "How long, Sovereign Lord, holy and true, until you judge the inhabitants of the earth and avenge our blood?"* <u>*Then each of them was given a white robe, and they were told to wait a little longer, until the number of their fellow servants and brothers who were to be killed as they had been was completed.*</u>

The fifth seal is when Jesus died on the cross. That is why in Rev 14:1 (below) He is called the Lamb standing on Mount Zion (Jerusalem). He is the Lamb because at this point, He had offered Himself up as a sacrifice. The Lamb standing on Mount Zion is the crucified and risen Jesus. When the *144,000* disembodied souls in the paradisiacal place of Hades observed Jesus being killed by such a cruel death, then becoming one of their numbers of the martyred, they cried out to God to judge the earth. It's like how much more do you need before you act? They killed the Lord of glory, just as they had done to us. However, it was then, when Jesus said, "it is finished" and gave up His Spirit that He went among them in Hades, gave them celestial bodies (white robes) and led them in a procession as the train of His robe out of Hades and out of their graves presenting them 40 days later to His Father, when He ascended to Heaven.

This was the most joyful and victorious moment in the history of history! These *144,000* were the very first celestial humans (the first fruits)! That is why in Rev 14:1 (below) it says, *and with Him 144,000 who had his name and his Father's name written on their foreheads.* Next, when it says they had His and His Father's name written on their foreheads, this is a reference to the above verse Rev 7:3 where it says, *we put a seal on the foreheads of the servants of our God.* Then going on to say, *Then I heard the number of those who were sealed: 144,000 from all the tribes of Israel.*

The Lamb and the 144,000

NIV Rev 14:1-5 Then I looked, and there before me was <u>the Lamb, standing on Mount Zion, and with him 144,000 who had his name and his Father's name written on their foreheads</u>. And I heard a sound from heaven like the roar of rushing waters and like a loud peal of thunder. The sound I heard was like that of harpists playing their harps. And they sang a new song before the throne and before the four living creatures and the elders. No one could learn <u>the song except the 144,000 who had been redeemed from the earth.</u> These are those who did not defile themselves with women, for they kept themselves pure. They follow the Lamb wherever he goes. <u>They were purchased from among men and offered as firstfruits to God and the Lamb.</u> No lie was found in their mouths; they are blameless.

The fact that they are in *Heaven* before the throne requires them to have received celestial bodies and to have been released from *Hades*. This was not even possible until Jesus died on the cross as the Lamb of God. Secondly, they are the first fruits so naturally, they are the first ones to be redeemed and receive celestial bodies. We are able to see what the above verses look like on earth through the verses recorded in Matthew concerning the death of Jesus (below).

The Death of Jesus

NIV Mt 27:50-54 And when Jesus had cried out again in a loud voice, he gave up his spirit. At that moment the curtain of the temple was torn in two from top to bottom. <u>The earth shook and the rocks split. The tombs broke open and the bodies of many holy people who had died were raised to life. They came out of the tombs, and after Jesus' resurrection they went into the holy city and appeared to many people.</u> When the centurion and those with him who were guarding Jesus saw the earthquake and all that had happened, they were terrified, and exclaimed, "Surely he was the Son of God!"

These, "holy people" in verse 52 are the first of whom were redeemed and given a celestial body—they are the *144,000* because it is said of them that they are the *first fruits*.

Finally, when it says in Rev 6:11 (above), *and they were told to wait a little longer, until the number of their fellow servants and brothers who were to be killed as they had been was completed.* It is talking about those who will die during the *great tribulation* to come and will, like them, be resurrected to life with a celestial body at the *first resurrection*.

This gives more evidence that the *144,000* were before the *great tribulation* including all the *end times* wrath poured out on both the saints and sinners for 7 years. It says it plainly that although they received a celestial body they had need to wait until the full number are killed as they were for justice to take effect. How could it be then, that these *144,000* are resurrected after or during the wrath of God which allows for the killing of the saints before punishing the world who kills them?

Again, it says as plain as day, they were given their celestial bodies then they had to wait for the full number of those who would be martyred before the Lord would carry out justice against the inhabitants of the earth. Clearly that will happen during the *great tribulation* when their fellow servants are killed during the first 3 ½ years of God's 7 years of wrath. For after that no more servants of God will be killed, and like the *144,000*, the surviving Christians will have a mark disallowing them to be harmed. That time of promised wrath proceeds after the full number are killed, immediately ending the *great tribulation* and starts the outpouring of God's wrath on the inhabitants of the earth who hated and killed the servants of God. The *144,000* are already in *Heaven* in fellowship with God and are the first of those redeemed by Jesus to have that privilege, and rightfully so, because of them the Christ was able to come and save us all.

The Seventh Seal and the Golden Censer

NIV Rev 8:1-5 When he opened the seventh seal, there was silence in heaven for about half an hour. And I saw the seven angels who stand before God, and to them were given seven trumpets. Another angel, *who had a golden censer, came and stood at the altar. He was given much incense to offer, with the prayers of all the saints, on the golden altar before the throne. The smoke of the incense, together with the prayers of the saints, went up before God from the angel's hand. Then the angel took the censer, filled it with fire from the altar, and hurled it on the earth; and there came peals of thunder, rumblings, flashes of lightning and an earthquake.*

Stood at the altar, this is where the 144,000 were when they became the first fruits of Jesus' redeeming work. *The smoke of the incense, together with the prayers of the saints, went up before God from the angel's hand. Then the angel took the censer, filled it with fire from the altar, and hurled it on the earth; and there came peals of thunder, rumblings, flashes of lightning and an earthquake.* Together with the prayers of the saints? What saints? The saints who were formerly at that altar and requested justice be poured out on the world. These saints, now including the full number of those who were also to be killed for their testimony, have been finally added to their numbers. *The smoke of the incense, together with the prayers of the saints, went up before God from the angel's hand.* Those prayers were the prayers of the *soul*s *under the Altar* looking for justice against the world. The smoke of the incense was the pleasing fragrance of the sacrifice of them having been martyred for the name of Christ. In the next verse (5) when it says that the angel hurled the censer down to the earth, it is from a Heavenly viewpoint we see the release of that justice and the beginning of the wrath of God poured out on the people of the earth who harmed His elect. This time period is at the end of the *great tribulation* and the start of the last 3½ years of wrath being poured out on the world.

Rev 8:1-5 (above) shows us what the release of God's wrath looks like from *Heaven* looking down, whereas Rev 6:14-17 (below) shows us what that looks like from the earth looking up.

NIV Rev 6:14-17 The sky receded like a scroll, rolling up, and every mountain and island was removed from its place. Then the kings of the earth, the princes, the generals, the rich, the mighty, and every slave and every free man hid in caves and among the rocks of the mountains. They called to the mountains and the rocks, "Fall on us and hide us from the face of him who sits on the throne and from the wrath of the Lamb! <u>*For the great day of their wrath has come, and who can stand?"*</u>

Finally, there will be hell to pay for the murders of God's people throughout history with the *great tribulation* being the capstone of those murders. Although the *144,000* and those who will die during the *great tribulation* are separated by a great deal of time, they are really only one group in the eyes of the Lord. They have a special place in the heart of God and together they will be given celestial bodies before the last day of judgment to be His bride and will rule with Him during His *millennium reign.*

Here is an interesting article taking note of the meanings of the names of this list of the 12 tribes mentioned who comprise the *144,000*:

In ancient times, the names given to children had significant meaning. In Genesis we find the meanings of the names listed in Revelation 7:7-8. In birth order they are:

Genesis 29:32 Reuben: "surely the LORD hath looked upon my affliction; now therefore my husband will love me."

Genesis 29:33 Simeon: "because the LORD hath heard… he hath therefore given me this son…"

Genesis 29:34 Levi: "now this time will my husband be joined unto me" (It should be noted that God is called Israel's husband in Isa 54:5)

Genesis 29:35 Judah: "now will I praise the LORD" [Dan is omitted in Revelation 7]

Genesis 30:8 Naphtali: "with great wrestlings…I have prevailed."

Genesis 30:11 Gad: "a troop cometh" [Gad in Hebrew means "good fortune"]

Genesis 30:13 Asher: "happy am I, call me blessed"

Genesis 30:18 Issachar: "God hath given me my hire" [Hebrew sakar – wages, compensation, reward]

Genesis 30:20 Zebulun: "now will my husband dwell with me"

Genesis 30:24 Joseph: "the LORD shall add"

Genesis 35:18 Benjamin: "the Son of the right hand"

Genesis 41:51 Manasseh: "for God hath made me forget all my toil."

The Order of the Names

Let's now rearrange the names in the order in which they are listed in Revelation 7:7-8 with the meaning next to each:

Judah: Praise the Lord,

Reuben: He has looked on my affliction

Gad: good fortune comes

Asher: happy and blessed am I

Napthali: my wrestling

Manasseh: has made me forget my sorrow

Simeon: God hears me

Levi: has joined me

Issachar: rewarded me

Zebulun: exalted me

Joseph: adding me

Benjamin: the Son of His right hand.

The Meaning of the Names in the Order of Revelation 7

Now let's string together the meaning of the names and read the message:

Praise the Lord. He has looked on my affliction [and] good fortune comes. Happy and blessed am I. My wrestling has made me forget my sorrow. God hears me, has joined me, rewarded me, exalted me [by] adding to me the Son of His right hand..[1]

Returning back to what Jesus spoke to Martha when He said,

I am the resurrection and the life. He who believes in me will live, even though he dies. . . Jesus went on to conclude what he was saying, *and whoever lives and believes in me will never die. Do you believe this?* I can understand why Jesus would say to Martha about His concluding statement, *Do you believe this?* He is saying that if you are still alive and you believe in Him, then you will never die—never experience death. Is this a mistranslation? He said, right before this incredible statement, that those who believe in Him and die will be resurrected back to life and live again. No, it is not a misprint! Here are a couple other occasions when Jesus claimed the same thing:

AMP Jn 5:24-25 I assure you, most solemnly I tell you, the person whose ears are open to My words [who listens to My message] and believes and trusts in and clings to and relies on Him Who sent Me has (possesses now) eternal life. And he does not come into judgment [does not incur sentence of judgment, will not come under condemnation], but he has already passed over out of death into life. Believe Me when I assure you, most solemnly I tell you, the time is coming and is here now when the dead shall hear the voice of the Son of God and those who hear it shall live.

When Jesus makes the above statement, and refers to the dead that hear His voice, on this occasion He is not talking about those who have died and passed away. He is talking about those in the world who are spiritually dead, who have as their fate to die and become disembodied, assigned to Hades. Notice that He says, *those who hear it shall live,* and not those who hear it shall rise to life. Basically, He is saying to those who listen to Him, you who are alive (but are spiritually dead, doomed to suffer death of the body), if you listen to Him and believe, then you will not die. You will continue to live without dying. That is why He says, *the time is coming and is here now* you shall spiritually live.

And again, during another occasion Jesus spoke:

AMP Jn 8:51-53 <u>I assure you, most solemnly I tell you, if anyone observes My teaching [lives in accordance with My message, keeps My word], he will by no means ever see and experience death.</u> The Jews said to Him, Now we know that You are under the power of a demon (insane). Abraham died, and also the prophets, yet <u>You say, If a man keeps My word, he will never taste of death into all eternity</u>. Are You greater than our father Abraham? He died, and all the prophets died! Who do You make Yourself out to be?

Again, just as with Martha when Jesus asked her, *do you believe this?* It is understandable why these people in verses 52-53 would be so astonished! He says if we believe in Him, we will never, by no means, ever see and experience death. They decided He was insane and brought up that even father Abraham died as well as the prophets. Likewise, it is the same for us. Looking back, we see that all Christians have died, even the miracle working apostles are all dead, right? So how can Jesus emphatically say this to the people on multiple occasions?

To answer this question, we must go back to the part where we explained death as God sees it. He sees it as a living soul becoming disembodied—naked, unclothed with flesh. Here is a certainty: if we are to escape judgment and the death of our flesh, our soul (mind/personality) must sooner or later be reborn with a celestial body, and thereby no longer have as a body, our flesh. Then we will live forever as celestial humans. After seeing death as God does, as having to experience that disembodied state of being, let's now look at what He said with that in mind. If we hear His words it means to take them to heart and believe them, and to believe (used as a verb in this case) is to obey and conform our lives to them; as opposed to having a mere conception of knowing they are true with no action behind it.

What does that look like? For the living who heard and believe His words, when it comes time for them to exchange their body of flesh to that of a celestial body, they will do so without ever experiencing that state of being where one is disembodied! Those who are in union with Christ possessing His Spirit will never die in the sense of being bodiless. They will not even taste death, disembodiment, for even a fraction of a second! *he will by no means ever see and experience death.* Even before their head hits the ground in death, the soul of the man in union with Christ is already in *Heaven* in His celestial body before the throne of the Father and His Son able to fellowship with them face-to-face! This is an advantage never before available. Not until the sacrificial death of Jesus and *spiritual union* with Him was possible.

Jesus Promises the *Holy Spirit*

NIV Jn 14:15-21 *"If you love me, you will obey what I command. And I will ask the Father, and he will give you another Counselor to be with you forever—the Spirit of truth. The world cannot accept him, because it neither sees him nor knows him. But you know him, for he lives with you and will be in you. I will not leave you as orphans; I will come to you. Before long, the world will not see me anymore, but you will see me. <u>Because I live, you also will live. On that day you will realize that I am in my Father, and you are in me, and I am in you.</u> Whoever has my commands and obeys them, he is the one who loves me. He who loves me will be loved by my Father, and I too will love him and show myself to him."*

On that day, the day which He is referring to is the day the world will see Him no more. Although most do not recognize Him, right now the world sees Him through those who have His Spirit and do His will, living for Him. He just finished saying that He would not leave us as orphans, meaning in the world without Him—without His Spirit in us. However, Jesus says there is a day coming in which He will depart from the world, *the world will not see me anymore.* When His Spirit departs from this world, Jesus calls that day a time of darkness when no one can work. On that day is the beginning of the *great tribulation.* For 3½ years, *Heaven* will be silent, inactive, and Jesus will no longer be in the earth in any form—not with His Spirit presence, and not in the body of His Church. Prayers will go unanswered during that time period. The believers who are not in union with Him, not living according to His promptings, will suffer at the hands of the world with no help from above until He returns 3½ years later. These are those who were forced into a crossroad of having to choose to follow the returned *antichrist* or Him, thereby no longer being lukewarm but have become apostates.

On the other hand, those who are in union with Him, those who obey Him through His Spirit, Jesus says, on that day we will realize that He is in His Father, and we are in Him, and He is in us. That day is the day you find yourself suddenly before the throne of God in Heaven, clothed in a celestial body. That is how we will see Him, but the world will not see Him. That is because we will be where He is at, in *Heaven*, the place which He prepares for our coming. The world will not see Him because He will not be in the world. What a day that will be! Jesus is describing the day of the *rapture,* and the time of the 3½ years of the *global desolation* called *the great tribulation*. That is the 1,335th day after the midpoint of the last seven, from the day the daily sacrifice is abolished, as told to us in Daniel (12:12).

This same experience awaits every Christian in union with Christ the day of his or her death up until the day of the *rapture*. As for the people around you, they see you fall to the ground and understand you to have died. However, you are not even there when death to the body happens and as a result, experience the separation of your living soul from your body of flesh. You are already in your new celestial body in Heaven before God. Hades, the realm of the dead (disembodied souls) is no longer the destination for those who are in union with Christ and are one with His Spirit.

Now this is truly a wonder and a gift from God! No one has left this world alive. However, the Lord of the universe died and was disembodied and sent to Hades for three days. Voluntarily He died and experienced death, so we would not have to, even for a moment. It is only in this way that the saying comes true, "*Jesus* died for me." This is not a symbolic statement, but it is literal and as a result we do not have to experience death, but instead, a simultaneous change of bodies.

How does His experience of death equate to our not experiencing death? Simple. Hundreds of years before the prophets told us their message from God. That message was that He would give us a new Spirit, a Spirit which would cause us to obey Him (Eze 36:26-27).

NIV Jn 12:24-28 <u>*I tell you the truth, unless a kernel of wheat falls to the ground and dies, it remains only a single seed. But if it dies, it produces many seeds. The man who loves his life will lose it, while the man who hates his life in this world will keep it for eternal life.*</u> *Whoever serves me must follow me; and where I am, my servant also will be. My Father will honor the one who serves me. "Now my heart is troubled, and what shall I say? 'Father, save me from this hour'? No, it was for this very reason I came to this hour. Father, glorify your name!" Then a voice came from heaven, "I have glorified it, and will glorify it again."*

When Jesus died His Spirit, the Holy Spirit of God, became disembodied. The water and blood that fell from His body was spilled out upon the ground. Because His disembodied Spirit spilled out in the earth leaving Him dead—disembodied—any human who desires to embody His Spirit, literally becomes the body of Christ, His bride—one with the Christ—Him in them, and them in Him. How does one embody the Spirit of Jesus? Voluntarily, out of love, a desire to be one with Him as in a marriage covenant by obeying every prompting of His Spirit as sensed through one's conscience. Obedience to the promptings of His disembodied Spirit binds us to Him. He wills, His Spirit inspires, then we as a matter of decision out of love for Him act on that inspiration. We then move together bound to Jesus as one whole person: His will, His Spirit inspiration and motive compelling our body to act it out.

Jesus is dead to His physical body but physically alive in ours, we die to our human spirit and become alive in His. With His (natural) body dead to His Spirit, and us dead to our lives in the body, together (His Spirit and our body) we are one whole person in union with each other when it is His Spirit that compels our deeds. The more we are compelled and moved by His Spirit instead of our own, the greater in union as one whole person we are with Him. That means to love Him and desire to be in union with Him can only be done one way, that is, by obeying Him. To obey His Spirit prompting is the chord which binds us to Him as one whole person; His Spirit promptings carried out through our life in the body. Therefore, to love Him is to obey Him!

It is then, after our union with Him, that when we die to our flesh as He did, we become the species of humans as He is—celestial. Right now, He is in Heaven at the right hand of the Father in His celestial body. He is in the earth by His Spirit embodied in our physical bodies. He truly is the last Adam, through Him a new species of humans (celestial humans) comes into being, just as through the first Adam a species of humans (natural humans) came into being. It took physical union between Adam and Eve to give birth to the human race. In the same way, it takes spiritual union with the last Adam (Jesus the Christ) for one to be reborn as a celestial human. No other kind of union can cause one to become a celestial human—one with Him. This explains why it was true when Jesus said:

AMP Jn 3:3-6 Jesus answered him, I assure you, most solemnly I tell you, that unless a person is born again (anew, from above), he cannot ever see (know, be acquainted with, and experience) the kingdom of God. Nicodemus said to Him, How can a man be born when he is old? Can he enter his mother's womb again and be born? Jesus answered, I assure you, most solemnly I tell you, unless a man is born of water and [even] the Spirit, he cannot [ever] enter the kingdom of God. What is born of [from] the flesh is flesh [of the physical is physical]; and what is born of the Spirit is spirit.

No other s*piritual union* with any other being will cause us to become a celestial human in fellowship with God. It is only celestial humans who will survive the judgment and the destruction of the natural world.

That is why only those who believe in Jesus will be saved from the destruction of everything. It is only through the metamorphosis of being a natural human through the first Adam to becoming a celestial human through the last Adam, can one escape. God is not mean and cruel by making only one religious system the only way to Him. It is not a religious system that will save you. It, likewise, is not about climbing up the mountain where all paths lead to the top.

The religious system of God is Judaism. If there was only one religious system that should be followed, it would be His, Judaism. The Church leaders in the first-century, who were all Jewish, realized that it was God's will to not yoke believers in union with Christ to a religion, even Judaism. They are quoted as saying this:

AMP Ac 15:5-19 But some who believed [who acknowledged Jesus as their Savior and devoted themselves to Him] belonged to the sect of the Pharisees, and they rose up and said, It is necessary to circumcise [the Gentile converts] and to charge them to obey the Law of Moses. The apostles and the elders were assembled together to look into and consider this matter. And after there had been a long debate, Peter got up and said to them, Brethren, you know that quite a while ago God made a choice or selection from among you, that by my mouth the Gentiles should hear the message of the Gospel [concerning the attainment through Christ of salvation in the kingdom of God] and believe (credit and place their confidence in it). <u>And God, Who is acquainted with and understands the heart, bore witness to them, giving them the Holy Spirit as He also did to us; And He made no difference between us and them, but cleansed their hearts by faith (by a strong and welcome conviction that Jesus is the Messiah, through Whom we obtain eternal salvation in the kingdom of God). Now then, why do you try to test God by putting a yoke on the necks of the disciples, such as neither our forefathers nor we [ourselves] were able to endure? But we believe that we are saved through the grace (the undeserved favor and mercy) of the Lord Jesus, just as they [are].</u> Then the whole assembly remained silent, and they listened [attentively] as Barnabas and Paul *rehearsed what signs and wonders God had performed through them among the Gentiles. When they had finished talking, James replied, Brethren, listen to me. Simeon [Peter] has rehearsed how God first visited the Gentiles, to take out of them a people [to bear and honor] His name. And with this the predictions of the prophets agree, as it is written, After this I will come back, and will rebuild the house of David, which has fallen; I will rebuild its [very] ruins, and I will set it up again<u>, So that the rest of men may seek the Lord, and all the Gentiles upon whom My name has been invoked,</u> Says the Lord, Who has been making these things known from the beginning of the world. <u>Therefore it is my opinion that we should not put obstacles in the way of and annoy and disturb those of the Gentiles who turn to God</u>. . .*

As for those who think God to be cruel if only one religious system can earn your salvation, they are barking up the wrong tree altogether. God made a way, and that way is to become reborn as a different species of humans, not to follow His religious system. The reality is that as with all natural humans who come from the first human—Adam, all celestial humans come from the first celestial human—Jesus. In addition, we can tell by the above verses, God is not at all being exclusive, but is making this way available to all who would take Him into their hearts. Even the Christians of that time had minds so small that it was hard for them to see that. Indeed, there is only one way, but it is available to all who would receive Him.

Yes, the *Church Corrupt* has made yet another religion out of salvation through Christ, however, it is through an individual's personal relationship and union with Christ that saves him from destruction. Although Christianity is the finest of religions and the most charitable, even honoring the one true God; and we are likewise instructed to not forsake the gathering of the brethren, it is not the religious system of Christianity that, when all things are said and done, saves us. It is the oneness of our spiritual marital union with Him. Jesus sums it all up:

NIV Jn 14:4-6 *You know the way to the place where I am going."* (To His Father in Heaven, in the spiritual realm, clothed in a *celestial* body and no longer in a natural body) *Thomas said to him, "Lord, we don't know where you are going, so how can we know the way?" Jesus answered, "I am the way and the truth and the life. No one comes to the Father except through me.*

The next question:

What about all those people who never knew Jesus or heard of Him while they were alive? The answer is that the original way of salvation is still open to them. They will be raised on the last day after being a disembodied soul in the realm of the dead, once again being clothed in a body. And while in that resurrected body they will stand before the judgment seat of God and be judged according to their deeds while in the body, and according to their own conscience. This is so they too have a chance to become a celestial human and survive the destruction of everything natural. This is the fairness of God. Although He judges humanity as a whole, which brings the destruction of all, He then judges all humans individually based on their own merit.

Jesus Promises the Holy Spirit

NIV Jn 14:15-21 "*If you love me, you will obey what I command. And I will ask the Father, and he will give you another Counselor to be with you forever—the Spirit of truth. The world cannot accept him, because it neither sees him nor knows him. But you know him, for he lives with you and will be in you. I will not leave you as orphans; I will come to you. Before long, the world will not see me anymore, but you will see me. Because I live, you also will live. On that day you will realize that I am in my Father, and you are in me, and I am in you. Whoever has my commands and obeys them, he is the one who loves me. He who loves me will be loved by my Father, and I too will love him and show myself to him."*

If one embodies His Spirit, His Spirit within is able to cause him to be reborn with a celestial body just like Him, and in that way be with

Him where He is at, a spiritual creature in the spiritual realm. When the time comes, God makes this exchange from a body of flesh to a celestial body before the heart in our body of flesh has stopped beating. For the person in union with Christ (meaning to possess and embody His Spirit), it is harder and more painful to endure a common cold than it is to pass from life-to-life into a new body.

He suffered death, disembodiment, He broke open His earthen vessel and released His Spirit so we can unite with it and never experience death (disembodiment) even for a fraction of a second. That makes it actual and literal that Jesus died for us who accept Him in our hearts, so that we do not have to experience death—disembodiment. That was His sacrifice, His act of love to us, to the those who would open their hearts to His disembodied Spirit and bind themselves to Him through being one with Him out of obedience. Again: for it is obedience to His Spirit, which binds us to His Spirit as one whole person—His Spirit given expression through our body and life.

Those who will be saved through one of the resurrections must die, first becoming disembodied and then be raised to life by His Spirit. The Israelites whose DNA and ancestry Jesus was able to come in human form through were the *firstfruits* of His work. They hold a most special place in His heart. They too died and were disembodied and were in need of being rescued from *Hades* (*Abraham's bosom*) and from their disembodied state. Even though those *144,000* were the very first to receive a white robe, a celestial body, they had to experience death (disembodiment—a mind without a body). However, after His work on the cross, we who believe Him, and all who have bound themselves to Him through His Spirit, never have tasted death since then! They have never been a disembodied soul, nor assigned to *Hades*, the realm of the dead. However, those after the cross who do not know Him or do not believe and are not in union with His Spirit, will, like those before the cross, become disembodied and have need to wait until the last day before receiving a new body and rescued from *Hades*, even if they are in that paradisiacal place, *Abraham's bosom*.

As *Jesus* promised, *"I assure you, most solemnly I tell you, if anyone observes My teaching [lives in accordance with My message, keeps My word], <u>he will by no means ever see and experience death.</u>"* And again: *"I assure you, most solemnly I tell you, the person whose ears are open to My words [who listens to my message] and believes and trusts in and clings to and relies on Him Who sent Me has <u>(possesses now)</u> eternal life. And he does not come into judgment [does not incur sentence of judgment, will not come under condemnation], <u>but he has already passed over out of death into life.</u>"*

At the last supper Jesus promised that we will be with Him forever and that He would never leave us or forsake us. Because of this promise those who are in union with Christ before they die must gain their spiritual body before their head hits the ground in death. Otherwise, His word would not be kept. We would not be where He is in Heaven at His Father's right side, we would be in the paradisiacal place in Hades, disembodied, even if it were just for a time. This gift and way of salvation is truly the best way to escape the doom and destruction in store for humanity and this world!

However, at closer inspection if all this is true, then one thing does not make sense at face value: what about those who die in the *great tribulation*? Why will they be in need of the *first resurrection* if what Jesus is saying is true and we as Christians do not taste death? If we get our celestial body even before our heart of flesh stops beating and our head hits the ground, why then will they who endure the *great tribulation* become disembodied souls who will require to be raised from among the dead, the disembodied? And why is this resurrection exclusively for them alone? Although we have covered this, this most important question bears repeating. Let's look closer at the scriptures which explain this seeming contradiction:

NIV Jn 9:4-5 As long as it is day, we must do the work of him who sent me. <u>Night is coming, when no one can work. While I am in the world, I am the light of the world.</u>"

"Night is coming," Jesus is talking about a time of spiritual darkness when the earth is left to its own devices without any restraint, interference, or intervention from Heaven above. *"While I am in the world"* Although Jesus died and rose and is seated in His celestial body at the right hand of His Father in Heaven, His Spirit, the Holy Spirit, remains here in the earth embodied by the saints. That being the case, Jesus is still in the world. We have to think differently than we do as superficial humans if we want to understand Jesus. He is a spirit being. He does not look to the body as the real man or person, but to the invisible immortal part of a person.

On the other hand, we know His physical body died and is not among us, so we tend to perceive Him as not here with us, but in Heaven seated next to the Father. Although it is true, Jesus is also here, present in the earth and that's how He understands Himself to be, present in the world—His Spirit, present and active in and among the saints who He is one with in *spiritual union*, intervening, and answering their prayers. They embody His Spirit and follow His promptings.

In the beginning, the person Jesus was the embodiment of the Spirit of God in the earth. However, and since the death of Jesus, the body of His Spirit are the saints. Jesus is literally here in the earth both in body and in Spirit! Jesus is the only being who has both a spiritual body in the spiritual realm, and through a marital *spiritual union* He has a body of flesh in the natural realm. He sits at the right hand of His Father clothed with His celestial body, and His Spirit is also in the earth clothed with the physical bodies of those in union with Him, those who would obey Him out of love, His bride, His Church. This is exactly why it is true for Jesus to call himself both the Son of God and the Son of Man.

AMP Eph 1:22-2:1 And He has put all things under His feet and has appointed Him the universal and supreme Head of the church [a headship exercised throughout the church], Which is His body, the fullness of Him Who fills all in all [for in that body lives the full measure of Him Who makes everything complete, and Who fills everything everywhere with Himself]. AND YOU [He made alive], when you were dead (slain) by [your] trespasses and sins

He is present, active, and powerful. His intervention restrains, to a certain degree, lawlessness and the lawless one. As long as He remains in the earth in the body of His believers, He is "the light of the world." However, He states spiritual darkness is coming. He is the light of the world and while He is here in the world, the world has light. Continuing with the logic of what He was saying, He is warning us that a time is coming when He will not be in the world. If He continued to be in the world then there would not be a time of darkness, for He is the world's light. However, He said, *Night is coming, when no one can work*. That means during that time of darkness, neither His Spirit nor His body (His bride, those in union with Him) will be in the world for a time.

NIV Rev 12:5 *She gave birth to a son, a male child, who will rule all the nations with an iron scepter. And her child was snatched up to God and to his throne.*

If Jesus, even after His death, has remained in the earth both with His Spirit and in His body (the Church), and if the contingency of the Church who embodied His Spirit results in them being the body of Christ, then when it says *and her child was snatched up to God*, it means those who are His body, giving expression to His Spirit, are the child who was snatched up. This is verified by the following verse:

NIV Mt 10:40-42 *"He who receives you receives me, and he who receives me receives the one who sent me. Anyone who receives a prophet because he is a prophet will receive a prophet's reward, and anyone who receives a righteous man because he is a righteous man will receive a righteous man's reward. And if anyone gives even a cup of cold water to one of these little ones because he is my disciple, I tell you the truth, he will certainly not lose his reward."*

NIV Mt 25:34-40 *"Then the King will say to those on his right* (on the last day), *'Come, you who are blessed by my Father; take your*

inheritance, the kingdom prepared for you since the creation of the world. For I was hungry and you gave me something to eat, I was thirsty and you gave me something to drink, I was a stranger and you invited me in, I needed clothes and you clothed me, I was sick and you looked after me, I was in prison and you came to visit me.'
"Then the righteous will answer him, 'Lord, when did we see you hungry and feed you, or thirsty and give you something to drink? When did we see you a stranger and invite you in, or needing clothes and clothe you? When did we see you sick or in prison and go to visit you?' "The King will reply, 'I tell you the truth, whatever you did for one of the least of these brothers of mine, you did for me.'

Revelation 12:5 (above) also verifies to us there is indeed a *pretribulation rapture*! When it will happen it will cause the time of darkness Jesus warned about. A time when He will not be in the world, neither in Spirit nor in body (His Church).

NIV Rev 8:1 *When he opened the seventh seal, <u>there was silence in heaven for about half an hour.</u> And I saw the seven angels who stand before God, and to them were given seven trumpets.*

"*There was silence in heaven,*" means inactivity. Heaven is still, silent, they will be inactive and will not interfere with the evil which goes on in the earth during this time of darkness. Half an hour is a half of a cycle of time. However, the cycle of time in question is a cycle of a week of years, meaning seven years. Half an hour is representative of 3½ years (42 months or *1,260* days as referring to the same time period in other parts of the Bible).

NIV Rev 13:5-10 *<u>The beast was given a mouth to utter proud words and blasphemies and to exercise his authority for forty-two months.</u> He opened his mouth to blaspheme God, and to slander his name and his dwelling place and those who live in heaven. <u>He was given power to make war against the saints and to conquer them. And he was given authority over every tribe, people, language and nation.</u> All inhabitants of the earth will worship the beast—all whose names have not been written in the book of life belonging to the Lamb that was slain from the creation of the world. He who has an ear, let him* *hear. <u>If anyone is to go into captivity, into captivity he will go. If anyone is to be killed with the sword, with the sword he will be killed. This calls for patient endurance and faithfulness on the part of the saints</u>*

There is a time coming which will last 3½ years in which the *antichrist* will be given complete authority over the earth without the restraint and intervention of God. Rev 13:10 (above) is telling us that during that time whatever is going to happen, will happen. It is a time of spiritual darkness; no prayers will be answered at this time. No intervention will take place. The Spirit of God will not at that time be among the elect who remain, nor will He be in them. They will be left alone, meaning; those elect who were found to be apostates and not in *spiritual union* with Christ at the time of the *rapture*, and therefore not His body in the world. Not only will they be totally subject to the *antichrist*, but they will endure this time without the Holy Spirit in their hearts. They will be on their own, and whatever happens, will happen, no intervention by *Heaven*, no exceptions. This is what the parable of the talents is speaking of:

NIV Mt 25:14-30 "Again, it will be like a man going on a journey, who called his servants and entrusted his property to them. To one he gave five talents (about 360 pounds of weight, as in pounds of gold, for example) *of money, to another two talents, and to another one talent* (between 66 and 77 pounds), *each according to his ability. Then he went on his journey. The man who had received the five talents went at once and put his money to work and gained five more. So also, the one with the two talents gained two more. But the man who had received the one talent went off, dug a hole in the ground and hid his master's money. "After a long time the master of those servants returned and settled accounts with them. The man who had received the five talents brought the other five. 'Master,' he said, 'you entrusted me with five talents. See, I have gained five more.' "His master replied, 'Well done, good and faithful servant! You have been faithful with a few things; I will put you in charge of many things. Come and share your master's happiness!' "The man with the two talents also came. 'Master,' he said, 'you entrusted me with two talents; see, I have gained two more.' "His master replied, 'Well done, good and faithful servant! You have been faithful with a few things; I will put you in charge of many things. Come and share your master's happiness!'* "<u>Then the man who had received the one talent came. 'Master,' he said, 'I knew that you are a hard man, harvesting where you have not sown and gathering where you have not scattered seed. So I was afraid and went out and hid your talent in the ground. See, here is what belongs to you.'</u> "*His master replied, 'You wicked, lazy servant! So you knew that I harvest where I have not sown and gather where I have not scattered seed? Well then, you should have put my money on deposit with the bankers, so that when I returned I would have received it back with interest.* "<u>Take the talent from him and give it to the one who has the ten talents. For everyone who has will be given more, and he will have an abundance. Whoever does not have, even what he has will be taken from him. And throw that worthless servant outside, into the darkness, where there will be weeping and gnashing of teeth.'</u>

Being thrown outside into the darkness, is reference to having to endure the *great tribulation*. The talents are a measure of the Holy Spirit. Whoever does not have, even what he has will be taken from him, is fulfillment of when Jesus said, you are lukewarm, and I will spew you out of my mouth. The withdrawal of the Holy Spirit from the earth leaving behind those elect who did not utilize the Holy Spirit in them and in fact, were proven to be apostates. The Holy Spirit is taken away from them by their own decision. As the Lord predicted, He will spew these apostates out of His mouth. However, for those who bore fruit it says of them, *come and share your masters happiness*, and they who receive a greater measure of His Spirit are those who are *raptured* or "caught up" to *Heaven* just as the *great tribulation* begins—which is the time of darkness. Listen to the contrast: to those who produce fruit He says *come*, and to those who do not, He says throw them *into the darkness*, into the time of darkness, the *great tribulation*. In addition, the undeveloped Spirit within them is taken from them because He departs this world. Thus,

He spews them out of His mouth and they are no longer in Him or Him in them—amounting to a spiritual divorce due to spiritual adultery, unfaithfulness. Because they were neither hot nor cold, and He wished that they were, the Lord had created these circumstances to come as a crossroads, to force His elect to show themselves as one or the other—faithful or an apostate, an adulterer.

The *Left Behind* series depicts during this time that the saints will rally together to fight the powers of the *antichrist*, and depicts that their prayers will be answered, angels will intervene on their behalf, and the presence of God will be with them. This notion, as romantic as it may be, is total fiction and runs counter to what scripture tells us.

NIV Rev 13:9-10 He who has an ear, let him hear. If anyone is to go into captivity, into captivity he will go. If anyone is to be killed with the sword, with the sword he will be killed. This calls for patient endurance and faithfulness on the part of the saints.

This will be a terrible time! It will be as they say, if it were not for bad luck, I would have no luck at all. Or everything that could go wrong will go wrong. What will happen, will happen, and calls for patient endurance on the part of the saints.

NIV Mt 24:15 "So when you see standing in the holy place 'the abomination that causes desolation,' spoken of through the prophet Daniel—let the reader understand—

Jesus not only calls the *antichrist*, "the abomination," but the "abomination that causes desolation." This way of reflecting on the *antichrist* is generally overlooked. With his appearance in the temple, it causes a desolation. One only needs to know what is meant by a desolation to understand how it is true, the things said above. A desolation is when God turns His face away from us, His Spirit is withdrawn, and He gives His people over to the evils of their sin. It says there were many desolations decreed by God which His people suffered, and His presence was gone from the temple during those time periods. However, this desolation (spoken about above) will be a global desolation—worldwide, there is no place to hide from it. Ezekiel prophesied about this time that will come:

NIV Eze 7:2-27 *"Son of man, this is what the Sovereign LORD says to the land of Israel: The end! The end has come upon the four corners of the land. The end is now upon you and I will unleash my anger against you. I will judge you according to your conduct and repay you for all your detestable practices. <u>I will not look on you with pity or spare you;</u> I will surely repay you for your conduct and the detestable practices among you. Then you will know that I am the LORD. "This is what the Sovereign LORD says: Disaster! <u>An unheard-of disaster is coming. The end has come! The end has come! It has roused itself against you. It has come!</u> Doom has come upon you—you who dwell in the land. The time has come, the day is near; there is panic, not joy, upon the mountains. I am about to pour out my wrath on you and spend my anger against you; I will judge you according to your conduct and repay you for all your detestable practices. <u>I will not look on you with pity or spare you;</u> I will repay you in accordance with your conduct and the detestable practices among you. Then you will know that it is I the LORD who strikes the blow. "The day is here! It has come! Doom has burst forth, the rod has budded, arrogance has blossomed! Violence has grown into a rod to punish wickedness; none of the people will be left, none of that crowd—no wealth, nothing of value. The time has come, the day has arrived. Let not the buyer rejoice nor the seller grieve, for wrath is upon the whole crowd. The seller will not recover the land he has sold as long as both of them live, <u>for the vision concerning the whole crowd will not be reversed. Because of their sins, not one of them will preserve his life.</u> Though they blow the trumpet and get everything ready, no one will go into battle, for my wrath is upon the whole crowd. "Outside is the sword, inside are plague and famine; those in the country will die by the sword, and those in the city will be devoured by famine and plague. All who survive and escape will be in the mountains, moaning like doves of the valleys, each because of his sins. <u>Every hand will go limp, and every knee will become as weak as water. They will put on sackcloth and be clothed with terror.</u>*

Their faces will be covered with shame and their heads will be shaved. They will throw their silver into the streets, and their gold will be an unclean thing. Their silver and gold will not be able to save them in the day of the LORD'S wrath. They will not satisfy their hunger or fill their stomachs with it, for it has made them stumble into sin. They were proud of their beautiful jewelry and used it to make their detestable idols and vile images. Therefore I will turn these into an unclean thing for them. I will hand it all over as plunder to foreigners and as loot to the wicked of the earth, and they will defile it. I will turn my face away from them, and they will desecrate my treasured place; robbers will enter it and desecrate it. "Prepare chains, because the land is full of bloodshed and the city is full of violence. I will bring the most wicked of the nations to take possession of their houses; I will put an end to the pride of the mighty, and their sanctuaries will be desecrated. When terror comes, they will seek peace, but there will be none. Calamity upon calamity will come, and rumor upon rumor. They will try to get a vision from the prophet; the teaching of the law by the priest will be lost, as will the counsel of the elders. The king will mourn, the prince will be clothed with despair, and the hands of the people of the land will tremble. I will deal with them according to their conduct, and by their own standards I will judge them. Then they will know that I am the LORD."

When the time of darkness comes and the Holy Spirit withdraws, those Christians who have the Holy Spirit and live by Him, will be *raptured* to Heaven before the throne of God receiving their new celestial bodies. However, those Christians who bear no fruit of the Spirit and become apostates will be left behind to endure the *great tribulation*. When the Holy Spirit goes up to *Heaven* abandoning the earth to the *antichrist*, those who possess Him, securely will be brought up as He goes up. Those who do not will lose what little Holy Spirit they have within them when He goes up without them— left in the time of darkness.

All this being the case, when believers die during the time of the absence of the Holy Spirit (during the 3 ½ years of the *great tribulation*), they will not receive a celestial body without experiencing disembodiment first. They will, like all other people who died before Jesus and without His Spirit, become disembodied souls held over in *Hades*. However, with one exception! During the *great tribulation,* those who hold fast to their testimony, do not worship the beast, or take his mark during this terrible time for Christians will raise from the dead, and as their brothers were before the *great tribulation,* be *raptured* in the *first resurrection* which is meant for them alone. Then, afterwards be lifted up into the sky to meet Jesus. This will happen after the 7-year time period of darkness is over. That is, 3 ½ years of God's wrath on the apostate believers followed by 3 ½ years of God's wrath on the world who hated and killed them. This accounts for all the Christians who would be in union with Christ, no accounts unsettled, the time of the *Church Age* finished and complete, down to the last believer. The rest of the believers who failed to be faithful in their union with Christ will be grouped with the rest of humanity and judged on the last day according to their deeds. However, their chances are good at becoming declared sheep and therefore saved at that time because surely they have met the minimum requirements of receiving that gift for giving even a glass of cold water to God's elect, knowing they were God's elect.

Those believers killed for their testimony during the first 3 ½ years will go to the paradisiacal place in *Hades* awaiting their resurrection after the 7 years. We are told that it will be days before the 7th trumpet is sounded that those believers who hang on to their testimony, who live through the first 3 ½ years will then receive a mark of God on their foreheads. Then, during the final 3 ½ years, when *Heaven* is again active in the earth, pouring out wrath on the world, these survivors cannot be killed or harmed. They are home free in that sense but must wait until the 7 years are finished.

As a quick note, although they will be protected from harm, the world will not be a nice place to reside in until the return of Jesus. It will be as the Israelites in Egypt who were protected while the Egyptians were being pummeled with wrath, neither was that time fun for the Israelites to endure. Although they were protected and exempt from what was happening to the Egyptians, it nevertheless was still a time of great peril, terror, and uncertainty for the Israelites. However, in retrospect their exemption was a cause for great celebration!

When that time period is over and the seventh and final trumpet is about to sound, first those who were killed during the first half will rise from the dead, and together with the survivors be raised up to the sky to meet Jesus, His Father, His angels, those believers who already have their celestial bodies, and the New Jerusalem. Then, together as the Lord's entourage will descend to the earth with Jesus touching down first on the Mount of Olives. His touch down will split the Mount in two, creating a huge valley that allows the worldly people to escape like cockroaches when the lights go on. His host and the New Jerusalem that is following right behind Jesus will occupy that land.

Those who are *raptured* without tasting death before the *great tribulation* and those who are *raptured* at the *first resurrection* of the dead will reign as the bride of Christ over the physical humans of the earth for 1,000 years. This is when Jesus comes down from the sky with His host of angels and celestial humans.

Revelation describes these two different ways of being harvested as His bride during the *end times*:

The first is in a *rapture* **before** the *great tribulation* (harvest of wheat)

Secondly is through the *first resurrection*, then *raptured* along with those who survived the *great tribulation* and the wrath poured out on the world (harvest of grapes).

NIV Rev 12:3-5 Then another sign appeared in heaven: an enormous red dragon with seven heads and ten horns and seven crowns on his heads. His tail swept a third of the stars out of the sky and flung them to the earth. The dragon stood in front of the woman who was about to give birth, so that he might devour her child the moment it was born. She gave birth to a son, a male child, who will rule all the nations with an iron scepter. And her child was snatched up to God and to his throne.

These verses (above) are speaking of the harvest by the *first rapture* taking place before the *great tribulation*—the wheat, when it said, *her child was snatched up to God and to his throne.* Also, those harvested through the *great tribulation*—the grapes, when it said, *an enormous red dragon with seven heads and ten horns and seven crowns on his heads. His tail swept a third of the stars out of the sky and flung them to the earth,* it is talking about those killed during the great tribulation.

AMP Rev 14:14-20 *Again I looked, and behold, [I saw] a white cloud, and sitting on the cloud One resembling a Son of Man, with a crown of gold on His head and a sharp scythe (sickle) in His hand. And another angel came out of the temple sanctuary, <u>calling with a mighty voice to Him Who was sitting upon the cloud, Put in Your scythe and reap, for the hour has arrived to gather the harvest, for the earth's crop is fully ripened. So He Who was sitting upon the cloud swung His scythe (sickle) on the earth, and the earth's crop (of wheat) was harvested.</u> Then another angel came out of the temple [sanctuary] in heaven, and he also carried a sharp scythe (sickle). And another angel came forth from the altar, [the angel] who has authority and power over fire, and he called with a loud cry to him who had the sharp scythe (sickle), <u>Put forth your scythe and reap the fruitage of the vine of the earth, for its grapes are entirely ripe. So the angel swung his scythe on the earth and stripped the grapes and gathered the vintage from the vines of the earth and cast it into the huge winepress of God's indignation and wrath. And [the grapes in] the winepress were trodden outside the city, and blood poured from the winepress, [reaching] as high as horses' bridles, for a distance of 1,600 stadia (about 200 miles).</u>*

The first *harvest of wheat* (inferred) made by Jesus (one *like a son of man with a crown of gold on his head)* is the *rapture* before the *great tribulation*. They are the first harvest and the product of the first swing of the scythe Jesus Himself harvests and gathers. The second harvest is of grapes which an angel reaps with his scythe. The grapes are the believers who suffer the *great tribulation* whose blood flowed like a river for 200 miles and is as deep as it is from the ground to a horse's bridle. That is an unprecedented amount of blood and death. The first verses above in Revelation Chapter 12 tells us it is 1/3 of the Christian population that are slain in the *great tribulation*.

Currently the Christian population is upwards of 3 billion. That is one billion Christians who are factory killed in just 3 ½ years. In fact, Jesus said if He did not bring an end to it there would be no one left alive. This group is resurrected and then *raptured* to meet Jesus in the sky just as the *two witnesses* had been killed and after 3 ½ days rose from the dead and were *raptured*. Likewise, after those who die in the *great tribulation* rise from the dead, along with those who held to their testimony but survived the *great tribulation* without being killed, will together, rise up to the sky to meet Jesus.

NIV Rev 7:9-17 After this I looked and there before me was a great multitude that no one could count, from every nation, tribe, people and language, standing before the throne and in front of the Lamb. They were wearing white robes and were holding palm branches in their hands. And they cried out in a loud voice: "Salvation belongs to our God, who sits on the throne, and to the Lamb." All the angels were standing around the throne and around the elders and the four living creatures. They fell down on their faces before the throne and worshiped God, saying: "Amen! Praise and glory and wisdom and thanks and honor and power and strength be to our God for ever and ever. Amen!" Then one of the elders asked me, "These in white robes—who are they, and where did they come from? I answered, "Sir, you know." And he said, "These are they who have come out of the great tribulation; they have washed their robes and made them white in the blood of the Lamb. Therefore, "they are before the throne of God and serve him day and night in his temple; and he who sits on the throne will spread his tent over them. Never again will they hunger; never again will they thirst. The sun will not beat upon them, nor any scorching heat. For the Lamb at the center of the throne will be their shepherd; he will lead them to springs of living water. And God will wipe away every tear from their eyes."

Note: A resurrection and a *rapture* (being caught up or snatched up) are two different events. A resurrection is when people are raised back to life. A *rapture* is when people are supernaturally brought up to *Heaven* and metamorphosized into a *celestial* human. They don't always follow each other. These two different phenomena generally are recorded to happen at different times, not as one event. For example, when the *144,000* patriarchs were resurrected and came out of their tombs, they went into Jerusalem and talked to the people (Mt 27:52-53). It was not until several days later that they were snatched up to *Heaven*, following Jesus to be presented to the Father as the *firstfruits* of His redeeming work. Once the *first resurrection* happens, after some undetermined time, a *rapture* happens with both those Christians alive and those who were risen back to life. They do not necessarily happen simultaneously. There are other occasions in the Bible that reflect that there is a time period between being resurrected and then being *raptured* or caught up. This interval between the two is meant to rattle the world when those they killed and thought they were through with, do not stay dead but rise back up. It will be a nightmare for them that will inspire terror in their hearts. Paul speaks of this event below.

We who are still alive, who are left till the coming of the Lord, will certainly not precede those who have fallen asleep When it says, *who are left till the coming of the Lord,* it is referring to those who are left behind and were not snatched up at the beginning of the *great tribulation*. Paul goes on to tell us that out of those who are left behind, the ones who die in the *great tribulation* will be resurrected first. Then, together with those who endured the *great tribulation* and survived, will rise to the sky to meet Jesus. If that does not inspire enough terror in the hearts of the people, one can only image what they will feel when the sky tears open and they all come back to the earth, including the Lord. The comfort here is that all the Christians will meet Jesus in the sky, descend to the earth and rule with Him. Jesus, the first born (of many brothers) to be resurrected becoming a celestial human, and the last believer born again and resurrected will as He, return to rule the earth for a thousand years. That is the end of the physical Christian humans (the Church). They all are accounted for, and for them, it is all said and done!

To summarize the fate of Christianity, it ends in these manners and the saints will reign over the earth with the Lord as celestial humans:

1) Those who did not taste death but gained their celestial bodies during the *Church Age*

2) The *Church Pure* is *raptured* before the *great tribulation* begins

3) The *Church Corrupt*, are Christians who became apostates by rejecting the Lord and His *two witnesses*. They are left to suffer the *great tribulation*. Given that they repent for doing so, they then hang on to their testimony in the face of suffering during the *great tribulation*. They are *raptured* in the days before the seventh trumpet sounds, which is after the *great tribulation* and wrath of God is poured out upon the world.

4) Those apostates who repented for rejecting the Lord and who die while hanging on to their testimonies during the *great tribulation*, will resurrect from the dead so they may join the survivors and likewise be *raptured* up together with them!

This is the fate of the Church as told to us in the Bible. Together, these groups will be the *great multitude*, His bride, and *celestial* humans who will rule the natural humans when Jesus comes into His Kingdom.

In review, here are the different circumstances by which one can become a celestial human, and avoid the second death:

1) Judged by your deeds and motives on the last day. If your motives and ultimately your deeds while in the body are acceptable to God, He will then grant you the gift of receiving a celestial body. This is the lowest standard of all. To so much as give a glass of cold water to one of the God's elect because he is God's elect, will give you favor enough from God to ultimately be saved from the second death (any friend of my children is a friend of Mine …as it is said).

2) Through relationship with Jesus. Those who are in union, or spiritual marriage with Jesus (possessing His Spirit and yielding to Him in obedience), will never taste death and will not be judged. On the contrary, they will be given thrones and assist Jesus in judging all of humanity on the last day. They will receive a celestial body even before the heart of their body of flesh stops beating. Not only will they not endure the second death, but neither will they (because of the sacrifice of Christ) endure the first death.

3) Being counted as God's elect—the followers of Christ. They are those Christians who are not in union with Christ, who are not His body by virtue of the fact that they lived their own lives according to their own desires. That is, those who lived and died before the *great tribulation*. They did not die to their life in the body or lived to be the expression and embodiment of the Holy Spirit within them. They are those who lost their first love! They, just as the Israelites, will endure the first death. They will wait until the last day and at that time before the judgment seat be declared the sheep of God, given their deeds qualify. It is then they will receive a celestial body and be citizens in the new heavens and the new earth in the spiritual realm for all of eternity. They will avoid the second death. However, unlike their brothers who did die to their lives in the body by obeying the promptings of the Spirit within, they will not have that "bride status," nor will they be the government of Christ for eternity in the new heavens and the new earth. They will have the gift of eternally being citizens of that reign.

4) Through profession of faith in Jesus. Those who hang onto their profession of faith during the *great tribulation*, even on to death and do not worship the beast or take his mark, will be given a celestial body. They will die and their disembodied souls will go to the paradisiacal place in *Hades*. Then, at the end of the *great tribulation* the *Holy Spirit* will become active in the world again. He will then raise this group from the dead in the *first resurrection*. After that, and together with those who lived but also hung on to their profession of faith, will gain their celestial bodies and be caught up to meet Jesus in the sky.

5) Through legalism. Those people who keep the laws of God will also receive a celestial body. However, as it was said;

NIV Mt 19:28-30 Jesus said to them, "I tell you the truth, at the renewal of all things, when the Son of Man sits on his glorious throne, you who have followed me will also sit on twelve thrones, judging the twelve tribes of Israel. And everyone who has left houses or brothers or sisters or father or mother or children or fields for my sake will receive a hundred times as much and will inherit eternal life. <u>But many who are first will be last, and many who are last will be first.</u>

God's people, the Israelites, were meant to be the bride of Christ in union with Him and the first to receive celestial bodies, ruling the earth with Him from the New Jerusalem for 1,000 years. However, they rejected Christ, causing Him to find a bride from among the Gentiles. Those who were first, who were meant to be celestial beings but did not believe in Christ, lost their place. The Israelites were the first to be called into salvation, however, during the *Church Age* the Israelites were in a state of pause.

The Church arose and was brought to completion, it is only then, during the 1,000-year reign, will the salvation of the Israelites become fulfilled and complete, making them the first that were last. And the believers the last who became first. The Israelites instead will suffer the first death; rise being judged on the last day with the promise that they might be found fit to become a celestial human avoiding the second death. However, they will have missed out on reigning with Christ as celestial humans for 1,000 years. They will be natural humans during that time period. Likewise, those Christians who were not in union with Christ, living by the promptings of His Spirit, will also have lost their place as His bride; just as the Israelites had. They too, like the Israelites, will have to endure the *great tribulation*, and wait until the last day after the *1,000-year reign* of Christ. Then, at that time, they will be declared sheep and gain a celestial body. The difference between the Israelites and the believers during the *great tribulation* and wrath against the world, is that the Israelites will be hidden away in the desert so that their population will be preserved as physical humans to participate in the *1,000-year reign of Christ* on the earth. For the *1,000-year reign of Christ* as their Messiah is a promise the Lord made to their forefathers that must be fulfilled.

NIV Mt 22:1-14 Jesus spoke to them again in parables, saying: "The kingdom of heaven is like a king who prepared a wedding banquet for his son. He sent his servants to those who had been invited to the banquet to tell them to come, but they refused to come. "Then he sent some more servants and said, 'Tell those who have been invited that I have prepared my dinner: My oxen and fattened cattle have been butchered, and everything is ready. Come to the wedding banquet.' "But they paid no attention and went off—one to his field, another to his business. The rest seized his servants, mistreated them and killed them. The king was enraged. He sent his army and destroyed those murderers and burned their city (the destruction of Jerusalem in 70 AD). *"Then he said to his servants, 'The wedding banquet is ready, but those I invited did not deserve to come. Go to the street corners and invite to the banquet anyone you find.' So the servants went out into the streets and gathered all the people they could find, both good and bad, and the wedding hall was filled with guests* (the Christians). *"But when the king came in to see the guests, he noticed a man there who was not wearing wedding clothes. 'Friend,' he asked, 'how did you get in here without wedding clothes* (those Christians who were not given celestial bodies nor were they raptured, because they did not die to their lives in the body nor did they give expression to the Spirit of Christ in them)?' *The man was speechless. "Then the king told the attendants, 'Tie him hand and foot, and throw him outside, into the darkness, where there will be weeping and gnashing of teeth* (they are doomed to endure the great tribulation).' *"For many are invited, but few are chosen."*

Both, the non-believing Israelites and Christ followers who have no wedding clothes (a celestial body) if judged as a sheep on the last day will receive the gift to be citizens in the new heavens and the new earth. But both of these groups as well as those who gain their citizenship because of their kindness to God's people will: Miss out on reigning with Christ for 1,000 years on the earth. They will have to die the first death, held over disembodied in Hades, raise back to life, face judgment, and the prospects of dying a second death. They will be citizens in the new heavens and the new earth, missing out on their opportunity to have been the bride of Christ. Who, after ruling the earth with Christ for 1,000 years, will go on to be the government over those celestial humans that will live in the new heavens and the new earth.

6) The *first fruits*, the *144,000*, 12,000 from every tribe of Israel. They have already been given new white robes—celestial bodies— and set free from disembodiment the day that Jesus died and broke open the prison doors—the gates of *Hades*—setting them free from their confinement. However, they were told that they must wait for the full numbers of those who will be martyred before receiving justice against those who killed them. The fullness of their numbers will come as a result of the *great tribulation*. Then after the *great tribulation*, the wrath of God will be poured out on the earth fulfilling that justice. Then the *144,000* will return with Jesus to co-rule the world who killed them. However, they will now be the government and judges over mortal men for 1,000 years and beyond. This is all fulfillment in answer to their prayers for justice.

Revelation, a message for the Church

The book of Revelation, once understood properly, ties all the other books of the Bible together in a way which does not contribute to seeming contradictions, but in fact clears them all up. We dare say that it is impossible to truly understand the Bible and know how to put all its pieces together without Revelation. It is the capstone! In addition, it is imperative to understand the above elementary concepts in order to understand the book of Revelation. This first volume will go on to give very important tools which will help give both context and interpretation to Revelation. The book of Revelation is written to the Church. A common misconception is, some believe that the book of Revelation is written for and about the:

- The decided (those who are professed Christians)
- The undecided (those who have not yet made a decision for or against Christ)
- The decided against (those who have decided against Christ)
They mistakenly see the *end times*, which Revelation speaks about, as a time to make a decision, a last chance for the undecided. This is not the case; it is a myth. The truth is the book of Revelation is written to and for the Church:

- The *Church Pure*
- The *Church Corrupt*
Jesus said:

NIV Jn 9:4 As long as it is day, we must do the work of him who sent me. <u>Night is coming, when no one can work.</u>

It is important to take note that the end will not be a time of evangelizing or convincing. It is as Jesus says, a time when no one can work. It will instead be a time of testing to show the true hearts of people:

AMP Da 11:33-35 And they who are wise and understanding among the people shall instruct many and make them understand, though some [of them and their followers] shall fall by the sword and flame, by captivity and plunder, for many days. Now when they fall, they shall receive a little help. Many shall join themselves to them with flatteries and hypocrisies. And some of those who are wise, prudent, and understanding shall be weakened and fall, [thus, then, the insincere among the people will lose courage and become deserters. <u>*It will be a test] to refine, to purify, and to make those among [God's people] white, even to the time of the end, because it is yet for the time [God] appointed.*</u>

Are you a God hater and consequently a hater of God's people like Cain? Or are you a lover of self? These times will experientially show the true depths of one's convictions. It will be a time when the elect, who are not in *spiritual union* with Christ, will remain in the world when the darkness comes. That darkness is a spiritual darkness and eventually becomes a physical darkness which engulfs the earth. It is a time when the Spirit withdraws from the earth bringing with Him those who are in *spiritual union* as well as the *two witnesses*. The Bible calls these times of darkness a "desolation." A desolation is an absence of the presence and intervention of God. Here in the verses below the Lord describes desolation:

NIV 2Ch 7:11-22 When Solomon had finished the temple of the LORD and the royal palace, and had succeeded in carrying out all he had in mind to do in the temple of the LORD and in his own palace, the LORD appeared to him at night and said: "I have heard your prayer and have chosen this place for myself as a temple for sacrifices. <u>*"When I shut up the heavens so that there is no rain, or command locusts to devour the land or send a plague among my people, if my people, who are called by my name, will humble themselves and pray and seek my face and turn from their wicked ways, then will I hear from heaven and will forgive their sin and will heal their land. Now my eyes will be open and my ears attentive to the prayers offered in this place.*</u> *I have chosen and consecrated this temple so that my Name may be there forever. My eyes and my heart will always be there. "As for you, if you walk before me as David your father did, and do all I command, and observe my decrees and laws, I will establish your royal throne, as I covenanted with David your father when I said, 'You shall never fail to have a man to rule over Israel.'* "But if you turn away and forsake the decrees and commands I have given you and go off to serve other gods and worship them, then I will uproot Israel from my land, which I have given them, and will reject this temple I have consecrated for my Name. I will make it a byword and an object of ridicule among all peoples. And though this temple is now so imposing, all who pass by will be appalled and say, 'Why has the LORD done such a thing to this land and to this temple?' *People will answer, 'Because they have forsaken the LORD, the God of their fathers, who brought them out of Egypt, and have embraced other gods, worshiping and serving them—that is why he brought all this disaster on them.' "*

NIV Dt 31:15-21 *Then the LORD appeared at the Tent in a pillar of cloud, and the cloud stood over the entrance to the Tent. And the LORD said to Moses: "You are going to rest with your fathers* (he will die becoming disembodied and go to the paradisiacal place in *Hades* and await the time when he can receive his celestial body), *and these people will soon prostitute themselves to the foreign gods of the land they are entering. They will forsake me and break the covenant I made with them.* On that day I will become angry with them and forsake them; I will hide my face from them, and they will be destroyed. Many disasters and difficulties will come upon them, and on that day they will ask, 'Have not these disasters come upon us because our God is not with us?' And I will certainly hide my face on that day because of all their wickedness in turning to other gods. *"Now write down for yourselves this song and teach it to the Israelites and have them sing it, so that it may be a witness for me against them. When I have brought them into the land flowing with milk and honey, the land I promised on oath to their forefathers, and when they eat their fill and thrive, they will turn to other gods and worship them, rejecting me and breaking my covenant. And when many disasters and difficulties come upon them, this song will testify against them, because it will not be forgotten by their descendants. I know what they are disposed to do, even before I bring them into the land I promised them on oath."*

AMP Jas 4:1-10 *WHAT LEADS to strife (discord and feuds) and how do conflicts (quarrels and fightings) originate among you? Do they not arise from your sensual desires that are ever warring in your bodily members? You are jealous and covet [what others have] and your desires go unfulfilled; [so] you become murderers. [To hate is to murder as far as your hearts are concerned.] You burn with envy and anger and are not able to obtain [the gratification, the contentment, and the happiness that you seek], so you fight and war. You do not have, because you do not ask. [Or] you do ask [God for them] and yet fail to receive, because you ask with wrong purpose and evil, selfish motives. Your intention is [when you get what you desire] to spend it in sensual pleasures. You [are like] unfaithful wives [having illicit love affairs with the world and breaking your marriage vow to God]! Do you not know that being the world's friend is being God's enemy? So whoever chooses to be a friend of the world takes his stand as an enemy of God. Or do you suppose that the Scripture is speaking to no purpose that says, The Spirit Whom He has caused to dwell in us yearns over us and He yearns for the Spirit [to be welcome] with a jealous love? But <u>He gives us more and more grace (power of the Holy Spirit, to meet this evil tendency and all others fully). That is why He says, God sets Himself against the proud and haughty, but gives grace [continually] to the lowly (those who are humble enough to receive it)</u>. So be subject to God. Resist the devil [stand firm against him], and he will flee from you. Come close to God and He will come close to you. [Recognize that you are] sinners, get your soiled hands clean; [realize that you have been disloyal] wavering individuals with divided interests, and purify your hearts [of your spiritual adultery]. [As you draw near to God] be deeply penitent and grieve, even weep [over your disloyalty]. Let your laughter be turned to grief and your mirth to dejection and heartfelt shame [for your sins]. Humble yourselves [feeling very insignificant] in the presence of the Lord, and He will exalt you [He will lift you up and make your lives significant].*

NIV Isa 54:6-8 *The LORD will call you back as if you were a wife deserted and distressed in spirit—a wife who married young, only to be rejected," says your God.* <u>*"For a brief moment I abandoned you, but with deep compassion I will bring you back. In a surge of anger I hid my face from you for a moment, but with everlasting kindness I will have compassion on you,"*</u> *says the LORD your Redeemer.*

I hid my face from you, this rich picture God depicts His turning away signifying that He is diverting His attention away from us and His presence is gone. This is a desolation! These verses also tell us the remedy that causes us to come out of a desolation when the Lord turns His face away from us. He instructs us that when we *seek His face* that is turned away from us, and repent, He will then turn His face back towards us, resulting in a healing and prosperity. To seek His face is to plead for His attention and care while we repent, changing our ways and thinking so that we no longer are an offense to our Creator.

NIV Da 9:26 *After the sixty-two 'sevens,' the Anointed One will be cut off and will have nothing. The people of the ruler who will come will destroy the city and the sanctuary. The end will come like a flood: War will continue until the end, and* <u>*desolations have been decreed.*</u>

In Daniel, as a part of the 70-7's we were told that because of God's judgment, He decreed multiple desolations, particularly over Jerusalem. However, this coming and final desolation is unique in that it will be a time of global desolation. God will turn His face away from the whole world and it will take 3½ years of suffering and crying out for Him before He will turn His face back towards His elect. No presence of God in the earth at all! What will happen will happen, no intervention, no answered prayer, no comfort of His Spirit within the souls of His elect who remain. The time of deciding will have passed. During the time of global desolation, Revelation tells us how the mettle, and the profession of faith of the believers who were left behind, will be tested, proved under horrific and unbearable circumstances. This is the test of fire Paul talked about that will burn away all the dross and make pure to the very core of the person, his love and faith in the Lord.

AMP 1Co 3:11-15 *For no other foundation can anyone lay than that which is [already] laid, which is Jesus Christ (the Messiah, the Anointed One). But if anyone builds upon the Foundation, whether it be with gold, silver, precious stones, wood, hay, straw, The work of each [one] will become [plainly, openly] known (shown for what it is); for the day [of Christ] will disclose and declare it, because it will be revealed with fire, and the fire will test and critically appraise the character and worth of the work each person has done. If the work which any person has built on this Foundation [any product of his efforts whatever] survives [this test], he will get his reward. <u>But if any person's work is burned up [under the test], he will suffer the loss [of it all, losing his reward], though he himself will be saved, but only as [one who has passed] through fire.</u>*

The time of deciding was "the Church Age," and again, it will have passed into the time of testing for those who are lukewarm (Rev 3:16)." Daniel is told about this time:

Da 11:34-35 *Now when they fall, they shall receive a little help. Many shall join themselves to them with flatteries and hypocrisies. And some of those who are wise, prudent, and understanding shall be weakened and fall, [thus, then, the insincere among the people will lose courage and become deserters. <u>It will be a test] to refine, to purify, and to make those among [God's people] white, even to the time of the end.</u>* . .

Even until the time of the end means that it is through tribulations that His people will be tested and refined from the time He said this, until after the *great tribulation*. It is right here He is telling us the purpose of why His people would have to endure such things. It will separate those who mean it with their whole heart from those who meant it only with their words. Our true nature will be exposed and the nature of what we truly love revealed with the ultimate test—our lives on the line. However, it is because of the corruptness of our faith that necessitates the testing of it through such life-or-death circumstances. The saints of God have brought this on themselves!

Then, Revelation speaks about the fate of those who are purified and made white during the time of darkness/*desolation*/the *great tribulation*:

NIV Rev 7:9 After this I looked and there before me was a great multitude that no one could count, from every nation, tribe, people and language, standing before the throne and in front of the Lamb. They were wearing white robes (celestial bodies) . . .

NIV Rev 7:13-17 Then one of the elders asked me, "These in white robes—who are they, and where did they come from?" I answered, "Sir, you know." And he said, "These are they who have come out of the great tribulation; they have washed their robes and made them white in the blood of the Lamb. Therefore, "they are before the throne of God and serve him day and night in his temple; and he who sits on the throne will spread his tent over them. Never again will they hunger; never again will they thirst. The sun will not beat upon them, nor any scorching heat. For the Lamb at the center of the throne will be their shepherd; he will lead them to springs of living water. And God will wipe away every tear from their eyes."

Revelation tells the whole story of salvation and judgment from its beginning, when humanity (Adam and Eve) were judged, to the end when judgment will be complete. It also tells us of the salvation of His elect in the midst of the passing of judgment. It promises the salvation of both the *Church Pure* and the discipline of the *Church Corrupt* resulting in their salvation as well. Likewise, it tells us of the nation of Israel, the *twelve stars* in the crown of the *woman clothed with the sun* and their redemption. Finally, He shows us exactly how that judgment of the world looks, who rejected His elect and persecuted them. It is a message that is told by Jesus to His Church. He is giving insight and warning His beloved of all which will take place. How do we know it is true that it is only them? Let's look at the following verse in Revelation:

NIV Rev 17:8 *The beast, which you saw, once was, now is not, and will come up out of the Abyss and go to his destruction.* <u>*The inhabitants of the earth whose names have not been written in the book of life from the creation of the world will be astonished when they see the beast, because he once was, now is not, and yet will come.*</u>

This verse is explaining that the *antichrist* (the beast) is someone who has lived and died in times of old and is currently dead. And that he will rise up from among the dead to rule the earth for a short time and then go to his destruction which, we find out, is to be thrown alive into the *lake of fire* for eternity. The verse goes on to say that every person alive and dead whoever lived on the face of the earth will be shocked, astonished at this happening. The disembodied souls in *Hades* will be in awe that one of them escaped the realm of the dead, finding a way to be embodied and walk the earth after death. Everyone alive and dead, "from the creation of the world" will be "astonished," meaning that when it happens, they will have no idea something like this would or even could happen.

However, it does mention an exception to those who will be astonished. They are those whose names are written in the Lamb's book of life. Those who are to be salvaged from among the condemned, they will not be surprised or astonished at this amazing turn of events. Why is that? It is because before it occurs, they are informed by the Lord, even in this message to them called the book of Revelation. This is more evidence that Revelation is written to God's elect, not the rest of the world. Unlike the rest of the living and the dead, the elect wait for this event and fully expect it to happen. What if unbelievers read this book? Even those of the world who read this book will either not believe it or not understand it. They will still be taken back unaware when this occurs. Jesus said:

NAS JN 12:35-40 *So Jesus said to them, "For a little while longer the Light is among you. Walk while you have the Light, so that darkness will not overtake you;* <u>*he who walks in the darkness does not know where he goes*</u>*. "While you have the Light, believe in the Light, so that you may become sons of Light." These things Jesus spoke, and*

He went away and hid Himself from them. But though He had performed so many signs before them, yet they were not believing in Him. This was to fulfill the word of Isaiah the prophet which he spoke: "LORD, WHO HAS BELIEVED OUR REPORT? AND TO WHOM HAS THE ARM OF THE LORD BEEN REVEALED?" <u>For this reason they could not believe, for Isaiah said again, "HE HAS BLINDED THEIR EYES AND HE HARDENED THEIR HEART, SO THAT THEY WOULD NOT SEE WITH THEIR EYES AND PERCEIVE WITH THEIR HEART, AND BE CONVERTED AND I HEAL THEM."</u>

Jesus has written the book of Revelation to His elect, but as for the world, God has blinded their eyes and hardened their hearts so they cannot understand. James tells us not just the world, but the proud.

NIV Rev 3:1-3 "To the angel of the church in Sardis write: These are the words of him who holds the seven spirits of God and the seven stars. I know your deeds; you have a reputation of being alive, but you are dead. Wake up! Strengthen what remains and is about to die, for I have not found your deeds complete in the sight of my God. Remember, therefore, what you have received and heard; obey it, and repent. <u>But if you do not wake up, I will come like a thief, and you will not know at what time I will come to you.</u>

It says, God resists the proud (those independent from God, living by their own power) but He gives grace to the humble (Jas 4:1-10). That includes the humble of the world who desire to be right with God and to submit to Him—to them also will He give His grace, as spoken below:

NIV Jn 6:43-44 "Stop grumbling among yourselves," Jesus answered. "No one can come to me unless the Father who sent me draws him, and I will raise him up at the last day.

An important phenomenon to take note of:

It was just shown that the truth is for believers only, and even though it is proclaimed throughout the entire world, it is hidden from the rest of the world. How is this the case when anyone has access to the word of God through the Bible?

AMP Mt 13:12-16 For whoever has [spiritual knowledge], to him will more be given and he will be furnished richly so that he will have abundance; but from him who has not, even what he has will be taken away. This is the reason that I speak to them in parables: because having the power of seeing, they do not see; and having the power of hearing, they do not hear, nor do they grasp and understand. In them indeed is the process of fulfillment of the prophecy of Isaiah, which says: You shall indeed hear and hear but never grasp and understand; and you shall indeed look and look but never see and perceive. For this nation's heart has grown gross (fat and dull), and their ears heavy and difficult of hearing, and their eyes they have tightly closed, lest they see and perceive with their eyes, and hear and comprehend the sense with their ears, and grasp and understand with their heart, and turn and I should heal them. But blessed (happy, fortunate, and to be envied) are your eyes because they do see, and your ears because they do hear.

To those not chosen and who are haters of God, the book of Revelation, and the entire Bible, for that matter, will be beyond their ability to understand. As Paul says, it will be as foolishness to them.

NIV 1Co 1:18-25 For the message of the cross is foolishness to those who are perishing, but to us who are being saved it is the power of God. For it is written: "I will destroy the wisdom of the wise; the intelligence of the intelligent I will frustrate." Where is the wise man? Where is the scholar? Where is the philosopher of this age? Has not God made foolish the wisdom of the world? For since in the wisdom of God the world through its wisdom did not know him, God was pleased through the foolishness of what was preached to save those who believe. Jews demand miraculous signs and Greeks look for wisdom, but we preach Christ crucified: a stumbling block to Jews and foolishness to Gentiles, but to those whom God has called, both Jews and Greeks, Christ the power of God and the wisdom of

God. For the foolishness of God is wiser than man's wisdom, and the weakness of God is stronger than man's strength.

The reason this is brought up is because Jesus says He will do the same to believers who have lost their first love, who do not follow the promptings of the Holy Spirit and instead follow their own will and desires. The same believers He tells everything to, through His prophets and His word, the Bible.

NIV Rev 3:1b-3 These are the words of him who holds the seven spirits of God and the seven stars. I know your deeds; you have a reputation of being alive, but you are dead. Wake up! Strengthen what remains and is about to die, for I have not found your deeds complete in the sight of my God. Remember, therefore, what you have received and heard; obey it, and repent. But if you do not wake up, I will come like a thief, and you will not know at what time I will come to you.

What does that look like? For we know Jesus and believe in Him! In these contemporary times the prophecies and the book of Revelation are so confusing that no one can agree on what exactly they mean. And what they think they mean are understandings based on mere fragments of verses which are taken out of context of the whole book or Bible. That applies especially to the book of Revelation. This divides and fragments the Church from each other, creating countless denominations. This has been the case early on in the history of the Church and because of the sin inside it, it necessitated the Protestant Reformation. In fact, many current scholars want to take the book of Revelation out of the Bible and no longer consider it canon because it leaves them scratching their heads over its meaning.

We Christians have and embrace the word of God and its record of exactly what the future brings and how to escape its woes, but we do not really understand it. In this one chapter we have pointed out a handful of elementary misunderstandings that skew our whole idea of what it means to be a Christian and the privileges and favor of God it affords the faithful. In fact, some denominations, especially the evangelicals, think that God no longer talks to us through dreams, visions and prophecy. And that Jesus will not come back to the earth and what the Bible says about His return has already happened and we are currently living in the *Millennium Reign* of Christ; including that we have or currently are enduring the *great tribulation*. By all this irrefutable evidence, we too (us Christians) are blind, and the truth is hidden from us in plain sight.

NIV Rev 18:4-8 *Then I heard another voice from heaven say: "Come out of her* (the Church), *my people, so that you will not share in her sins, so that you will not receive any of her plagues; for her sins are piled up to heaven, and God has remembered her crimes. Give back to her as she has given; pay her back double for what she has done. Mix her a double portion from her own cup. Give her as much torture and grief as the glory and luxury she gave herself.* <u>In her heart she boasts, 'I</u> (the Church) <u>sit as queen</u> (the bride of Christ); <u>I am not a widow, and I will never mourn.</u>' *Therefore in one day her plagues will overtake her: death, mourning and famine. She will be consumed by fire, for mighty is the Lord God who judges her.*

Jesus says of us about our self-delusion:

AMP Rev 3:17-22 *For you say, I am rich; I have prospered and grown wealthy, and I am in need of nothing; and* <u>you do not realize and understand that you are wretched, pitiable, poor, blind, and naked.</u> *Therefore I counsel you to purchase from Me gold refined and tested by fire* (enduring the great tribulation), *that you may be [truly] wealthy, and white clothes to clothe you and to keep the shame of your nudity* (being dead without a body) *from being seen, and salve to put on your eyes, that you may see. Those whom I [dearly and tenderly] love, I tell their faults and convict and convince and reprove and chasten [I discipline and instruct them]. So be enthusiastic and in earnest and burning with zeal and repent [changing your mind and attitude]. Behold, I stand at the door and knock; if anyone hears and listens to and heeds My voice and opens the door, I will come in to him and will eat with him, and he [will eat] with Me. He who overcomes (is victorious), I will grant him to sit beside Me on My throne, as I Myself overcame (was victorious)* and sat down beside My Father on His throne. He who is able to hear, let him listen to and heed what the [Holy] Spirit says to the assemblies (churches).

It is not too late, for Jesus says to His Church, His bride:

AMP Rev 2:4-5 But I have this [one charge to make] against you: that you have left (abandoned) the love that you had at first [you have deserted Me, your first love]. Remember then from what heights you have fallen. Repent (change the inner man to meet God's will) and do the works you did previously [when first you knew the Lord], or else I will visit you and remove your lampstand from its place, unless you change your mind and repent.

AMP Rev 3:2-3 Rouse yourselves and wake up, and strengthen and invigorate what remains and is on the point of dying; for I have not found a thing that you have done [any work of yours] meeting the requirements of My God or perfect in His sight. So call to mind the lessons you received and heard; continually lay them to heart and obey them, and repent.

Indeed, the book of Revelation is a message meant for the Church, the elect of Jesus and no one else.

Notes

[1] Abbott, S. (2015) Is there a hidden Message in Revelation 7? Why is Dan missing? Retrieved October 2017, from Reasons for Hope*Jesus: https://reasonsforhopejesus.com/is-there-a-hidden-message-in-revelation-7/

CHAPTER FIVE

The Bride and the Woman who Rides the Beast

The bride and the woman who rides the beast are one and the same, or rather they are both the Church of Christ. The bride, we refer to as the *Church Pure*, and the woman who rides the beast, or the great prostitute we refer to as the *Church Corrupt*. The difference between the two is that the *Church Pure* has as its spiritual power the Holy Spirit. As for the *Church Corrupt*, the *devil*, and the *antichrist* are its source of power. In fact, the Pope and the Catholic Church are the 7th king and kingdom (respectively) of the *beast* and of the *devil*. They sit on the throne of the beast. The *Church Corrupt* has merged into Babylon and the Vatican/Rome is currently the great city.

It is just as spoken in Nebuchadnezzar's vision in Daniel.

NIV Da 2:31-45 "*You looked, O king, and there before you stood a large statue—an enormous, dazzling statue, awesome in appearance. The head of the statue was made of pure gold, its chest and arms of silver, its belly and thighs of bronze, its legs of iron, its feet partly of iron and partly of baked clay. While you were watching, a rock was cut out, but not by human hands. It struck the statue on its feet of iron and clay and smashed them. Then the iron, the clay, the bronze, the silver and the gold were broken to pieces at the same time and became like chaff on a threshing floor in the summer. The wind swept them away without leaving a trace. But the rock that struck the statue became a huge mountain and filled the whole earth. "This was the dream, and now we will interpret it to the king. You, O king, are the king of kings. The God of heaven has given you dominion and power and might and glory; in your hands he has placed mankind and the beasts of the field and the birds of the air. Wherever they live, he has made you ruler over them all. You are that head of gold. "After you, another kingdom will rise, inferior to* *yours. Next, a third kingdom, one of bronze, will rule over the whole earth. Finally, there will be a fourth kingdom, <u>strong as iron—for iron breaks and smashes everything—and as iron breaks things to pieces, so it will crush and break all the others. Just as you saw that the feet and toes were partly of baked clay and partly of iron, so this will be a divided kingdom; yet it will have some of the strength of iron in it, even as you saw iron mixed with clay. As the toes were partly iron and partly clay, so this kingdom will be partly strong and partly brittle. And just as you saw the iron mixed with baked clay, so the people will be a mixture and will not remain united, any more than iron mixes with clay.</u> "In the time of those kings, the God of heaven will set up a kingdom that will never be destroyed, nor will it be left to another people.</u> It will crush all those kingdoms and bring them to an end, but it will itself endure forever. This is the meaning of the vision of the rock cut out of a mountain, but not by human hands—a rock that broke the iron, the bronze, the clay, the silver and the gold to pieces. "The great God has shown the king what will take place in the future. The dream is true and the interpretation is trustworthy."*

First, to point out is that this dream only describes 5 kingdoms when there are 7 heads of the beast (Rev12:3) and 7 shepherds of the kingdom of *Nimrod*, the Assyrian (Micah 5:5). Some may speculate that this dream is therefore not talking about the 7 heads of the *devil*. It is, in fact, referring to those 7 heads of the dragon, the *devil*. The reason there are only 5 in Nebuchadnezzar's dream is because 2 of those heads/shepherds and kingdoms of the beast have already passed. Nebuchadnezzar and his Babylonian Empire are the third. The first two were respectively, *Nimrod* of Babylon, the original and first kingdom who subdued other nations. Second, was the Assyrian Empire. When that fell it was Nebuchadnezzar's Babylonian Empire whose dream it is and was the head of gold on the statue. To be thorough, Micah in his 5th chapter predicted 7 kings and even an 8th. Then Revelation says a similar thing:

NIV Rev 17:10-11 **They are also seven kings. Five have fallen, one is, the other has not yet come; but when he does come, he must remain for** *a little while. The beast who once was, and now is not, is an eighth king. He belongs to the seven and is going to his destruction.*

The one that "is", was a king during the time that John penned Revelation. That king and kingdom was Caesar and the Roman Empire who was the sixth head. The 7th, who was *yet to come* as of when John wrote Revelation, is now in place. It is the Pope and the Holy Roman Empire with its head the Roman Catholic Church. In Nebuchadnezzar's dream it says the legs of iron (the Roman Empire) will end with feet of clay mixed with iron. A phenomenon that does not by nature mix together well. Those feet of clay mixed with the iron before them, represents the last of the seven kingdoms and it is the Roman Catholic Church. This combination of iron and clay, not something that can mix, represents a secular empire that does not by nature mix with the Lord's spiritual church. However, it is still, nevertheless, mixed to form the Holy Roman Empire, a combination of the Roman Empire (the iron) and the Roman Catholic Church (the clay).

The destruction of the Roman Catholic Church, the seventh head, cannot happen until the end because it is the last, and it is from her that the 8th king, who was the first, *Nimrod*, comes back as the *antichrist*. The corrupted Catholic Church is the bridge and source that brings back from the *Abyss*, the *antichrist*. Besides even that, the Lord is letting the Church grow and mature to help distinguish between individuals in the Church, the pure, and the corrupt. Just as the Lord said:

NIV Mt 13:25-30 But while everyone was sleeping, his enemy came and sowed weeds among the wheat, and went away. When the wheat sprouted and formed heads, then the weeds also appeared. "The owner's servants came to him and said, 'Sir, didn't you sow good seed in your field? Where then did the weeds come from?'" "'An enemy did this,' he replied. "The servants asked him, 'Do you want us to go and pull them up?'" "'No,' he answered, 'because while you are pulling the weeds, you may root up the wheat with them. Let both grow together until the harvest. At that time I will tell the harvesters:

First collect the weeds and tie them in bundles to be burned; then gather the wheat and bring it into my barn.'"

It must be kept in mind that the *great tribulation* is not simply what the world evolves into. It is the plan of God to polarize the people of the world. All are sinners; however, God is not condemning individuals on that basis. By polarizing the people of the world, God can identify the souls that desire to be reconciled with Him, from those who do not.

AMP Jas 4:4 You [are like] unfaithful wives [having illicit love affairs with the world and breaking your marriage vow to God]! Do you not know that being the world's friend is being God's enemy? So whoever chooses to be a friend of the world takes his stand as an enemy of God.

Although John the Baptist (who paved a path for the Lord) was from a priestly family, a family that had both stature and means and was an important part of the temple system, he abandoned it all. He did not use his family's stature to communicate and spread his message, but gave it all up because of the corruption within. Jesus, likewise, did not work through the Jewish government or the temple system. Instead Jesus called people out of it, and its corruption. However, Babylon, the kingdom of the devil, has entered into and empowers the Lord's beloved bride, His Church. The lines have been blurred. The distinction that came through polarization has been erased. His Church is not in one clear camp or the other but has become integrated with the world and his people do not know the difference and have not chosen with clarity one camp or the other. They have one foot on each side of the fence. They have become one with the world starting with the Roman Catholic Church, including those denominations that broke free through the Reformation. They, as well as we, in these contemporary times are ignorant of where that line is.

NIV Rev 3:15-22 I know your deeds, that you are neither cold nor hot. I wish you were either one or the other! So, because you are lukewarm—neither hot nor cold—I am about to spit you out of my mouth (about to, does not mean I am considering it, it means soon I am going to). *You say, 'I am rich; I have acquired wealth and do not need a thing.'* <u>But you do not realize that you are wretched, pitiful, poor, blind and naked.</u> *I counsel you to buy from me gold refined in the fire* (of the great tribulation), *so you can become rich; and white clothes to wear* (become a celestial human), *so you can cover your shameful nakedness; and salve to put on your eyes, so you can see. Those whom I love I rebuke and discipline. So be earnest, and repent. Here I am! I stand at the door and knock. If anyone hears my voice and opens the door, I will come in and eat with him, and he with me.* <u>To him who overcomes, I will give the right to sit with me on my throne, just as I overcame and sat down with my Father on his throne. He who has an ear, let him hear what the Spirit says to the churches."</u>

The two witnesses are meant to save the saints and separate them from the world as the end comes. However, they will divide it by making the boundaries clear again, forcing the saints to choose one side or the other. Many of the saints (the weeds [according to the parable above]) when forced to a crossroads will choose to join the world and thus become apostates. With them, they will support the Pope (the *false prophet*) to bring back from the dead, *Nimrod*, so he can kill the *two witnesses*. Then celebrate their death. This is the predicted great falling away—the *great apostasy*.

AMP 2Th 2:3-4 Let no one deceive or beguile you in any way, for that day will not come except the apostasy comes first [unless the predicted great falling away of those who have professed to be Christians has come], and the man of lawlessness (sin) is revealed, who is the son of doom (of perdition), Who opposes and exalts himself so proudly and insolently against and over all that is called God or that is worshiped, [even to his actually] taking his seat in the temple of God, proclaiming that he himself is God.

In an effort to save even the apostates, the Lord *raptures* those of His saints who do not become apostates and brings on the *great tribulation*.

NIV Rev 17:11-18 *The beast who once was, and now is not, is an eighth king. He belongs to the seven and is going to his destruction. "The ten horns you saw are ten kings who have not yet received a kingdom, but who for one hour will receive authority as kings along with the beast. They have one purpose and will give their power and authority to the beast. They will make war against the Lamb, but the Lamb will overcome them because he is Lord of lords and King of kings—and with him will be his called, chosen and faithful followers." Then the angel said to me, "The waters you saw, where the prostitute sits, are peoples, multitudes, nations and languages. <u>The beast and the ten horns you saw will hate the prostitute. They will bring her to ruin and leave her naked; they will eat her flesh and burn her with fire. For God has put it into their hearts to accomplish his purpose by agreeing to give the beast their power to rule, until God's words are fulfilled.</u> The woman you saw is the great city* (the Vatican) *that rules over the kings of the earth."*

He turns the world against the apostates to push them back to their first love. Even after they betray Him and denounce the Lord, He creates a way to save them. Just as He prophesies through Hosea and demonstrated by how He turned the heart of Gomer back to her husband, Hosea. The *great tribulation* is the refinement in the fire Jesus counsels us to be purified in, saying, I discipline the ones I love. Make no mistake, He does not discipline to punish the ones He loves, but to save them from themselves and their deluded ignorance that would have them doomed for eternity if not for the time of the great tribulation.

AMP Rev 7:9-14 *After* <u>*this I looked and a vast host appeared which no one could count, [gathered out] of every nation, from all tribes and peoples and languages. These stood before the throne and before the Lamb; they were attired in white robes*</u> (celestial bodies), <u>*with palm branches in their hands.*</u> *In loud voice they cried, saying, [Our] salvation is due to our God, Who is seated on the throne, and to the Lamb [to Them we owe our deliverance]! And all the angels were standing round the throne and round the elders [of the heavenly Sanhedrin] and the four living creatures, and they fell prostrate* before the throne and worshiped God. Amen! (So be it!) they cried. Blessing and glory and majesty and splendor and wisdom and thanks and honor and power and might [be ascribed] to our God to the ages and ages (forever and ever, throughout the eternities of the eternities)! Amen! (So be it!) Then, addressing me, one of the elders [of the heavenly Sanhedrin] said, Who are these [people] clothed in the long white robes? And from where have they come? I replied, Sir, you know. And he said to me, <u>These are they who have come out of the great tribulation (persecution), and have washed their robes and made them white in the blood of the Lamb</u>

Yes, if not for the divided hearts of the saints there would be no tribulation! It is meant as a last resort to save.

NIV Lk 14:16-24 *Jesus replied: "A certain man was preparing a great banquet and invited many guests. At the time of the banquet he sent his servant to tell those who had been invited, 'Come, for everything is now ready.' "But they all alike began to make excuses. The first said, 'I have just bought a field, and I must go and see it. Please excuse me.' "Another said, 'I have just bought five yoke of oxen, and I'm on my way to try them out. Please excuse me.' "Still another said, 'I just got married, so I can't come.' "The servant came back and reported this to his master. Then the owner of the house became angry and ordered his servant, 'Go out quickly into the streets and alleys of the town and bring in the poor, the crippled, the blind and the lame.' "'Sir,' the servant said, 'what you ordered has been done, <u>but there is still room.' "Then the master told his servant, 'Go out to the roads and country lanes and make them come in, so that my house will be full.</u> I tell you, not one of those men who were invited will get a taste of my banquet.'"*

"But they all alike began to make excuses, these are the Jews who reject Jesus. *Then the owner of the house became angry and ordered his servant, 'Go out quickly into the streets and alleys of the town and bring in the poor, the crippled, the blind and the lame.* These are the Christians—the *Church Pure*—whom He offers salvation to, and they accept. *But there is still room, 'Go out to the roads and country lanes and make them come in, so that my house will be full.* This is speaking about those the Lord gathers during the *great tribulation*.

As for the *Church Pure* it is as *Jesus* spoke:

^{NAS JN 18:36} *Jesus answered, "<u>My kingdom is not of this world.</u> If My kingdom were of this world, then My servants would be fighting so that I would not be handed over to the Jews; but as it is, <u>My kingdom is not of this realm.</u>"*

The city the New Jerusalem, the mountain it sits on, and the Lord's seat of power is within that city. They come with Him upon His return to the physical earth. Jesus, His Father and His court of celestial beings, angels, and celestial humans all come down to earth from the spiritual realm. Truly His entire Kingdom is spiritual in nature even the buildings and walls and the mountain it sits on consists of spiritual matter and not of natural matter. At just the right time Jesus and His Kingdom will come down to the earth, not from another place in the physical universe, but from a totally different dimension.

It will be at that time within the walls of the New Jerusalem that He will hold His *wedding feast*. When it is finished, Jesus with His host, will come out of the New Jerusalem and by force subdue the earth after winning the *battle of Armageddon*. Then He will remake the nation of Israel with all 12 tribes represented and cause the whole world to serve them, as He promised to their forefathers. However, even this is temporal and will last only 1,000 years. After which everything consisting of natural matter, including all natural elements of the universe, will melt in the *lake of fire*. The Kingdom of Jesus will remain for eternity and be unscathed by this event, because it does not consist of natural matter but of spiritual matter.

In the meantime, the kingdom of the natural world has been ordained by God to be the kingdom of the *devil* and his beast/*antichrist*/*Nimrod* who in his day, the whole world made him king over themselves. When he rises from the dead to kill the *two witnesses*, the whole world will once again make him king over them. That is with the exception of the Jews who are hidden in the desert out of his reach, the Christians that are consequently *raptured*, and the apostates who come to their senses after being left behind and thereby refuse to worship or take the mark of the beast.

Since his beginning, Nimrod's seat of authority has been restrained from having its granted total global power until after the end of the 70-7's, or 70 weeks of years. When the *Church Age* (the delay between the 62-7's and the 1-7) is finished there are only seven years (the last 7) before he takes that place. However, the spirit of *Nimrod*'s obsession to conquer the whole world influences the kings of the earth throughout history, the 7 kings and kingdoms are his legacy. Nimrod is the earthly agent the devil gives that power to. Again, Jesus said, as it is (as it stands right now) My Kingdom is not of this realm. Ever since Jesus lived on this earth, He is to bring His Kingdom to rule the earth at the appointed time. However, His Kingdom, as He spoke, is not of this world, but comes down from Heaven. The new Jerusalem that comes down with Him is a Heavenly city made of celestial matter; the celestial angels come with Him, even the human beings who populate His Kingdom are and must be celestial humans. It is only when that Kingdom comes to the earth that it is time to take rulership of the world away from the devil and his antichrist. As such, and since the beginning of the *New Covenant*, His servants do not fight to rule over, take over, or protect their piece of the pie in this present world. That being the case, if one has a seat of power during these times, that seat of power and authority is under the devil and his antichrist, even though God uses those leaders for His good and to carry out His plan of salvation.

It is important to realize that aside from those God calls for special purposes to affect change in the world, whoever fights for or takes a place in this world over the leaders of this world is under the power of the antichrist. However, even the wicked God calls to carry out His plan of salvation. Case in point; God called Nebuchadnezzar, His wicked servant. This state of affairs is because it is their ordained time of power, and man has desired for them to rule over themselves. It says of the *Church Corrupt*:

NIV Rev 17:18-18:10 <u>The woman you saw is the great city that rules over the kings of the earth."</u> *After this I saw another angel coming down from heaven. He had great authority, and the earth was illuminated by his splendor. With a mighty voice he shouted: "Fallen! Fallen is Babylon the Great! She has become a home for demons and a haunt for every evil spirit, a haunt for every unclean and detestable bird.* <u>*For all the nations have drunk the maddening wine of her adulteries. The kings of the earth committed adultery with her, and the merchants of the earth grew rich from her excessive luxuries."*</u> *Then I heard another voice from heaven say:* <u>*"Come out of her, my people, so that you will not share in her sins, so that you will not receive any of her plagues; for her sins are piled up to heaven, and God has remembered her crimes.*</u> *Give back to her as she has given; pay her back double for what she has done. Mix her a double portion from her own cup. Give her as much torture and grief as the glory and luxury she gave herself.* <u>*In her heart she boasts, 'I sit as queen; I am not a widow, and I will never mourn.'*</u> *Therefore in one day her plagues will overtake her: death, mourning and famine. She will be consumed by fire, for mighty is the Lord God who judges her. "When the kings of the earth who committed adultery with her and shared her luxury see the smoke of her burning, they will weep and mourn over her. Terrified at her torment, they will stand far off and cry: "'Woe! Woe, O great city, O Babylon, city of power! In one hour your doom has come!'*

In her heart she boasts, I sit as queen; I am not a widow, and I will never mourn, It must be asked, who could say this and believe it? The only one who is in a position to have such a confidence is the bride of Christ—the Church. The Church will never be a widow and as a result, never mourn. Her husband is the Lord and source of life which makes her a queen! However, in her quest for power here on earth, she became one with the Roman Empire. She is the feet of iron mixed with clay. The Roman Catholic Church is guilty of conducting wars of conquest and mass genocide destroying whole cultures in an effort to destroy her rivals. Throughout history those she has killed is estimated between 60 million to over 100 million. That is not only against the mandate of the Christ, but is, likewise, adultery to be in league with the Roman Empire (including the Holy Roman Empire which the Catholic Church revived and reestablished). All of which makes her the great prostitute!

Jeremiah warned the people of Jerusalem in vain that because of their sin and spiritual adultery the Lord planned to have Babylon overtake the city and lead the captives away to Babylon as slaves; with the purpose of ejecting them out of the promised land. They scorned Jeremiah and punished him, even tossing him into jail. They boasted in their hearts that Jerusalem was the city with the Lord's temple, and He would never let invaders have the city. So too will the false confidence of the Roman Catholic Church be brought to humiliation and suffer the consequences of her sins. That is why the Lord admonishes His saints to come out of her, so they will not suffer her doom.

In the Bible, God sometimes refers to cities as women (even nations or certain groups of people for that matter). Similarly, some men might refer to their machines or cars as a *she* or a *woman*. This kind of association runs much deeper for God to do so. When we think of a certain city we think of the landscape, the skyline, what it is known for, its food, culture, buildings, and infrastructure. God sees a city, its people, the infrastructure which ties all its people together to make the city function, the activities of the people, and what those activities produce as a single living organism, like a woman. Or like a human body whose living cells, organs, and different members all work together, giving life to the entire body which clothes the spirit and soul of a person.

The city, the New Jerusalem, is called the bride of Christ in the Bible. The New Jerusalem is the center, home, and natural habitat for Jesus, His angels, and the celestial humans He had saved from death.

NIV Rev 21:2 <u>I saw the Holy City, the new Jerusalem, coming down out of heaven from God, prepared as a bride beautifully dressed for her husband.</u>

Now, listen to how the Lord talks about natural Jerusalem from its inception as a city, as well as other cities:

NAS EZE 16:1-8 Then the word of the LORD came to me, saying, "Son of man, make known to Jerusalem her abominations and say, <u>'Thus says the Lord GOD to Jerusalem, "Your origin and your birth are from the land of the Canaanite, your father was an Amorite and your mother a Hittite.</u> "As for your birth, on the day you were born your navel cord was not cut, nor were you washed with water for cleansing; you were not rubbed with salt or even wrapped in cloths. "No eye looked with pity on you to do any of these things for you, to have compassion on you. Rather you were thrown out into the open field, for you were abhorred on the day you were born. "When I passed by you and saw you squirming in your blood, I said to you while you were in your blood, 'Live!' Yes, I said to you while you were in your blood, 'Live!' "I made you numerous like plants of the field. Then you grew up, became tall and reached the age for fine ornaments; your breasts were formed and your hair had grown. Yet you were naked and bare. <u>"Then I passed by you and saw you, and behold, you were at the time for love; so I spread My skirt over you and covered your nakedness. I also swore to you and entered into a covenant with you so that you became Mine," declares the Lord GOD.</u>

In the highlighted verse above the Lord is describing how He betrothed, Jerusalem, even though Jerusalem was a city located in a heathen land and was originally created and built by godless people. However, like Boaz who, by covering Ruth (of heathen origin) with his robe (skirt), the Lord is making Jerusalem His wife—His bride, bringing prosperity and order to her.

NAS EZE 16:9-46 "Then I bathed you with water, washed off your blood from you and anointed you with oil. "I also clothed you with embroidered cloth and put sandals of porpoise skin on your feet; and

I wrapped you with fine linen and covered you with silk. "I adorned you with ornaments, put bracelets on your hands and a necklace around your neck. "I also put a ring in your nostril, earrings in your ears and a beautiful crown on your head. "Thus you were adorned with gold and silver, and your dress was of fine linen, silk and embroidered cloth. You ate fine flour, honey and oil; so you were exceedingly beautiful and advanced to royalty. "Then your fame went forth among the nations on account of your beauty, for it was perfect because of My splendor which I bestowed on you," declares the Lord GOD. <u>"But you trusted in your beauty and played the harlot because of your fame, and you poured out your harlotries on every passer-by who might be willing.</u> "You took some of your clothes, made for yourself high places of various colors and played the harlot on them, which should never come about nor happen. "You also took your beautiful jewels made of My gold and of My silver, which I had given you, and made for yourself male images that you might play the harlot with them. "Then you took your embroidered cloth and covered them, and offered My oil and My incense before them. "Also My bread which I gave you, fine flour, oil and honey with which I fed you, you would offer before them for a soothing aroma; so it happened," declares the Lord GOD. "Moreover, you took your sons and daughters whom you had borne to Me and sacrificed them to idols to be devoured. Were your harlotries so small a matter? "You slaughtered My children and offered them up to idols by causing them to pass through the fire. "Besides all your abominations and harlotries you did not remember the days of your youth, when you were naked and bare and squirming in your blood. "Then it came about after all your wickedness ('Woe, woe to you!' declares the Lord GOD), that you built yourself a shrine and made yourself a high place in every square. "You built yourself a high place at the top of every street and made your beauty abominable, and you spread your legs to every passer-by to multiply your harlotry. "You also played the harlot with the Egyptians, your lustful neighbors, and multiplied your harlotry to make Me angry. "Behold now, I have stretched out

My hand against you and diminished your rations. And I delivered you up to the desire of those who hate you, the daughters of the Philistines, who are ashamed of your lewd conduct. "Moreover, you played the harlot with the Assyrians because you were not satisfied; you played the harlot with them and still were not satisfied. "You also multiplied your harlotry with the land of merchants, Chaldea, yet even with this you were not satisfied.""' "How languishing is your heart," declares the Lord GOD, "while you do all these things, the actions of a bold-faced harlot. "When you built your shrine at the beginning of every street and made your high place in every square, in disdaining money, you were not like a harlot. "You adulteress wife, who takes strangers instead of her husband! (Again the Lord references Jerusalem as His wife) *" Men give gifts to all harlots, but you give your gifts to all your lovers to bribe them to come to you from every direction for your harlotries. "Thus you are different from those women in your harlotries, in that no one plays the harlot as you do, because you give money and no money is given you; thus you are different." Therefore, O harlot, hear the word of the LORD. Thus says the Lord GOD, "Because your lewdness was poured out and your nakedness uncovered through your harlotries with your lovers and with all your detestable idols, and because of the blood of your sons which you gave to idols, therefore, behold, I will gather all your lovers with whom you took pleasure, even all those whom you loved and all those whom you hated. So I will gather them against you from every direction and expose your nakedness to them that they may see all your nakedness. "Thus I will judge you like women who commit adultery or shed blood are judged; and I will bring on you the blood of wrath and jealousy. "I will also give you into the hands of your lovers, and they will tear down your shrines, demolish your high places, strip you of your clothing, take away your jewels, and will leave you naked and bare. "They will incite a crowd against you and they will stone you and cut you to pieces with their swords. "They will burn your houses with fire and execute judgments on you in the sight of many women. Then I will stop you from playing the harlot, and you will also no longer pay your lovers. "So I will calm My fury against you and My jealousy will depart from you, and I will be pacified and angry no more. "Because you have not remembered the days of your youth but have enraged Me by all these things, behold, I in turn will bring your conduct down on your own head," declares the Lord GOD, "so that you will not commit this lewdness on top of all your other abominations. "Behold, everyone who quotes proverbs will quote this proverb concerning you, saying, 'Like mother, like daughter.' "You are the daughter of your mother, who loathed her husband and children. You are also the sister of your sisters, who loathed their husbands and children. Your mother was a Hittite and your father an Amorite. "Now your older sister is Samaria, who lives north of you with her daughters; and your younger sister, who lives south of you, is Sodom with her daughters.*

It can get confusing when your mind is thinking about people and not cities. However, God is visualizing the citizens of a city as one. Coupled with their combined pursuits and the unanimous direction the people of that city take; God relates to the citizens as a single organism in His eyes. The people in it are the city. However, as Peter points out, when judgment comes, the Lord can and does save the individuals in it that are in opposition to the direction the majority pursue. Their directions and pursuits make up the personality and soul of the city. God simply sees:

- The city as the embodiment of the people who occupy it.
- The walls and buildings as the clothing which covers them.
- Their deeds and pursuits as the jewelry which adorns it (Rev 18:8).
- Its beliefs as the foundations upon which it stands (Rev 21:14).
- Its integrity as the columns which support its structures (Rev 3:12).

NAS EZE 16:47-63 *"Yet you have not merely walked in their ways or done according to their abominations; but, as if that were too little, you acted more corruptly in all your conduct than they. "As I live," declares the Lord GOD, "Sodom, your sister and her daughters have not done as you and your daughters have done. "Behold, this was the guilt of your sister Sodom: she and her daughters had arrogance, abundant food and careless ease, but she did not help the poor and* needy. *"Thus they were haughty and committed abominations before Me. Therefore I removed them when I saw it. "Furthermore, Samaria did not commit half of your sins, for you have multiplied your abominations more than they. Thus you have made your sisters appear righteous by all your abominations which you have committed. "Also bear your disgrace in that you have made judgment favorable for your sisters. Because of your sins in which you acted more abominably than they, they are more in the right than you. Yes, be also ashamed and bear your disgrace, in that you made your sisters appear righteous. "Nevertheless, I will restore their captivity, the captivity of Sodom and her daughters, the captivity of Samaria and her daughters, and along with them your own captivity, in order that you may bear your humiliation and feel ashamed for all that you have done when you become a consolation to them. "Your sisters, Sodom with her daughters and Samaria with her daughters, will return to their former state, and you with your daughters will also return to your former state. "As the name of your sister Sodom was not heard from your lips in your day of pride, before your wickedness was uncovered, so now you have become the reproach of the daughters of Edom and of all who are around her, of the daughters of the Philistines—those surrounding you who despise you. "You have borne the penalty of your lewdness and abominations," the LORD declares. For thus says the Lord GOD, "I will also do with you as you have done, you who have despised the oath by breaking the covenant. "Nevertheless, I will remember My covenant with you in the days of your youth, and I will establish an everlasting covenant with you. "Then you will remember your ways and be ashamed when you receive your sisters, both your older and your younger; and I will give them to you as daughters, but not because of your covenant. "Thus I will establish My covenant with you, and you shall know that I am the LORD, so that you may remember and be ashamed and never open your mouth anymore because of your humiliation, when I have forgiven you for all that you have done," the Lord GOD declares.*

In Chapter 17 of Revelation the Lord calls the woman on the beast a prostitute who rides the beast. To ride the beast is likened to riding a horse. With bit and bridle, we can use and direct a horse as a beast of burden. We can use and direct the horse's power and strength to empower ourselves while accomplishing things we could not otherwise do, by our own power. Why call her a prostitute? Because the woman is the bride of Christ, married to God, but in spiritual adultery she empowers herself by joining with the devil and the beast, using their power to rule. This woman, this great prostitute, uses and directs the power of the devil and of the beast to do her own will and bidding, instead of using the power of God, to do His will and bidding.

Both the devil and the beast have the same ordained destiny, a legacy which originates and comes out of their defiance of God. The empirical center of Babylon is referred to in the Bible as *the great city*. Micah tells us that the Empire of Babylon has been ongoing, however, it has been conquered resulting in that ordained destiny being transferred to seven different kingdoms (empires), one subduing the next. These seven different empires were originated and established by seven different kings, the first being *Nimrod*. Each one of these seven kings were driven in their hearts to conquer and rule the entire world. That drive is the spirit of the devil within them and is expressed through a human agent, making each one of those kings a type of antichrist. However, the first of those seven kings is *Nimrod*. He is the *antichrist*.

Nimrod built the Tower of Babel inventing idols, worshiping celestial beings (gods), and their physical offspring, the giants of old (demigods). He made them objects of worship out of a hatred and a rejection of the Creator who wiped them out with the flood. He was the originator of *astrology*. The whole world and every culture adopted these gods and *demigods* to worship and that we know today as mythology. However, these gods and *demigods* were real *preflood* beings that virtually ruled the earth, abusing humans while regarding them as sheep or cattle. It was *Nimrod* who invented the post-flood spiritual system of gods and *demigods* believing himself to be one of them. He seduced and forced the world to worship them. In fact, Abraham's father, Terah, was *Nimrod*s top general and in charge of imposing on his conquered people this system of worship. Terah had a shop that sold idols and made Abraham work in it. Abraham ended up destroying the idols in his father's shop.

The reason behind the pursuit of these activities was because *Nimrod* himself was a giant among men, perhaps the first in the post-flood world. This was due to the hybriding through incest of his grandparents Ham and his wife to create a clan of giants—a super race—to be the superior race to rule the world as it would repopulate. A quest that Adolf Hitler tried to accomplish as well, a master race.

Nimrod identified with those giants, seeing himself as a descendant of them who perished in the flood. This caused him to hate God for killing them. *Nimrod* saw himself as a self-proclaimed savior—a christ, protecting the people against God, who might bring about another flood because of their defiance (in his thinking). He was known for proclaiming, "do as you will, and I will protect you from Yahweh." *Nimrod* is the *antichrist.* His life's goal was to fight God in a battle and kill Him. *Nimrod* was constantly challenging and seeking out this battle, insulting and mocking God in a most blasphemous manner. He created the first urban center in an effort to rule over the people. After the destruction of the Tower of Babel which *Nimrod* had built, he was the first to defy the boundaries that God set in place when God divided up the globe, assigning territories to 70 different clans, each with their own language. *Nimrod* did so by invading his neighboring territory, Assyria. This is why *Nimrod*, from the land of Babylon (Ur), was called "the Assyrian." He settled there, making several great cities, one of which was Nineveh where he resided and made the capital of his empire.

It was he, *Nimrod*, who built the first great urban centers. This too was in defiance of God. For God wanted the people to spread out around the globe, while living in peace having their own share of land and "subdue the land." We see in Isaiah that when the Lord establishes His Kingdom on the earth, with the exception of Jerusalem, large urban centers will not be.

NIV Isa 65:17-25 *For I am about to create new heavens and a new earth; the former things shall not be remembered or come to mind. But be glad and rejoice forever in what I am creating; for I am about to create Jerusalem as a joy, and its people as a delight. I will rejoice in Jerusalem, and delight in my people; no more shall the sound of weeping be heard in it, or the cry of distress. No more shall there be in it an infant that lives but a few days, or an old person who does not live out a lifetime; for one who dies at a hundred years will be considered a youth, and one who falls short of a hundred will be considered accursed. They shall build houses and inhabit them; they shall plant vineyards and eat their fruit. They shall not build and another inhabit; they shall not plant and another eat; for like the days of a tree shall the days of my people be, and my chosen shall long enjoy the work of their hands. They shall not labor in vain, or bear children for calamity; for they shall be offspring blessed by the LORD—and their descendants as well. Before they call I will answer, while they are yet speaking I will hear. The wolf and the lamb shall feed together, the lion shall eat straw like the ox; but the serpent—its food shall be dust! They shall not hurt or destroy on all my holy mountain, says the LORD.*

It is the legacy of *Nimrod*, the *antichrist*, that the others of the seven kings and seven kingdoms have their empire. These subsequent kingdoms are the continuation of what he established. *Nimrod* will come back for seven years and reclaim his legacy only this time he will rule the entire earth. It has been ordained by God as a part of His plan for salvation of the human race that *Nimrod* will attain his quest to rule the entire earth and have his showdown with the Lord.

AMP Isa 14:24-27 *The Lord of hosts has sworn, saying, Surely, as I have thought and planned, so shall it come to pass, and as I have purposed, so shall it stand—That I will break (crush) the Assyrian in My land, and upon My mountains I will tread him underfoot. Then shall the [Assyrian's] yoke depart from [the people of Judah], and his burden depart from their shoulders. This is the [Lord's] purpose that is purposed upon the whole earth [regarded as conquered and put under tribute by Assyria]; and this is [His omnipotent] hand that is stretched out over all the nations. For the Lord of hosts has purposed, and who can annul it? And His hand is stretched out, and who can turn it back?*

Micah tells us:

AMP Mic 5:5-8 *And this [One* (the Christ/Messiah)*] shall be our peace. When the Assyrian* (as represented by the Assyrian Empire because he had long since passed) *comes into our land and treads upon our soil and in our palaces, then will we raise against him seven shepherds and eight princes among men. And they shall rule and waste the land of Assyria with the sword and the land of Nimrod within her [Assyria's own] gates. Thus shall He [the Messiah] deliver us from the Assyrian [representing the opposing powers] when he comes into our land and when he treads on our borders. Then the remnant of Jacob shall be in the midst of many peoples like dew from the Lord, like showers upon the grass which [come suddenly and] tarry not for man nor wait for the sons of men. And the remnant of Jacob shall be among the nations in the midst of many peoples like a lion among the beasts of the forest, like a young lion [suddenly appearing] among the flocks of sheep which, when it goes through, treads down and tears in pieces, and there is no deliverer.*

The Assyrian, *Nimrod* along with his father the *devil*, have been given by God the destiny of ruling the whole world ending with a final battle with the Lord over the supremacy of the earth. It is destined to be fought on His Holy Mountain (the *battle of Armageddon*). This destiny is what drives the heart of the *devil* and his *antichrist, Nimrod*. When the Assyrians invaded the land of Israel, this destiny was compelling and driving them to do so. Being utterly successful, they lastly came upon Jerusalem and laid siege to conquer this last vestige of the land of Israel. Although it was their God ordained destiny, the timing was not right according to the plan of God. Even though they had superior numbers sufficient to conquer Jerusalem, and because it was not the right time, God killed

185,000 soldiers of their army with disease, sending them back home.

To ensure the proper timing of when the Assyrian, *Nimrod*, becomes the global leader, and present in the body to fight the Lord in battle, God put in place some obstacles to impede that from happening until the ordained time, like the example mentioned above of killing 185,000 soldiers. This is also the purpose of God's decree to Micah. The empire of *Nimrod* starting in Babylon moving to Assyria is continuous from its inception until the *end times*. Only God had given the power for six other empirical kings to conquer the ones before them, to prevent them from growing to global rule, before the ordained time. The Babylonian Empire of Nebuchadnezzar defeated the Assyrian Empire, returning the *great city* back to Babylon from Nineveh. Then the Persians conquered Babylon; the Greeks conquered the Persians; the Romans conquered the Greeks; the Germanic tribes conquered Rome. Finally, the Germanic tribes and the Franks who through the plot of Pope Leo III of the Roman Catholic Church in 800AD, reinstated and revived the Roman Empire, which evolved into the Holy Roman Empire, and is the seventh kingdom of the beast.

Interesting to note that the leader or king of Germany was called, Kaiser. When translated it means Ceasar. The head of Germany first held by Charlemagne of the Franks was crowned by Pope Leo III as the Ceasar of the Holy Roman Empire. Currently and as a result, *Nimrod*'s Babylonian Empire is present in the world as the Roman Catholic Church with its leader the Pope. The city-state, the Vatican, presently serves as the *great city*. This is the last transfer of power before the 8th king, *Nimrod*, who was the first, and will come back to life because of a dastardly deed of the Pope. It is then that the *great city* will become Jerusalem. It will be then that the timing will be right for both the global dominance of *Nimrod*, the *antichrist*, with the world divided into 10 districts, and for the promised battle with the Lord because he (*Nimrod*) desires to save the people from Yahweh.

Returning to the woman who rides the beast. The beast she rides is described in the vision exactly as is the devil and the beast out of the water, which encapsulates their ordained destiny. We are even told in the book of Revelation that the colors of this woman, scarlet and purple, further identifying her as the Catholic Church, which are the colors of its leadership.

This all means her power comes from the beast and *antichrist*, not the Lord and Christ. The beast she rides and draws her power from has seven heads and crowns, we are told. The position being the authority of ruling the kings of the earth is the power of the beast. Those seven heads which represent the seven kings and kingdoms of Babylon, John is told, also represent the seven hills of Rome she sits on. This is another prophecy identifying the Roman Catholic Church as the great prostitute and the city-state, the Vatican, as the great city or center of Babylon. The seventh king and kingdom is the Pope and the Catholic or Universal Church (the Holy Roman Empire). Again, that makes "the great city" Rome, more specifically the Vatican city-state, the place where the woman sits and derives her power from.

The Pope held an authority which is above the kings. As such, the United States has always been reluctant, even set against, electing a Catholic president for fear that the Pope would yield his power through the presidency. The Church of Rome is the Holy Roman Empire. Pope Leo III revived the Roman Empire 300 years after its demise for the expressed purpose to empower the Church over the nations of the world and who he defied and rebelled against, the headquarters of Christianity, Constantinople.

Pope Leo III

Pope Leo III was a corrupt pope from the beginning. While in a Roman procession, being accused of adultery and perjury, he was attacked by some citizens who wanted to blind him and cut his tongue out. This was an effort to have him removed from the office of Pope. He was able to escape the attack and fled to the Franks, led by their king, Charlemagne. This experience made Leo painfully and fearfully aware of the fact that as Pope, he had no force to protect himself and no ability to enforce any of his authority. At the time Charlemagne was the major power in western Europe. They became allies and Charlemagne brought him back to Rome and restored him back to power as the Pope, protecting him with his military might.

Given all this, Leo hatched a plan to extend his power by taking advantage of the might of King Charlemagne of the Franks. His plan was to revive the Roman Empire, which had been deposed some 300 years earlier, by ordaining Charlemagne as Caesar and reinstating its form of government. In addition, and under the guise of unity, Leo declared all the independent countries that formed after the combined Germanic tribes conquered Rome, as now the revived Roman Empire.

On December 25, 800AD during Christmas Mass that Charlemagne was in attendance for, and to his utter shock, Pope Leo turned the Mass into an ordination and crowned Charlemagne as Caesar of the Roman Empire, which had been destroyed some 300 years earlier. Charlemagne graciously accepted the crown but left the Church in anger and was very upset, taken back by this move. However, it gave him an authority over lands that without a shot fired were now subject to him. The reason why He was so angry was that Charlemagne realized that by Leo crowning him, it made the Pope a higher authority over him.

By reviving the Roman Empire and subordinating Charlemagne and his military might as its Ceasar, the Pope of the Roman Catholic Church now became the higher but spiritual authority over both Ceasar Charlemagne and his empire. Thus, this paper lion, the powerless Pope of the Roman Church (the feet of clay), now had a subordinate military force to impose his rule over people and kingdoms (the legs of iron). Never again would people be able to disobey or attack him without consequence, as had happened to him before. The Roman Catholic Church in league with the newly revived Roman Empire now fulfilled the prophecy predicted in Nebuchadnezzar's dream of the statue and its last kingdom of the beast which was the feet made of iron mixed with clay—the Holy

Roman Empire. The only thing left before the return of Christ is for the eighth king, who was one of the seven, to appear by coming back among the living. The one who was, is not now, but will be again after he is called out of the *Abyss* and given a body by the Pope and *false prophet* of the 7th kingdom—the Holy Roman Empire.

Now in those days the center of Christendom was the city built for that purpose by Ceasar Constantine. The position called Pope in Rome was really just a bishop over that region. There were many bishops of the Catholic Church that were a Church authority over the many different regions Christianity had spread to and fell under the organized Church that Constantine helped organize and made a working structure or government out of. In those days, it was through the agreement of all the bishops that rules, ordinances, and structures were decided and set into rule. No one person ruled as a supreme leader or dictator over the Church of Christ.

As a quick note, there were many pockets of believers throughout who, even though they had bishops over them, did not subscribe to the Church structure that Constantine inspired and helped form for his own political purpose of using Christianity to unite and win the hearts and minds of his subjects. In fact, the bishops who did respond to his call were a minority. However, given the clout, the financial support, the secular authority, protection, and having been lavished with buildings, even a city to have as its capitol, this minority of bishops under the Roman government's auspices became known as the real Church, the only credible and universal authority of Christendom; "universal" is the meaning of the word "Catholic," as in the Universal Church of Christ.

The bishop of Rome, Leo, was one of this body of bishops who, in agreement, governed the organized Universal (Catholic) Church. However, after reviving the Roman Empire and becoming empowered through Charlemagne, the Pope claimed universal jurisdiction and Rome as the place of See. As a result, schisms developed between Rome and Constantinople. The body of bishops in Constantinople ordered all Latin Churches in Constantinople to be closed. In 1054 Pope Leo IX of the Roman Church exchanged excommunications with Constantinople. Both excommunicating the other.

From 800 AD on, and through the rebellion, defiance, arrogance, hunger for power, and union with the secular powers of the sixth head of the beast (the Roman Empire), Pope Leo III married the Roman Catholic Church in league with, becoming the embodiment of the *antichrist*; making the Holy Roman Empire the seventh head of the beast—the woman who rides the beast.

More irrefutable prophetic and historical proof that the Roman Catholic Church is the seventh head of the beast:

Ever since the fall of the Roman Empire, Italy and its peninsula had not been a continuous nation. Through territories given as gifts from Charlamagne, in addition to intrigue and war in his newly found power, Leo controlled and ruled, as a nation, most of central Italy which divided northern and southern Italy. The Roman Catholic Church had become a sovereign nation making the Pope a king. Daniel predicts this approximately 1,300 years before it occurred, before there was a Catholic Church:

NIV Da 7:7-8 *"After that, in my vision at night I looked, and there before me was a fourth beast—terrifying and frightening and very powerful. It had large iron teeth; it crushed and devoured its victims and trampled underfoot whatever was left. It was different from all the former beasts, and it had ten horns. "While I was thinking about the horns, there before me was another horn, a little one, which came up among them; and three of the first horns were uprooted before it. This horn had eyes like the eyes of a man and a mouth that spoke boastfully*

NIV Da 7:23-26 *"He gave me this explanation: 'The fourth beast is a fourth kingdom that will appear on earth. It will be different from all the other kingdoms and will devour the whole earth, trampling it down and crushing it. The ten horns are ten kings who will come from this kingdom. After them another king will arise, different from* the earlier ones; he will subdue three kings. He will speak against the Most High and oppress his saints and try to change the set times and the laws. The saints will be handed over to him for a time, times and half a time. "'But the court will sit, and his power will be taken away and completely destroyed forever.*

The fourth beast in Daniel's vision is the Roman Empire. The ten horns are ten kings who are the Germanic tribes that consolidated and took over the Roman Empire. It was the same kind of prophetic picture as Alexander the Great who was depicted as a goat with him being the one horn and how after his death (*his large horn was broken off*), his empire was taken over by four kings (*and in its place four prominent horns grew up toward the four winds of heaven*).

NIV Da 8:5-8 As I was thinking about this, suddenly a goat with a prominent horn between his eyes came from the west, crossing the whole earth without touching the ground. He came toward the two-horned ram (Persian Empire) *I had seen standing beside the canal and charged at him in great rage. I saw him attack the ram furiously, striking the ram and shattering his two horns* (Persians and Medes). *The ram was powerless to stand against him; the goat knocked him to the ground and trampled on him, and none could rescue the ram from his power.* <u>*The goat became very great, but at the height of his power his large horn was broken off, and in its place four prominent horns grew up toward the four winds of heaven.*</u>

In the previous case of the fourth beast who was the Roman Empire, the 10 horns had taken over the Empire. They were the combined forces of the Germanic tribes that defeated Rome. Then it says, *While I was thinking about the horns, there before me was another horn, a little one, which came up among them.* That little horn is Pope (Leo III) of the Roman Catholic Church that arose in the aftermath of power void left behind of the fourth beast. It was the Pope of the Catholic Church who changed the times, shifting the Sabbath Day from Saturday to Sunday, totally against what God had established. It was Pope Gregory who established the Gregorian

Calendar, changing the date system given to the Hebrews. Likewise, it was the Pope who changed the Ten Commandments (the Law) by eliminating one commandment and dividing another in two, in order to keep 10 of them. In addition, the office of Pope reworded one of the commandments to change the context of its meaning.

Then it continues, *and three of the first horns were uprooted before it* (the little horn). *This horn had eyes like the eyes of a man and a mouth that spoke boastfully.* These three uprooted horns by the little one became the sovereign territories of the Pope and were called the Papal States because it was not the Roman Catholic Church who became ruler over these three, but the Pope, and all the succeeding popes that have taken his seat. All of this identifies the Pope and His Church as coming up from and as the power of the fourth beast (and seventh head of the *antichrist*).

However, in Italy's effort to unite the territories of its peninsula as a sovereign nation, they warred with the Pope so that they could include central Italy, uniting the whole of the peninsula as one nation. As the war ground on, the Pope and his armies lost more and more of its Papal States to the Italians. Finally, the unification of Italy, known as the Risorgimento, culminated in the capture of Rome by Italian troops on September 20, 1870. When Italian troops succeeded in defeating the Pope and finally seized Rome, Pope Pius IX retreated to the Vatican declaring himself a "prisoner." Out of reverence towards God, the Italians stopped short of capturing the final remnants of the Papal States, the Vatican City in Rome. It was from then on, that the Pope did not take a single step outside the city for fear of being captured. It was not until February 11, 1929, when Benito Mussolini, as the Prime Minister of Italy, signed the Lateran Treaty with Pope Pius XI, establishing the Vatican City as an independent state—recognizing the Vatican as a Sovereign city-state continuing the rulership of the Pope as a king.

Although the Roman Catholic Church and its popes is to this very day considered as a representation of the authority of Christ (the Vicar of Christ) and an establishment of peace and charity, the Lord remembers all her crimes and she will be exposed for who and what she truly is—the seventh head and kingdom of the beast. In all the crimes and independent defiance and empowering herself with the spirit of the *antichrist* the Lord says:

NIV Rev 18:4-10 *Then I heard another voice from heaven say: "Come out of her, my people, so that you will not share in her sins, so that you will not receive any of her plagues; for her sins are piled up to heaven, and God has remembered her crimes. Give back to her as she has given; pay her back double for what she has done. Mix her a double portion from her own cup. Give her as much torture and grief as the glory and luxury she gave herself. In her heart she boasts, 'I sit as queen; I am not a widow, and I will never mourn.' Therefore in one day her plagues will overtake her: death, mourning and famine. She will be consumed by fire, for mighty is the Lord God who judges her. "When the kings of the earth who committed adultery with her and shared her luxury see the smoke of her burning, they will weep and mourn over her. Terrified at her torment, they will stand far off and cry: "'Woe! Woe, O great city, O Babylon, city of power! In one hour your doom has come!'*

Even before this time, the Lord warned in one of His seven letters,

NIV Rev 2:20-26 *Nevertheless, I have this against you: You tolerate that woman Jezebel, who calls herself a prophetess. By her teaching she misleads my servants into sexual immorality and the eating of food sacrificed to idols. I have given her time to repent of her immorality, but she is unwilling.* <u>*So I will cast her on a bed of suffering, and I will make those who commit adultery with her suffer intensely, unless they repent of her ways. I will strike her children dead.*</u> *Then all the churches will know that I am he who searches hearts and minds, and I will repay each of you according to your deeds. Now I say to the rest of you in Thyatira, to you who do not hold to her teaching and have not learned Satan's so-called deep secrets (I will not impose any other burden on you): Only hold on to what you have until I come. To him who overcomes and does my will to the end, I will give authority over the nations . . .*

I have this against you: You tolerate that woman Jezebel, who calls herself a prophetess. The Lord is talking to His saints, that He holds it against the congregation of the Roman Catholic Church for tolerating and being willfully blind to her sins against God and union with the *antichrist*. He further tells them, *I have given her time to repent of her immorality, but she is unwilling. <u>So I will cast her on a bed of suffering</u>, and I will make those who commit adultery with her suffer intensely, unless they repent of her ways. <u>I will strike her children dead</u>. Then all the churches will know that I am he who searches hearts and minds, and I will repay each of you according to your deeds.* This warning was fulfilled by the Black Plague spreading across all of Europe taking the lives of millions. This punishment on the Roman Church, in turn, spawned the Reformation in the aftermath. Christians and nations succeeded from under the power of the Pope in an effort to break free from the deception and power of the Holy Roman Empire. We only need to await for God to force the hand of the Pope in the near future through the *two witnesses*. They will expose him as the *false prophet* and the one who not only brings back to life *Nimrod*, the *antichrist*, to kill the two witness, but because of the proverbial cat coming out of the bag, gives up his deception and declares that anyone who does not become an apostate and instead worship the risen beast, will be put to death kicking off first the great falling away (apostasy) spoken of 2 Thessalonians 2:3, then, the *great tribulation.*

Going back to the beginning of the corruption of the Catholic Church

The Roman Church slowly became the woman who rides the beast from the times of the emperor Constantine who embraced the Church thereby making it the state religion to control the hearts and minds of its population. The church began to regarded Constantine as a declared saint, and "equal-to-the-Apostles." Since then, starting in the early 300's (AD), the Church had been empowered by (riding) the power of the legacy of the beast—the Roman Empire. From that time forward the Roman Church survived, was protected by, and had her authority enforced by the Roman Empire. The Church and the Empire began to think of themselves as the right and left arms of God. It became the Empire's job to protect and enforce the authority of the Church. The Church went along with this becoming the woman or the prostitute who rides the beast.

However, around 500 AD, right before the turn of the century, the Roman Empire was no more. 300 years later in 800 AD, Pope Leo III revived Rome and its empire in order to enforce his authority. It was then that the prostitute took things a step further. By that deed the Catholic Church became the seventh and last kingdom, and Pope Leo III (and the succeeding popes) are the seventh king—the feet of clay mixed with iron. That's why this bio starts with her riding the beast, with bit and bridle in her hands controlling the beast, committing adultery on God. Then ends with her being the great city, Babylon, she became the seventh king and kingdom who had to *remain a little while.*

In chapter 17 it says the origin of this legacy, the beast or *Nimrod*, is dead, but God has agreed to let him come back from the dead to be the 8th and final king because He has put it in his heart to utterly destroy the Church (the woman) and all the churches who follow in her footsteps. *Nimrod* will walk the earth again, it says, until he has accomplished the purposes of God—to destroy the worldly church through the *great tribulation.*

Moving forward in chapter 17 it says this about the great prostitute:

NIV Rev 17:18 *The woman you saw is the great city that rules over the kings of the earth."*

This is a tricky statement to understand in its proper context. Rome indeed is the great city, the city where the seat of the power of the beast currently resides and was when John had this vision. The great city always is the city or city-state where the seat of the power of the beast and the reigning king of the seven kings wield their power from. The great city has been Rome since the Roman Empire began and will remain Rome until the beast comes up out of the *Abyss.*

However, the above verse is not so much saying that the woman is a city and that city is Rome, thereby concluding the woman is not the worldly Church but the city of Rome. No, it is saying the woman who prostitute's herself (the Roman Catholic Church) is Babylon! She sits on the seat of the power of the beast, and that seat resides in the city of seven hills (Rome). She has become more than an adulterer, prostituting herself by climbing in bed with the beast to empower herself with, as how her bio starts out. The end of her bio tells us that in the end, she becomes that power, the seventh king and kingdom.

The Roman Catholic Church now is the seventh king of the beast! The seven heads are seven kings of which she becomes the seventh, and the heads are also seven hills upon which she sits, which is Rome (specifically, the Vatican City from the time of Pope Leo III), her place of residence and the center from which she wields her power.

NIV Rev 17:9 "*... The seven heads are seven hills on which the woman sits.*

Again, verse 9 is saying she, the great prostitute and Roman Catholic Church, has become Babylon—the Church is Babylon! She had become Babylon because she first used the power of the beast, the Roman Empire, to control the kings. Then later, she became the next king 300 years after the Empire was destroyed. To control the kings of the earth and be the authority of the entire earth is a power God granted *Nimrod*, the beast, and his legacy of seven kings. Although God has granted *Nimrod* to rule the entire globe, He has frustrated and retarded the seven kings and kingdoms from attaining full autonomy of the globe until it serves His purposes.

The Catholic Church stepped into that position and became the seventh king and kingdom on that fateful Christmas Day, December 25, 800AD, when Pope Leo III crowned king Charlemagne of the Franks, emperor of the Holy Roman Empire. Although the Germanic tribes had united to defeat the Roman Empire, afterwards they had returned to being fragmented and independent of each other. It is safe to believe that God had wiped out this empirical scourge over so many nations by a people that were not an empire, thereby relieving them from slavery and domination. It had been 300 years after its destruction that Pope Leo III organized the Germanic tribes, who had destroyed the Roman Empire, into a rebuilding of it. Since it was, he, the Pope, who revived the Rome Empire and chose to crown him, the Pope therefore became the authority over the emperor and the Holy Roman Empire he just instituted.

The Emperor Charlemagne then became subordinate to the Pope because he did not conquer and take the empire by his military might, but it was bestowed upon him by the Pope (a paper lion, one who speaks boastfully). Charlemagne immediately recognized this fact and became very angry feeling manipulated, but in the end conceded to this subordinate position.

In Review:

Pope Leo III revived the Roman Empire so as to empower and secure his own position as Pope. There were factions of the church who wanted him removed as Pope because of his adultery and perjury. He had been attacked on the streets of Rome, and his attackers attempted to cut out his tongue. Pope Leo escaped and sought refuge from Charlemagne, who through military might put him back in power over the Church. It was then that Pope Leo hatched his plan by joining the military might of Charlemagne to the Church under his recreation of the Roman Empire. He did so by crowning Charlemagne as Emperor of the Holy Roman Empire and declaring the territories of the other nations under the new Caesar. Without a single battle, Charlemagne became ruler over many nations. The Pope continues the throne and legacy of what originated from and was set into motion by the first king, *Nimrod*.

Note: It was not until some time later that the newly reformed Roman Empire was called the Holy Roman Empire. However, that is the name we are using to identify it from its inception on December 25, 800AD.

When the eighth king, who was the first (*Nimrod*), comes to take what is his ordained destiny and the legacy which he himself established, he will have to take it from the worldly church, the Catholics in particular. He will take it in the fashion that God had ordained from the beginning, how each of the 7 kingdoms were to be taken—with the sword! In each case the next king/shepherd of the seven takes that empirical throne from the previous king by destroying the former, and the empirical legacy of the beast continues through the next of the seven. It is with the sword that the risen *Nimrod* will take by force his ordained kingdom from the Church and destroy her. When he does and because the Roman Catholic Church is both the great prostitute, and the seventh head/king, it will be the *great tribulation* when he kills the elect in order to take his seat of power.

NIV Mic 5:5-6 *When the Assyrian invades our land and marches through our fortresses, <u>we will raise against him seven shepherds, even eight leaders of men. They will rule the land of Assyria with the sword, the land of Nimrod with drawn sword.</u> He will deliver us from the Assyrian when he invades our land and marches into our borders.*

After making that condemning and concluding statement at the end of chapter 17 of Revelation, it tells us that the adulterous *Church Corrupt* has become the 7th king and its organization/congregation, Babylon, with the city-state, the Vatican as the *great city*. After identifying the Roman Catholic Church as the woman who rides the beast, chapter 18 starts with the *great tribulation* and the destruction of the Church. All of *Heaven* cheers on as Babylon in the Church is destroyed. How horrific is this that God condemns the Church as being Babylon (the great city). Some may say how harsh that the authors speak that the congregation of the Roman Catholic Church are the people of Babylon. Besides God having just said it in the 18th chapter, God admonished His elect to come out of her, the Church, so that they will not share in her sins and suffer her punishment. He is calling for His elect to abandon the Church and by doing so, come out of Babylon.

NIV Rev 18:4-5 *Then I heard another voice from heaven say: "Come out of her, my people, so that you will not share in her sins, so that you will not receive any of her plagues; for her sins are piled up to heaven, and God has remembered her crimes.*

The ones who heed His admonishment will be caught up and *rapture*d the very day the *great tribulation* begins. The ones who do not heed, becoming apostates, will endure and perhaps die in the *great tribulation*.

Note: Even the reform churches, the Protestants and Lutherans and so on, have gone the way of the Catholic Church by making their kingdoms of this world. However, Jesus said His Kingdom is not of this world and it will be one which comes down from the Heavens to this world. It is only then at the ordained time, that Jesus will subdue the nations and rule the globe with an iron scepter.

AMP Rev 10:10-11:3 *So I took the little book from the angel's hand and ate and swallowed it; it was as sweet as honey in my mouth, but once I had swallowed it, my stomach was embittered. Then they said to me, You are to make a fresh prophecy concerning many peoples and races and nations and languages and kings. A REED [as a measuring rod] was then given to me, [shaped] like a staff, and I was told: <u>Rise up and measure the sanctuary of God and the altar [of incense], and [number] those who worship there. But leave out of your measuring the court outside the sanctuary of God; omit that, for it is given over to the Gentiles (the nations), and they will trample the holy city underfoot for 42 months (three and one-half years)</u>. And I will grant the power of prophecy to My two witnesses for 1,260 (42 months; three and one-half years), dressed in sackcloth.*

"You can only serve one master"

The measuring and numbering John is told to do, the measuring rod he is given to do it with, and the words he hears from the seven thunders that he is told not to write down but is to prophesize later, reveals him as one of the *two witnesses*. He is the voice of thunder along with his brother James, who was the first Apostle to be martyred by being thrown off the top of the temple—an ironic thing, especially considering they are called to perform this task. Jesus called John and his brother, the sons of thunder. Just as they wanted to call down fire on a city who did not receive Jesus, the *two witnesses* are given power to do many miraculous things including the ability to close up the sky so it does not rain, and to call down fire to consume anyone who attempts to kill them. By their testimony and prophecy, they will divide even the church as against the Christ and for the *antichrist*, or convict as true worshipers of Christ. The worshipers in the sanctuary is a metaphor for those who worship the Lord wholeheartedly and are true to Him, the *Church Pure*—the ones they are supposed to count/identify by how they receive their testimony. They will be *rapture*d at the onset of the *great tribulation*. John is further told not to measure (count) the outer court of the sanctuary. This is a metaphor representing the worldly Christians or the *Church Corrupt* that, because of the testimony of the *two witnesses*, become apostates. They are left behind and will be trampled on—martyred for 3 ½ years (the *great tribulation*).

It is important to keep in mind that when the *two witnesses* force ALL Christians (Catholic or not) to a crossroads of decision, those who support the Pope in bringing back *Nimrod* to kill them, denounce Christ, and worship the beast (*Nimrod*), are the ones who will not come out of her and then suffer the *great tribulation*. That is because the Pope and his leadership will themselves become apostates and follow the beast, while demanding under the penalty of death that all their followers fall away from Christ with them. The ones who choose to be loyal to Christ, condemning the Pope for bringing back *Nimrod*, and refuse to worship the beast, are the ones who *come out of her*, so they do not share in her sins and punishment. They will be taken up/*rapture*d so as not to endure the time of the *great tribulation*. The time of the *two witnesses* is the time of the great falling away, also known as the apostasy, that Paul tells us about in 2 Thessalonians.

Similarly, in Revelation concerning the great city:

NIV Rev 11:8 Their bodies *(*two witnesses) *will lie <u>in the street of the great city</u>, which is figuratively called Sodom and Egypt, where also their Lord was crucified.*

Earlier, the church of Rome and the Vatican City of Rome was called the great city (Babylon). In calling Jerusalem the *great city* God is now calling Jerusalem; Babylon, and a city with the same sin profile as Sodom, and Egypt. How can this be? Sodom attempted to create a giant. Egypt enslaved His people and fought against God. Now in Jerusalem the Pope calls a giant back from the *Abyss* while making a body out of the parts of men he kills. Is God contradicting Himself? No. At this point, God is calling Jerusalem, the *great city*, Babylon. It is now the seat and center or capital of the 8th kingdom of the beast—the risen *Nimrod*. Jerusalem will be Babylon, the great city where the beast, *Nimrod*, rules from when He comes back to life from among the dead, in the temple.

However, the *Church Corrupt*, particularly the Roman Catholic Church (the great prostitute and the woman who rides the beast located in Rome) is now currently Babylon, the 7th kingdom with the Pope as the 7th king and has been since Christmas Day 800 AD. The great city, the center of Babylon will move from the Vatican (the 7th kingdom) to Jerusalem (the 8th kingdom) after the last seven years of the 70-7's. Likewise, the power of the Pope (the 7th king), will shift to *Nimrod* (the 1st and 8th king of the world). He then will have to destroy the 7th and former kingdom (the Church) to establish himself as the eighth. This is destined to happen from the city of Jerusalem.

NIV Isa 14:24-27 *The LORD Almighty has sworn, "Surely, as I have planned, so it will be, and as I have purposed, so it will stand. <u>I will crush the Assyrian in my land; on my mountains</u> I will trample him down. His yoke will be taken from my people, and his burden removed from their shoulders." <u>This is the plan determined for the whole world; this is the hand stretched out over all nations.</u> For the LORD Almighty has purposed, and who can thwart him? His hand is stretched out, and who can turn it back?*

Almost 2,000 years (so far) have passed between the 69th-7, and the 70th or final 7 years. That gap between them, which we are currently in, is the *Church Age*. It is the time for Jesus to find and make a bride of *celestial* humans for Himself. Jesus needed to do so because Israel had rejected Him and their place as His bride. Going forward, the 70-7's has ended (after the coming 1-7), and the end has come. The beast has risen from the dead by coming up out of the *Abyss*. He is standing in the temple after the *false prophet* (the Pope) has given his image breath. *Nimrod* goes out and kills the *two witnesses* that the whole world wants dead but cannot kill. He succeeds, however, left lying 3 ½ days in the street, they rise to their feet from the dead. The whole world had celebrated their death and exchanged gifts, relieved after having finally been freed of the *two witnesses* and all the ways they had interrupted life with droughts and plagues like Moses did in Egypt.

Now that the *two witnesses* have come back to life, the people of the world are terrified over what they might do. However, after an undetermined but short time, there is a voice from *Heaven* which calls them up. Along with them the Holy Spirit departs from the world and brings with Him the contingency of the elect who are in union with the Holy Spirit, the *Church Pure* who did not become apostates. As they depart there is a severe earthquake causing 10% of Jerusalem to collapse, leaving 7,000 people dead. The people become in such awe and fear that they acknowledge that God is real and had done this.

Although they are all called the elect, or the Church, not all are snatched up to *Heaven* and transformed into celestial humans at this time. Those who are part of the worldly church and have taken their stand as apostates, are left behind. These verses in Revelation describe this happening:

NAS REV 14:14-16 Then I looked, and behold, a white cloud, and sitting on the cloud was one like a son of man, having a golden crown on His head and a sharp sickle in His hand (Jesus). *And another angel came out of the temple, crying out with a loud voice to Him who sat on the cloud, "Put in your sickle and reap, for the hour to reap has come, because the harvest of the earth is ripe." Then He who sat on the cloud swung His sickle over the earth, and the earth was reaped.*

There are two different harvests of the Lord's elect in the verses above and below (14:14-20). Both harvests result in being snatched up or a *rapture* of those involved. This first harvest of the elect (above) is, as it infers, a harvest of wheat. Above is Jesus sitting on a cloud with a crown on His head having been released by the Father to collect wheat for His barn. In other words, the catching up in a *rapture* those who are in union with Him, saving them from having to endure the *great tribulation*. Jesus does this personally because He is one whole person in *spiritual union* with this group. They are His body and the very expression of His own Spirit. It is said in the Bible that the Holy Spirit is in and among the saints. It is this group of people who embody His Spirit.

Another thing to take note of is Jesus patiently waits with sickle in hand. It is only when He is released by His Father (through a messenger angel) that He finally harvests His wheat. This is in line with what Jesus told us:

NIV Mt 24:36 "No one knows about that day or hour, not even the angels in heaven, nor the Son, but only the Father.

Then (below) is the second harvest, however, this is a harvest of grapes. Why grapes? Because grapes are crushed and their blood like juice spills out. This is a fitting allegory. This is again the harvest of the elect; however, these share in the guilt of and suffer the punishment of the woman who rides the beast and became the seventh king of the legacy of the beast. There are so many Christians killed during the *great tribulation* that it says their blood will create a river about 4 to 6 feet deep for 200 miles. A single human body holds about 6 quarts of blood. It boggles the imagination how many people will die in the *great tribulation* in order that enough blood would be spilled so that if it was all put in the same place, it would create a river 200 miles long, and 4 to 6 feet deep.

NAS REV 14:17-20 *And another angel came out of the temple which is in heaven, and he also had a sharp sickle. Then another angel, the one who has power over fire, came out from the altar; and he called with a loud voice to him who had the sharp sickle, saying, "Put in your sharp sickle and gather the clusters from the vine of the earth, because her grapes are ripe." So the angel swung his sickle to the earth and gathered the clusters from the vine of the earth, and threw them into the great wine press of the wrath of God.<u> And the wine press was trodden outside the city, and blood came out from the wine press, up to the horses' bridles, for a distance of two hundred miles.</u>*

This group of people will, likewise, be snatched up to meet Jesus in the sky. However, it will only happen after there is a resurrection of those who perished in the *great tribulation* but clung to their testimony in Christ, did not worship the beast, or take his mark. This is called in the book of Revelation, the *first resurrection* of the dead. Some time after they are resurrected and along with those who survive the *great tribulation*, who likewise clung to their testimony in Christ, didn't worship the beast or take his mark, will together be snatched up to meet Jesus in the sky. When this happens and like the group of wheat before them, they will transform into celestial humans. John the Baptist (below) speaks of this two-part harvest of the elect of Jesus:

NAS MT 3:11-12 *"As for me, I baptize you with water for repentance, but He who is coming after me is mightier than I, and I am not fit to remove His sandals; <u>He will baptize you with the Holy Spirit and fire.</u> "His winnowing fork is in His hand, and He will thoroughly clear His threshing floor; and <u>He will gather His wheat into the barn, but He will burn up the chaff with unquenchable fire."</u>*

He will thoroughly clear His threshing floor; this is telling us the time of the Church is complete with every single Christian accounted for and sorted through having been assigned to their eternal fate. There is no more Church left on the earth. His wheat is gathered to His barn and the chaff, the grapes, have been purified through the *great tribulation* or proven unredeemable. The only thing left is to keep His promises to the Israelites during His 1,000-year reign.

According to John, Jesus' baptism of the Holy Spirit is like the double-edged sword of Hebrews 4:12 (the Spirit words of Jesus) which cuts both ways; it will purify and save you for eternal life, but will also purify you by exposing, and convicting the thoughts and purposes of the heart. John says, he only baptizes us with water, Jesus will baptize us with the Holy Spirit and with fire. The Holy Spirit will heal and save but watch out! Unlike water, the water baptism of John's, Jesus' baptism of the Holy Spirit is powerful and pure and will test your heart through its purifying fire. Jesus is in charge of the harvest and the harvest is at hand, according to John. The wheat are those who are caught up to *Heaven*, and the chaff of the wheat which are purified in the fire are those who endure the *great tribulation*. This is the baptism of fire John the Baptist spoke of concerning Jesus! Both Jesus and Paul witness to this:

NIV Rev 3:16-22 So, because you are lukewarm—neither hot nor cold—I am about to spit you out of my mouth. You say, 'I am rich; I have acquired wealth and do not need a thing.' But you do not realize that you are wretched, pitiful, poor, blind and naked. <u>I counsel you to buy from me gold refined in the fire, so you can become rich; and white clothes to wear, so you can cover your shameful nakedness; and salve to put on your eyes, so you can see. Those whom I love I rebuke and discipline.</u> So be earnest, and repent. Here I am! I stand at the door and knock. If anyone hears my voice and opens the door, I will come in and eat with him, and he with me. To him who overcomes, I will give the right to sit with me on my throne, just as I overcame and sat down with my Father on his throne. He who has an ear, let him hear what the Spirit says to the churches."

NRSV 1Co 3:10-17 According to the grace of God given to me, like a skilled master builder I laid a foundation, and someone else is building on it. Each builder must choose with care how to build on it. For no one can lay any foundation other than the one that has been laid; that foundation is Jesus Christ. Now if anyone builds on *the foundation with gold, silver, precious stones, wood, hay, straw—<u>the work of each builder will become visible, for the Day will disclose it, because it will be revealed with fire, and the fire will test what sort of work each has done.</u> If what has been built on the foundation survives, the builder will receive a reward. <u>If the work is burned up, the builder will suffer loss; the builder will be saved, but only as through fire.</u> Do you not know that you are God's temple and that God's Spirit dwells in you? If anyone destroys God's temple, God will destroy that person. For God's temple is holy, and you are that temple.*

"It will become visible, for the Day will disclose it," is referring to the illuminating and convicting power of the Holy Spirit as each person's heart is experientially tested and proved. That fire is the coming *great tribulation*, and those who survive with their lives being burnt up are those who partake in the *first resurrection* and become the *great multitude* of celestial humans. In John, Jesus helps us understand this further:

NAS JN 3:19-21 "This is the judgment, that the Light has come into the world, and men loved the darkness rather than the Light, for their deeds were evil. "For everyone who does evil hates the Light, and does not come to the Light for fear that his deeds will be exposed. "But he who practices the truth comes to the Light, so that his deeds may be manifested as having been wrought in God."

Jesus too, likens this time to a harvest of wheat.

NIV Mt 13:24-30 Jesus told them another parable: "The kingdom of heaven is like a man who sowed good seed in his field. But while everyone was sleeping, his enemy came and sowed weeds among the wheat, and went away. When the wheat sprouted and formed heads, then the weeds also appeared. "The owner's servants came to him and said, 'Sir, didn't you sow good seed in your field? Where then did the weeds come from?' "'An enemy did this,' he replied. "The servants asked him, 'Do you want us to go and pull them up?' "'No,' he answered, 'because while you are pulling the weeds, you may root up the wheat with them. Let both grow together until the harvest. At that time I will tell the harvesters: First collect the weeds and tie them in bundles to be burned; then gather the wheat and bring it into my barn.'"

The wheat is the *Church Pure*. The weeds are the *Church Corrupt* who the *devil* planted within the Church and who will burn in the fires of the *great tribulation*. Revelation tells the Church (those who remain faithful to Jesus during the *great tribulation*) that they must endure the fires of the *great tribulation* steadfastly even onto death and they will be rewarded by becoming celestial humans:

NIV Rev 14:12-13 This calls for patient endurance on the part of the saints who obey God's commandments and remain faithful to Jesus. Then I heard a voice from heaven say, "Write: Blessed are the dead who die in the Lord from now on." "Yes," says the Spirit, "they will rest from their labor, for their deeds will follow them."

Then it says about those of the elect who endure the fires of the *great tribulation*:

NAS REV 20:4-6 Then I saw thrones, and they sat on them, and judgment was given to them. And <u>I saw the souls of those who had been beheaded because of their testimony of Jesus and because of the word of God, and those who had not worshiped the beast or his image, and had not received the mark on their forehead and on their hand; and they came to life and reigned with Christ for a thousand years.</u> The rest of the dead did not come to life until the thousand years were completed. This is the first resurrection. Blessed and holy is the one who has a part in the first resurrection; over these the second death has no power, but they will be priests of God and of Christ and will reign with Him for a thousand years.

And again:

1Th 4:15-17 For this we declare to you by the Lord's [own] word, that we who are alive and remain until the coming of the Lord shall in no way precede [into His presence] or have any advantage at all over those who have previously fallen asleep [in Him in death]. For the

Lord Himself will descend from heaven with a loud cry of summons, with the shout of an archangel, and with the blast of the trumpet of God. <u>And those who have departed this life in Christ will rise first. Then we, the living ones who remain [on the earth], shall simultaneously be caught up along with [the resurrected dead] in the clouds to meet the Lord in the air;</u> and so always (through the eternity of the eternities) we shall be with the Lord!

When it comes to the Church, both the *Church Pure* and the *Church Corrupt*, they will be caught up and *raptured*, they are the bride of Christ that He woos for over 2,000 years. Whether it is the:

- *Church Pure* who is caught up before the fires of the *great tribulation*
- Or the *Church Corrupt* who endure the *great tribulation* and are caught up after it is finished
- Or those who die during the *great tribulation* and partake in the *first resurrection* rising back to life and then are caught up along with those who did not die and are *raptured* to *Heaven*.

The whole Church is accounted for, and they are all caught up and given a celestial body so they can rule the world and its mortal humans for 1,000 years with Jesus from the New Jerusalem.

Although both the *Church Pure* and the *Church Corrupt* have the same destination and relationship with Christ in the New Jerusalem, there is a great advantage to being part of the *Church Pure* and avoiding the pain of death and the fires of the *great tribulation*. If only the thought of having to live life without the Holy Spirit within one's heart for 3 ½ years while living in a world God has turned His face away from, makes it important, even urgent, to be on the right side of things. As a result, these two questions suddenly become important:

- What does it mean to be in union with Christ?
- How did the worldwide Church get so far away from God that they actually became Babylon?

The next chapter will be devoted to these questions.

CHAPTER SIX

What is Spiritual Union with Christ?

AMP Gal 3:27 For as many [of you] as were baptized into Christ [into a spiritual union and communion with Christ, the Anointed One, the Messiah] <u>have put on (clothed yourselves with) Christ.</u>

". . . (clothed yourselves with) Christ." This is an interesting statement concerning *spiritual union* with Christ. Jesus said to the church in Laodicea:

WEB Rev 3:17-18 Because you say, 'I am rich, and have gotten riches, and have need of nothing,' and don't know that you are the wretched one, miserable, poor, blind, and <u>naked</u>; I counsel you to buy from me gold refined by fire, that you may become rich; and white garments, <u>that you may clothe yourself, and that the shame of your nakedness may not be revealed;</u> and eye salve to anoint your eyes, that you may see.

With the finest clothes, Jesus calls these Christians naked. The next highlighted part says, *that you may clothe yourself, and that the shame of your nakedness may not be revealed*; He is saying that we should clothe ourselves with Christ, so that on the day we die the shame of our nakedness may not be revealed. The shame of our nakedness being revealed, is us being in a state of death where we have become a disembodied soul. Meaning, our *soul* is no longer clothed with a body.

However, if we clothe ourselves with Christ, even before our head hits the ground, we will never taste death (disembodiment) but be clothed with a celestial body; absent from our natural body before our heart stops beating. Therefore, we never even taste death or experience it. However, if we are not clothed with Christ, we are told above, the shamefulness of being found dead, a disembodied soul, will be our state of being until the last day. At which time we will once again be clothed with a body, having been resurrected from being dead, so that we may face God and be judged.

To say that we are clothed with Christ is a very curious statement that Jesus and Paul make. This is because Jesus is currently in the earth as a disembodied Spirit—the Holy Spirit. We, the Church—His bride—who are in *spiritual union* with Him, are His embodiment, His clothes, in the world. We are the body of Christ, if we live to carry out His promptings and not live out our own desires. In other words, technically He, the Spirit of Christ, is clothed with us. We are the body of His Spirit in the world; that is, we who are in union with Him. Paul sums up how this would make sense in his statement:

NAS GAL 2:19-20 *"For through the Law I died to the Law, so <u>that I might live to God.</u> "I have been crucified with Christ; and it is no longer I who live, but Christ lives in me; and the life which I now live in the flesh I live by faith in the Son of God, who loved me and gave Himself up for me.*

NIV Gal 3:26-27 *You are all sons of God through faith in Christ Jesus, for all of you who were baptized into Christ have clothed yourselves with Christ.*

When it says, "it is no longer I who live, but Christ lives in me; and the life which I now live in the flesh I live by faith. . ." it verifies that our flesh is the embodiment of the Spirit of Christ. As Paul would say, we are the temple of God. But to say, "the life I live in the flesh I live by faith," is to say that even though my flesh is still alive, my life in the flesh I have forfeited and give it over to the expression of the Spirit of Christ. Therefore, what you now see me living out is no longer my life, my choices and desires, but His. Make no mistake about it, in spite of the fact that my flesh didn't die, and I look and sound the same (with the same soul/personality), what has expression through the works and words of my flesh is not what I desire. It is instead the expression of the Holy Spirit in me. So, it's true it is no longer I who live, but Christ in me—I have died to my life in the body.

If this is true and we yield to the Spirit promptings of Christ, giving our flesh over to the expression of His Spirit, then it is His Spirit which animates us. Our life in the flesh is now His, given as a gift to Him. This makes it the case that our soul, our personality and mind, are clothed with Christ. When it says, *to be clothed with Christ* it is to be in union with Christ. The two phrases are both synonymous and literal. Listen again to what Galatians says about being clothed with Christ:

NIV Gal 3:26 *You are all sons of God through faith in Christ Jesus*

NIV Gal 4:6 *Because you are sons, God sent the Spirit of his Son into our hearts, the Spirit who calls out, "Abba, Father."*

NIV Gal 3:27 *for all of you who were baptized into Christ have clothed yourselves with Christ*

What these verses (above) are saying is that if we are baptized into Christ, we have become sons of God just as Christ is. And if we are sons of God, God sends the Spirit of His Son, Jesus' own Spirit, into our hearts. Because Jesus is God's Son, when we are given His Spirit, we too become God's Son, spiritually speaking. That Spirit that He gives us cries out from our hearts, *Abba, Father*. Because of this, we are reconciled to God. This is due to the fact that from the bottom of our hearts, the Spirit within us sincerely and rightfully both perceives and longs for God as our Father. It is an honest, sincere, and actual cry from within us that already knows God as our Father; because it is the Spirit of His Son which has become our Spirit—the Spirit within us. This is in contrast to our human spirit, our sin nature, which identifies with and strives to be independent from God, to be a law unto ourselves, free to do our own will.

As a result of us becoming sons in the truest sense, from that deepest place in our hearts which is beyond words, verse 27 says, *we have put on Christ*. In other words, we have clothed ourselves with Christ.

So when we die to our lives in the body and decide when we wake up in the morning, that today I commit to giving expression to His Spirit in me, following every prompting, doing what He says to do and speaking what He says to say, that means today we die to our own lives in the body, and come alive in Him. When we do this and follow through in our commitment, we have put on Christ, we have clothed ourselves with Christ. Our body is the temple of God. The Spirit of Christ is embodied by our flesh and the work that He wants done, gets done through our lives in the body.

NAS EZE 16:7-14 *"I made you numerous like plants of the field. Then you grew up, became tall and reached the age for fine ornaments; your breasts were formed and your hair had grown. Yet you were naked and bare. "Then I passed by you and saw you, and <u>behold, you were at the time for love; so I spread My skirt over you and covered your nakedness. I also swore to you and entered into a covenant with you so that you became Mine,"</u> declares the Lord GOD. "Then I bathed you with water, washed off your blood from you and anointed you with oil. "I also clothed you with embroidered cloth and put sandals of porpoise skin on your feet; and I wrapped you with fine linen and covered you with silk. <u>"I adorned you with ornaments, put bracelets on your hands and a necklace around your neck. "I also put a ring in your nostril, earrings in your ears and a beautiful crown on your head. "Thus you were adorned with gold and silver, and your dress was of fine linen, silk and embroidered cloth. You ate fine flour, honey and oil; so you were exceedingly beautiful and advanced to royalty.</u> "Then your fame went forth among the nations on account of your beauty, for it was perfect because of My splendor which I bestowed on you," declares the Lord GOD.*

In making that commitment when we awake in the morning means we have put on Christ for that day. Since the spiritual is invisible to the natural when we clothe ourselves with Christ, the people in the world will not see our garment of His Spirit. The people we know will think they know us, and who we are, and judge us according to our past. However, it's not us who they speak with and judge. It is not us who decides what we do and say to them. It is Him who we have committed to clothe ourselves with when we rose up from our bed. Since we have put on the invisible nature of Christ, with their natural eyes and natural ears it is Him they unwittingly speak with and judge as being the same old person we formerly were, however, in reality we are not.

NIV Jn 17:20-23 "*My prayer is not for them alone. I pray also for those who will believe in me through their message, that all of them may be one, Father, just as you are in me and I am in you. May they also be in us so that the world may believe that you have sent me. I have given them the glory that you gave me, that they may be one as we are one: I in them and you in me. May they be brought to complete unity to let the world know that you sent me and have loved them even as you have loved me.*

When we are in union with Christ, we are in Him (meaning we are clothed with Him) and He is in us (meaning He is clothed with our body). When we are clothed with Him, we are not naked, and we will not be caught shamefully naked when our bodies die. We will find ourselves before the throne of both the Father and the Son, clothed in a celestial body; which is never subject to death for eternity.

NIV Rev 7:15-17 *Therefore, "they are before the throne of God and serve him day and night in his temple; and he who sits on the throne will spread his tent over them. Never again will they hunger; never again will they thirst. The sun will not beat upon them, nor any scorching heat. For the Lamb at the center of the throne will be their shepherd; he will lead them to springs of living water. And God will wipe away every tear from their eyes."*

Never again will they hunger; never again will they thirst. The sun will not beat upon them, nor any scorching heat. This is the case because they no longer have a natural body of flesh but a celestial body which is not subject to the natural elements.

NIV Ge 2:24 *For this reason a man will leave his father and mother and be united to his wife, and they will become one flesh.*

Surprisingly, what it said in Genesis (above) was prophetic and could not be fully attained until Christ came. Union, or a marriage between a natural man and a natural woman does not truly result in the two becoming one flesh. There are two people with two bodies of flesh having between them, two different lives. After they come together in marital union, God does reconcile the two as having one life in the flesh and no longer two.

When a couple gets married, they give up their individual goals and aspirations, and through their love for each other they begin a single common life. The two work for a common goal, and what they both do provides, nurtures, and perpetuates this common life they now share. She may stay home and manage the house they share and care for the children, instead of spending her time living for herself. He may go out to work, but his earnings are now devoted to their common life and not his individual enrichment. Both their agendas and plans are made for the promotion of their common life and no longer to please their individual selves. They have one life between them and God has reconciled the two as only having one life in the flesh, although they have two bodies.

Paul tells us that should one of them die, the other is released from that common life and is free to go into marital union with another.

NIV Ro 7:2-3 For example, by law a married woman is bound to her husband as long as he is alive, <u>but if her husband dies, she is released from the law of marriage</u>. So then, if she marries another man while her husband is still alive, she is called an adulteress. But if her husband dies, she is released from that law and is not an adulteress, even though she marries another man.

This is not the case when it comes to *spiritual union* with Christ. In fact, *spiritual union* cannot even occur until one of the two dies to His body. In the case of marital union between a man and a woman, it is two people, two bodies, and one life. If one of the two bodies die, then the other is no longer bound by their union. In the case of *spiritual union*, it does not end when one dies, the fact is that it does not begin until one dies.

In *spiritual union* with Christ, there are two individuals, one body, and one life. He dies to His body and becomes a disembodied Spirit in the earth. We die to our life in our body of flesh and voluntarily give expression to His Spirit through our body of flesh, instead of our own desires. After coming into union, we do not do or say what we want or plan, but what He prompts us to do or say.

NIV 1Co 14:32 *The spirits of prophets are subject to the control of prophets.*

Unlike our bondage to sin, we do not do what the Holy Spirit compels us to do out of a slavery or addiction, having little control over ourselves, like with sin. In union with Christ, it is an expression of freedom on our part and an act of love when we voluntarily speak and act out the promptings of the Holy Spirit in preference to our own feelings and desires (as an independent person). The more we are obedient to the Spirit's promptings in us, the more we are bound as one whole person to the One we love, Jesus. Our life in the flesh is no longer our own, but we are living out His Spirit expressions and will. Our will has become to do His will. This is the nature of *spiritual* (marital) *union*.

In the case of *spiritual union* with Christ, the verse in Genesis finally becomes true! The two become one flesh. Two individuals (souls/minds/personalities/wills) not only share one life which has been reconciled by God as such but go further and share only one flesh—one life in one body, which also is reconciled by God as such. Again, unlike marriage in the world that ends when one of the two dies, *spiritual union* does not begin until one dies, Christ. In union with Christ, the two actually become one whole person and no longer two different individuals. The two become one!

AMP 2Co 3:17-18 *Now the Lord is the Spirit, and where the Spirit of the Lord is, there is liberty (emancipation from bondage, freedom). And all of us, as with unveiled face, [because we] continued to behold [in the Word of God] as in a mirror the glory of the Lord, are constantly being transfigured into His very own image in ever increasing splendor and from one degree of glory to another; [for this comes] from the Lord [Who is] the Spirit.*

Spiritual union with Christ is the plan of God to save us from the judgement and destruction of the earth and everything in it, which has already been determined.

This message and understanding was lost as early as before the end of the first-century. Even during the time of the Reformation if one was to claim that he was one with God or Christ, that person would be burned at the stake or killed as a heretic in a most cruel and painful manner. Still yet, some would have their tongue cut out or a hole burned through it with a red-hot poker, so you could never talk again and speak such things. To make yourself equal with God by claiming to be one with Him was considered a heinous blasphemy which was unforgivable. However, even though there is the union which makes the two individuals one whole person together, Christ is still the head and we, as a part of that union, are the body and the bodily expression of our head. To act as an individual without honoring the will of God within is to be in spiritual adultery. Jesus says about this:

AMP Rev 2:2-5 I know your industry and activities, laborious toil and trouble, and your patient endurance, and how you cannot tolerate wicked [men] and have tested and critically appraised those who call [themselves] apostles (special messengers of Christ) and yet are not, and have found them to be impostors and liars. I know you are enduring patiently and are bearing up for My name's sake, and you have not fainted or become exhausted or grown weary. But I have this [one charge to make] against you: that <u>you have left (abandoned) the love that you had at first [you have deserted Me, your first love]</u>. Remember then from what heights you have fallen. Repent (change the inner man to meet God's will) and do the works you did previously [when first you knew the Lord], or else I will visit you and remove your lampstand from its place, unless you change your mind and repent.

Paul says about our state of being in union that we have put on or clothed ourselves with Christ. Look at the following verses and see the Biblical significance of such a statement:

Amp Rev 7:15-16 *. . . He Who is sitting upon the throne will protect and <u>spread His tabernacle (tent) over and shelter them with His presence.</u> They shall hunger no more, neither thirst any more; neither shall the sun smite them, nor any scorching heat.*

NAS EZE 16:8 *"Then I passed by you and saw you, and behold, you were at the time for love; <u>so I spread My skirt over you and covered your nakedness.</u> I also swore to you and entered into a covenant with you so that you became Mine," declares the Lord GOD.*

NIV Ru 3:7-11 *When Boaz had finished eating and drinking and was in good spirits, he went over to lie down at the far end of the grain pile. Ruth approached quietly, uncovered his feet and lay down. In the middle of the night something startled the man, and he turned and discovered a woman lying at his feet. "Who are you?" he asked. "I am your servant Ruth," she said. <u>"Spread the corner of your garment over me, since you are a kinsman-redeemer."</u> "The LORD bless you, my daughter," he replied. "This kindness is greater than that which you showed earlier: You have not run after the younger men, whether rich or poor. And now, my daughter, don't be afraid. I will do for you all you ask.*

When Ruth asked Boaz to spread the corner of his garment over her, she literally was asking him to marry her. Boaz did what she had asked and indeed they got married. To give these verses even more context and significance let's look at the following verse:

NAS LEV 18:7-8 *'You shall not uncover the nakedness of your father, that is, the nakedness of your mother. She is your mother; you are not to uncover her nakedness. 'You shall not uncover the nakedness of your father's wife; it is your father's nakedness.*

In the Old Testament when it is said to uncover the nakedness of someone, it means to have sexual intercourse with their wife. We can see by how most translations do not interpret this verse literally, word for word, but translate its meaning. Here below are how many translations of the Bible translate the same verse above:

NIV Lev 18:7-8 *"'Do not dishonor your father by having sexual relations with your mother. She is your mother; do not have relations with her.* *"'Do not have sexual relations with your father's wife; that would dishonor your father.*

To cover someone with your robe is the same as asking their hand in marital union, for the two to become one. Paul said as a result:

NAS EPH 5:28-30 *So husbands ought also to love their own wives as their own bodies.* <u>*He who loves his own wife loves himself;*</u> *for no one ever hated his own flesh, but nourishes and cherishes it, just as Christ also does the church, because we are members of His body.*

The man is the covering, and the woman is the one who is clothed with her husband. Afterwards they are one. In light of that, to see a man's wife naked or to have sex with her is to see her husband's nakedness, because God has reconciled them as one, according to His word and His view. His word and view are actually reality! What a romantic and poetic view to see union as the two becoming one, and for the head to clothe or spread his robe to cover his bride as him doing so for his very own body. Then, to understand this gesture as a marriage or as a commitment to a marital union, we can understand our life in union with Christ in the way the Lord beholds it! Because in the spiritual realm it is not just a romantic or poetic metaphor, but a reality. Therefore, when it says that God covered us with His skirt to cover our nakedness, He is choosing to become in union, or married to us just as Boaz did for Ruth. And we are becoming one with Him—clothed with Him.

To cover with our robe as a sign of marriage is indeed a poetic gesture, a romantic symbol of a desire to have one life together in a natural marriage. When we do as Paul asks (above) concerning our wives, God does reconcile the two as one. This again reflects that the *two become one flesh* in this fashion, however, it is not literal in the physical realm, there are still two bodies of flesh in this type of union.

This is just like when the Israelites made animal sacrifices to atone for sin, and they were declared ceremonially clean. It was not until Jesus came and sacrificed His life as a sin offering that we were actually and literally cleansed of our sin. It is the same with natural marriage. Natural marital union may bind us together, reconciling us in the eyes of God as being one in spirit, having a single life together. We know this because if one of the two dies, they are no longer bound by their marital union. The one who survives is free to marry another. For the two to become one flesh does not have its actual and literal manifestation until we become one whole person with the One who died to His body of flesh, so we can become *one flesh* in the body. In a physical marriage there are two bodies, one life, and when one dies, the other is released. In a spiritual marriage, the union does not even begin until the One dies and they together become *one flesh*. Since through our faithfulness and obedience, our body is moved by His Spirit, then by nature, He is the head, and we are the body. This (spiritual) type of union transcends the physical and is eternal.

In the Ephesians verses above, Paul calls husbands to love and nurture their wives *as* their very own body just as Christ loves the Church. In saying this, he is pointing out that because you are in marital union, that to neglect your wife is tantamount to neglecting the needs of your very own body. Continuing, Paul points out that no one neglects the needs of his very own body, for that would make one miserable and in constant pain. No, we instead nourish, comfort, and cherish our body doing everything in our power to preserve it and make it comfortable. Paul requires of us that we do the same for our wives who have their own body of flesh in this type of union.

Now think about this, Paul tells us to love this way; as Christ does His body, the members of His Church. Since in the case of *spiritual union* with Christ, we are actually and literally one flesh with Jesus, He would be hating, neglecting, or despising Himself, causing self-inflicting pain if He were not to nurture His body, the Church. No, He loves and nurtures and cherishes His body of which our body of flesh is His body. He does not nurture and cherish us *as* His own body, He nurtures and cherishes us because we *are* His body! Accordingly, those verses end with, *because we are members of His body*. This means that on the day of Pentecost, Jesus returned to the earth, not in the body of Jesus, but in the bodies of His believers who possess and obey His Holy Spirit within them. Ironically, the powers at be tried to stop Him by killing Him, thinking they had gotten rid of Him. However, instead, they succeeded in making Him manifest in millions of bodies, the believers He is one whole person with. This is a literal spiritual phenomenon that the world does not understand. So, when you read in the Bible, and it makes a statement like this:

NIV Rev 12:5 She gave birth to a son, a male child, who will rule all the nations with an iron scepter. And her child was snatched up to God and to his throne.

With the child being Jesus and us being His body, it means we get snatched up to God and to His throne. This is most definitely a reference to the *rapture*!

In the midst of your pain, sorrow, or needs, have you ever felt alone in your misery? Did you ever question where Jesus was while you are going through it all? In our overwhelming agony it is difficult at best, to have a sense of it, however, if you are in *spiritual union* with Jesus, the answer is, He is right there with you! He is going through every painful and agonizing moment with you, not as a friend or husband who holds your hand in sympathy, but experiencing it in His own body as you, because the two of you are actually and literally *one flesh*.

Understanding covering and nakedness in this way gives an entirely different context to the following verses about Ham, the son of Noah:

NIV Ge 9:22-25 Ham, the father of Canaan, <u>saw his father's nakedness</u> and told his two brothers outside. But Shem and Japheth took a garment and laid it across their shoulders; then they walked in backward and covered their father's nakedness. Their faces were turned the other way so that they would not see their father's nakedness. When Noah awoke from his <u>wine and found out what his youngest son had done to him,</u> he said, <u>"Cursed be Canaan!</u>

Here are a few things to consider in interpreting this:

- It says three times *his father's nakedness*, why doesn't at least one of these occasions call Noah by name? Because it's not referring to Ham doing something to Noah but to his wife.
- Why does the story start with, *Ham, <u>the father of Canaan</u>, saw his father's nakedness?* Why not simply say Ham saw his father's nakedness? Because Noah's wife had a child as a result of Ham having sex with his mother, while Noah was drunk and passed out.
- The word, done, is significant because it says when Noah found out what his youngest son (Ham) had *done*, he used the word *done,* not what his youngest son had seen. If all that happened was that he saw Noah naked, then it was something he had seen, not something he had done. And after it says what Ham had, *done*, to his father, Noah says cursed be Canaan. Noah is not cursing Ham for what he had done (had sex with his mother), but he is cursing Canaan, the child his wife had borne that was not his but his son's (Ham), remember, this narrative starts out with, *Ham the father of Canaan saw His father's nakedness*.
- It should be further noted that this story starts out with:

NAS GE 9:18-19 Now the sons of Noah who came out of the ark were Shem and Ham and Japheth; and <u>Ham was the father of Canaan</u>. These three were the sons of Noah, and from these the whole earth was populated.

Why take this occasion to mention that Canaan was the son of Ham if he wasn't a son of Noah, especially considering they do not mention Ham's other children or the children of his other sons, Shem, or Japheth? Furthermore, why mention Canaan there when Chapter 10 which immediately follows, begins with the genealogy of the sons of Noah?

According to the other verses we went over, it would say of this story that Noah got drunk, passed out, and Ham came in his tent and had sex with his own mother—Noah's wife. This would make sense considering how severe this event is beheld. It doesn't make sense if all Ham did was notice his father was drunk and naked, then mock about it to his brothers. That would seem more like Noah's wrongdoing than Ham's. But for Ham to take advantage of Noah's drunken state, go in his tent and have sex with his mother, while Noah is passed out drunk, then brag about it to his brothers, this would be a wrongdoing on Ham's part. This is far worse than any wrong doing on Noah's part by getting drunk, and being naked in his own tent (in his own private bedroom).

These verses started giving context to this story by saying Canaan is the son of Ham, and end with Noah cursing Canaan for what Ham had done. Even before that, when it gave a list of the sons of Noah, Canaan was included in that list. It is therefore reasonable to believe Canaan is being called a son of Noah, or better said, a stepson, the son of his wife whose real father was Ham. To curse Canaan for what Ham had done and if it was only to see his father's nakedness and mock it, doesn't seem reasonable. However, for Noah to eventually find out that his son Ham had sex with his wife, then realize the baby she had is Ham's and not his own, this is a very good reason to curse the child his wife borne, because it was not his own and was born outside of their marriage. All this makes the meaning of having our nakedness being clothed by a husband or by Christ, gives us so much more of an ability to understand the meaning of scripture.

Now when Jesus said:

AMP Rev 3:17-18 *For you say, I am rich; I have prospered and grown wealthy, and I am in need of nothing; and you do not realize and understand that you are wretched, pitiable, poor, blind, and naked. Therefore I counsel you to purchase from Me gold refined and tested by fire, that you may be [truly] wealthy, and white clothes to clothe you and to keep the shame of your nudity from being seen, and salve to put on your eyes, that you may see.*

He means we are not faithful to Him—we are not clothed with Him, we are actually in adultery while in union with Him. When we die to our body, we will be like everyone else on earth and become dead—a naked or disembodied soul. When Jesus said, *I counsel you to buy from me gold refined by fire, that you may become rich; and white garments, that you may clothe yourself, and that the shame of your nakedness may not be revealed*; He is saying that we would do well to be in union with Him and then we will never be disembodied and shamefully shown as a disembodied soul—naked, proving our relationship with Christ was merely a pretense—a false persona. With the salve for our eyes that He offers next, seeing spiritually and not superficially, we would also see the truth about the condition and fate of those who are alive in the world. This all comes about through being in union with Him.

The following will help us further understand spiritual nakedness.

In ancient Jewish writings it says that Adam and Eve were made by God naked out of the dust of the earth but were clothed in light reflecting their high spiritual stature and nature. When they had sinned against God, becoming in rebellion separated from Him, they lost their Heavenly stature and their covering of spiritual light. It was then that they knew they were naked—a spiritual nakedness, that is—a nakedness of the soul. The Bible agrees with this Heavenly stature when in Revelation it describes Eve as:

NIV Rev 12:1 *". . . a woman clothed with the sun . . ."*

It was then when they sinned that they were no longer clothed by the light of God's spiritual power which gave them Heavenly stature, authority, and protection. Thus, they became self-conscious and painfully aware of the loss of both their covering by God and their Heavenly stature. So in their shameful spiritual nakedness (as Jesus described above), they felt so vulnerable and exposed they did the only thing they could, they covered their natural bodies from the shame and vulnerability they felt in their souls.

However, it did not help much because when God came into the garden to be with them, they hid because they knew they were naked and felt very exposed. Something important to take note of is that they already had sewn coverings for their physical nakedness. In spite of that fact, they were ashamed and hid in the bushes and said they were afraid because they were naked, yet they had clothes on.

WEB Gen 3:7-10 Their eyes were opened, and they both knew that they were naked. <u>They sewed fig leaves together, and made coverings for themselves</u>. They heard Yahweh God's voice walking in the garden in the cool of the day, and the man and his wife hid themselves from the presence of Yahweh God among the trees of the garden. Yahweh God called to the man, and said to him, "Where are you?" The man said, "I heard your voice in the garden, and <u>I was afraid, because I was naked; so I hid myself.</u>"

It was said that after the reality of no longer being clothed in light and possessing the spiritual stature and authority they were originally clothed in, they then experienced the scorching heat of the sun during the day, and the cold of the night. They began to fear the night because previously, the spiritual light that came out from within them kept them full of light and safe from the blackness of the dark, and the coldness of separation from God.

This is an important point. God has no problem with natural nudity, He actually made us that way (we temper this by saying as long as the nudity is not serving sin). It is spiritual nakedness which reflects the rebellion, separation, and independence from God that He has a problem with. Spiritual nakedness not only makes Adam and Eve vulnerable and more subject to the natural elements, it means they are willfully free from God's rule and spiritual sustenance. The reason God gave them coverings of skin was because they lost their covering of light. It was painful for Adam and Eve to be so exposed to the point they could not stand before God and have relationship with Him. Even though they had rebelled against Him, God still wanted to have a relationship with them and to work out their reunion with Him—their salvation.

We are so superficial and naturally-minded that we don't understand or even have a sense of our spiritual nakedness, not being clothed with God's spiritual light. As such, we make the whole issue of nakedness about the natural body, thereby missing the whole point. That's why Jesus also said, at the same time, that we are blind. Again, He is not talking about natural blindness but blind to the spiritual. In the same way, He is talking to people who are financially affluent (rich), yet He is telling them that they are spiritually impoverished. If He was talking about being physically blind, and being financially impoverished, then in that case He would also be talking about being physically naked. But as it is, He is saying that we are in a spiritually miserable state; impoverished spiritually; spiritually blind; and spiritually naked. We are completely ignorant and unaware of what Adam and Eve were so painfully aware of when, in fear and trembling, they hid in the bushes. It is a terrible statement about us that we are in a state that He would say to His Church:

WEB REV 3:16-18 So, because you are lukewarm, and neither hot nor cold, I will vomit you out of my mouth. Because you say, 'I am rich, and have gotten riches, and have need of nothing,' and <u>don't know that you are the wretched one, miserable, poor, blind, and naked;</u> I counsel you <u>to buy from me gold refined by fire, that you may become rich; and white garments, that you may clothe yourself, and that the shame of your nakedness may not be revealed;</u> and eye salve to anoint your eyes, that you may see.

We, contemporary Christians, think we are so spiritual and in right standing with God. What Adam and Eve were so painfully aware of and caused them to tremble and hide and cover in some manner—any manner—Jesus notes that we are oblivious to. As His Church, we make it about the natural body and outward appearances.

WEB LUKE 12:22-23 *He said to his disciples, "Therefore I tell you, don't be anxious for your life, what you will eat, nor yet for your body, what you will wear. Life is more than food, and the body is more than clothing.*

We must face the truth; our current state of spiritual nakedness is the new normal. It feels normal to us that which sent Adam and Eve running to hide realizing that to cover that body—the superficial—did nothing towards covering their nakedness of the soul. Jesus says that this is a wretched and pitiful state that we are so bankrupt spiritually and are blind to. Our sight has dropped from the spiritual, to the natural.

We are blind to the spiritual and now make every concern about the body and behavior. We continue the mistake Adam and Eve made, thinking if we just cover the body, we will no longer be naked in our soul. We cover the body, and we think we have solved the problem of spiritual nakedness. We create a pretentious persona and think we have covered the darkness and misery of our soul. Then we believe the outward persona we have invented about ourselves and in doing so, delude ourselves of our true state of being. However, and because of this mindset, we are oblivious to the fact that our souls have no covering from God. As a result, we have become superficial, and we look only to the things of the natural as to what the problems are and what needs to be remedied—the outward appearance of following God. Those who comprise the *Church Pure* are as the woman was seen, clothed with the sun, with the light of the Spirit of Jesus shining from the inside out.

Those who clothed themselves with the light of Jesus' Spirit actually have exposed by that Spirit, everything in their soul which is not of or in union with Him. This is why it is said that the word of God is sharper than a double-edged sword; it cuts both ways. That is the nature of the light which clothes them. It is a painful process to see this self-knowledge. As each conflicting idea about self and life comes up as a result, it gives us opportunity to acknowledge our false perception that leads to sin and repent, thereby deciding to change.

Conversely, to clothe oneself with darkness is to cover with the superficial, to cover the physical nakedness. With lies and darkness, in denial, we cover our soul, so we do not feel vulnerable like Adam and Eve did after they sinned. Having been on both sides, they felt the huge contrast of light and darkness and it disturbed them greatly causing them to hide and cover their bodies.

Clothing ourselves with darkness and lies keeps us in denial or blind to our sin (our unrighteousness), and our rebellious independence from God. This darkness resides in our soul because of the corrupt nature of the human spirit. The human spirit was made corrupt by the sin of Adam and Eve. Our human spirit causes our mind, which is our soul, to perceive life in a light that is, as James calls it, *false to the truth*. By nature, we do not want to see the sin in ourselves and therefore avoid being convicted by our own conscience. Then blind and naked and spiritually bankrupt, we feel normal. Like a "basically good person," totally self-righteous, completely ignorant of our true spiritual condition. Unwittingly, this is the type of religion the contemporary Church practices and thinks will save them. This idea is fundamentally wrong, as Jesus pointed out above, and will leave us short of the mark to be in union with Christ and therefore be saved.

AMP Jn 3:17-21 For God did not send the Son into the world in order to judge (to reject, to condemn, to pass sentence on) the world, but that the world might find salvation and be made safe and sound through Him. He who believes in Him [who clings to, trusts in, relies on Him] is not judged [he who trusts in Him never comes up for judgment; for him there is no rejection, no condemnation—he incurs no damnation]; but he who does not believe (cleave to, rely on, trust *in Him) is judged already [he has already been convicted and has already received his sentence] because he has not believed in and trusted in the name of the only begotten Son of God. [He is condemned for refusing to let his trust rest in Christ's name.] The [basis of the] judgment (indictment, the test by which men are judged, the ground for the sentence) lies in this: <u>the Light has come into the world, and people have loved the darkness rather than and more than the Light, for their works (deeds) were evil. For every wrongdoer hates (loathes, detests) the Light, and will not come out into the Light but shrinks from it, lest his works (his deeds, his activities, his conduct) be exposed and reproved. But he who practices truth [who does what is right] comes out into the Light; so that his works may be plainly shown to be what they are—wrought with God [divinely prompted, done with God's help, in dependence upon Him].</u>*

. . . he who does not believe (cleave to, rely on, trust in Him) is judged already [he has already been convicted and has already received his sentence] because he has not believed in and trusted in the name of the only begotten Son of God. [He is condemned for refusing to let his trust rest in Christ's name. What this is telling us is that humanity has already been judged and condemned for the second time, first it was with water and soon the second will be with fire. God saved eight on the ark from the flood, however, that did not save their souls from their inherent corrupt human spirit, and they started over again led by sin. As such, all of humanity and the world they live in has been condemned to melt and burn in the heat of the *lake of fire*. However, on this occasion of judgment, numbers beyond counting throughout history all the way up to the end will be saved. They will be saved from the fire by being given a new and incorruptible spirit, and then a celestial body made of spiritual matter because there will be no longer physical matter. It will all burn up in the fire!

Who will be saved and how? No human has the power to correct the sinful perception of the human spirit, it is irreparably damaged. We see who and how in the verses above that those who open up to and receive the light into their souls, by becoming in union with the light that came into the world is through Jesus. To take on, be bound to, to act and perceive out of His Spirit—the Holy Spirit—makes us in a spiritual marital union with Jesus. Through Christ, who is the second or last Adam, a new species of humans are created, celestial humans, just as physical humans came out of the first Adam. Out of the first Adam, humans are born with the corrupt human spirit. Out of union with the second or last Adam, celestial humans come who have an incorruptible spirit.

Celestial humans are not born taking their first breath of life as a child of the first Adam. Celestial humans are the children of the first Adam who are corrupt, but have experienced a rebirth of a new spirit, the spirit of Christ, metamorphosizing into a celestial human. There never has been, nor will there be for all of eternity any celestial human created from birth, but only those who have been born as children of wrath and afterwards experience a rebirth. Jesus is the ark of the covenant that through spiritual marital union saves numbers beyond counting, and not the wooden ark that saved eight only to continue as sinners on this side of the flood.

However, all the others who refuse the light and the opportunity of rebirth will parish because they (the entire human race) are already under judgment, condemned to perish even before they were born. Why? Because they are born out of sin with a sinful and corrupt human spirit hopelessly and most often ignorantly independent and in rebellion to God. Their only hope is to open up to and receive the light and spirit of rebirth into Christ. However, when they reject and refuse that way out, they remain under the destruction of the human race.

Note: Witches are able to see the shining Spirit of the Holy Spirit on Christians in union with Jesus and are offended by it. They can discern the Holy Spirit in a person's heart without hearing their words.

AMP 1Jn 4:1 **BELOVED, DO** *not put faith in every spirit* (person), *but prove (test) the spirits* (on the person) *to discover whether they proceed from God; for many false prophets have gone forth into the world.*

But the majority of Christians are spiritually blind and cannot discern the Spirit on their own people. They judge by outward appearances or mere professions of faith.

AMP Jn 7:24 *Be honest in your judgment and do not decide at a glance (superficially and by appearances); but judge fairly and righteously.*

NIV Jn 7:24 *Stop judging by mere appearances, and make a right judgment."*

This is one of the reasons Jesus has us giving this message while naked. He wants His Church to stop being concerned only with the superficial, the outward, and become concerned with and aware of the Holy Spirit, a person's spiritual condition, and their union with Him. In that case it's not by our outward naked appearance that people would judge us or our message as being from God or not. They instead would be sensitive to the Holy Spirit and recognize that our words are from Him and His Spirit is in us.

AMP Lk 24:32 *And they said to one another, Were not our hearts greatly moved and burning within us while He was talking with us on the road and as He opened and explained to us [the sense of] the Scriptures?*

It will witness in their hearts when our words proceed from the Holy Spirit. That is if they do not willfully have a closed mind to anything but their own worldly understanding.

AMP 1Co 3:1-4 **HOWEVER, BRETHREN,** *I could not talk to you as to spiritual [men], but as to nonspiritual [men of the flesh, in whom the carnal nature predominates], as to mere infants [in the new life] in Christ [unable to talk yet!] I fed you with milk, not solid food, for you were not yet strong enough [to be ready for it]; but even yet you are not strong enough [to be ready for it], For you are still* *[unspiritual, having the nature] of the flesh [under the control of ordinary impulses]. For as long as [there are] envying and jealousy and wrangling and factions among you, are you not unspiritual and of the flesh, behaving yourselves after a human standard and like mere (unchanged) men? For when one says, I belong to Paul, and another, I belong to Apollos, are you not [proving yourselves] ordinary (unchanged) men?*

If an individual has a discerning sense of the Holy Spirit and they don't have a sense of the Spirit in us, they will not listen to us and discount us as not from God. However, if they do have a sense of the Holy Spirit in us and our words, in spite of our nudity, they will listen to us. This is how God wants it. Those who set aside their personal and superficial judgments of what God would and would not ask of His messengers and instead recognize the Spirit in us, approving of us, they will know our words are from God and God will enlighten them with the words we speak.

We are in an age where it is imperative that we stop looking at the wrapping of the package and start being sensitive to God's Spirit and how He is prompting us. Because there are so many wolves in sheep clothing, wolves who make themselves look and seem much more believable than those who would speak naked out of obedience to God. It is imperative that we recognize and decide according to the Holy Spirit's judgment.

Spiritual Union

It is essential to understand *spiritual union* in order to understand tribulations, the measures God takes to purify His bride in a way that binds her to Him for her own salvation. Contrary to popular belief, it takes more than a one-time declaration of faith to be in union with Christ. As such, we must spend more time on *spiritual union* in order to be able to understand the message of love, called Revelation.

Clearing up another common delusion: Once we have received Christ, it is a common perception that our sins have been forgiven and from now on we must watch our "p's and q's," we have to be a "good person" now, as it were. However, this is not the case when we are baptized into His death.

WEB Ro 6:2-4 *May it never be! We who died to sin, how could we live in it any longer?* <u>*Or don't you know that all of us who were baptized into Christ Jesus were baptized into his death?*</u> *We were buried therefore with him through baptism into death, that just as Christ was raised from the dead through the glory of the Father, so we also might walk in newness of life.*

Salvation is a process, a multistep event.

Although after coming into Christ we have the same physical body, we have a new life. This is literal and not figurative. We actually are born again of a new spirit and have died to the old. So it becomes about living for the new Spirit and no longer being moved by the old, our corrupt human spirit. At the moment of confessing that Jesus is Lord we receive a new spirit, the Spirit of our Lord that binds us in *spiritual union* with Jesus. However, we still possess our corrupt human spirit for a time. That is until we die to our physical human body. This process is described in Hebrews:

NIV Heb 4:9-13 *There remains, then, a Sabbath-rest for the people of God; for anyone who enters God's rest also rests from his own work, just as God did from his. Let us, therefore, make every effort to enter that rest, so that no one will fall by following their example of disobedience.* <u>*For the word of God is living and active. Sharper than any double-edged sword, it penetrates even to dividing soul and spirit, joints and marrow; it judges the thoughts and attitudes of the heart. Nothing in all creation is hidden from God's sight.*</u> *Everything is uncovered and laid bare before the eyes of him to whom we must give account.*

Humans are triune beings, spirit, soul, and body. We are created in the image of God just as He is, Father, Son, and Holy Spirit. The Father is the soul or mind of God, the Holy Spirit is the spirit of God and the Son, or the Word of God, is the embodiment of God, the outward manifestation of God. Just as we have three different natures but are a single person, God has three natures but is one being. In light of Him being a triune being, the Bible tells us that God is one.

What this passage is telling us is that by God's word He can sever our corrupt human spirit (our awareness, life-principle, which is the power of animation) from our body (joints and marrow) like a surgeon with a scalpel which renders our body as dead. Likewise, by His word He can surgically sever our corrupt human spirit from our very soul (our mind, the seat of reason, and decision and personality). Then, give us first, a new Spirit, that renews the mind by convicting the thoughts and purposes of our heart (our soul/mind) having a whole new perspective or worldview of our life. Then to complete the process, by His word our life-giving human spirit is severed from the body, and we die to it, but not without giving us a new body, an incorruptible body that never dies, a spiritual or celestial body.

Herein lies the short-sightedness of the majority of Christians: our corrupt human spirit gives life and animation to our physical body. The moment it is severed from our body, the body dies. The Holy Spirit of Christ we receive is given us to animate our new and promised celestial body. However, we possess that spirit while still in the physical body. Possessing it while still in the body serves to purify our worldview and purposes, convicting our soul/mind of wrongdoing. Possessing the Holy Spirit while still in the body also serves as a promise that when we die to the physical body, we will not spend a single moment as a disembodied soul. It is just as Jesus stated, we will in no way taste or experience death (disembodiment).

AMP Jn 5:24 I assure you, most solemnly I tell you, the person whose ears are open to My words [who listens to My message] and believes and trusts in and clings to and relies on Him Who sent Me has (possesses now) eternal life. And he does not come into judgment [does not incur sentence of judgment, will not come under condemnation], but he has already passed over out of death into life.

AMP Jn 11:25-26 Jesus said to her, I am [Myself] the Resurrection and the Life. Whoever believes in (adheres to, trusts in, and relies on) Me, although he may die, yet he shall live; <u>And whoever continues to live and believes in (has faith in, cleaves to, and relies on) Me shall never [actually] die at all.</u> Do you believe this?

And as Paul reflects:

AMP 2Co 4:6-7 For God Who said, Let light shine out of darkness, has shone in our hearts so as [to beam forth] the Light for the illumination of the knowledge of the majesty and glory of God [as it is manifest in the Person and is revealed] in the face of Jesus Christ (the Messiah<u>). However, we possess this precious treasure [the divine Light of the Gospel] in [frail, human] vessels of earth,</u> that the grandeur and exceeding greatness of the power may be shown to be from God and not from ourselves.

AMP 2Co 1:21-22 But it is God Who confirms and makes us steadfast and establishes us [in joint fellowship] with you in Christ, and has consecrated and anointed us [enduing us with the gifts of the Holy Spirit]; <u>[He has also appropriated and acknowledged us as His by] putting His seal upon us and giving us His [Holy] Spirit in our hearts as the security deposit and guarantee [of the fulfillment of His promise].</u>

And again:

AMP Eph 1:13-14 In Him you also who have heard the Word of Truth, the glad tidings (Gospel) of your salvation, and have believed in and adhered to and relied on Him<u>, were stamped with the seal of the long-promised Holy Spirit. That [Spirit] is the guarantee of our inheritance [the firstfruits, the pledge and foretaste, the down payment on our heritage], in anticipation of its full redemption and our acquiring [complete] possession of it—to the praise of His glory.</u>

NIV 1Co 15:35-55 But someone may ask, "How are the dead raised? With what kind of body will they come?" How foolish! What you sow does not come to life unless it dies. When you sow, you do not plant the body that will be, but just a seed, perhaps of wheat or of something *else. But God gives it a body as he has determined, and to each kind of seed he gives its own body. All flesh is not the same: Men have one kind of flesh, animals have another, birds another and fish another. There are also heavenly bodies and there are earthly bodies; but the splendor of the heavenly bodies is one kind, and the splendor of the earthly bodies is another. The sun has one kind of splendor, the moon another and the stars another; and star differs from star in splendor. So will it be with the resurrection of the dead. The body that is sown is perishable, it is raised imperishable; it is sown in dishonor, it is raised in glory; it is sown in weakness, it is raised in power; <u>it is sown a natural body, it is raised a spiritual body. If there is a natural body, there is also a spiritual body. So it is written: "The first man Adam became a living being"; the last Adam, a life-giving spirit. The spiritual did not come first, but the natural, and after that the spiritual. The first man was of the dust of the earth, the second man from heaven. As was the earthly man, so are those who are of the earth; and as is the man from heaven, so also are those who are of heaven. And just as we have borne the likeness of the earthly man, so shall we bear the likeness of the man from heaven.</u> I declare to you, brothers, that flesh and blood cannot inherit the kingdom of God, nor does the perishable inherit the imperishable. Listen, I tell you a mystery: <u>We will not all sleep, but we will all be changed—in a flash, in the twinkling of an eye, at the last trumpet.</u> For the trumpet will sound, the dead will be raised imperishable, and we will be changed. <u>For the perishable must clothe itself with the imperishable, and the mortal with immortality. When the perishable has been clothed with the imperishable, and the mortal with immortality, then the saying that is written will come true: "Death has been swallowed up in victory." "Where, O death, is your victory? Where, O death, is your sting?"*</u>

Having the Holy Spirit in us is a *guarantee* in the sense that when our process of salvation is complete and we die to the physical body, at the same moment we will be clothed with a celestial body; meaning, we already possess the spirit that will animate the celestial body when the time comes. Having the Holy Spirit in us as a *deposit* means, although the process of our salvation is not yet complete, as long as we are clothed with the physical body, we already have the essential element that will give life to and animate our celestial body when we are finished with the physical body. We have now, while still alive in the body, the first stage of our metamorphosis into a celestial being.

Now here is where the shortsightedness comes in: Our physical body cannot remain alive if we are severed from our corrupt human spirit because it is the very life principle that animates it. As a result, when we receive the deposit of having a new spirit, which is the very element that will animate our promised celestial body, we still have not yet been severed from our corrupt human spirit. What this means is that while still in the physical body and after we become born again, we have two opposing spirits in our hearts influencing our soul or mind, those opposing spirits are the corrupt human spirit and the Holy Spirit. Likewise, until we receive our celestial body, we live in our corrupt physical body which is subject to decay (illness) and death and has corrupt sinful desires. Paul calls the combination of our corrupt human spirit and our corrupt physical body and impure mind, our *sin nature*. It is not until we die to our physical body that we can shed our corrupt human spirit. Why? Because when we die to our physical body, we no longer have need of that which animates it with life, our corrupt human spirit. However, while we are alive in the physical body, we must have that corrupt life-giving spirit to remain alive in the physical body.

The next question would naturally be: Why then do we have to stay in our physical body keeping us tied to our sinful nature, having to fight against it? The answer is for at least two reasons; the first being that we do not get a new soul, but are eventually severed from the body we gave expression to sin with and that is doomed for death, and severed from that spirit that gives life, perception, inspiration, and motivation (the power and life to make our mind active and alive) which is also corrupt. However, the scripture says that the new spirit renews our mind and convicts the thoughts and purposes of the heart. If we were to die to our soul/mind, we would not exist as the person and personality that we are. Given that, our soul/mind needs to be purified of the way it sees life and responds to it in its sinful manner.

As the plan and process of salvation goes, we are given a new spirit that will cause us to see things in a new light that makes us sensitive to the Lord's will and causes us to obey Him, thus weaning us away from seeing life from a sinful perspective, or as James says, *according to the wisdom of this world.* That makes the time left in the physical body an important part of the process of salvation. To live in the celestial universe as an uncorrupted being, our minds need to go through the process of being purified and operating out of the (again, as James says) *wisdom that comes down from heaven.* Having more time in our physical body gives us the time, through conviction of our new spirit, to convert from perceiving and acting out of the wisdom of the world.

The second purpose is that Jesus died to His physical body. However, He desires to save the whole world by filling everything everywhere with His Spirit. His Spirit remains in the world because we are in union with Him and since He died to His body in the world, and we died to our life in the world, we are literally His body and one whole person with Him.

AMP Eph 1:17-2:2 *[For I always pray to] the God of our Lord Jesus Christ, the Father of glory, that He may grant you a spirit of wisdom and revelation [of insight into mysteries and secrets] in the [deep and intimate] knowledge of Him, By having the eyes of your heart flooded with light, so that you can know and understand the hope to which He has called you, and how rich is His glorious inheritance in the saints (His set-apart ones), And [so that you can know and understand] what is the immeasurable and unlimited and surpassing greatness of His power in and for us who believe, as demonstrated in the working of His mighty strength, Which He exerted in Christ when He raised Him from the dead and seated Him at His [own] right hand in the heavenly [places], Far above all rule and authority and power and dominion and every name that is named [above every* *title that can be conferred], not only in this age and in this world, but also in the age and the world which are to come. <u>And He has put all things under His feet and has appointed Him the universal and supreme Head of the church [a headship exercised throughout the church], Which is His body, the fullness of Him Who fills all in all [for in that body lives the full measure of Him Who makes everything complete, and Who fills everything everywhere with Himself].</u> AND YOU [He made alive], when you were dead (slain) by [your] trespasses and sins In which at one time you walked [habitually].*

AMP Gal 2:20 I have been crucified with Christ [in Him I have shared His crucifixion]; it is no longer I who live, but Christ (the Messiah) lives in me; and the life I now live in the body I live by faith in (by adherence to and reliance on and complete trust in) the Son of God, Who loved me and gave Himself up for me.

It is through our union with Him that He is still in the world saving it. It is our new purpose and destiny that while we remain in the physical body, He is in the world in a body, and for as long as He can use our lives to minister to those in the world (according to His plan), we will stay in our physical body. In turn, during that time, we must remain in the physical body, we will have to contend with the two different spirit influences (the Holy Spirit and our corrupt human spirit) and our sin nature so the Lord may have an active body in the world.

AMP Gal 5:16-18 But I say, walk and live [habitually] in the [Holy] Spirit [responsive to and controlled and guided by the Spirit]; then you will certainly not gratify the cravings and desires of the flesh (of human nature without God). <u>For the desires of the flesh are opposed to the [Holy] Spirit, and the [desires of the] Spirit are opposed to the flesh (godless human nature); for these are antagonistic to each other [continually withstanding and in conflict with each other]</u>, so that you are not free but are prevented from doing what you desire to do. But if you are guided (led) by the [Holy] Spirit, you are not subject to the Law.

As such, moment by moment, decision by decision, and act by act while in the body we must choose to perceive, purpose, and be moved by one spirit in our hearts over the other during this interim time; before we are free of our corrupt human spirit and physical body—our sin nature. Not only has the Lord *stamped* (us) *with the seal of the long-promised Holy Spirit,* but we have also bound ourselves to His Spirit in a spiritual marital union.

AMP Mt 6:24 No one can serve two masters; for either he will hate the one and love the other, or he will stand by and be devoted to the one and despise and be against the other

It is spiritual adultery to serve our sin nature while we wait patiently for freedom from it and the receipt of our celestial body.

AMP Jas 4:2B-10 You do not have, because you do not ask. [Or] you do ask [God for them] and yet fail to receive, because you ask with wrong purpose and evil, selfish motives. Your intention is [when you get what you desire] to spend it in sensual pleasures. You [are like] unfaithful wives [having illicit love affairs with the world and breaking your marriage vow to God]! Do you not know that being the world's friend is being God's enemy? So whoever chooses to be a friend of the world takes his stand as an enemy of God. Or do you suppose that the Scripture is speaking to no purpose that says, The Spirit Whom He has caused to dwell in us yearns over us and He yearns for the Spirit [to be welcome] with a jealous love? But He gives us more and more grace (power of the Holy Spirit, to meet this evil tendency and all others fully). That is why He says, God sets Himself against the proud and haughty, but gives grace [continually] to the lowly (those who are humble enough to receive it). So be subject to God. Resist the devil [stand firm against him], and he will flee from you. Come close to God and He will come close to you. [Recognize that you are] sinners, get your soiled hands clean; [realize that you have been disloyal] wavering individuals with divided interests, and purify your hearts [of your spiritual adultery]. [As you draw near to God] be deeply penitent and grieve, even weep [over your disloyalty]. Let your laughter be turned to grief and your mirth to dejection and heartfelt shame [for your sins]. Humble yourselves [feeling very insignificant] in the presence of the Lord, and He will exalt you [He will lift you up and make your lives significant].

We know by the parable of the sower that this new Spirit comes in the form of a seed which needs to be nurtured, or it will die, or the life will be choked out of it. With our superficial, non-spiritual minds, like Nicodemus, it's hard for us to grasp how we can actually become a new person when we have the same old life, same old body, the same old job, and same old friends. However, from a spiritual perspective the very essence of life-principle that gives us awareness and power to be animated is completely new and different from the former. We become celestial humans and no longer mortal humans.

AMP 1Pe 1:23 You have been regenerated (born again), not from a mortal origin (seed, sperm), but from one that is immortal by the ever living and lasting Word of God.

AMP 1Jn 3:9 No one born (begotten) of God [deliberately, knowingly, and habitually] practices sin, for God's nature abides in him [His principle of life, the divine sperm, remains permanently within him]; and he cannot practice sinning because he is born (begotten) of God.

Yes, we do eventually get an immortal body and become a celestial human, but until then, it is the very essence of life that first begins our transformation into a different species of humans—celestial humans. However, in order for that seed of life to grow and become the spirit essence which rules every aspect of our soul, we must purposefully identify with and nurture the seed of the new Spirit within our hearts. We must, in a determined way, not identify with or be motivated by the full-grown and mature corrupt spirit of this world we were born with and have lived by our whole life.

NIV Ro 8:12-16 Therefore, brothers, <u>we have an obligation—but it is not to the sinful nature, to live according to it.</u> For if you live according to the sinful nature, you will die; but if by the Spirit you put to death *the misdeeds of the body, you will live, because those who are led by the Spirit of God are sons of God. For you did not receive a spirit that makes you a slave again to fear, but you received the Spirit of sonship. And by him we cry, "Abba, Father." The Spirit himself testifies with our spirit that we are God's children.*

What this means is our Christian walk is not a behavioral conformity to a set of religious rules. It is a conformity to and living from a new Spirit essence, while dying to the former. We do this by starving our human spirit (which is our sin nature) from having expression. Denying its power to move us with its inspirations, motivations, perceptions, outlook, bondages, and power. Then progressively we desire to and are focused on being moved by the Holy Spirit within. It is a spiritual thing of identifying with one spirit over another.

Are we capable of never sinning once we have the Holy Spirit? And what if I make a mistake?

AMP Ro 7:15-25 For I do not understand my own actions [I am baffled, bewildered]. I do not practice or accomplish what I wish, but I do the very thing that I loathe [which my moral instinct condemns]. Now if I do [habitually] what is contrary to my desire, [that means that] I acknowledge and agree that the Law is good (morally excellent) and that I take sides with it. However, it is no longer I who do the deed, but the sin [principle] which is at home in me and has possession of me. For I know that nothing good dwells within me, that is, in my flesh. I can will what is right, but I cannot perform it. [I have the intention and urge to do what is right, but no power to carry it out.] For I fail to practice the good deeds I desire to do, but the evil deeds that I do not desire to do are what I am [ever] doing. Now if I do what I do not desire to do, it is no longer I doing it [it is not myself that acts], but the sin [principle] which dwells within me [fixed and operating in my soul]. So I find it to be a law (rule of action of my being) that when I want to do what is right and good, evil is ever present with me and I am subject to its insistent demands. For I endorse and delight in the Law of God in my inmost self [with my new nature]. But I discern in my bodily members [in the sensitive appetites and wills of the flesh] a different law (rule of action) at war against the law of my mind (my reason) and making me a prisoner to the law of sin that dwells in my bodily organs [in the sensitive appetites and wills of the flesh]. O unhappy and pitiable and wretched man that I am! Who will release and deliver me from [the shackles of] this body of death? O thank God! [He will!] through Jesus Christ (the Anointed One) our Lord!

We will make mistakes by perceiving and acting out of our sin nature out of our fears and because of the pressures of life, even our sinful desires that we are trying to overcome. They will cause us to stumble from time to time. However, as it says above, *He gives us more and more grace (power of the Holy Spirit, to meet this evil tendency and all others fully). That is why He says, God sets Himself against the proud and haughty, but gives grace [continually] to the lowly (those who are humble enough to receive it). So be subject to God. Resist the devil [stand firm against him], and he will flee from you. Come close to God and He will come close to you.*

And again:

AMP Ro 14:4 *Who are you to pass judgment on and censure another's household servant? It is before his own master that he stands or falls. And he shall stand and be upheld, for the Master (the Lord) is mighty to support him and make him stand.*

The above verse must be weighed against this verse:

AMP 1Jn 3:6 *No one who abides in Him [who lives and remains in communion with and in obedience to Him—<u>deliberately, knowingly, and habitually] commits (practices) sin</u>. No one who [habitually] sins has either seen or known Him [recognized, perceived, or understood Him, or has had an experiential acquaintance with Him].*

John is not saying that we never sin if we have the Holy Spirit, but he is pointing out that one in unity with the Spirit of the Lord does not *deliberately, knowingly, and habitually] commits (practices) sin.* If we possess the Holy Spirit, in union with Jesus, our new spirit gives us different motives and different desires, and a whole new way of perceiving life that is no longer false to the truth. Possessing these new qualities we, through our conscious, are convicted with truth, giving us the power and leading us to not knowingly and deliberately and habitually sin anymore. Despite this, while still in the physical body, we will stumble from time to time. However, that is why it says:

AMP Jn 1:16-17 *For out of His fullness (abundance) we have all received [all had a share and we were all supplied with] one grace after another and spiritual blessing upon spiritual blessing and even favor upon favor and gift [heaped] upon gift. For while the Law* (with its blessing for keeping them and its curses for breaking them) *was given through Moses, grace (unearned, undeserved favor and spiritual blessing) and truth came through Jesus Christ.*

We must realize that when we were reconciled to Christ and our sins forgiven, we were forgiven for all our sins, past, present, and future. We were forgiven for seeing our life through the false to the truth worldly wisdom of our corrupt human spirit and are in process of being saved from it. That is why when the Bible tells us, Jesus died to set us free from the sin of the world, it uses the singular. It does not say, He saves us from the *sins* of the world.

How does God's grace account for future sins? It says that through Jesus, He brought *grace* and *truth*. Truth so that we no longer see things according to the false to the truth wisdom perceptions, and grace because He knows we will not be fully free from our sin nature until the death of our physical body, in spite of the fact that His Spirit resides in our hearts. That is why James says, God gives *grace upon grace to the humble*. Those who are painfully aware that their sin nature from time to time influences their decisions and their deeds. The Lord knows we are not totally free from our sin nature until we die to the physical body. But as we mature, we become stronger in our integrity under more and more trying circumstances in operating out of the Holy Spirit in us. As such, His initial forgiveness and grace extends to our future sins for those who humbly recognize they are sinners and make every effort to seek out His will and comply with that.

It is a fixed law of nature that when we are growing and becoming alive with one spirit in us by nurturing and identifying with it, we are at the same time starving and dying to the other. Our Christian walk is about choosing with every decision we make, which spirit within us we will grow in and which we will die to. Again, it's not simply about being a good person by human standards.

AMP Ro 7:6 *But now we are discharged from the Law and have terminated all intercourse with it, having died to what once restrained and held us captive. So now we serve not under [obedience to] the old code of written regulations, <u>but [under obedience to the promptings] of the Spirit</u> in newness [of life].*

Here are some good scriptures that explain *spiritual union*:

AMP Col 2:6 *As you have therefore received Christ, [even] Jesus the Lord, <u>[so] walk (regulate your lives and conduct yourselves) in union with and conformity to Him.</u>*

WEB Gal 2:20 *I have been crucified with Christ, and <u>it is no longer I who live, but Christ lives in me.</u> That life which I now live in the flesh, I live by faith in the Son of God, who loved me and gave himself up for me.*

WEB Jn 6:38 *For I have come down from heaven, <u>not to do my own will, but the will of him who sent me.</u>*

AMP 2Co 5:14-15 *For the love of Christ controls and urges and impels us, because we are of the opinion and conviction that [if] One died for all, then all died; And He died for all, <u>so that all those who live might live no longer to and for themselves, but to and for Him</u> Who died and was raised again for their sake.*

The above scriptures explain *spiritual union* with Christ. They are not metaphors, but literal in their meaning. When Paul says, it is no longer I who live, but Christ in me, he means that he stopped living out the life he willed and desired for himself (dead to his life in the body). But instead, he follows every prompting that the Lord gave him. This is so whatever the Holy Spirit wanted accomplished, at the sacrifice of his own agenda, he did not do what he wanted or what was beneficial to himself (in his own estimation). But out of love and a desire to be one with the Lord, he did whatever the Spirit wanted done. In this way, the disembodied Spirit of Jesus has a body in the world by which the Lord could do what He wills.

AMP Phil 1:21A For to me, to live is Christ . . .

AMP Phil 3:7-16 But whatever former things I had that might have been gains to me, I have come to consider as [one combined] loss for Christ's sake. Yes, furthermore, I count everything as loss compared to the possession of the priceless privilege (the overwhelming preciousness, the surpassing worth, and supreme advantage) of knowing Christ Jesus my Lord and of progressively becoming more deeply and intimately acquainted with Him [of perceiving and recognizing and understanding Him more fully and clearly]. For His sake I have lost everything and consider it all to be mere rubbish (refuse, dregs), in order that I may win (gain) Christ (the Anointed One), And that I may [actually] be found and known as in Him, not having any [self-achieved] righteousness that can be called my own, based on my obedience to the Law's demands (ritualistic uprightness and supposed right standing with God thus acquired), but possessing that [genuine righteousness] which comes through faith in Christ (the Anointed One), the [truly] right standing with God, which comes from God by [saving] faith (obedience to His Spirit promptings). *[For my determined purpose is] that I may know Him [that I may progressively become more deeply and intimately acquainted with Him, perceiving and recognizing and understanding the wonders of His Person more strongly and more clearly], and that I may in that same way come to know the power outflowing from His resurrection [which it exerts over believers], and that I may so share His sufferings as to be continually transformed [in spirit into His likeness even] to His death, [in the hope] That if possible I may attain to the [spiritual and moral] resurrection [that lifts me] out* *from among the dead [even while in the body]. Not that I have now attained [this ideal], or have already been made perfect, but I press on to lay hold of (grasp) and make my own, that for which Christ Jesus (the Messiah) has laid hold of me and made me His own. I do not consider, brethren, that I have captured and made it my own [yet]; but one thing I do [it is my one aspiration]: forgetting what lies behind and straining forward to what lies ahead, I press on toward the goal to win the [supreme and heavenly] prize to which God in Christ Jesus is calling us upward. <u>So let those [of us] who are spiritually mature and full-grown have this mind and hold these convictions</u>; and if in any respect you have a different attitude of mind, God will make that clear to you also. Only let us hold true to what we have already attained and walk and order our lives by that.*

Paul threw away all his aspirations and future, as we hear in Philippians. He did this to use his time, resources, reputation on whatever Jesus wanted done and said, at no concern with the repercussions it had on his person—leaving no time to nurture his own life. Many would believe this type of following Christ is extreme and only for the Monastics. However, this is the way to follow and be in *spiritual union* with Christ. It is the way which is taught in the Bible, and it is the only way to be truly one with Christ.

When Paul says, *[For my determined purpose is] that I may know Him [that I may progressively become more deeply and intimately acquainted with Him, perceiving and recognizing and understanding the wonders of His Person more strongly and more clearly], . . . and that I may so share His sufferings as to be continually transformed [in spirit into His likeness even] to His death . . .* he is expressing that he wants to obey every prompting he senses from the Lord's Spirit to the point that the people of the world would react to him (Paul) as they would react to Jesus standing before them, while he is doing and saying the things Jesus wants said and done. However, in their spiritual blindness the world sees Paul thinking that they know him from his past, seeing him according to his human weaknesses as Paul. Judging in such a superficial way, they think he is just a mere human, and they do not recognize Jesus in Him. They do not perceive that the acts he performs and the words he speaks are not his own or from his own desires and will, but prompted by the Holy Spirit in him.

KJ Heb 13:2 Be not forgetful to entertain strangers: for thereby some have entertained angels (messengers from God) *unawares.*

In another respect, what Paul is aware of is that when he does and speaks what the Holy Spirit is prompting him, people will react to him as they would react to Jesus because he is being moved in words and deed by the Lord's Spirit. Now, because of that, when the people react to Paul when he is led by the Spirit, they are actually reacting to Jesus in him.

AMP 1Co 2:1-6 AS FOR myself, brethren, when I came to you, I did not come proclaiming to you the testimony and evidence or mystery and secret of God [concerning what He has done through Christ for the salvation of men] in lofty words of eloquence or human philosophy and wisdom; For I resolved to know nothing (to be acquainted with nothing, to make a display of the knowledge of nothing, and to be conscious of nothing) among you except Jesus Christ (the Messiah) and Him crucified. And I was in (passed into a state of) weakness and fear (dread) and great trembling [after I had come] among you (not powered up with his own passions and judgments matching theirs). *And <u>my language and my message were not set forth in persuasive (enticing and plausible) words of wisdom, but they were in demonstration of the [Holy] Spirit and power [a proof by the Spirit and power of God, operating on me and stirring in the minds of my hearers the most holy emotions and thus persuading them]</u>, So that your faith might not rest in the wisdom of men (human philosophy), but in the power of God. Yet when we are among the full-grown (spiritually mature Christians who are ripe in understanding), we do impart a [higher] wisdom (the knowledge of the divine plan previously hidden); but it is indeed not a wisdom of this present age or of this world nor of the leaders and rulers of this age, who are being brought to nothing and are doomed to pass away.*

The people may break down in tears of repentance, joy, and undying gratitude, they may reject argue and discount him calling him a fool, they might get offended, shun, persecute, and attack Paul. However, Paul did not take it personal because he knew that their reaction to him was not only a judgment of his person, but was provoked and inspired by Jesus in him, prompting him to do and speak what he did—they were reacting to Jesus, not so much him!

This is something contemporary Christian's neglect to realize. Furthermore, and most importantly, Paul understood that in absorbing the reactions of those he related to, he was able to share the greatest, closest type of intimacy possible with Christ. In essence, Paul was walking a mile in Jesus' sandals! Paul was able to experientially know exactly the feelings and emotions, joys, and pain that Jesus feels! Why? Because in real time Paul went through everything as one whole person with Jesus. *That I may [actually] be found and known as in Him. [For my determined purpose is] that I may know Him [that I may progressively become more deeply and intimately acquainted with Him, perceiving and recognizing and understanding the wonders of His Person more strongly and more clearly and that I may so share His sufferings as to be continually transformed [in spirit into His likeness even] to His death.* How can anyone be more intimate with another person? Even physical sex cannot match the oneness of this kind of spiritual intimacy! Jesus died to His body and Paul died to his life in his body, thus it is no longer Paul who lives but Jesus in him. Being moved in his mind (soul) and body by the Spirit of Jesus and Jesus having expression in the body of Paul. By Paul's obedience, the two are one flesh—together they are one whole person bound in *spiritual union*, marriage. We as believers, Jesus shares His Spirit with us, and we share our body with Jesus. And the two will become one flesh.

AMP 1Co 2:14-16 *But the natural, nonspiritual man does not accept or welcome or admit into his heart the gifts and teachings and revelations of the Spirit of God, for they are folly (meaningless nonsense) to him; and he is incapable of knowing them [of progressively recognizing, understanding, and becoming better* *acquainted with them] because they are spiritually discerned and estimated and appreciated. But the spiritual man tries all things [he examines, investigates, inquires into, questions, and discerns all things], yet is himself to be put on trial and judged by no one [he can read the meaning of everything, but no one can properly discern or appraise or get an insight into him]. For who has known or understood the mind (the counsels and purposes) of the Lord so as to guide and instruct Him and give Him knowledge? <u>But we have the mind of Christ (the Messiah) and do hold the thoughts (feelings and purposes) of His heart.</u>*

How can we be intimate and show our love to Jesus?

AMP Jn 14:15-21 <u>*If you [really] love Me, you will keep (obey) My commands*</u>*. And I will ask the Father, and He will give you another Comforter (Counselor, Helper, Intercessor, Advocate, Strengthener, and Standby), that He may remain with you forever—The Spirit of Truth, Whom the world cannot receive (welcome, take to its heart), because it does not see Him or know and recognize Him. But you know and recognize Him, for He lives with you [constantly] and will be in you. I will not leave you as orphans [comfortless, desolate, bereaved, forlorn, helpless]; I will come [back] to you. Just a little while now, and the world will not see Me any more, but you will see Me; because I live, you will live also. At that time [when that day comes] you will know [for yourselves] that I am in My Father, and you [are] in Me, and I [am] in you.* <u>*The person who has My commands and keeps them is the one who [really] loves Me; and whoever [really] loves Me will be loved by My Father, and I [too] will love him and will show (reveal, manifest) Myself to him. [I will let Myself be clearly seen by him and make Myself real to him.]*</u>

The more we obey Jesus and His promptings as a choice because we love Him, the more intimately one we are with Him, bound as one through His Spirit. To obey is our experiential act of love and our intimacy with Him. The more we are moved by His Spirit, the more we are one.

Many Spirit-filled Christians would like to believe they do the will of God, even though they might pray and fast for the general direction the Lord would have them take in their lives. They most often have an agenda and look for affirmation from the Lord in the direction they wish. Doing this is not the same thing. Dying to self and being alive in Christ is not a superficial thing and a matter of simple outward behavioral conformity, or vocational choice. No, it is a spiritual thing—an act of your will to (by choice) totally surrender it to that of the Lord's.

You can judge for yourself how spiritually in union you are with the Lord by if your thoughts and prayer time are about you sorting things out in your own mind, according to what you think should happen. If that is the case, then you are like a married person keeping things to yourself and deciding by yourself what to do, without sharing and allowing your partner to be involved. Or to just tell them what you need them to do without being in agreement with what needs to be done. You have not died to self by living out His promptings if you decide what the problems are, decide the solutions, make God aware (as if He did not know), tell Him the problems and ask Him to grant the solutions you have decided are needed. This holds true even if you are successful at the things He has called you to do, but are done in your own ability and wisdom, because you are judging what success is by your own superficial perceptions, standards, and estimations. In addition, if you find yourself constantly presenting to God your requests, your desires, and concerns leaving no time to search out His will, except on rare occasions for general directions, then you have not died to self nor do you live for His purposes more than a small degree.

Truly dying to self is something that happens in your soul (your mind) to your spirit, not just in your outward behavior. Many people say, "If I could just know God's will for me in this or that situation, I would do it." We fool ourselves when we believe this about ourselves. When we give all the focus of our thought life towards seeking out what the Spirit will have us do or say, it is then that we can say we want to do the will of God. That doesn't mean to just wait around asking Him for things you want while assuming God will interrupt the focus of your concerns to tell you what He wants.

AMP Jn 7:17 If any man desires to do His will (God's pleasure), he will know (have the needed illumination to recognize, and can tell for himself) whether the teaching is from God or whether I am speaking from Myself and of My own accord and on My own authority.

Our relationship with God is based on freedom; out of sheer love and a desire to be one with Him, we obey Him and His Spirit. That is the only way to have intimacy with Jesus. To wait for God to make His will known to us, while we go about our lives, is not showing love for Him or a desire to die to self to let His Spirit have expression through our lives and thus be one with Him in union. We must hearken to His will. This means we must actively seek to find out what it is. Not passively wait for Him to tell us, nor does it mean we tell Him what His will is or how we should accomplish it.

After seeking His will out so His Spirit has expression and not our own will, we must have a commitment to not move until we receive marching orders from His Holy Spirit. This holds true even if we are in a situation where we are uncomfortable or incurring loss. If we don't have this heart, He is not our righteousness. We are deciding what is right and wrong or what God would or would not ask of us.

AMP Gal 2:19B-20 . . . so that I may [henceforth] live to and for God. I have been crucified with Christ [in Him I have shared His crucifixion]; <u>it is no longer I who live, but Christ (the Messiah) lives in me; and the life I now live in the body I live by faith in (by adherence to and reliance on and complete trust in) the Son of God</u>, Who loved me and gave Himself up for me . . .

Spirit-filled or not, contemporary Christians do not understand dying to their life and becoming alive in Christ any more than Nicodemus understood how he could be reborn spiritually and be a new creation without having a new physical life or body. He thought in natural terms only. Likewise, we do not understand how it was a spiritual, not a physical nakedness that Adam and Eve were looking to cover.

Jesus died to His physical body; we did not die to ours. For our part we die to our corrupt spirit and pursuits to have a life that will gratify our own will and desires. Jesus came alive in our hearts and body as we become alive to His Spirit and carry out His concerns.

In other words, we die not physically but to the life we once lived in the body for our own happiness, but came alive to carry out the life Jesus cannot because He died to His body. In this way we become one with Him as He is one with the Father. It is in this way that we don't understand dying to self any more than Nicodemus understood being reborn spiritually.

AMP 2Co 5:15 And He died for all, so that all those who live might live no longer to and for themselves, but to and for Him Who died and was raised again for their sake.

If we fall short of this type of love relationship, Jesus tells us that we are not worthy of His love.

NLT Mt 10:37-38 If you love your father or mother more than you love me, you are not worthy of being mine; or if you love your son or daughter more than me, you are not worthy of being mine. If you refuse to take up your cross and follow me, you are not worthy of being mine.

And again:

NLT Lk 14:26-30 "If you want to be my follower you must love me more than your own father and mother, wife and children, brothers and sisters—<u>yes, more than your own life.</u> Otherwise, you cannot be my disciple. And you cannot be my disciple if you do not carry your own cross and follow me. "But don't begin until you count the cost. For who would begin construction of a building without first getting estimates and then checking to see if there is enough money to pay the bills? Otherwise, you might complete only the foundation before running out of funds. And then how everyone would laugh at you!

They would say, 'There's the person who started that building and ran out of money before it was finished!'

The above verse is for those who say they are Spirit-filled, however, after finding out what it really means in giving up their lives to live out the Spirit's promptings, they feel like they didn't "sign-on for that" kind of commitment, and have an attitude of, "you've got to have balance." They built a solid foundation of faith but are unwilling to pay the price to build their life on that foundation. They say things like, "that kind of radical Christianity is not for everyone." And the ones who do it are "over the top." The truth is they are the ones who can't finish the work they started in their own hearts. In other words, they want the benefits, but don't want to pay the price.

Likewise, many Spirit-filled Christians claim forever that they desire to do the will of God and that's what they think they do, but don't. It is not that they do not want to do the Lord's will as it may appear. The problem is that over time, the Lord's will quickly becomes second in preference and priority to their own will.

NIV Rev 2:3-4 You have persevered and have endured hardships for my name, and have not grown weary. Yet I hold this against you: You have forsaken your first love.

AMP Mt 6:24 No one can serve two masters; for either he will hate the one and love the other, or he will stand by and be devoted to the one and despise and be against the other.

It is through developing a discipline to have a command of our thoughts that we train ourselves to spend all of our focus using all of our thoughts to search out His will. That is instead of allowing our focus to naturally drift, then concentrate and consider our own desires. In this way we can actually become one with Him.

AMP Dt 6:4-5 Hear, O Israel: the Lord our God is one Lord [the only Lord]. And you shall love the Lord your God with all your [mind and] heart and with your entire being and with all your might.

There are many that have a maturity problem.

AMP 1Co 13:11 *When I was a child, I talked like a child, I thought like a child, I reasoned like a child; now that I have become a man, I am done with childish ways and have put them aside.*

Maturing as a Christian is not unlike maturing as a person. When we are children and since birth, everything is about us and our needs. Our parents take care of every need we have, but we do not take care of the needs of others, and rightfully so because we are helpless. They also discipline us to do right and good until we learn to discipline ourselves into doing right and good. Older people will always acknowledge children and be concerned with how they are doing, lavishing them with gifts and good things, but the child does not reciprocate. Adults bend down and greet children, asking how they are doing. The children respond by telling them about their day and experiences but do not ask them about theirs. Adults remember, acknowledge, and bring gifts or cards to children for the important anniversaries and significant days in the lives of children, but grateful as they are, they do not reciprocate doing the same for the lives of others.

Adults do not take it personally when it comes to children not reciprocating. In fact, because they are children, they neither demand nor expect them to do so. However, when the child matures into an adult, and still acts as a child in this manner, they are considered rude, uncaring of others, ill-mannered, selfish, self-centered and self-absorbed, out only for number one. As we mature in life we are trained by our parents and expected to not just live for ourselves, but to live bigger than ourselves. To be aware of and consider the feelings and needs of others. A mature adult is expected to be considerate of and contribute, to do our part within our family unit, friends, neighbors, community and country, even strangers.

It is the same as we mature in our Christian faith. Most often when we become born again in union with Christ, we are lavished by the Lord. Our life becomes miraculous, taking miraculous turns. We are saved from the direction our lives have taken because of all the bad and sinful choices of the past we have made. Everything is turned around and our fellowship helps us at every turn, just as the needs of a child are met by their family. They not only help us with our needs but teach us so we grow in the knowledge of Christ. However, just as there are individuals who do not mature and learn to live bigger than themselves, there are Christians who do not mature and live a life bigger than themselves and continue depending on the Lord and their fellowship to make their lives content, making that their focus.

As a Christian, Paul points out that there is a time to put away the childish ways of being lost in indulging and living for self, concerned with personal needs. That time is not after our lives become perfect without needs, problems, and challenges, which most perceive is the case. One of the major reasons we are not brought up to Heaven when we receive the Spirit of Christ, is so that we become His body in the world so that He may save others in the world. The Lord does allow us as new believers to mature into that way of living. However, just as it is imperative for us to grow up and take our place in this world, being a productive part of it, we are likewise expected to mature taking our place as the body of Christ, serving the salvation and welfare of others. Because that is the nature and motives of the Spirit we are born again with.

***Spiritual union* is an inward spiritual condition not just a behavioral conformity.**

It is so important to understand what spirit is and the faculties it possesses as a part of our triune-being. After all, the new spirit we are born again with is the most important part of our salvation. Without it there is no salvation. Spirit is life, energy, power, awareness, feelings (which differs from the emotions of the mind) perception, inspiration, and motivation. Since spirit is awareness, it is also memory. Spirit does not think with words as the mind or soul does. Its natural language and communication are according to the quality and power of spirit energy which it senses or expresses. Another term we can use is to describe the language of spirit are feelings. Whereas the soul thinks by assigning word descriptions to its spirit's feelings and concerns, then uses words to reason, and consider. Spirit makes the body alive, animated, and the five senses conscious. It makes the soul, which is the mind, alive with life, awareness, or consciousness.

Note: The soul/mind is not the physical brain. The brain interacts with the mind; however, the brain is more geared towards managing the functions of the physical body.

The way that the man's spirit interacts with his mind is that it fills it with awareness and life—spirit energy (feelings) to function with. Wisdom is a faculty of the spirit whereas intelligence is a faculty of the mind. Wisdom differs from intelligence just as feelings are different from emotions. Wisdom is more of an understanding that is experiential. We call wisdom a set of values by which to perceive through so that we can know or distinguish a thing as something.

To understand the above statement, it is like a person blind his whole life then he suddenly is given sight. Although he may see clear as a bell, everything might appear as one object with things blending into each other and as shifting light and darkness. He could still walk right into a wall not realizing it is an obstacle separate from all the other stuff in front of him—where one object ends and another begins. He must learn to distinguish one object from another and define them. Likewise, he will need to incorporate and develop his perception of depth and judgement of the distance between them. It is the same with the wisdom values of our spirit awareness. We must have a set of values by which to perceive through to know one thing from another. That is whether it is something we sense spiritually or emotionally through the soul or through the five senses of the body. Another good word to describe wisdom as used in the Bible is a German word, "Anschauung [AHN-shou-əng]." *Anschauung is a German concept that is usually translated as "intuition". It, however, connotes a more nuanced definition especially when the concept is applied to philosophical discourse, including quantum theory. Some of the translations include actual, sense impressions, contemplation, view, opinion, and notion. Anschauung is also an important component of Johann Gottlieb Fichte's doctrine of knowledge. An application of Anschauung as experience is the perception of fire and immediately recognizing it as fire.* _{Wikipedia & word Genius}

It also includes in its meaning an intuition of what is perceived through the five senses of the body.

Again, perception—to see or sense things in one light or another—is a highly important component of wisdom or Anschauung. The way one person perceives something can be utterly different from the next person. According to the Bible and how the word Anschauung is used, this level of perception is called wisdom. It is the wisdom or Anschauung of the man's spirit that was corrupted by Adam and Eve ingesting the spirit of the devil—the fruit of the knowledge of good and evil. Once they did, they corrupted the human spirit for all and that is why we suffer from the misdeed they did. We perceive our life through corrupted wisdom, Anschauung. As for the devil, this is what the Lord said to him.

_{NIV Eze 28:17} *Your heart became proud on account of your beauty, and <u>you corrupted your wisdom because of your splendor</u>.*

And this is what was said about Eve:

_{NIV Ge 3:5-6} *"For God knows that when you eat of it your eyes will be opened, and you will be like God, knowing good and evil." When the woman saw that the fruit of the tree was good for food and pleasing to the eye, and <u>also desirable for gaining wisdom</u> (Anschauung), she took some and ate it. She also gave some to her husband, who was with her, and he ate it.*

This is what James tells us about our corrupt human spirit and its wisdom (Anschauung):

_{AMP Jas 3:13-17} *Who is there among you who is wise and intelligent? Then let him by his noble living show forth his [good] works with the [unobtrusive] humility <u>[which is the proper attribute] of true wisdom. But if you have bitter jealousy (envy) and contention</u>*

(rivalry, selfish ambition) in your hearts, do not pride yourselves on it and thus be in defiance of and false to the Truth. This [superficial] wisdom is not such as comes down from above, but is earthly, unspiritual (animal), even devilish (demoniacal). For wherever there is jealousy (envy) and contention (rivalry and selfish ambition), there will also be confusion (unrest, disharmony, rebellion) and all sorts of evil and vile practices. *But the wisdom from above is first of all pure (undefiled); then it is peace-loving, courteous (considerate, gentle). [It is willing to] yield to reason, full of compassion and good fruits; it is wholehearted and straightforward, impartial and unfeigned (free from doubts, wavering, and insincerity).*

Who is wise and intelligent, James is not being redundant by using both of these terms. We will show that they are two separate qualities that we possess as humans. We can be the most intelligent person in the world, possessing greater knowledge than anyone, however, all our knowledge and intelligence of the mind can only be applied to our spirit perception of a matter. Because our spirit wisdom is corrupt as James calls it, worldly (superficial, considering only what our five senses can take in, blind to the spiritual), we will consider and reason a matter in a corrupt and false to the truth way. Our outcome will be twisted and perverted from the actual truth of the matter, rendering our superior intelligence and knowledge ineffective and faulty. However, our decisions will make perfect sense according to the wisdom values we perceive through, even if they are false to the truth. Wisdom of the spirit and the intelligence of the mind must work together to be truly wise and intelligent. A good example is a person who is upset believing you have done something to hurt them. They will verbalize that you did *this* and *that*, thus it means you regard them with ill will. However, how they interpreted what they observed is perceived incorrectly and is completely out of context. They may say, "I know it is true because I saw it with my own eyes." Their spirit perception and feelings have given their mind (intellect) a perception to understand the matter. Their intelligence of the mind can only understand within the perception that their spirit provides it with. Then, you become astonished that someone who knows you would think your motives were ingenuine and would let themselves believe you would do such a thing to purposely harm them because what you did in your mind was intended for their good. It's like James says, that person's wisdom values are *false to the truth*. Even with superior intelligence that person will conclude you are out to harm them given their perception of the matter.

Albert Einstein once said that truth is relative to the observer. This is a contemporary concept that allows everyone to have their own truth, making no truth absolute. However, this is wrong! Truth is absolute and it is according to how the Creator of all things made, gave life to, and perceives things. To adjust Einstein's concept, it is correct to say, perception is relative to the observer. Perception varies and shifts depending on the spirit wisdom of the observer and their limiting point of perspective. Truth is immovable and does not shift—it is absolute.

This is why human resources no longer look only to the IQ (intelligence quotient) of a perspective employee. They now highly rely on a person's EQ (emotional quotient), as they call it. Having no concept of spirit perception or wisdom they call it your emotional quotient. Emotions are an attribute of the soul. In reality, what they are trying to measure is the person's spirit wisdom.

Wisdom of the spirit also differs from intelligence of the mind/soul in that the mind can accumulate a bank of knowledge that it can draw from to consider a matter. For all intents and purposes that knowledge is a fixed thing the mind can draw from. Whereas wisdom of the spirit and its perception can be fleeting. It can be like a profound dream that you think you can never forget, however, get out of bed and go to the bathroom and by the time you finish, you forget. All you remember is that you had a profound dream but for the life of you, you cannot remember. That is because you had the dream while in a spiritual state according to that wisdom and once you fully get back into your body and start perceiving according to the wisdom of the physical world, the spiritual escapes you.

We teach that you should not reevaluate or judge a Heavenly decision with worldly wisdom. During a church service, or a counseling session with a person of wisdom, or during a time of deep contemplation, we may have an extreme clarity about a matter and then make a decision about it with total confidence. Then later, the more that we think about it the more we doubt and eventually totally change our mind. The perception of spiritual wisdom is elusive like the dream, not like the accumulated word knowledge of the mind. We return to our worldly wisdom perceptions and understandings, then the spirit wisdom we had during our moment of clarity completely escapes us, causing us to see in a totally different light. Then we doubt and for the life of us cannot make any sense out of the former way of seeing things.

It doesn't matter how long and experienced you are in perceiving things through the eyes of an enlightened spiritual perspective; all you need to do is fall back into a worldly perspective and the former view of things no longer makes any sense. Change the spirit you operate out of, and you will change your perspective. You may find it hard to understand why you thought something you realized in a moment of spiritual clarity is a sound idea or makes any sense at all. Again, the intelligence of the mind can only function within the perception the spirit fills the mind with. This is why James emphasizes that there is a difference between worldly wisdom which is false to the truth and the wisdom that comes down from Heaven. They are in conflict with each other, and it becomes the individual's choice which wisdom values they decide to perceive through.

You could say that the human spirit is collective. And for the corrupt human spirit to be passed down to those we give birth to is just as our corrupt human DNA is passed down. Both determine the defects in body and spirit perception. This is why we require both a new and uncorrupted body and spirit to be saved. It is our soul that is an individual personality. That cannot be replaced like spirit and body but has need of being renewed, convicted and shown the errors of its thinking and perception.

Although we possess a corrupt human spirit that skews our perception of life, we also can be influenced in our perception and empowered by the spirit wisdom and power of the demonic. The Bible mentions fourteen different demonic spirits that if empowered with and perceived through will dictate our worldview and can alienate us from God bringing death to both our soul and body.

1 the *spirit of infirmity*

2 the *spirit of fear*

3 the *spirit of divination*

4 the *spirit of whoredom*

5 the *spirit of bondage*

6 the *spirit of haughtiness*

7 the *spirit of perverseness*

8 the *spirit of antichrist*

9 the *spirit of deaf and dumbness*

10 the *spirit of heaviness*

11 the *spirit of lying*

12 the *spirit of jealousy*

13 the *spirit of stupor or slumber*

14 the *spirit of error*

These spirits are comprised of and work like all spirits, including the human spirit. *Spirit* is life-principle and awareness. The attributes of which are a sense of self and its surroundings; it is memory, and its power is motivation, inspiration, feelings, wisdom (a set of values by which to perceive through). Each of these 14 different root spirits have their own unique motives and perceptions of life that given the chance, they can become the eyes of our understanding and rule our thoughts and behavior. *Spirit* does not inherently have an embodiment. Spirits without an embodiment are forever looking for an opportunity, particularly the ones listed above, to search out and embody themselves with a human host to have expression through.

This extreme condition is referred to as being possessed. This is a condition that the soul or mind, its reason and conscience are completely bypassed causing those individual hosts to be spirit led. People in bondage to this extreme are animalistic in nature and are quite often referred to as being soulless. This is reflected by how these individuals react by what the world calls instinct, just as an animal does. Words, logic, reasoning, conscience, compassion, sensitivity to the feelings of others are all faculties of the soul and are not employed by a person who is spirit led/possessed. Psychology would label this person as a sociopath. This is extreme possession, however, there are many different degrees of spirit influence that taint our perceptions and cause us to respond in a sinful, "look out for number one," sort of way. James says these spirits are demonical and perceive things in a false to the truth animalistic way.

In contrast, we are told in the Bible:

2Ti 1:6-8 That is why I would remind you to stir up (rekindle the embers of, fan the flame of, and keep burning) the [gracious] gift of God, [the inner fire] that is in you by means of the laying on of of my hands [with those of the elders at your ordination]. For God did not give us a spirit of timidity (of cowardice, of craven and cringing and fawning fear), but [He has given us a spirit] of power and of love and of calm and well-balanced mind and discipline and self-control. Do not blush or be ashamed then, to testify to and for our Lord, nor of me, a prisoner for His sake, but [with me] take your share of the suffering [to which the preaching] of the Gospel [may expose you, and do it] in the power of God.

For God did not give us a spirit of fear. . . the motive of the spirit of fear is to control and it often employs the spirit of lies and deaf and dumbness and the ensuing confusion of false to the truth perceptions to do so. When a person who is trying to control has a powerful and overwhelming spirit, it overwhelms us, makes us doubt and can cause us to see the logic and sense of their wisdom reasoning which is false to the truth, while going blank to our own. This happens most often to people in codependent relationships. Dominant personalities can intimidate us, causing us to lose sight of true wisdom and a true perception of things; making us timid, afraid and powerless to correct; in order to stand up for truth. This demonstrates how wisdom is fleeting and is dependent on what spirit perception our mind/soul is filled with or encounters in others.

However, the gift of the Spirit of God gives us a power and a love and calm and a well-balanced mind, discipline and self-control. That power Paul is referring to is a power of spirit—spirit perception, and wisdom values. In this case it is the power of the Holy Spirit within. Power and wisdom values that are so strong and overwhelm with clarity in the face of any worldly spirit, that it cuts right through the overwhelmingly false and deceptive perception power of all demonic spirits. The result is we see right through confusion and falsehood of demonic reasoning without being afraid and intimidated or losing sight of the true reality of their faulty but powerful deception.

Here's an example; have you ever knowingly did wrong as a child, or as an adult, but worked out a justification that made total sense in case you were caught? Then, when your authority or parents discover the wrong and confront you concerning it, you then tell them your rehearsed justification? However, even while it is leaving your lips you realize how utterly idiotic and nonsensical your reasoning is and you have no power to stop it from leaving your lips while knowing it is transparently wrong and a lie, and only a fool would believe it?

The reason this is the case is because the spirit wisdom on your authority or parents is powerful, much more powerful than yours was, in this case. Even though they may not have even retorted to your justification yet, the powerful spirit on them cuts right through and its light exposes your words as nonsense. It gives them the power of clarity and truth, leaving you intimidated and exposed as being deceitful. It's feeling that you are standing before them and they can plainly see that you are telling a lie. This is the kind of unintimidatable power the Holy Spirit provides for you that doesn't leave you floundering and forgetful of your own sound understanding in the face of a powerfully deceptive person.

We ignorantly empower ourselves with these 14 demonic spirit energies and perceptions as we learn how to empower ourselves to deal with different circumstances. When we do, they have an influence in the physical world and expression through a physical body, which they do not have on their own. Each spirit has a unique way of perceiving things that is according to their false to the truth wisdom values. Each spirit has a unique quality to their spirit energy.

For example, the quality of the power/energy of the spirit of fear is dread and anxiety. The motive of the spirit of fear is to control. When it cannot control circumstances, it will exert itself in power in an effort to control or bend the direction things are leading to something of its own desire. This is what we feel when empowered by that spirit.

Anger, even a murderous rage, is the energy quality of the spirit of jealousy that we feel when we do not possess what we falsely believe we are entitled to. Cain was jealous of his brother Abel and murdered him. Each spirit has a unique motive that empowers and inspires it. The motive of the spirit of jealousy is to have something it did not earn, perceiving that it is entitled to possess a thing. These are just a couple of examples to help give understanding how demonic spirits influence our soul and worldview.

Whenever we perceive things in life with the eyes of the understanding of these demonic spirits (through their wisdom values and motives), we call them down to protect, empower, and achieve whatever it is we are trying to attain. We ignorantly abandon God as our wisdom and source of power. This is what original sin has done to us and what our parents have modeled.

Here are other misinterpretations of scripture:

AMP 1Co 2:11 *For what person perceives (knows and understands) what passes through a man's thoughts except the man's own spirit within him? Just so no one discerns (comes to know and comprehend) the thoughts of God except the Spirit of God.*

Some teach this means that the devil cannot know our thoughts. This understanding is wrong! If the spirit perception (wisdom) within the man is the spirit of the devil or of demons, empowering him, and causing his understanding to perceive things through a demonic perception, then the devil and demons indeed know and understand the thoughts that pass through that man. What Paul was trying to communicate above was that if we perceive and empower ourselves with the Spirit of God, we can know His thoughts:

AMP 1Co 2:12 *Now we have not received the spirit [that belongs to] the world, but the [Holy] Spirit Who is from God, [given to us] that we might realize and comprehend and appreciate the gifts [of divine favor and blessing so freely and lavishly] bestowed on us by God.*

AMP 1Co 2:16 *For who has known or understood the mind (the counsels and purposes) of the Lord so as to guide and instruct Him and give Him knowledge? But we have the mind of Christ (the Messiah) and do hold the thoughts (feelings and purposes) of His heart.*

Secondly, it is erroneously taught that if we have the Spirit of God, then we cannot have the spirit of the devil because where the Holy Spirit is, evil spirits cannot be. This could not be further from the truth. First of all, when we receive the Holy Spirit, He must live in our hearts with our corrupt and sinful human spirit until we die to our bodies. It is then that we are set free of our human spirit, and only the Holy Spirit influencing us, including our perception and deeds. Inside of our heart of hearts, we desire to be reconciled with God.

AMP Eze 11:19 *And I will give them one heart [a new heart] and I will put a new spirit within them; and I will take the stony [unnaturally* hardened] heart out of their flesh, and will give them a heart of flesh [sensitive and responsive to the touch of their God], And I will put my Spirit within you and cause you to walk in My statutes, and you shall heed My ordinances and do them.

AMP Eze 36:28-31 And you shall dwell in the land that I gave to your fathers; and you shall be My people, and I will be your God. I will also save you from all your uncleannesses, and I will call forth the grain and make it abundant and lay no famine on you. And I will multiply the fruit of the tree and the increase of the field, that you may no more suffer the reproach and disgrace of famine among the nations. Then you shall [earnestly] remember your own evil ways and your doings that were not good, and shall loathe yourselves in your own sight for your iniquities and for your abominable deeds.

AMP Eze 18:31 (I will) Cast away from you all your transgressions by which you have transgressed against Me, and make you a new mind and heart and a new spirit.

AMP Ro 6:20-23 For when you were slaves of sin, you were free in regard to righteousness. But then what benefit (return) did you get from the things of which you are now ashamed? [None] for the end of those things is death. But now since you have been set free from sin and have become the slaves of God, you have your present reward in holiness and its end is eternal life. For the wages which sin pays is death, but the [bountiful] free gift of God is eternal life through (in union with) Jesus Christ our Lord.

The desire in our heart of hearts to be reconciled with God and to be free of our own bondage to sin is what invites and binds us with the Holy Spirit. However, and once again, we are not separated from our corrupt human spirit until we die. Now possessing the Holy Spirit within, we start out our new life perceiving according to sinful understandings which evolve into a Holy Spirit understanding and it becomes purified over time through experience and different choices. Yes, we have a life-changing revelation when we are saved that allows us to see life in a totally different light. Although that new perception of life starts out with a big, eye-opening bang, it continues to evolve our minds into purity over time. Our bodies continue out of bondage, habit, conditioning, and desire to gratify self. This too evolves into purity over time and continual practice of relating to the Holy Spirit inside, instead of our sinful human spirit. Salvation is a process. It is a process that is never fully attained while in the physical body. Although we are made clean by the presence of the Holy Spirit, who is evolving us into an ever-greater purity until we are completely free of our sin nature, which doesn't happen until we die, and it is no longer needed to animate our (now dead) body. In the meanwhile, the Holy Spirit lives in our hearts, side-by-side with our sin nature, competing with it to fully influence our soul.

AMP Gal 5:16-25 But I say, walk and live [habitually] in the [Holy] Spirit [responsive to and controlled and guided by the Spirit]; then you will certainly not gratify the cravings and desires of the flesh (of human nature without God).

This first verse verifies that we have a cage match within, fighting for our souls. The verse makes it clear that the Holy Spirit and our sinful human spirit, for a time, inhabit the same heart.

Continuing: *For the desires of the flesh are opposed to the [Holy] Spirit, and the [desires of the] Spirit are opposed to the flesh (godless human nature); <u>for these are antagonistic to each other [continually withstanding and in conflict with each other], so that you are not free but are prevented from doing what you desire to do.</u> But if you are guided (led) by the [Holy] Spirit, you are not subject to the Law. Now the doings (practices) of the flesh are clear (obvious): they are immorality, impurity, indecency, Idolatry, sorcery, enmity, strife, jealousy, anger (ill temper), selfishness, divisions (dissensions), party spirit (factions, sects with peculiar opinions, heresies), Envy, drunkenness, carousing, and the like. I warn you beforehand, just as I did previously, that those who do such things shall not inherit the kingdom of God. <u>But the fruit of the [Holy] Spirit [the work which His presence within accomplishes</u>* (evolving our souls into)*] is love, joy (gladness), peace, patience (an* *even temper, forbearance), kindness, goodness (benevolence), faithfulness, Gentleness (meekness, humility), self-control (self-restraint, continence). Against such things there is no law [that can bring a charge]. And those who belong to Christ Jesus (the Messiah) have crucified the flesh (the godless human nature) with its passions and appetites and desires. If we live by the [Holy] Spirit, let us also walk by the Spirit. [If by the Holy Spirit we have our life in God, let us go forward walking in line, our conduct controlled by the Spirit.]*

The fact that Paul is admonishing us to *go forward walking in line, our conduct controlled by the Spirit,* means that we must make a choice of what spirit within we go forward with, which in turn infers that we have two spirit forces within us, for the time being.

Next, while we possess both spirits, the Holy Spirit is constantly convicting our minds to see, think, and act differently than we were accustomed to, according to our sin nature. And it is a progressive process ongoing all the way up to our death that we learn not to perceive and empower ourselves out of our sin nature which is influenced by demonic spirits. In other words, to not rely on our sin nature, our corrupt human spirit and the demonic to navigate through our life experiences or to perceive our lives through our old worldview as the Holy Spirit within convicts and enlightens us to do otherwise.

While alive in the body, the Holy Spirit living in our hearts is like a man who is chase and morally pure but has to enter into a den of drug users with orgies going on to save his friend, whom he loves, from self-destruction. It surely would be a clash of spirits for him to enter in and very uncomfortable to say the least. However, he must be in that same home in order to help his friend escape that place. It is the same for the Holy Spirit to reside in our sinful hearts along with all the other spirit influences we are moved by. However, He loves us and has bound Himself to us to lead us out of that life of self-destruction until He can convict and convince us to fully operate out of His Spirit. Yes, He who is pure must enter in and for a time reside where it is impure even sometimes demoniacal, for the sake of His love for us.

AMP 1Co 6:15-20 *Do you not see and know that your bodies are members (bodily parts) of Christ (the Messiah)? Am I therefore to take the parts of Christ and make [them] parts of a prostitute? Never! Never! Or do you not know and realize that when a man joins himself to a prostitute, he becomes one body with her? The two, it is written, shall become one flesh. But the person who is united to the Lord becomes one spirit with Him. Shun immorality and all sexual looseness [flee from impurity in thought, word, or deed]. Any other sin which a man commits is one outside the body, but he who commits sexual immorality sins against his own body. Do you not know that your body is the temple (the very sanctuary) of the Holy Spirit Who lives within you, Whom you have received [as a Gift] from God? You are not your own, You were bought with a price [purchased with a preciousness and paid for, made His own]. So then, honor God and bring glory to Him in your body.*

Below are a few more verses among the many in the Bible that tell us the true nature of our relationship with Jesus.

AMP Jn 15:4-10 <u>*Dwell in Me, and I will dwell in you.*</u> *[Live in Me, and I will live in you.] Just as no branch can bear fruit of itself without abiding in (being vitally united to) the vine, neither can you bear fruit unless you abide in Me. I am the Vine; you are the branches. Whoever lives in Me and I in him bears much (abundant) fruit. However, apart from Me [cut off from vital union with Me] you can do nothing. If a person does not dwell in Me, he is thrown out like a [broken-off] branch, and withers; such branches are gathered up and thrown into the fire, and they are burned. If you live in Me [abide vitally united to Me] and My words remain in you and continue to live in your hearts, ask whatever you will, and it shall be done for you. When you bear (produce) much fruit, My Father is honored and glorified, and you show and prove yourselves to be true followers of Mine. I have loved you, [just] as the Father has loved Me; abide in My love [continue in His love with Me]. If you keep My* commandments *[if you continue to obey My instructions]*, *you will abide in My love and live on in it, just as I have obeyed My Father's commandments and live on in His love* . . .

AMP Jn 14:15-23 *If you [really] love Me, you will keep (obey) My commands.* And I will ask the Father, and He will give you another Comforter (Counselor, Helper, Intercessor, Advocate, Strengthener, and Standby), that He may remain with you forever— The Spirit of Truth, Whom the world cannot receive (welcome, take to its heart), because it does not see Him or know and recognize Him. But you know and recognize Him, for He lives with you [constantly] and will be in you. I will not leave you as orphans [comfortless, desolate, bereaved, forlorn, helpless]; I will come [back] to you. Just a little while now, and the world will not see Me any more, but you will see Me; because I live, you will live also. At that time [when that day comes] you will know [for yourselves] that I am in My Father, and you [are] in Me, and I [am] in you. *The person who has My commands and keeps them is the one who [really] loves Me; and whoever [really] loves Me will be loved by My Father, and I [too] will love him and will show (reveal, manifest) Myself to him.* [I will let Myself be clearly seen by him and make Myself real to him.] Judas, not Iscariot, asked Him, Lord, how is it that You will reveal Yourself [make Yourself real] to us and not to the world? *Jesus answered, If a person [really] loves Me, he will keep My word [obey My teaching]; and My Father will love him, and We will come to him and make Our home (abode, special dwelling place) with him (spiritually united).*

AMP Eph 1:22-2:6 And He has put all things under His feet and has appointed Him the universal and supreme Head of the church [a headship exercised throughout the church], *Which is His body, the fullness of Him Who fills all in all [for in that body lives the full measure of Him Who makes everything complete, and Who fills everything everywhere with Himself].* AND YOU [He made alive], when you were dead (slain) by [your] trespasses and sins In which at one time you walked [habitually]. You were following the course and fashion of this world [were under the sway of the tendency of *this present age], following the prince of the power of the air. [You were obedient to and under the control of] the [demon] spirit that still constantly works in the sons of disobedience [the careless, the rebellious, and the unbelieving, who go against the purposes of God]. Among these we as well as you once lived and conducted ourselves in the passions of our flesh [our behavior governed by our corrupt and sensual nature], obeying the impulses of the flesh and the thoughts of the mind [our cravings dictated by our senses and our dark imaginings]. We were then by nature children of [God's] wrath and heirs of [His] indignation, like the rest of mankind. But God—so rich is He in His mercy! Because of and in order to satisfy the great and wonderful and intense love with which He loved us, <u>Even when we were dead (slain) by [our own] shortcomings and trespasses, He made us alive together in fellowship and in union with Christ; [He gave us the very life of Christ Himself, the same new life with which He quickened Him, for]</u> it is by grace (His favor and mercy which you did not deserve) that you are saved (delivered from judgment and made partakers of Christ's salvation). <u>And He raised us up together with Him</u> and made us sit down together [giving us joint seating with Him] in the heavenly sphere [by virtue of our being] in Christ Jesus (the Messiah, the Anointed One).*

Although Jesus has a body and is in Heaven sitting at the righthand of the Father, at His request the Father granted that Jesus could return to the world in the disembodied form of His Spirit.

WEB 2 Co 3:17 Now the Lord is the Spirit; and where the Spirit of the Lord is, there is liberty (freedom).

The *Church Pure* are those who are in *spiritual union* with Christ. Through personal tribulation they have become detached from what keeps them bound to the spirit of this world. They no longer seek out their own desires, and agendas for their lives. They live as the embodiment of Jesus' Spirit in the earth. They are obedient to every prompting of His Spirit no matter the effect it has on their person. They no longer consider their lives as their own anymore, rather, they have died so that Christ may live through them.

The delusion of balance

AMP 2Co 5:20 *So we are Christ's ambassadors, God making His appeal as it were through us. We [as Christ's personal representatives] beg you for His sake to lay hold of the divine favor [now offered you] and be reconciled to God.*

We are not the Lord; we are servants of the Lord; we are His ambassadors. Jesus is not our co-pilot but our pilot. We often take on too much responsibility of saving the lives of others, however, we are admonished by the Lord to help others and lead them to Him. How do we know how far to go in helping others? What is the right balance of living for others and not ourselves so we do not neglect our families? Where is the line that helping others enable them to sin and lead destructive lives instead of saving them?

AMP Ro 14:4B *It is before his own master that he stands or falls. And he shall stand and be upheld, for the Master (the Lord) is mighty to support him and make him stand.*

AMP 2Co 5:18-20 *But all things are from God, <u>Who through Jesus Christ reconciled us to Himself</u> [received us into favor, brought us into harmony with Himself] and gave to us the ministry of reconciliation [that by word and deed we might aim to bring others into harmony with Him]. <u>It was God [personally present] in Christ, reconciling and restoring the world to favor with Himself</u>, not counting up and holding against [men] their trespasses [but cancelling them], and committing to us the message of reconciliation (of the restoration to favor). <u>So we are Christ's ambassadors, God making His appeal as it were through us.</u> We [as Christ's personal representatives] beg you for His sake to lay hold of the divine favor [now offered you] and be reconciled to God.*

When we take on too much responsibility for the salvation of others, we begin to take their choices personally. In some cases, we end up judging them because they are not responding the way we judge they should. In other cases, we get frustrated and blame ourselves for not doing the right thing or doing enough to persuade them. In yet other cases we force ourselves on them and eventually condemn them, even giving up and writing them off when they do not respond as we judge they should. Eventually we will them so powerfully to think and act a certain way that we want to move their arms and legs the way we think they should. However, they are individuals with their own will, held accountable by God for their own choices and actions. Even Jesus said to His own followers at a moment of doubt and disbelief:

AMP Jn 6:66-67 After this, many of His disciples drew back (returned to their old associations) and no longer accompanied Him. Jesus said to the Twelve, Will you also go away? [And do you too desire to leave Me?]

Many Christian pastors burn themselves out in service to the Lord and it quite often takes its toll on their families, sometimes destroying them. Likewise, individuals will sometimes dive so deep into their relationship with the Lord that it divides their families.

In the worldly church they counsel that one must have *balance* between the spiritual and life in the world. A common saying is, *don't be so spiritually-minded that you are no earthly good.* Christian counselors and pastors will recommend honoring your wife and family first as a means to avert divorce because the Bible says that God hates divorce. However, if you really look at that solution that counsel is offering, it is saying to ignore what the Lord is prompting you to do because your wife or husband might divorce you and if they do, that makes it your fault.

When it is the wife or husband that objects to your obedience to the Lord and His prompting, they are in sin or in disobedience to the Lord, even if they do not believe. So, do we likewise fall into disobedience to preserve the marriage and go down with the ship (as it were) because that is supposedly what the Lord prefers? However, that is exactly what this type of solution is unwittingly advising.

AMP Lk 14:25-35 Now huge crowds were going along with [Jesus], and He turned and said to them, <u>If anyone comes to Me and does not</u>

hate his [own] father and mother [in the sense of indifference to or relative disregard for them in comparison with his attitude toward God] and [likewise] his wife and children and brothers and sisters—[yes] and even his own life also—he cannot be My disciple. Whoever does not persevere and carry his own cross and come after (follow) Me cannot be My disciple. For which of you, wishing to build a farm building, does not first sit down and calculate the cost [to see] whether he has sufficient means to finish it? Otherwise, when he has laid the foundation and is unable to complete [the building], all who see it will begin to mock and jeer at him, Saying, This man began to build and was not able (worth enough) to finish. Or what king, going out to engage in conflict with another king, will not first sit down and consider and take counsel whether he is able with ten thousand [men] to meet him who comes against him with twenty thousand? And if he cannot [do so], when the other king is still a great way off, he sends an envoy and asks the terms of peace. So then, any of you who does not forsake (renounce, surrender claim to, give up, say good-bye to) all that he has cannot be My disciple. Salt is good [an excellent thing], but if salt has lost its strength and has become saltless (insipid, flat), how shall its saltness be restored? It is fit neither for the land nor for the manure heap; men throw it away. He who has ears to hear, let him listen and consider and comprehend by hearing!

NIV Lk 12:49-53 "I have come to bring fire on the earth, and how I wish it were already kindled! But I have a baptism to undergo, and how distressed I am until it is completed! Do you think I came to bring peace on earth? No, I tell you, but division. From now on there will be five in one family divided against each other, three against two and two against three. They will be divided, father against son and son against father, mother against daughter and daughter against mother, mother-in-law against daughter-in-law and daughter-in-law against mother-in-law."

The entire plan of salvation has always been to create a division, an enmity or hatred between sinners; for all humanity are sinners. A separation between those sinners who desire to conform to God from those sinners who desire to do their own will. This is not to say that you should not honor your wife and family, but you should not do so at the expense of not honoring God and doing the work He has given you to do.

In spite of how the contemporary church tries to resolve this type of discord in families, the real problem is not a matter of *balance* and not knowing how to manage your time properly. The problem is that we run out in front of God and do our God tasks in our own power and wisdom, according to our own passions and fears. We end up employing God to give us the things we need to help Him, and by doing so we steal away the headship of our relationship from Him and take it on for ourselves. Then, quite often we are left perplexed, scratching our heads, wondering why things did not work out according to our plans.

The solution is to learn how to better hear from God before acting, while not trying to be smarter at managing our time. Then be obedient to how the Spirit instructs you to spend your attention. Sometimes it will be for your family and sometimes it will be for His purposes. But it will always be the most productive thing for both family and God's work. For the Spirit knows what is best in serving all things. We are responsible for honoring our union with the Lord first and He will guide us into all things, for the good of all things. The Lord loves and cares for even our own children and spouses infinitely more than we do. We need to trust Him especially with the outcome of everything! In fact, the love and nurturing care we feel for our own children is God's love and care for them as expressed through us as their parents.

When we sacrifice and nurture our children in deeds, we give expression to the nurturing love God has for them and as a result, we sense and feel the powerful love of God for the child as it flows through us. We then feel it as our own because we own, conform, and act on it. It is said that God is love. Can we reject giving nurturing sacrificial love in favor of our own self-absorbed needs—can we give a dysfunctional or ill motivated or self-serving or resentful expression of God's love towards the objects of our love? Yes! Because we are all sinners and most often lack the capacity to love others in its purest form. For love pours out its energies and resources to nurture the object of its love without conditions or expectations or payment.

^{AMP 1Jn 4:19} *We love Him, because He first loved us.*

^{AMP Ro 5:6-10} *While we were yet in weakness [powerless to help ourselves], at the fitting time Christ died for (in behalf of) the ungodly.* <u>*Now it is an extraordinary thing for one to give his life even for an upright man, though perhaps for a noble and lovable and generous benefactor someone might even dare to die. But God shows and clearly proves His [own] love for us by the fact that while we were still sinners, Christ (the Messiah, the Anointed One) died for us*</u>*. Therefore, since we are now justified (acquitted, made righteous, and brought into right relationship with God) by Christ's blood, how much more [certain is it that] we shall be saved by Him from the indignation and wrath of God.* <u>*For if while we were enemies we were reconciled to God through the death of His Son,*</u> *it is much more [certain], now that we are reconciled, that we shall be saved (daily delivered from sin's dominion) through His [resurrection] life.*

Too many times, leadership condemns a person because of his devotion to God at the neglect of his wife. Then they will counsel him to instead, honor her with his time and find a *healthy balance*. Often in these circumstances is a spouse who is self-serving, concerned with their own needs, at the expense of not following the Lord's will—having a, *what have you done for me lately*, love. The wife (in this example) refuses to step into what God is calling her to do and demands her husband's attention in a way that prevents him, also, from doing what he is called to do. This can be a very deceitful situation in that the wife may not want to do something criminal, immoral, or a sin as outlined in the Ten Commandments, however, she is not willing to live her life in union with Christ doing His will, but living for herself doing her own will and pleasure. Whereas without exception the husband is condemned and is told to please his wife because God hates divorce, resulting in neither of them living to do the Lord's will instead of their own, breaking union with the Lord. In a worldly perspective, this course of action makes perfect sense because it preserves the marriage. However, from a spiritual perspective, the one has corrupted the other into no longer honoring their spiritual marriage, their New Covenant relationship with the Lord, which is dependent on dying to self and living out the Lord's will and thus being one with Him. It's exactly what happened in the garden. Eve ingested the fruit of the knowledge of good and evil in direct disobedience towards God. Then Adam did the same, not because he desired to, but to remain in harmony with his wife. Adam broke union with God in order to remain in union with Eve. Because of Eve's sin and defiance, she put Adam in a position where He had to choose union with God or with her. Eve's primary sin was to ingest that fruit, and Adam's primary sin was as we are told by God below:

NIV Ge 3:17-19 To Adam he (God) said, "Because you listened to your wife and ate from the tree about which I commanded you, 'You must not eat of it,' "Cursed is the ground because of you; through painful toil you will eat of it all the days of your life. It will produce thorns and thistles for you, and you will eat the plants of the field. By the sweat of your brow you will eat your food until you return to the ground, since from it you were taken; for dust you are and to dust you will return."

In the case of Old Covenant believers, to not follow the law is sin! However, when it comes to New Covenant believers that is not sin, for we have been set free from the law. According to the New Covenant relationship, for us to not do the Lord's will above our own, is sin and spiritual adultery. In fact, it is the only sin we can commit and the only (for a lack of a better word) law we can break. To do so is to, in spiritual adultery, break free from union with Jesus just as Eve did, followed by Adam. We forsake our first love; we worship the created and no longer the Creator.

AMP Ro 14:22-23 *Your personal convictions [on such matters]—exercise [them] as in God's presence, keeping them to yourself [striving only to know the truth and obey His will]. Blessed (happy, to be envied) is he who has no reason to judge himself for what he approves [who does not convict himself by what he chooses to do]. <u>But the man who has doubts (misgivings, an uneasy conscience) about eating, and then eats [perhaps because of you], stands condemned [before God], because he is not true to his convictions and he does not act from faith. For whatever does not originate and proceed from faith is sin [whatever is done without a conviction of its approval by God is sinful].</u>*

The whole concept of trying to figure out how to please everyone by having *balance* is futile, including the counseling of it. As shown, above it is also wrong to think that if one's spouse is so self-centered and in rebellion to God, that He hates divorce so much, the Lord would say to the other spouse, *go ahead and live in sin and fall short of My call on your life in order to cleave to your spouse because, I hate divorce more than I hate disobedience.* That is just plain ignorant, however, if one was to stand back and look, this is exactly the thinking that is in line with most of the counsel out there.

Note: Even though the example made the wife the one outside of God's will and the husband trying to do God's will, it works the other way around too. It could be the wife trying to do the Lord's will and leadership admonishing her to have *balance* and appease her husband who is not interested in doing the Lord's will. In fact, this is more often the case than the other way around. The only reason it was worded that way was because we were focusing on pastors who are advised to find proper *balance*. For the most part, pastors are males.

In every case in the Bible without exception, God puts the disobedient one on the outside and demands the loyalty of the other. There is no scripture that reflects something different than to hold God as a first priority.

Appeasing self-centered selfishness by finding a compromise of balance is not a Biblical answer. This seems wrong to the worldly-minded, but those in *spiritual union* with Christ never compromise. That is not the way to bring true peace and unity to any diverse groups. To compromise the promptings of the Lord for the sake of unity and peace is to be jointly in disobedience to the Lord, breaking free from Him to join with others. In all cases, no matter what the cost, believers follow what they believe the Spirit is saying. To compromise values for the sake of peace will bring superficial peace between people, but it will never make hearts in one accord with each other or with the Lord. To accept someone else's values for the sake of peace is to betray one's own conscience and values.

The worldly-minded would say at that point, well then, how could there be any peace or unity between individuals without compromise? To hang on to your own values divides people, causing us to judge and that is why Judeo-Christian Biblical values are the blame of all violence in the world. We should respect the truth of others as their truth. First of all, the first recorded act of violence was not perpetrated by those who believed Biblical values and followed the will of God. It was the one who followed his own will and insisted on acceptance without conformity to God that committed the first act of violence. It was out of jealousy and anger Cain killed his brother Abel who had acceptance through conforming to the will of God.

AMP Ge 4:3-16 And in the course of time Cain brought to the Lord an offering of the fruit of the ground. And Abel brought of the firstborn of his flock and of the fat portions. And <u>the Lord had respect and regard for Abel and for his offering. But for Cain and his offering He had no respect or regard. So Cain was exceedingly angry and indignant, and he looked sad and depressed. And the Lord said to Cain, Why are you angry? And why do you look sad and depressed and dejected? If you do well, will you not be accepted? And if you do not do well, sin crouches at your door; its desire is for you, but you must master it. And Cain said to his brother, Let us go out to the</u>

field. And when they were in the field, Cain rose up against Abel his brother and killed him. And the Lord said to Cain, Where is Abel your brother? And he said, I do not know. Am I my brother's keeper? And [the Lord] said, What have you done? The voice of your brother's blood is crying to Me from the ground. And now you are cursed by reason of the earth, which has opened its mouth to receive your brother's [shed] blood from your hand. When you till the ground, it shall no longer yield to you its strength; you shall be a fugitive and a vagabond on the earth [in perpetual exile, a degraded outcast]. Then Cain said to the Lord, My punishment is greater than I can bear. Behold, You have driven me out this day from the face of the land, and from Your face I will be hidden; and I will be a fugitive and a vagabond and a wanderer on the earth, and whoever finds me will kill me. And the Lord said to him, Therefore, if anyone kills Cain, vengeance shall be taken on him sevenfold. And the Lord set a mark or sign upon Cain, lest anyone finding him should kill him. So Cain went away from the presence of the Lord and dwelt in the land of Nod [wandering], east of Eden.

My punishment is greater than I can bear. In typical fashion of those who do their own will and demand acceptance without conformity, they see the consequence of their action as unjust punishment heaped upon them. According to the Bible, this murder was the first death. On top of that, it was a death of jealous violence perpetrated on an individual whose only crime was in conforming to the will of God. Abel, by nature of his conformity, contrasted the one who did not. Why is Cain surprised that he is alienated from his family who loved the brother he murdered—that they are shocked, horrified, and angry? Why is he likewise surprised that there are those who desire to kill him over what he did? And most telling about his mind set; why does Cain see his family's reaction as a punishment and not a consequence of the unthinkable deed he committed? And why does he not show any signs of remorse for what he did to his brother, but only feels sorry for himself?

Secondly, to respect the perception of the truth of others as, "their truth," is to rest in the idea that there is no absolute truth.

Unwittingly that includes your own idea of truth; that notion by default makes your truth as not absolute. Einstein's famous observation that states; truth is relative to the observer makes the universe chaotic and random, giving us all rationales and justifications to do as we will. Truth is absolute and it is established by Him who created all things and has formed and brought order to all things according to His intent and creativity.

It is perception that is relative to the observer, not truth. Perception varies from one point of perspective to another because it cannot see all holistically, but only fragments. A holistic truth can never accurately be observed or understood by perceiving only a fragment of anything. Even the greatest intelligence like Einstein cannot derive truth from a fragmented perception. It will aways fall short and be false to the truth based on assumptions, even if it gets some small part of the whole correct. It is like one claiming to have made a perfect model of a dinosaur from a single bone.

True unity can only come from one perception and one truth—absolute truth—the truth of the Creator.

Agreeing on mutual compromise to accommodate the truth and ideas of others can never bring about true unity. However, with the superficial worldly-minded people possessing chaotic, random, and self-serving principles, compromise is the closest individuals can get to being unified.

The true and only way of unity is if all individuals were to abandon their own perceptions, motives, and self-serving notions, then instead, adopt those of a single spirit—the Holy Spirit. In this way, they can finally achieve true and absolute unity with each other and God. Yes, it does not have to be the perceptions and motives of the Holy Spirit but those of a single spirit to truly unify. For us to adopt the spirit of those who desire acceptance without conformity doing as they will, is for the whole world to be united, however, united in rebellion and alienated from the absolute truth of God.

AMP Eph 1:18-2:3 By having the eyes of your heart flooded with light, so that you can know and understand the hope to which He has called you, and how rich is His glorious inheritance in the saints (His set-apart ones), And <u>[so that you can know and understand] what is the immeasurable and unlimited and surpassing greatness of His power in and for us who believe</u>, as demonstrated in the working of His mighty strength, Which He exerted in Christ when He raised Him from the dead and seated Him at His [own] right hand in the heavenly [places], Far above all rule and authority and power and dominion and every name that is named [above every title that can be conferred], not only in this age and in this world, but also in the age and the world which are to come. <u>And He has put all things under His (Jesus') feet and has appointed Him the universal and supreme Head of the church [a headship exercised throughout the church], Which is His body, the fullness of Him Who fills all in all [for in that body</u> (the Church, His followers that He is in spiritual union with) *<u>lives the full measure of Him Who makes everything complete, and Who fills everything everywhere with Himself]</u>. AND YOU [He made alive], when you were dead (slain) by [your] trespasses and sins In which at one time you walked [habitually]. You were following the course and fashion of this world [were under the sway of the tendency of this present age], following the prince of the power of the air. [You were obedient to and under the control of] the [demon] spirit that still constantly works in the sons of disobedience [the careless, the rebellious, and the unbelieving, who go against the purposes of God]. Among these we as well as you once lived and conducted ourselves in the passions of our flesh [our behavior governed by our corrupt and sensual nature], obeying the impulses of the flesh and the thoughts of the mind [our cravings dictated by our senses and our dark imaginings]. We were then by nature children of [God's] wrath and heirs of [His] indignation, like the rest of mankind.*

Instead of compromising the values and perceptions of individuals that hang on to and believe their perceived truth, we all abandon our own and adopt those of the one individual who knows absolute truth.

We then can all be in perfect unity, single-minded in concord agreement.

AMP Ac 4:31-33 *And when they had prayed, the place in which they were assembled was shaken; and they were all filled with the Holy Spirit, and they continued to speak the Word of God with freedom and boldness and courage. Now the company of believers was of one heart and soul, and not one of them claimed that anything which he possessed was [exclusively] his own, but everything they had was in common and for the use of all. And with great strength and ability and power the apostles delivered their testimony to the resurrection of the Lord Jesus, and great grace (loving-kindness and favor and goodwill) rested richly upon them all.*

AMP Phil 2:1-2 *SO BY whatever [appeal to you there is in our mutual dwelling in Christ, by whatever] strengthening and consoling and encouraging [our relationship] in Him [affords], by whatever persuasive incentive there is in love, by whatever participation in the [Holy] Spirit [we share], and by whatever depth of affection and compassionate sympathy, Fill up and complete my joy by living in harmony and being of the same mind and one in purpose, having the same love, being in full accord and of one harmonious mind and intention.*

AMP Jas 3:11-4:2 *Does a fountain send forth [simultaneously] from the same opening fresh water and bitter? Can a fig tree, my brethren, bear olives, or a grapevine figs? Neither can a salt spring furnish fresh water. Who is there among you who is wise and intelligent? Then let him by his noble living show forth his [good] works with the [unobtrusive] humility [which is the proper attribute] of true wisdom. But if you have bitter jealousy (envy) and contention (rivalry, selfish ambition) in your hearts, do not pride yourselves on it and thus be in defiance of and false to the Truth. This [superficial] wisdom is not such as comes down from above, but is earthly, unspiritual (animal), even devilish (demoniacal). For wherever there is jealousy (envy) and contention (rivalry and selfish ambition), there will also be confusion (unrest, disharmony, rebellion) and all sorts of evil and vile practices. But the wisdom from above is first of all pure (undefiled); then it is peace-loving, courteous (considerate, gentle). [It is willing to] yield to reason, full of compassion and good fruits; it is wholehearted and straightforward, impartial and unfeigned (free from doubts, wavering, and insincerity). And the harvest of righteousness (of conformity to God's will in thought and deed) is [the fruit of the seed] sown in peace by those who work for and make peace [in themselves and in others, that peace which means concord, agreement, and harmony between individuals, with undisturbedness, in a peaceful mind free from fears and agitating passions and moral conflicts]. WHAT LEADS to strife (discord and feuds) and how do conflicts (quarrels and fightings) originate among you? Do they not arise from your sensual desires that are ever warring in your bodily members? You are jealous and covet [what others have] and your desires go unfulfilled; [so] you become murderers. [To hate is to murder as far as your hearts are concerned.] You burn with envy and anger and are not able to obtain [the gratification, the contentment, and the happiness that you seek], so you fight and war.*

In the case of relationship and community, the one in *spiritual union* with Jesus always follows what both parties of the relationship and the community agrees the Spirit is saying, not what makes sense to some, according to their own perceived wisdom; even if they are experts in the given field. They never take action until they unanimously agree with what the Spirit is saying, how the Spirit of Jesus perceives, feels, and wills. This is the remedy, not to compromise, enable, and appease.

AMP 1Co 2:12-3:5 Now we have not received the spirit [that belongs to] the world, but the [Holy] Spirit Who is from God, [given to us] that we might realize and comprehend and appreciate the gifts [of divine favor and blessing so freely and lavishly] bestowed on us by God. And we are setting these truths forth in words not taught by human wisdom but taught by the [Holy] Spirit, combining and interpreting spiritual truths with spiritual language [to those who possess the Holy Spirit]. But the natural, nonspiritual man does not accept or *welcome or admit into his heart the gifts and teachings and revelations of the Spirit of God, for they are folly (meaningless nonsense) to him; and he is incapable of knowing them [of progressively recognizing, understanding, and becoming better acquainted with them] because they are spiritually discerned and estimated and appreciated. <u>But the spiritual man tries all things [he examines, investigates, inquires into, questions, and discerns all things], yet is himself to be put on trial and judged by no one [he can read the meaning of everything, but no one can properly discern or appraise or get an insight into him]. For who has known or understood the mind (the counsels and purposes) of the Lord so as to guide and instruct Him and give Him knowledge? But we have the mind of Christ (the Messiah) and do hold the thoughts (feelings and purposes) of His heart.</u> HOWEVER, BRETHREN, I could not talk to you as to spiritual [men], but as to nonspiritual [men of the flesh, in whom the carnal nature predominates], as to mere infants [in the new life] in Christ [unable to talk yet!] I fed you with milk, not solid food, for you were not yet strong enough [to be ready for it]; but even yet you are not strong enough [to be ready for it], For you are still [unspiritual, having the nature] of the flesh [under the control of ordinary impulses]. <u>For as long as [there are] envying and jealousy and wrangling and factions among you, are you not unspiritual and of the flesh, behaving yourselves after a human standard and like mere (unchanged) men? For when one says, I belong to Paul, and another, I belong to Apollos, are you not [proving yourselves] ordinary (unchanged) men?</u> What then is Apollos? What is Paul? Ministering servants [not heads of parties] through whom you believed, even as the Lord appointed to each his task:*

Question: When does the *spiritual man* act outside of agreement with what the community is saying, or what their authority or husband or wife or the other people in any other relationship are saying?

Answer: When those who they are in relationship with are not seeking the will and perception of God in a matter but are going by their own desires and sense of right and wrong. That is, even if they back it up with scripture, expertise, or by their own agendas, or desires. If the Lord says, spend less time doing ministry work and more time with the wife and family, then in that case we counsel for the husband to do so. Likewise, we never take it for granted we know what is right, but bring all things to God. If we all are in agreement the Spirit says work harder in ministry, forsaking your family and wife, then we counsel that. Even if it means the other spouse who is operating out of their own agenda says they will divorce.

The same goes for churches who decide to merge with sister churches or unite as a core group of churches to attain unity in the body. The church has become so worldly in making peace that churches will find a common ground through compromise to make unity, while ignoring what the Spirit is saying to do, which in some cases would be to divide from one another. To co-depend and difunctionally bind your church to another church outside of what the Spirit is saying will cause your church to take on demonic forces that are ruling that church religiously. This will bring you in a superficial harmony with each other, but spiritually together, outside of the will of God.

The Bible says, let the unbelieving spouse leave if they want because we are people of peace (1 Co 7:15). The Church has to get it out of their heads that what we believe He is saying to do will always result in harmony and peace. That is just plain unscriptural. It is true we are people of peace who disarm, sacrifice, even suffer by letting our lives be poured out as a drink offering to bring others into harmony and unity with Christ. However, it is never at the compromise of not following the Spirit's solutions. We follow the Spirit while at the same time knowing His solutions may, on occasion, bring division and loss into our lives. Sometimes even more than it brings harmony, peace, and prosperity because we live in a world whose mentality is to take care of number one.

WEB Mt 10:34-39 "*Don't think that I came to send peace on the earth. I didn't come to send peace, but a sword. For I came to set a man at odds against his father, and a daughter against her mother, and a daughter-in-law against her mother-in-law. A man's foes will be those of his own household. He who loves father or mother more than me is not worthy of me; and he who loves son or daughter more than me isn't worthy of me. He who doesn't take his cross and follow after me isn't worthy of me. He who seeks his life will lose it; and he who loses his life for my sake will find it.*

The prayer life of those in *spiritual union* vs. those who practice a Christian religion

What have you done for me lately? love relationship. . . Union with Jesus is not a one-sided relationship. In fact, Jesus gives us the respect and dignity of an equal. He says, He will forgive who we forgive, and whoever we do not forgive, they will not be forgiven. Likewise, He tells us that whatever we ask in His name, it will be granted to us. What we bind on earth will be bound in *Heaven*, what we loose on earth will be loosed in *Heaven*. And again, the spirit of prophecy is subject to the prophet. Meaning, we have the final say whether we give expression to the Spirit or any other spirit perception and motivation, even when it is compelling for us to say or do a certain thing.

The Lord is not up there on a throne wagging His finger waiting to see if we get it right or wrong, then condemns us. The Lord Himself is determined to keep connected and in unity with us. Add to the heart of His relationship with us (the above outlined) that we are no longer judged by the law, what is right and wrong. Being in union with Him changes that. We are now judged by whether or not the course of action we take is something we believe His Spirit is prompting us to do. And at that, we are not judged whether we hit the mark or totally miss His urging.

AMP Ro 4:3 *For what does the Scripture say? Abraham believed in (trusted in) God, and it was credited to his account as righteousness (right living and right standing with God).*

AMP Ro 8:26-28 *So too the [Holy] Spirit comes to our aid and bears us up in our weakness; for we do not know what prayer to offer nor how to offer it worthily as we ought, but the Spirit Himself goes to meet our supplication and pleads in our behalf with unspeakable yearnings and groanings too deep for utterance. And He Who searches the hearts of men knows what is in the mind of the [Holy] Spirit [what His intent is], because <u>the Spirit intercedes and pleads [before God] in behalf of the saints according to and in harmony with God's will. We are assured and know that [God being a partner in their labor] all things work together and are [fitting into a plan] for good to and for those who love God and are called according to [His] design and purpose.</u>*

NLT Jn 20:23 *If you forgive anyone's sins, they are forgiven. If you refuse to forgive them, they are unforgiven."*

NAS MT 16:19 *"I will give you the keys of the kingdom of heaven; and whatever you bind on earth shall have been bound in heaven, and whatever you loose on earth shall have been loosed in heaven."*

AMP 1Co 2:11-16 *. . . no one discerns (comes to know and comprehend) the thoughts of God except the Spirit of God. Now we have not received the spirit [that belongs to] the world, but the [Holy] Spirit Who is from God, [given to us] that we might realize and comprehend and appreciate the gifts [of divine favor and blessing so freely and lavishly] bestowed on us by God. And we are setting these truths forth in words not taught by human wisdom but taught by the [Holy] Spirit, combining and interpreting spiritual truths with spiritual language [to those who possess the Holy Spirit]. But the natural, nonspiritual man does not accept or welcome or admit into his heart the gifts and teachings and revelations of the Spirit of God, for they are folly (meaningless nonsense) to him; and he is incapable of knowing them [of progressively recognizing, understanding, and becoming better acquainted with them] because they are spiritually* *discerned and estimated and appreciated. <u>But the spiritual man tries all things [he examines, investigates, inquires (the Lord), into questions, and discerns all things]</u>, yet is himself to be put on trial and judged by no one [he can read the meaning of everything, but no one can properly discern or appraise or get an insight into him]. For who has known or understood the mind (the counsels and purposes) of the Lord so as to guide and instruct Him and give Him knowledge? <u>But we have the mind of Christ (the Messiah) and do hold the thoughts (feelings and purposes) of His heart.</u>*

When we do what we believe He is leading us to do as being the body to His Spirit in this world, we are judged as righteous. When we do whatever we desire to do, we are in sin and in spiritual adultery—we are acting independent and not in union with the Lord's Spirit. All we need to do is, in all sincerity, our due diligence in seeking out His heart and what response or course of action He is inspiring us to do, and do that. If after that we miss the mark, it is still accredited to us as righteous because we believed.

The Lord is such a big and powerful God that His promise is to make all things work for our good. Jesus will carry out His plans using the course of action we take however misguided and counterproductive it mistakenly is. Why? Because He is determined to do His part to stay in union with us and will not divide even if we mistakenly get it wrong.

NIV 1Sa 3:19 The LORD was with Samuel as he grew up, and he let none of his (prophetic) words fall to the ground.

That is why He will bind and loose whatever we bind and loose, forgive or not forgive who we forgive or not forgive and consider it as righteous if we do what we sincerely believe He is prompting us to do, and make it work for our good. Indeed, Jesus gives us the respect and dignity of an equal, and the grace, due to our limited ability to see Him clearly!

AMP 1Co 13:9-12 <u>For our knowledge is fragmentary (incomplete and imperfect), and our prophecy (our teaching) is fragmentary</u>

<u>(incomplete and imperfect)</u>. But when the complete and perfect (total) comes, the incomplete and imperfect will vanish away (become antiquated, void, and superseded). When I was a child, I talked like a child, I thought like a child, I reasoned like a child; now that I have become a man, I am done with childish ways and have put them aside. <u>For now we are looking in a mirror that gives only a dim (blurred) reflection [of reality as in a riddle or enigma], but then [when perfection comes] we shall see in reality and face to face!</u> Now I know in part (imperfectly), but then I shall know and understand fully and clearly, even in the same manner as I have been fully and clearly known and understood [by God].

However, the majority of contemporary Christians relate and pray to Jesus as a *fix it all guy*. Like a *sugar daddy*, there to care for our every whim as we desire or see fit. This is hard to hear, however, if we are honest with ourselves, this is most often the case. We pray as if we need to appraise Him of things He did not know, and we inform Him of the solutions. And our solutions are mostly self-serving, concerning the best outcome for our own agendas and desires. If you want to disagree with this, and you are thinking, *I do want to do God's will, and I always ask Him what it is*. It would be a good challenge for you to inspect yourself to see what percentage of your prayer time is about your own needs and desires and what percentage is about finding out what He is saying for you to do and say.

^{WEB 1Co 13:11} *When I was a child, I spoke as a child, I felt as a child, I thought as a child. Now that I have become a man, I have put away childish things.*

When we talk to children, we greet them and ask how they are doing. They will tell us all about what is going on with them. We are fascinated by them. However, it doesn't occur to the child to ask how we are doing. We give the child gifts for many occasions and take our joy in their happiness to receive them. Yet they do not make gifts for us or think to give even a card. We are ok with this. We don't expect it from them. However, as they grow up and mature, we do teach them to give back to relationships. As well, to not just be concerned with receiving, but to be concerned with giving, honoring others, and caring about their wellbeing.

It works much the same with our relationship with Jesus. When we are a new or immature Christian, almost every prayer we pray is answered, and all things, for the most part, go in our favor. We look to God to fix our personal issues, and quite often it is our personal issues that God saved us from that led us into relationship with Him. Our relationship and prayers to God are all about what we are going through. At this point we think as a child, reason as a child, and relate to God as a child.

There is a point in time, however, that we need to mature in our union with Him, and our life begins to serve Him. We then concern ourselves not with our own needs and wellbeing. We in fact learn to abandon them, and are concerned with searching out His heart, what will please Him, giving ourselves over to His concerns, and focusing on giving honor to Him. Also, spending ourselves on what will further His cause, at the neglect of our own. This is what is supposed to transpire once we become mature enough to serve Him with our bodies and lives. Love pours itself out for the object of its love. In this way, we become one in our relationship with Jesus, which is worthy of the kind of love, dignity, and respect He gives us.

NIV Lk 9:23-26 Then he said to them all: "If anyone would come after me, he must deny himself and take up his cross daily and follow me. For whoever wants to save his life will lose it, but whoever loses his life for me will save it. What good is it for a man to gain the whole world, and yet lose or forfeit his very self? If anyone is ashamed of me and my words, the Son of Man will be ashamed of him when he comes in his glory and in the glory of the Father and of the holy angels.

It has to be asked by every Christ follower, *What does this look like?* That is so we can shape the focus of our prayer time and thought life in a way that matures us as a lover who pours himself out for the object of his love. One of the ways this kind of reflection and prayer looks like with a mature believer in union with Jesus, is that they discipline their thoughts causing them to all but ignore concerns about their own needs. They believe God will be jealous to take care of their needs, then feeling safe enough, they let go of control and concern for their own lives being free to live for Him. Then, they purposefully seek out the needs of Jesus. They become progressively more still and quiet in their prayer time; meaning less verbal, as they try to get a sense of Jesus' Spirit and what He may be communicating. They wait on Him to find out what priorities He has and what promptings need to be carried out.

Here are some traits of the prayers of a mature Christian:

- Listening in prayer and not speaking
- Caring more about His concerns than one's own
- Wanting to serve more than be served
- In the quiet of one's own heart to actively listen with a heart posture that desires to search out His will, having this in mind—to *hearken*.
- Through a disciplined prayer life become a person who is unconflicted; meaning, pure in his heart in wanting to serve Jesus, with no mind to serve himself.

All these things reflect a mature believer who is actively and faithfully in *spiritual union* with Jesus; all of which make him His body and a member of the *Church Pure*.

AMP Jn 7:18 *He who speaks on his own authority seeks to win honor for himself. [He whose teaching originates with himself seeks his own glory.] But He Who seeks the glory and is eager for the honor of Him Who sent Him, He is true; and there is no unrighteousness or falsehood or deception in Him.*

It is with this understanding of our relationship with Jesus that we can know what is in His heart when He spoke these words:

AMP Mt 6:24 *No one can serve two masters; for either he will hate the one and love the other, or he will stand by and be devoted to the one* (at the expense of) *and despise and be against the other.*

And:

AMP Rev 2:2-4 *I know your industry and activities, laborious toil and trouble, and your patient endurance, and how you cannot tolerate wicked [men] and have tested and critically appraised those who call [themselves] apostles (special messengers of Christ) and yet are not, and have found them to be impostors and liars. I know you are enduring patiently and are bearing up for My name's sake, and you have not fainted or become exhausted or grown weary. But I have this [one charge to make] against you: that you have left (abandoned) the love that you had at first [you have deserted Me, your first love].*

2Co 5:13-18 *For if we are beside ourselves [mad, as some say], it is for God and concerns Him; if we are in our right mind, it is for your benefit, For the love of Christ controls and urges and impels us, because we are of the opinion and conviction that [if] One died for all, then all died; And He died for all, so that all those who live might live no longer to and for themselves, but to and for Him Who died and was raised again for their sake. Consequently, from now on we estimate and regard no one from a [purely] human point of view [in terms of natural standards of value]. [No] even though we once did estimate Christ from a human viewpoint and as a man, yet now [we have such knowledge of Him that] we know Him no longer [in terms of the flesh]. Therefore if any person is [ingrafted] in Christ (the Messiah) he is a new creation (a new creature altogether); the old [previous moral and spiritual condition] has passed away. Behold, the fresh and new has come! But all things are from God, Who through Jesus Christ reconciled us to Himself [received us into favor, brought us into harmony with Himself] and gave to us the ministry of reconciliation [that by word and deed we might aim to bring others into harmony with Him].*

Glossary

1,000-Year Reign of Christ (Millennium Reign of Christ): The promised global celestial reign over the earth led by King Jesus when He returns with His entourage including His celestial humans who are His bride. He will have sole rulership and dominion over mortal men while being King of the Israelites. A time period promised to the patriarchs of old fulfilled as the Lord's Chosen People. It immediately follows the battle of Armageddon, which is fought and won by the Lord Himself annihilating His opposition with the breath of His mouth. His reign ends with the final battle of Gog Magog when the Lord shows that He has always loved and defends His people. After which time the devil is condemned into the lake of fire. All of the elements of the natural universe melt in the lake of fire with a tremendous crash leaving humanity extinct. It is followed by the last day of judgment when ALL will rise and be judged and entry into the new heavens and new earth for those who are righteous and deemed sheep, and eternal damnation in the lake of fire for those who are cursed and deemed goats along with all natural elements of the universe and Hades, the realm of the dead.

1,260 days: (also referred to as 42 months, 3 ½ years) is mentioned on multiple times in scripture. They always describe the midpoint of a 7-year time period of a movement of God when those particular seven years have a contrasting point in the middle.

The 70-7's is a time period of grace for the Israelites to make themselves presentable before the Lord, as told in Daniel. The end cannot come or begin until after this time period is fulfilled. From the beginning of the last seven years of the 70-7's prophesied by Daniel, 1,260 days later will be the midpoint of that last seven. It is then that the sacrifices at the temple will be prohibited. The prohibition of sacrifices in the temple marks the midpoint of the last seven of the 70-7's and is the most instrumental event in creating an accurate timeline going forward and backwards of the end times and the return of Christ.

Within days after the midpoint of the last seven a time of power is granted by God for the two witnesses to prophecy for 1,260 days, dressed in sackcloth bringing us past the end of the last 7 of the 70-7's (Rev 11:3). When they have finished their appointed time appealing to the world, marks the beginning of the end.

1,260 days will also divide into two the time of God's seven years of wrath poured out on all the inhabitants of the earth. These seven years begin after the time of the two witnesses, which is a different 7-year period than that of the last seven of the 70 years of Daniel's prediction. It will consist of 1,260 days of tribulation poured out onto God's elect, *Church Corrupt*, who became apostates during the time of the two witnesses. They will be genocide by the one world government of the antichrist (Nimrod) and his false prophet (the Pope of the Catholic Church). An additional 1,260 days of wrath follows and is poured out by celestial beings on the world who persecutes God's elect, together totaling 7 years. This models the events that happened in Egypt when the Lord preserved His people while bringing disaster upon the Egyptians who persecuted and enslaved His people.

1,290 days (Dan 12:11)**:** The time period between when the daily sacrifice is abolished until the abomination that causes desolation is set up in the temple—the bringing back to life Nimrod, the beast and antichrist.

1,335 days (Dan 12:12)**:** The time period between when the daily sacrifice is abolished and when the pretribulation rapture (the first of two raptures) occurs. This happens 45 days after the appearance of the antichrist who comes back to life in the temple killing the two witnesses requiring patient courage and integrity on the part of believers who do not become apostates under the pressure of the world, the Catholic Church (the false prophet, the Pope), and the risen antichrist (Nimrod).

144,000: First fruits of God's redeeming work. Patriarchs of Israel who paved the way for Jesus to come and died through martyrdom. 12,000 from every tribe of Israel. Pure in worship and genealogy as

God's chosen people. They were the first to be resurrected and receive their celestial bodies, coming out of their tombs and appeared to many people immediately following Christ's crucifixion (Mt 27:52-53).

Abraham's Bosom (Under the altar, Paradise): The paradisiacal compartment within Hades used to hold disembodied souls of those who would eventually be redeemed and therefore recipients of a celestial body and citizens of the new heavens and the new earth, on the Last Day.

Abyss (bottomless pit): Third compartment of Hades is primarily made to confine the devil, fallen angels, hybrids of humans and angels, and demons until the last day of judgement. Their confinement is so they are no longer able to influence the affairs of mortals on the earth.

Angel: Simply a messenger from God (human or celestial). The Bible uses *angel* to depict a special messenger from God. It is also used incorrectly as a general term for celestial beings (of which there are many kinds). In this series of books there are occasions when we describe celestial beings as angels using it as a general term for the ease of understanding for our readers.

Antichrist (beast out of the sea, Nimrod): The antithesis of Christ who is currently dead, a bodiless soul, in the Abyss. His obsession is to be a savior of the people. His intention is to save people from Almighty God and to bring the world back to preflood conditions. Granted by God, the false prophet (the Pope) will be given the power to give life to Nimrod bringing him back among the living to kill the two witnesses and save the world from Yahweh and His elect. God grants him seven years to carry out God's purposes of giving His elect who become apostates their "Gomer experience" which will hem them in and turn them back to their first love, the Lord. This is a last-ditch effort of the Lord's to save even those who He spewed out of His mouth (divorced) to include them as His bride. After using the antichrist and false prophet to do His will, the antichrist will gather the world in rebellion to fight against the Lord upon His return at the

Battle of Armageddon, the world will fall and become the Kingdom of the Lord when He defeats them, and both the antichrist and false prophet will be thrown into the lake of fire. They will be the only occupants in the lake of fire for 1,000 years preceding the Day of Judgment after the Millennial Reign of Christ.

Apostacy/Apostates: Apostate is someone who abandons or renounces their faith in Christ. The apostacy is the collective group of apostates that Paul (2Th 2:3) speaks of when he says *the apostacy* or *the great falling away*. He states that Christ cannot return until this predicted event happens. The facilitation of the *great falling away* of Christians from their faith will occur as a result of the activities and prophecy of the two witnesses. They will do many wonders that will be a huge strain on the inhabitants of the earth gaining the attention of the two witnesses. The world will hate them and will want them killed. Only anyone who attempts will be swallowed up by fire. Among the many things they expose about the world is that they will expose the Pope and the leadership of the Catholic Church whose ulterior agenda is to lead Christians away from Christ and under the antichrist. The Pope becomes the false prophet and by the demand of the world, will bring the antichrist back to life in order to kill the two witnesses. The Christians who do not abandon their faith in favor of the antichrist will be raptured to Heaven and those who align with the great prostitute—the Catholic Church—will suffer in her plagues by enduring the *great tribulation*.

Astrology: The study of the movements and relative positions of celestial bodies (stars, moons, constellations and planets) interpreted as having an influence on human affairs and the natural world. It draws from a spirit of divination. Recorded in antiquity as invented by Nimrod as a point of reference to associate the fallen angels and their offspring, the giants of the preflood times as now stars and constellations, so they might be worshiped as gods and demigods still lording over the inhabitants of the earth. All the mythologies of the world have their roots in this system developed and imposed by Nimrod.

Astronomy: The scientific study of celestial objects; stars, moon, galaxies, space, the physical universe and beyond. Recorded in antiquity as a science started by Nimrod in order to develop his system of astrology and worship of the fallen gods and demigods. Astronomy (the study of space) is a legitimate scientific field, however, its origins were developed for the reason above—to make the dead giants and the confined fallen angels in the Abyss represented as stars in the heavens thereby keeping them alive as an influence over humanity in the minds of his (Nimrod's) subjects; for example, the entire pantheon of Roman and Greek gods as well as all the mythological gods and demigods in every culture on the earth. They were all instituted by Nimrod before the fall of the tower of Babel and the spreading out of the postflood population over the face of the earth given by God 70 different nations, territories, and languages. The names, exploits, and characteristics of these gods and demigods shifted over time depending on the language and cultures of the different nations who worshiped them.

Battle of Armageddon: Is the ultimate battle between Jesus and the antichrist/Nimrod/the Assyrian. Nimrod had insisted on having this showdown in his first carnation a couple of generations after the flood. All of prophecy and Israeli history from the beginning has led up to this battle of good annihilating evil on the earth. It will take both Nimrod and Jesus to rise and return to the earth for this final battle of good and evil to happen. It finally occurs after the seventh and final trumpet blows following the return of Christ and His Wedding Feast. Nimrod the antichrist has already, at this time, returned from the Abyss. In an effort to continue their rule of the earth, the antichrist, his false prophet, and the devil (now manifest on earth) will seduce the world into a war against the returned Jesus and His entourage of angels and celestial humans (all of which are now manifest and visible to mortal humans). It is their goal to eject God, Jesus and His government including the new Jerusalem off the face of the earth to claim it as their own and to save the people from God. This battle will be a futile attempt resulting in their defeat by the breath of the Lord's mouth. It is then having defeated the global empire of the antichrist that the Lord will, from the new Jerusalem, become everything He promised to the patriarchs of the Israelites. Jesus will begin His global Kingdom on the earth beginning His Millennium Reign and continuing His Kingdom afterwards for eternity in the new heavens and the new earth.

Beast out of the sea: (Nimrod, the antichrist) who was, is not now, but will rise up out of the Abyss to rule the earth for 7 years and then go to his final destruction in the lake of fire. The reason he is called the beast out of the sea is because he is the seed of Ham and his wife who were on the Ark would give birth to Nimrod (the beast) after the flood waters (the sea) recede. Ham and his wife (who possessed giant DNA) plotted to create a master race to ensure that their clan would rule the earth as it repopulated. They did this through hybriding the DNA of his wife, resulting in the giant Nimrod, the beast.

Beast out of the earth: (false prophet, Pope of the Roman Catholic Church): who will deceive and lead the whole earth (even the saints) into the great apostasy—the great falling away, and forces them to worship the beast, the risen Nimrod. He will create a body for and give life through witchcraft, satanic powers, modern medicine, and science. The reason he is called the beast out of the earth is because the false prophet is a mortal man not possessing celestial DNA such as the risen Nimrod. He is just a man who rises up to the position of Pope from among the population of mortal men. And who facilitates the return of Nimrod (the beast out of the sea).

Blueprint: a drawing or design of a plan, or model. In this series it refers the design and plan of God for salvation and judgment of mankind.

Body: is the physical or celestial embodiment of the invisible (immaterial) spirit and or soul of a creature. Celestial beings are spirit and celestial bodies, animals are spirit and physical bodies, humans are spirit, soul, and physical bodies. In the case of humans, they possess a physical (not celestial) body. Having a body made of the same matter of its environment, along with its 5 senses, allows the spirit and soul of the person to interact within its environment, the physical universe. When one dies to that body, the Bible often refers to that individual as a "soul", or as "naked," without an outward (material) embodiment. When humans die, they do not automatically have a celestial or spiritual body, they become a disembodied soul (which is the mind) and are retained in Hades (the realm of the dead) until the day of judgment. On that day of judgment, God grants the soul a celestial embodiment in order to interact in the celestial realm, their new environment, so that we may face Him and be judged by Him to either live on for eternity with Him in the celestial realm or experience a second death in that celestial body by being thrown in the lake of fire for eternity. The exception is, however, those who are in a New Covenant relationship with Jesus. They do not experience death, disembodiment. Before their heart stops beating in their physical body, they are translated into a celestial body, to live with Christ in His realm, the spiritual realm, and therefore never experience death, disembodiment. They therefore avoid being disembodied and confined in the realm of the dead, Hades. This makes the saying true, "death, where is your sting."

Celestial: [1]supernatural or spiritual realm (beyond the natural). The heavenly, or from the heavenly realm, belonging to or coming from God and His domain. It is a domain that is outside of the physical universe and the laws that govern it, including outside of time. Thus, it cannot be observed or quantified by natural means, other than it has become obvious that the physical universe has been created by intelligent design (as they term). Since science, by nature, demands observable proof, they blind themselves with tunnel vision by that principle of observation to the possibility of a realm outside the physical universe and therefore are ignorant of its existence. [2]Depending on context, the celestial is also used to describe space, including the stars and planets in the natural universe. The sky and earth's atmosphere are termed the first heaven, space and the rest of the physical universe are the second heaven, the third heaven is outside of the physical universe and is the realm of God, the spiritual or celestial realm.

Church: the Church is referring to the bride or body of Christ in the earth, who are those individuals who are in a New Covenant relationship with Christ, obeying the promptings and inspirations of the Spirit of Jesus Christ, the Holy Spirit. That relationship is a marital spiritual relationship where the individual forsakes his own will and desires and instead carries out that of his covenant partner's, Jesus, becoming one with Him. Church refers to either the all-encompassing Christian fellowship at large or a single fellowship of a Christian community or denomination. Often distinguished by the use of a capital "C" in its spelling to signify all Christians and a small "c" referring to a single community of believers.

Church Age: Can only be understood in context to Daniel's timeline (Dan 9:20-25). The *Church Age* is the delayed time between the 62-7's and the last week of years. A week of years being 7 years of which Daniel was told there would be 70. They are divided into 3 segments with delays between them. 7 weeks of years (49 years) then a gap or delay, 62 weeks of years (434 years) then a delay, finally 1 week of years (7 years) (Dan 9:25). Daniel was told that the 62 weeks of years or the second segment would be complete at the appearance and death of Jesus. God knowing that the Jews, His chosen people, would reject and have Jesus killed, assigned the delay between the end of the second segment and final segment of the 70 weeks of years, as a time to gather to Himself a new bride from among the Gentiles—the non-Israelites. This decision is given because the Jews rejected that place by rejecting Jesus. That delay is referred to as the *Church Age*, a time when the rest of the world is given opportunity to come into a New Covenant relationship with Jesus—His bride. That delay has so far lasted approximately 2,000 years while He gathers from all nations those who would be His bride. Once this has been accomplished the 70 weeks of years (70-7's) will resume with only the last segment left, which is 1 week of years or 7 years. Once completed, the end will come. This includes first; the return to the earth of Nimrod, the antichrist, and then the return of Jesus, the Christ for the final showdown of good and evil.

Crucifixion of Jesus: The death of Jesus involving being nailed to the cross. In voluntarily submitting to being crucified, Jesus was showing His sacrificial love by making reconciliation between God and man. Through His spilt blood, it created a way to release His Spirit into the earth, making all things new, while washing away the sin of the world. Enduring the cross in obedience to His Father's will is an example we must all take as believers to commit our lives to His will and purposes, no matter what the cost, in order to be worthy of being His disciples.

Death: is the cessation of life in the physical body and the lower nature of man's triune being, leaving him a disembodied but living soul, severed from his body. The soul departs its natural embodiment on the earth, and the living soul is confined to Hades, the realm of the dead, while awaiting judgment.

> **The First Death:** is death of the physical body. Death entered into the world because of the sin of Adam and Eve. This Results in the soul's disembodiment and confinement in Hades, awaiting to become embodied once again on the last day with a celestial body, so as to face judgment of either eternal life or to suffer a second and eternal death.

> **The Second Death:** is to suffer a second but eternal death. Not because of the original sin of Adam and Eve that ushered death into the world, but a result of being judged for one's own sins while in the body. It is a sentence of eternal punishment in the lake of fire, following the last day of judgment.

Delay: is a pause in God's plan of salvation and judgment of the earth. His judgment of fire, which will utterly disintegrate the earth and the physical universe ending mortal humanity, was determined and began to be carried out just a few generations after the judgement of the flood. Pauses or delays had been issued by God as a part of His plan and sentence to allow his chosen people, the Israelites, to right themselves before the end comes; to give opportunity for the full numbers of Gentiles, non-Israelites, to reconcile themselves to God; to release all prophesy throughout history informing those who reconcile with God to become aware and understand how and why the end will come; to allow both salvation and sin to evolve into their zenith, globally, before the last day comes making a clear line of demarcation, distinguishing by their deeds, individuals who desire to do God's will from those who desire to do their own will. There were two delays built into Daniel's 70 weeks of years and others throughout history. In Rev 10:6 Jesus proclaims that there will be no more delays, the end is finally at hand. This happens before the seventh and final trumpet is sounded which is immediately followed by the return of Christ and the battle of Armageddon launching His 1,000-year reign.

Demigods: are physical individuals who are hybrids of fallen angels and mortal/physical women, resulting in what is referred to as giants or Nephilim or men of renown. Because of their stature and size, they dominated mortal men and brought chaos during the preflood era. Their presence made life on earth a living hell and is the cause of God's judgment to bring the flood. In Genesis, God referred to them as *mere men*, because they had physical bodies which were subject to death as was all living things on earth. This is unlike the celestial bodies of their fathers, the fallen angels, or as they became known, the gods, that spawned them. These giants died as a result of the flood and were jailed disembodied in the Abyss, along with the celestial beings that fathered them (who were confined in the Abyss, embodied [not experiencing death to their celestial bodies]). The Bible tells us there were giants also after the flood (Gen 6:4). Postflood giants were a result of the incestual hybriding of Ham's wife (2 of the 8 survivors of the flood) to bring out those giant genes his wife possessed to make their clan a superior race of giants to rule the earth as it repopulated after the flood. It was one of that clan's offspring, Nimrod a giant, who in his hatred of God for destroying the giants of old, declared the preflood fallen angels and their spawn as gods and demigods to be worshiped and spiritually empowered by. Although they were defeated, killed, arrested and jailed in the Abyss, these figures, through Nimrod, became the mythological characters in all mythologies around the world as devised and invented by Nimrod, the antichrist, to sway people away from God the Creator.

Demigod worship: The worship of the pre-flood giants who have died and are confined in the Abyss, instituted by Nimrod in the post-flood era.

Desolation: A time period when the Lord turns His face away from any intervening help while giving people over to their own devices.

Devil (Satan)**:** Defier and adversary of God. Known by such names as; the lord of the flies or of dung (Jesus' term), Beelzebub, the father of lies, the deceiver, the accuser of the brethren, the red dragon, or serpent, the tempter, the prince of the power of the air, Lucifer. He is the supreme spirit of evil, a fallen cherub. It is written, *Eze 28:14b-17 You were on the holy mount of God; you walked among the fiery stones. You were blameless in your ways from the day you were created till wickedness was found in you. So I drove you in disgrace from the mount of God, and I expelled you, O guardian cherub, from among the fiery stones. Your heart became proud on account of your beauty, and you corrupted your wisdom because of your splendor.*

End times: The period of time that immediately follows Daniel's seventy weeks of years. The two witnesses finish their appointed time; the great falling away (the apostasy) happens; Nimrod is risen from the dead for 7 years; the first rapture and the two witnesses are called to Heaven leaving the earth in a *global desolation* for 3-1/2 years. This is the first half of the 7 years of God's wrath. In its conclusion, Jesus returns with celestial humans; the ultimate battle of good and evil happens at Armageddon; Jesus conquers and begins His 1,000 year reign on the earth; the final battle of evil happens with Gog Magog; the earth is destroyed by fire, and the day of judgment comes determining who gets eternal life and who suffers a second and eternal death by being cast into the lake of fire.

False prophet (beast out of the earth)**:** The Pope of the Roman Catholic Church who deceives and leads the earth (even the Christian believers) into the great apostasy—the great falling away and under penalty of death, forces them to worship the beast, the risen Nimrod, who the Pope, false prophet, created a body for and gave the breath of life to so Nimrod could rise back to life, and kill the two witnesses then rule the earth.

Father: The aspect of God's triune being that would be the mind and will of God, the Creator of ALL in Heaven and the earth. The ultimate divine Ruler of human destiny, its judgment, and redemption.

Fear: In the spiritual sense, fear is worship by yielding your will to the will of another. To fear God is not to be afraid of Him, but to have a reverence and respect, yielding to His will. When fearing man we have a feeling of dread, but to fear God gives a feeling of belonging, safety, strength, and joy. This is reflected in the Psalms of David.

First fruits: the first and best part of the harvest. When sacrificing, it is the first fruits we are to give God. The first fruits of the Lord's redeeming work were those disembodied souls who were resurrected and freed from the confines of Hades, specifically under the altar, the moment Jesus died on the cross. They rose out of their graves with their new bodies and appeared to many people. They were 12,000 from each of the tribes of Israel who were martyred as a sacrifice to pave the way for the Messiah, Jesus, to come into the world. They were the 144,000, the patriarchs of the Israelites, described in Matthew 27:52-53 and in Revelation 6:9-11, 7:1-8, and 14:1-5. They were as the train of His robe when Jesus returned to the Father after His death, presenting them as the first fruits of the many who would now be saved because of what He accomplished. Many might argue against this point, believing the 144,000 have yet to be redeemed until the end-times. In answer, the question must be asked; how can the patriarchs, disembodied souls, break out of Hades, the realm of the dead, come out of their graves having received clean white robes (celestial bodies) being resurrected the moment Jesus cried out, "It is finished!" if they are not indeed the first fruits of His redeeming work?

The Four Horsemen of the Apocalypse: The Four Winds of God's Destruction (Rev 6, 7:1-3). A judgment released over humanity a few generations after the flood, which followed the destruction of the tower of Babel. It was one of the initial steps of the release of God's judgement of fire—which in its completion will bring the final destruction of the earth, the physical universe, and all of physical mankind. It is a result of man unanimously choosing to line up under Nimrod and his invented pantheon of gods and demigods in order to do their own will (not God's) and be protected by Nimrod the antichrist for doing so. Nimrod's battle cry was, "Do as you will and I will protect you from Yahweh," any retribution God might visit upon them for rebelling against Him. This was one of the purposes of the tower, a refuge to save man in the case God would bring another flood because of their rebellion. However, God had promised to Noah to never again bring a global flood. Instead, this time it is of fire. This final judgment of fire by our Creator was the sentence on man in large part because it was Nimrod's declared intention to bring back the giants of old and their dominance over mankind as was before the flood. The very hell on earth that God had saved humanity from through the flood, and now unanimously they wanted to return to those circumstances! It is the curse of the four horsemen that has come down on man since then that has put us under evil dictators bent on conquest, with an ongoing 25% of humanity prematurely dying before their time due to constant wars, starvation/famine, disease, hostility from the animal kingdom, with Hades following close behind, scooping up and confining all the resulting disembodied souls.

>**First/White Horse:** Conquest
>
>**Second/Red:** War and bloodshed
>
>**Third/Black:** Famine and scarcity
>
>**Fourth/Pale:** Death by wild beasts, disease, war, and famine, followed by Hades (the realm of the dead) collecting all the disembodied souls.

Note: Jesus was quoted as saying to people who followed Him because they wanted the bread and healing of His miracles, "You follow me because you want the bread, but you do not understand My miracles (Jn 6:25-27)!" What escapes the majority is that all the miracles He did were His bona fide (certificate, credential) that He was the Savior, the Messiah, because it was Him alone who had an authority over the power and curses of the 4 horsemen, even over death, as demonstrated by the kinds of miracles He preformed. Yet He is still doubted, then and now . . .

Fourteen Root Spirits: The fourteen different demonic spirits that are mentioned in the Bible. The devil will try to find ways to manifest and bear fruit for darkness in our lives through different open doors to separate us from God. Based off of Dr. Henry Malone's 2-5-14 deliverance strategy described in His book, *Shadow Boxing*.

> **Spirit of Infirmity:** Lk 13:11
>
> **Spirit of Fear:** 2Timothy 1:7
>
> **Spirit of Divination:** Acts 16:16-18
>
> **Spirit of Whoredoms:** Hosea 4:12
>
> **Spirit of Bondage:** Romans 8:15
>
> **Spirit of Haughtiness:** Proverbs 16:18-19
>
> **Spirit of Perverseness:** Isaiah 19:14
>
> **Spirit of Antichrist:** 1 Jn 4:3
>
> **Spirit of Deaf and Dumbness:** Mark 9:25-27
>
> **Spirit of Heaviness:** Isaiah 61:3
>
> **Spirit of Lying:** 2 Chronicles 18:22
>
> **Spirit of Jealousy:** Numbers 5:14
>
> **Spirit of Stupor (Slumber):** Romans 11:8

Spirit of Error: 1 Jn 4:6

Spirit of Death (acts as a root spirit): Hebrews 2:14-15

Gehenna (Hell): The hellish place where the evil disembodied souls of humans await judgment before continuing their punishment in the permanent lake of fire.

Global desolation: A desolation is a time period when the Lord turns His face away from any intervening help while giving the people over to their own devices. A desolation against the Israelites for their unfaithfulness and spiritual adultery is described in 2 Chronicles 7:11-22. This has happened throughout history, and many desolations have been decreed by God, as spoken in Daniel 9:26. The majority of desolations have been against peoples and cultures on a local and remote level. However, when the false prophet, the Pope, sacrifices the bodies of men to make a Frankenstein type of embodiment for Nimrod the antichrist to return from the dead and occupy (the image of the beast), the Lord describes it as the abomination that cause desolation. When that happens, coupled with the great falling away of His believers, God and the heavens will turn away from the earth leaving it suffer in a global desolation for 3 ½ years. Revelation refers to this global desolation as *a half an hour of silence in heaven*, just as the silence from above when Jesus hung on the cross as depicted in Psalm 22. *MY GOD, my God, why have You forsaken me? Why are You so far from helping me, and from the words of my groaning?* When He gives humanity over to their own devises and ungodly strivings, they will kill the Christians in a mass genocide while God does not intervene. NIV Mt 8:12 *But the subjects of the kingdom will be thrown outside, into the darkness, where there will be weeping and gnashing of teeth."*

> **Note:** Knowing what a global desolation is and that it will happen, becomes proof that there is a pretribulation rapture. For at the last supper Jesus promised that He would return in the form of His Holy Spirit not ever leaving His true believers as orphans, but that He would be with them for all of eternity. It would break His promise if heaven, including

the Holy Spirit, turning away from the faithful when leaving the earth in a global desolation. It is for this reason, to keep His promise, that it would require the Lord to rapture from the earth His faithful who do not become apostates. The apostates in the mass falling away, He spews out of His mouth dooming them to suffer the great tribulation. Then they will be saved after their Gomer experience of the world turning against them which will lead to the return to their first love (Jesus) and salvation.

Grave: The burial place in the ground for the physically dead body.

Great apostasy: The great falling away, rebellion (2Th 2:3), of Christians who reject the Lord's Spirit and His chosen two witnesses and as a result will be *left behind* to endure the great tribulation.

Great Multitude: Are all of the Christians (the apostate Christians who repent of their unfaithfulness) that die, as a result of their faithfulness in Christ during the 3½ years of the great tribulation. They will eventually be raised from the dead as celestial humans and be called up to meet Jesus in the sky immediately preceding His return to the earth in the second rapture, along with those believers who faithfully survived the great tribulation while standing firm on their profession of Jesus, not taking the mark of the beast, and not worshiping the beast during the great tribulation.

Great Tribulation: It is the greatest time of trial and suffering, persecution and judgment over the *Church Corrupt,* the apostates who are left behind to endure this time, in an effort to persuade them from being apostates. Jesus tells us it is a mercy to purify God's elect in an effort to yet save them as His elect. Jesus likens it as a time to be purified like gold in the furnace during this time period (Rev 3:18-19). The global desolation is the great tribulation. It is the silence or inactivity for the first half of the 7-year period of God's wrath poured out on the earth. When Heaven will be silent the antichrist will rule the earth (Rev 8:1).

Hades: The temporary confinement for the disembodied or naked souls—the realm of the dead.

Harvest: reaping of souls on the earth for God's Eternal Kingdom (Revelation 14)

> **Harvest of Wheat (first harvest):** symbolic depiction of the *Church Pure* being raptured at the onset of the great tribulation (Rev 14:14-16).
>
> **Harvest of Grapes (second harvest):** symbolizes the wrath of God being poured out on Babylon in the *Church Corrupt*, the apostates, resulting in a multitude of souls being saved to populate Heaven. Revelation likens this multitude as grapes crushed in a wine press resulting in a river of blood 200 miles long. Those martyred for their profession during the great tribulation (Rev 14:17-20).

Hearken: To attentively listen, not just "hear."

Heaven: The dwelling place of God, the celestial realm. An eternal realm of peace, love, and glory. Also, where the righteous humans reside after this life.

Hell (Gehenna): A compartment of Hades (the realm of the dead) for the souls who are being held over to be resurrected, judged on the last day, and thrown alive into the lake of fire, doomed to endure a permanent but second death.

Holy Spirit: The Holy Spirit of God released through the death of Christ on the cross. He is alive on the earth in and with the saints of God who have repented and have received Christ's gift of salvation through the remission of sin. He is the comforter, counselor, advocate, stand by, wisdom of God, and attributes of God; the Holy Spirit is the Spirit of Christ returned to embody his bride, the Church, His body in the earth, His believers who He is in union with as one.

Idol worship (idolatry): Worship of idols, which are images or representatives or deities, or excessive admiration of a person, or thing. It can also be excessive devotion to material things, worldly achievements, or self-worship. Nimrod was the first to introduce idol worship post-flood.

Jesus: The Word of God, the Son of God, the manifestation of God, the Messiah, the Savior of the World. Having sacrificed His life on the cross for the salvation of men, He will return to the earth to rule for 1,000 years over both the natural and supernatural realm. He is currently seated on His throne in the eternal realm at the right hand of His Father possessing a celestial body but is likewise active and embodied in the earth via His Spirit that abides in his faithful believers. He will continue to rule eternally in the new heavens and the new earth which are yet to come. He is the Spirit of Prophecy, and the Author and Finisher of our faith.

John: Apostle of Christ, author of the book of Revelation, author of the gospel of John and the letters he wrote to the Churches that are a part of the cannon of the Bible.

Judgment: God's divine verdict and pronouncement, legal decision, and final reckoning.

> **First judgment:** In the garden when Eve and Adam ate the fruit of the knowledge of good and evil (Gen 3).
>
> **Second judgment:** Global flood (Genesis 6-9)
>
> **Third judgment:** Started a few generations after the flood with Nimrod and his antichrist movement. It ends with Nimrod and his antichrist movement at the battle of Armageddon (Rev 6:1-8).
>
> **Final judgment:** Last Day when all will rise and be judged, all flesh, the earth, and natural universe will be destroyed. All people who ever drew breath will rise and be separated as sheep and goats. Goats will go to eternal damnation in the lake of fire. Sheep will go to eternal salvation in the new heavens and the new earth (Mt 25:31-46, Rev 20:11-15).

Lake of Fire: The eternal destination of everything which will not survive the last day of judgment becoming extinct forever (the earth, the universe, all it's physical elements (matter), natural humans (bodies of the dead), Hades, fallen angels, demons, fallen humans, even death itself. It is the instrument of the second death.

Last Day (Day of Judgment): The day of judgment at the end of time when ALL humanity will arise to be judged by God. Some to everlasting life, others to eternal damnation in the lake of fire. Mt 25: 31-46, Rev 20:11-15).

Millenium Reign (1,000-Year Reign of Christ): The celestial comes down to the natural realm to rule the mortal men of the world led by King Jesus, having sole rulership and dominion over mortal men as King of the Israelites. The Lord brings with Him His own city to rule from, the New Jerusalem, complete with its own hill to rest on. All of which are not constructed of physical matter from this world but of spiritual matter from the celestial realm. And with Him when He touches down is His entourage consisting of His Father, His army angels, and His bride, the celestial humans. Those in covenant relationship with Him who will co-rule and be the ministers of His government, including those who lived and died while hanging on to their testimony during the great tribulation. This was a position in His Kingdom that the Jews had rejected when they had rejected Jesus. It is a time period promised to the patriarchs of old fulfilled for the Lord's Chosen People, even though they are merely mortal citizens and not the celestial humans who co-rule with Him. When His Kingdom touches down Jesus will have His wedding feast in the city, the New Jerusalem for a time, while outside the city walls is 24-7 darkness, weeping, and gnashing of teeth, people begging to enter in the city to no avail. As the wedding feast is taking place the devil, the false prophet (the Pope), and the antichrist (risen Nimrod, the beast), will seduce the entire globe, (his kingdom) together and march on the New Jerusalem to the place of Armageddon for a battle of dominance over control of planet earth. When the feast is over the Lord will come out of the city to meet them in battle with his army angels and celestial humans behind. Only the Lord single handedly with the words out of His mouth slays all who have gathered to oppose him. The false prophet (the Pope), and the antichrist (risen

Nimrod, the beast) are prematurely thrown into the Lake of Fire 1,000 years before anyone else will enter. The devil is chained and confined in the Abyss for a thousand years, the mortal men that followed them into battle, die. Scavenger birds feast on the bodies which is called in the Bible, "The Great Supper of God." Their naked souls are confined in Hades awaiting the day of judgment. Immediately following the battle of Armageddon, the Lord takes command of the entire globe and all the nations establishing His Kingdom on earth as the Messiah and defender of the Israelites re-establishing their nation with representation from all 12 tribes. This starts His 1,000-year millennial reign when all nations will be required pay tribute to Israel. A time that brings back to earth utopian conditions and healing, including the river of life that flows from the New Jerusalem bringing healing to the nations and making the dead sea teem with life. The Millenium Reign ushers in freedom from the curse of the Four Horsemen as defeated by Jesus. The Lord's Kingdom on earth ends with the final battle of Gog Magog. When the devil is released from the Abyss to lead this final battle of opposition to weed out all who would still oppose the Lord before the books are closed. Then sometime after, the earth is destroyed by fire, and the last day comes with the Judgement of the living and the dead, the Lord continues His Kingdom in the celestial realm for eternity.

> **Note:** His city, the New Jerusalem, will not be destroyed or the celestial beings in it when every element of the universe was dissolved in the fire, because neither the city, the hill it sat on, nor the celestial beings were made of physical matter and the end of natural universe.

Narrative: a spoken or written account of connected events; a story. In this book the word "narrative" is used to distinguish between the different accounts of prophetic history in the book of Revelation of which there are four narratives. The story of Revelation is told four times over and is not one continuous story, as most take for granted it is. This style of writing Revelation is akin to the way the Gospel is told, with four different narratives.

First Narrative: (Rev 6:1-11:18): Reveals the execution of God's plan for redemption and judgement according to the structure of sevens. Breaking of the seven seals on the scroll.

Second Narrative: (Rev 11:19-16:21): Begins when Adam and Eve sinned. It opens this narrative with the reaction in Heaven when they sinned. The theme is to introduce us to the main players of Revelation who altered history and form the story of humanity. The temple of God, the Ark of the Covenant, the Woman Clothed with the Sun, The Red Dragon, The beast out of the sea, the beast out of the earth, the Lamb and the 144,000. After introducing the main characters, this second narrative skips forward to the new beginning post-flood with the 8 on the ark introducing and giving context to the rest of the main characters and their role in human fate and alignment. Then the narrative tells the rest of the story in sequential order.

Third Narrative (Rev 17:1-21:8): Covers in great detail what happens during the 6th and 7th seals, beginning with the corruption of the Church, then beyond, to the end.

Fourth Narrative (Rev 21:9-22:21): This final narrative is the shortest one, concerning itself with life eternal and where we will live life when all is said and done. John begins with the New Jerusalem and the 1,000-year reign, the last day, then the promise that awaits afterwards. This fourth narrative finishes with closing words from both Jesus and John.

Nephilim: The Bible tells us that they are hybrid beings created from celestial beings and human women. They were known also as giants, men of renown, the demigods of mythology. The flood was meant to wipe them out as well as the people who had genes in their DNA that were from these giants. Because of their great stature and strength, they dominated humans and taught them dark spiritual arts, war, metallurgy (weapons), astrology, and cosmetics. They took for themselves whatever women they fancied and eventually ate humans. Mythologies around the world have stories of cannibalistic giants and they are most likely the roots of cannibalism in some of the tribes around the world.

> **Note:** homosexuals quite often blame God for their condition siting that there is a homosexual gene assuming God created it. When the celestial beings procreated with natural women it is important to keep in mind that celestial beings, by nature, do not procreate and therefore do not have genders. Jesus verified that when correcting the Pharisees about husbands and wives in the afterlife. *Mt 22:30 At the resurrection people will neither marry nor be given in marriage; they will be like the angels in heaven* (genderless). God did not create humans with homosexual genes, or hermaphrodites, the mixing of the celestial and physical humans created these and all other genetic defects, and humanity suffers from this abomination to this very day.

New Covenant: The New Covenant was instituted by God to reconcile man to Himself in order to save as many as possible before the destruction of the earth. There was a previous covenant (the Old Covenant), but because of a defect in man it proved insufficient to save (as told in the book of Hebrews). The New Covenant provides a spiritual union, a spiritual marriage between Jesus and believers who become guided by His will while dying to their own and thus become together one whole person. The Lord died to His body in this world and the believer dies to his life in the body, living for the expression of His Spirit in the world. Thus, Christians are called His bride and His body. This is a literal, not metaphoric, description of the relationship between Christ and His elect.

New Jerusalem: A city made out of supernatural matter that supersedes the natural world where the Lord and the Father reside in the celestial/heavenly realm. It will descend to the natural world and rest on the location of the current Jerusalem for the Lord's 1,000-year reign. Although that is the case, it will not eliminate or interfere with the natural city of Jerusalem because the New is of different matter than that of the physical world. It will occupy the same space in two different frequencies of existence. It will then depart this earth when all of natural matter is destroyed, continuing eternally in the celestial realm, a part of the New Heavens and New Earth.

Nimrod (beast out of the sea, the antichrist): the grandson of Canaan the son of Noah, who Ham fathered by having sex with His mother (Noah's wife), Canaan was cursed by Noah for this reason. Through continued incestual hybriding the giant genes, possessed by the wife of Ham, Nimrod was born a giant. He was the first king on the earth causing the whole world to rebel against God post-flood. He was the first conqueror of nations. When he comes back from the dead, he will rule the earth as antichrist for 7 years and will be defeated by Christ at the battle of Armageddon. He will gather the world in rebellion to fight against the Lord in that final battle of Armageddon. He will be defeated and will be the first to be thrown into the lake of fire 1,000 years before the rest of the unsalvageable humans and fallen celestial beings.

Post-flood (New Beginning): Era of time beginning after the ark of Noah landed on dry land and the judgment of water was completed. Humanity started over from the 8 survivors on that ark.

Pre-flood: Era of time from beginning of creation including the fall in the garden of Eden through the corruption and breakdown of God's design over mankind and the animal kingdom resulting in the flood. All events occurring before the flood. Time period of giants (Nephilim), dinosaurs and abominable perversions of natural and supernatural roamed the earth.

Rapture: A calling up to heaven from earth living humans that, in transition, metamorphize from having natural bodies to celestial bodies. There are two raptures spoken of in the Bible.

> **Pre-tribulation rapture** (harvest of wheat, first rapture): a rapture that occurs when the global desolation known as the great tribulation comes, and Jesus removes His Spirit from the earth for 3 ½ years. It will occur at the same time that the two witnesses are raised back to life then called up. Those who are one with His Spirit will go up to heaven, the harvest of wheat (Rev 14: 14-16). Those left-behind will endure the

great tribulation (Rev 14:18-20). This event will happen 1,335 days after the mid-point of the last week of years, 45 days after the return of Nimrod, the abomination that causes desolation (Da 12:11, 12).

Post-tribulation rapture (harvest of grapes, second rapture)**:** a rapture that occurs after the great multitude are resurrected from the dead and walk the earth for an undetermined time, then are called up to Heaven along with those who are still alive on the earth with a mark of God protecting them from the wrath being poured out on to the world (1Th 4:13-18) they are the grapes of the harvest in Rev 14:18-20.

Red Dragon (the Devil)**:** Is the deceiver, the architect and spirit of rebellion against God. He is the father of lies, and is both the tempter and the accuser of the brethren.

Redemption: Being saved from the bondage of sin through Christ's death as our ransom.

Religion of Cain: A co-exist religion that seeks harmony outside of God giving acceptance without conformity to the divine structure of God's design and purposes and rules started with and by Cain.

Resurrection/Resurrected: when a disembodied soul is raised from Hades (the realm of the dead) with a new body. On the third day following Jesus' crucifixion, Jesus rose from the dead and appeared to His disciples and many others in the earth prior to His rapture to Heaven 40 days later. He was lifted up on a cloud, and we are told that He will return the same way.

The first recorded Resurrection: preceded the First resurrection. This resurrection immediately followed Jesus' death on the cross when the tombs of many holy people broke open and were raised from the dead and walked the earth before they ascended to Heaven as the train of Jesus' robe to be with the Father (Mt 27:52-53). They are the first fruits of the redeeming work of Jesus. They are those under the altar in the paradisiacal place of Hades (Abraham's bosom), who were given clean white robes (celestial bodies) and told to wait for justice. They are the 144,000, 12,000 from every tribe of Israel, the first fruits.

The first Resurrection: as called in the Bible occurs 7 years after the start of the great tribulation. When those who were martyred for their testimony of Jesus during the first 3½ years called the great tribulation rise from the dead and join those who stood firm on their testimony but survived. Together, in the days before the 7th trumpet blows, they receive their celestial bodies and ascend to meet Jesus in the sky, joining Him in His return. Along with all the other celestial humans they come down and rule the earth with Jesus for 1,000 years (Rev 20:5-6).

Final Resurrection: This happens on the last day when all the living suddenly find themselves disembodied when with a thunderous crash every natural element in the universe melts in the final judgment of fire. Everyone who ever lived in all of history and is disembodied, confined in Hades, along with those who died on the last day will receive a celestial body and face judgment before God. This is the end of mortal men. Those approved will go on to everlasting life in the new heavens and earth in the celestial realm. Those not found worthy will be condemned to a second death by being thrown alive into the lake of fire for eternity (Mt 25: 31-46).

Salvation: The deliverance of sin and what results from sin including bondage, death, and separation from God achieved through putting your faith in Jesus Christ.

Seven bowls: the set of seven bowls of wrath described in Revelation 16 poured out on to the earth by seven angels to avenge those who persecuted God's elect during the great tribulation. This occurs in the last 3 ½ years of God's 7 years of wrath. The bowls symbolize the finality and perfection of judgment against Babylon in the world (the kingdom of the beast). The first half of those 7 years of wrath is against Babylon in the Church—the apostates who join the Pope and his antichrist aligning with them against the Lord and His two witnesses. The bowls are poured out as the seven trumpets release each segment/bowl of wrath. The trumpets are told about in one narrative. The same event described in another narrative speaks of the ensuing bowels/plagues poured out after the corresponding trumpet is blown. They are not 2 separate events, as many would believe. Knowing that there are 4 narratives of the same story in Revelation using 4 different perspectives surrounding their own main subject, goes a long way in recognizing when the same event is described using different wording and perspective.

> **Bowl 1:** Sores break out on those who have the mark of the beast and worship him (Rev16:2).
>
> **Bowl 2:** The sea turns into blood, and all living things in the sea die (Rev16:3).
>
> **Bowl 3:** The rivers and springs of water turn to blood (Rev 16:4).
>
> **Bowl 4:** The sun scorches people with fire (Rev 16:8).
>
> **Bowl 5:** The entire world is first moved into the spirit realm like a baby's head crowning out of the birth cannel, causing 8 hours of daylight, 8 hours of night sky, and 8 hours of the spiritual realm where there are no heavenly bodies to illuminate the earth with light. That is except for the heavenly sight of Jesus arraying with His entourage while preparing to return to the earth. What follows is as a baby fully exiting the womb into the world, the earth fully enters into the celestial realm and is plunged into total darkness— no light of the sun, no reflected light of the moon, no light from the stars, all of which is left behind in the physical universe where the earth is no more. This causes people to grope about in pitch blackness, while in agony, and pain, blaspheming God from those who insist on cursing God, not repenting of their ways (Rev16:10-11).

Bowl 6: The Euphrates River is dried up preparing the way for the kings of the East.

Bowl 7: A great earthquake destroys cities and mountains, and hailstones weighing around 100 pounds fall from the sky (Rev 16:17-21).

Seven Lampstands: Represent the Spirit of His bride among the seven Churches throughout the history of the *Church Age*. Jesus walks among them throughout time, warning the Spirit of His bride of the errors of her ways and admonishing to turn back to Him before it is too late. Within those individual lampstands burn the Spirit of the bride. When the full number of individuals who are to embody that Spirit, currently embodied in those lampstands, He will then have the fullness of the souls and faces that the Lord will love and call His own, His bride. When that number has been achieved, the Spirit that currently burns in those lampstands will finally be in the hearts of His elect and no longer in those lampstands. The Lord knows the Spirit of His bride intimately, but until it is fully embodied in the hearts of his people, He cannot enjoy it until it is adopted, having the faces and personalities, and souls of those who would accept His Spirit into their hearts and be His bride.

Seven Letters of Revelation: The seven letters of Revelation are a compilation of letters written by Jesus (through John) to His Church giving prophetic insight concerning its current condition and the direction it is taking throughout history future. Each letter describes what Jesus is approving of, and what He is warning against. They express His double-edged sword (words) that give life, and words that give judgment. These letters, likewise, reveal the characteristics of His person to each specific Church, especially those of Him that reflect authority over the admonitions He gives to each church. Throughout these letters Jesus reveals the future progression of His Church, encouraging her, but warning her at the same time that she has left her first love and is serving herself. Babylon enters the Church like a cancer until he finally must divorce her in the final or 7th *Church Age* because she rejects Him, becoming apostates in spiritual adultery, unfaithful to Him, giving Him the right to spew her out of His mouth (divorce). Out of love and in a last-ditch effort to cause her to return to Him, He gives the unfaithful apostates over to the world they chase after, just as Hosea did to his wife Gommer. He does this while causing her lovers (the world) to turn against her, in hopes that she will return to her first love (Jesus). It is for this purpose that the Lord gives the *Church Corrupt* over to the *great tribulation*.

> **Church in Ephesus:** First *Church Age*. She is persevering while doing good works, however, she has lost her first love, which is the root cause of every problem and seduction the church faces going forward in time. The Nicolaitans are infecting the Church is an example of this. The Church of Ephesus, at this point, is resisting and is appalled by them.
>
> **Church in Smyrna:** Second *Church Age* when the Lord acknowledges her works, her oppression, and poverty, describing her as rich in the Kingdom of God. Warning her to not fear what she is about to suffer, great persecution, even telling her how long she will have to suffer, 10 days. Each day represents the rulership of one Caesar of the Roman Empire. It is with the eleventh, Caesar, Constatine, that her persecution ends. Likewise, her persecution lasts for 10 years. The Lord ends this letter encouraging her by informing her that He will give her the crown of life for her faithfulness even to death.
>
> **Church in Pergamum:** Third *Church Age* Jesus gives credit for being strong and faithful in the face of persecution during the second *Church Age*, but we also see the devil's plan to infiltrate the ranks by seducing the people unwilling to fully conform to God's will, co-mingling the ways of the Roman Empire with the Church, in this age. As the old saying goes, "if you can't beat'em, join'em," thus the devil spreads darnell among the good seed the Apostles planted. The ways of the Romans included sexual activities as a part of their worship of false gods. It is this that was being introduced into the Christian "lovefeast." Obviously, they were perverting the kind of love Jesus promoted by making it something sexual. The Nicolaitans promoted and practiced such

activities. He warns against this *Church Age* for their spiritual adultery, that He will make war against her with the sword of His mouth. The Church has officially lost her first love. 300 AD Constanine brings the ways of Balaam into the Church government, seducing her into becoming a power in the secular world by Constantine declaring Christianity as the state religion. However, because of Constanine, the martyrdom of Christians stop, thereby causing Christians to lose sight of the first-century Christianity Jesus and the Apostles spread and practiced.

Church of Thyatira: Fourth *Church Age* and is the most profoundly pivotal of all the Church ages. Jezebel has entered the Church through Constantine we see in the third *Church Age,* however, Pope Leo III seals the deal on December 25, 800AD by crowning king Charlamagne the king of the Franks, emperor of the Roman Empire, reviving it from its destruction a few hundred years earlier. This officially makes the Church the 7th kingdom of the beast, the Church, ruled by the Pope, is officially the great prostitute and Babylon enters the Church who uses it as her power to rule and enforce her domination. Jesus warns against this Church age that because of her vial terrible deeds, conquering, torturing, killing, becoming a world power, He will intervene. The Lord states that He will put her children (the congregates and subjects of the Roman Catholic Church) on a bed of suffering and kill them. The reason being is because of their complacency and compliance with the departure from the Lord and reliance on the Holy Spirit. Instead, the Church is now empowered by the beast through Pope Leo III. Because of spiritual adultery, the Lord's Church is seduced, even hijacked, becoming the head of the Holy Roman Empire and thus she is the great prostitute, and she is the woman who rides (is empowered by) the beast. This warning of the Lord to the followers of the Catholic Church was fulfilled by the Black Plague some 1,100 years after the Lord prophesied and warned through John's book of Revelation, which went brazenly unheeded. The Black Death killed an estimated 30% to 66% of Europe's population between 1347 and 1351, wiping out tens of millions causing a loss of faith and trust in the Catholic Church. While at the same time this disaster became the very catalyst of the ensuing Reformation, including nations and kings taking themselves out from under the spiritual authority of the Catholic Church.

Church of Sardis: Jesus is officially saying that the Church is dead spiritually and they don't even know it. He tells them to "Wake up! Strengthen what remains and is about to die, for I have not found your deeds complete in the sight of my God." The Church is deluded and thinks itself to be alive and well and serving. Even after the Lord's judgment of the Bubonic (Black) Plague, the Church is still dead, only now, it is showing its cracks and greed. The Church enjoys world dominance and holds the hearts and souls of men in the palm of her hands, but the people are quickly becoming disillusioned. This fifth Church age begins in the aftermath of the Black Plague around 1400AD. The Lord sends His prophets and reformers to speak up and expose the Church, leading to the Reformation Movement. A demand for change and renewal cries out from the voices of such men like for example, Luther, Calvin, Huss, Tyndale, George Fox, and many others to break from the corruption and strive to return to first-century values of Christianity by calling people out of the *Church Corrupt. Remember, therefore, what you have received and heard; obey it, and repent,* the Lord admonishes this Church age. The Bible previously was kept from the common people, with church leadership believing it would be like casting pearls before swine. Putting their lives on the line, the reformers issued copies of the Bible making it available to the common people, translating it in the vernacular for everyone to study for themselves. The Church resisted by burning at the stake those who made it available to the common people.

Church of Philadelphia: The Church age that, as a result of the Reformation, finally brought the Church back to her *first love* and first-century values. The pinnacle of the Reformation came through George Fox and the Quakers in

1647AD, England. The Quakers sacrificed their lives in this world and refused to bow down to any of the ways the government and the Church of England demanded that countermanded the teachings of Jesus. Although compliant with the law, they refused to idolize people or officials by things as common as calling authority figures, Lord, or to bow down to them, nor to call buildings the Church, but they insisted that the Church was the people who embodied the Spirit through obedience to Him. These seemingly small things, during those times, caused them to be thrown in jail and persecuted constantly. Eventually William Penn was given an inheritance of Pennsylvania by the king of England to pay a debt the king owed to Penn's deceased father. Coincidentally, they named its center or capital, Philadelphia. The Quakers found religious freedom there. They designed their government in line with biblical principles, which not only caused its citizens to prosper far above other colonies, but became a model that the United States government, in large part, designed itself after. Not superficially seen, but the blessings and prosperity this country enjoys from the Creator, are due to the godly Quaker social structure and the works they have accomplished in their act to ease the worldwide suffering of mankind. The Quakers spoke out against the *Church Corrupt* and lived a sustained life of quiet prayer, being moved by a first-century New Covenant understanding of Christianity. They obeyed not their own ambitions, but the Lord and His Spirit promptings, as interpreted through their conscience. They lived not for this world, but for the world to come. In the contemporary world when one approaches adulthood and graduates school, they are asked what they are going to do with the rest of their lives, what career they intend to pursue? How they will achieve success in this world? However, when Quakers reach maturity, they ponder how and what part of the world they feel called to serve humanity and ease their suffering. The percentage of Quakers who become missionaries is infinitely greater than other Christians from different denominations. They successfully brought a contingency of the Church back, becoming the *Church Pure*. The Lord finds nothing wrong with this Church age that produced the Quaker Church headquartered in Philadelphia, PA, and admonishes them to hold tight to everything they have attained because He is coming soon!

Church of Laodicea: This is the Church age that we find ourselves in during these contemporary times! In this final letter and because the end is in sight, Jesus addresses the elect who are of the *Church Corrupt* (the worldly church, the church of Babylon). There was something recaptured during the sixth Church age that was pure, even if it did not correct the entire body of Christians. Otherwise, this age would not be the precursor to the great falling away—the apostasy. In fact, even the Quakers have splintered into different groups, some calling themselves Quakers but have taken on the ways of the worldly church. Nevertheless, it did make a course correction that has affected the entire Church pointing it in the right direction. However, for many it is too little too late because the salvation and judgment of God is a moving train speeding towards its completion. It is through this age that the Lord is bringing back to a head the dividing enmity and distinction between those who desire to do His will, and those who desire to do the will of their own (as He declared in the garden). It has been the nature of the world to blur those lines, but the adversarial stances of these two opposing world views will be forced to a crossroad that every individual will have to choose sides—thus the end. The *Church Corrupt* will, by their decisions, show themselves either for or against, lovers of the will of God or apostates. It is then, at this apex, that the end will come, but not before Jesus spews them out of His mouth by granting the divorce they seek in their spiritual adultery. Those who ignore His admonishment to, *come out of her my people, so that you will not share in her sins, so that you will not receive any of her plagues; for her sins are piled up to heaven, and God has remembered her crimes* will indeed share in her suffering. He will rapture the *Church Pure* to insulate them from her suffering and condemn the apostates to endure the *great tribulation* in hopes they will finally return to their *first love*—Jesus—and be saved.

Seven seals: Reveals God's plan of execution for redemption and judgment through the *structure of sevens*. It seals the fate of humanity, the world, and the entire universe (Rev 5-6).

> **Seals 1-4:** The release of the four horsemen also known as the four horsemen of the apocalypse, or the winds of God's destruction are the initial installment of the judgment of fire that will destroy mankind forever, saving those only who would receive salvation. This judgment was released during the time of Nimrod due to rebellious man who unanimously put themselves under him, the antichrist, who brazenly proclaimed, "Do as you will and I will protect you from God." We have and will continue, to the end, suffer under these curses and granted powers. By the demonstrations of His miracles, Jesus showed Himself as the true Savior by exerting an authority over every plague we suffer under by the power granted to the devil and his antichrist—the four horsemen.
>
>> **Seal 1:** White horse with a rider given bow given a crown to conquer (Rev 6:1-2).
>>
>> **Seal 2:** Fiery red horse with a rider given power to make war (Rev 6:3-4).
>>
>> **Seal 3:** Black horse with a rider given a scale to judge the measure of necessities people receive or are withheld. However, this horse is given limitations on his cruelty and deprivation when it comes to the power to destroy or withhold (Rev 6:5-6).
>>
>> **Seal 4:** Pale green (like a corpse) horse and its rider, death, given power to prematurely kill an ongoing ¼ of the population of earth by means of the powers granted the other horsemen—war, famine, plague (pestilence, disease), and wild beasts of the earth (Rev 6:7-8).

Seal 5: Is the redemption of God amidst His judgment. It is when the Lord dies on the cross to save mankind. It is here at the fifth seal that Jesus becomes the sacrificial Lamb of God by dying on the cross. When returning to His Father in heaven He brought with Him the 144,000, the first fruits, parading in heaven before the Father the resulting triumph of His redeeming work (Rev 6:9-11).

Seals 6 and 7: Wrath poured out on Babylon on the earth (Rev 6:12-17)

Seal 6: Wrath of God poured out first on Babylon in the Church, or the *Church Corrupt* which are those apostates left behind to endure the great tribulation. It is the first segment imposed by God for the first 3 ½ years of the 7 years of wrath which is preparation for the return of Christ. This time of punishment is facilitated by those in the world led by the returned antichrist, the Pope, and the 10 nations who rule the globe and are under the authority of the antichrist.

Seal 7: The second half or last 3 ½ years of God's wrath poured out on Babylon in the world directed against those who opposed and killed God's elect. It begins with the release of the seventh trumpet blasts which are the progressive release of their punishment. These punishments are facilitated by cosmic events and supernatural beings loosed on the earth ending with the return of Christ and His entourage of celestial humans; many of which they had just finished killing during the first 3 ½ years.

Seven Stars: Represent seven specific angels that have been assigned to oversee each individual Church age throughout history as described in His seven letters written by Jesus in Rev 2:1-7.

Seven Trumpets: A new cycle of seven within the seventh seal. It is the justice that the 144,000 disembodied souls under the altar requested at the time they received their clean white robes, their celestial bodies. It is when they were told they would have to wait a little while until the full numbers of their brothers are martyred, finally fulfilled during the great tribulation. It is the judgment of God against those who hated and killed His elect—the global kingdom of the beast, Babylon (Rev 8: 11:15-19). It also precedes the return of Christ.

> **First trumpet:** Hail, fire, and blood hurled down, destroying a third of the earth, trees, and grass burned up (Rev 8:7).
>
> **Second trumpet:** A burning mountain thrown into the sea, turning a third of it to blood, a third of sea creatures die, a third of ships destroyed (Rev 8:8).
>
> **Third trumpet:** A great star called Wormwood poisons freshwater making the water poisonous/bitter causing many people to die and making fresh water scarce (Rev 8:10).
>
> **Fourth trumpet:** A third of the sun, moon, and stars are darkened. It is at this time that the earth is pushed up out of the physical realm and into the spiritual realm. At first, one-third, like a baby's head crowning out of the womb. This results in a shift of our 24-hour day: 8 hours of the day sky with the sun, 8 hours of the night sky with the stars and moon, then 8 hours of the spiritual realm, each from horizon to horizon. Eventually it shifts entirely into the spiritual realm, bringing the earth to a place of total darkness with no illuminating bodies to shine light on it. However, one only needs to look up to see the sight of the Lord gathering His entourage before descending back to the earth causing people to panic. Eventually at the Lord's return, He will be the light of the world, and light will shine out from inside of Him. This fourth trumpet comes with a warning of the three "woes" that are yet to come (Rev 8:12-13).
>
> **Fifth trumpet (first woe):** the devil is thrown out of Heaven down to the earth. On his way, he releases out of the Abyss, bringing with him an army of demonic locust-like creatures

to torment those on the earth who do not have the seal of God. They sting the people with scorpion like stings causing them to suffer from those stings for five months (Rev 9:1-12).

Sixth trumpet (second woe): Again from the Abyss an army of 200 million demonic creatures kills 1/3 of humanity, except for those who have the mark of God, those who were faithful to their testimony during the great tribulation (Rev 9:13-21).

Seventh trumpet (third woe): This trumpet marks the end of the seven years of wrath poured out on Babylon in the earth. In the days before it sounds the resurrection from the dead occurs of those killed during the great tribulation. Then together with those who survived and received a mark of protection from God are raptured to the sky joining Jesus before His return. As a part of this trumpet blast, the Lord returns to the earth with His entourage and the supernatural city, the New Jerusalem to have His wedding feast, then take possession of the government of the earth, beginning His 1,000-year Kingdom. One may ask, where is the woe in that? The woe is that the world will resist His takeover. They will organize themselves into a great army and march against the Lord. And at the battle of Armageddon by the His words of His mouth, He will annihilate all those who would stop Him from establishing His Kingdom on the earth. (Rev 11:15-19).

Sheol (Hades, realm of the dead): Temporary confinement for disembodied souls.

Son (Son of God, Son of Man, Word of God, Jesus): The one and only offspring of the Father, Jesus, the Messiah. The Savior of the World sent to pay the wrath due to fallen man making reconciliation between man and the Father, facilitating eternal salvation. The Word of God.

Soul (mind): The essence of a man, the real man. This is what Jesus came to die and save eternally. It is the personality, the seat of decision, the intellect, rationale, and the conscience. Better known as the mind of the man.

Soul power (emotional power): using self-empowerment, intellectual power, to fulfill agendas in life. Source of witchcraft as opposed to subordination to God's Spirit and being moved by His will and one with His Spirit.

spirit: an invisible or unmanifested force of consciousness and life power that gives the soul awareness and animates the body whether celestial or physical.

Spiritual adultery: doing any deed that breaks union with Christ and His Spirit.

Spiritual Union: Being the bride of Christ by receiving His Spirit into one's heart. Being the body of Christ in the world and the expression of His invisible Spirit through one's life. True intimacy and expression of oneness as the bride of Christ in the earth is to obey every prompting of His Spirit. To obey is our act of intimacy with the Lord, the better we do so, the more in oneness we are with Him. It is the New Covenant relationship with Christ.

Structure of Sevens: The order and organization of God, with seven representing divine perfection and completion. His process and organization of it divided into 7 segments or cycles.

Twelve Stars: The twelve stars of the crown on the head of the woman clothed with the sun described in Rev 12:1 are the twelve tribes of Israel who paved the way for the Messiah to come into the world. They are Eve's (the woman clothed with the sun) crowning achievement after having brought sin then death into the world.

Two Witnesses: key figures in the end times called to prophesy for 1,260 days clothed in sackcloth. They are the witnesses of the Lord given to the world as both a last effort to save those who would listen from enduring the end time plagues about to be poured out on the world, and to widen the blurred gap between true believers and those who would by their own choice become apostates. To separate the wheat from the darnel to be burned with a purifying fire for the end times harvest. Those who would be saved are also represented as the harvest of wheat and grapes. The two witnesses will preach repentance, exposing the facade of the Church. They will call down judgment and fire as they deem fitting to complete their mission and message and thus pronounce and widen the gap between the faithful and the apostates. They are the two olive trees, lampstands, standing between the Lord and the earth. If anyone tries to harm them fire comes from their mouths to devour their enemies. They have the power to shut up the skies, turn water to blood, and strike the earth with plagues. It is only the risen Nimrod the beast, the abomination that causes desolation, who will come and kill them, thereby facilitating the global desolation that brings on the rapture of the faithful and the great tribulation of the apostates. (Rev 11:1-6).

Wedding Feast: the promised and anticipated Wedding Supper of the Lamb. It is when Jesus, the bridegroom, and His bride, the Church, have their long-anticipated celebration of a wedding feast at their return to the earth in the New Jerusalem (including both Jesus and His celestial humans who have died but are now alive and complete in numbers). Meanwhile, outside the wall of the New Jerusalem on the earth, the world suffers, groping around in total darkness and plots to destroy them in a battle—the battle of Armageddon.

Wisdom (vs. Intelligence): is a set of values by which to perceive through. Wisdom is a faculty of the spirit; it is a wordless understanding based on spirit feelings and experiences. Thus, the term experiential knowledge. Whereas intelligence is a faculty of the mind/soul and utilizes word knowledge to consider with. Wisdom, because it is a wordless reasoning, can be called instinct or a knowing. The mind/soul uses logic to organize word knowledge to conclude an understanding. However, intelligence of the mind, no matter how powerful and insightful, is always subject to spirit feelings and perceptions to work its faculties within. Faulty spirit perception results in rendering even the most superior intelligence as insufficient. The word knowledge of the mind/soul is a stable and accumulated bank of information by which to draw from. Wisdom perception, on the other hand, is wordless and can shift from self-centered to centered on the things outside of self, perceiving from a selfish light to a selfless light; from worldly/superficial perspective to a spiritual perspective. Wisdom can be like an elusive dream where you can see clearly in a spiritual moment then, the next moment, when your spirit returns to a superficial or self-centered perception, not at all remember or relate to the clarity or reasoning of the former. Understanding is always dependent on one's perception as dictated by their attitude, feelings, and worldview or the height one views things from. Since the spirit nature of man is not understood or recognized by science or psychology, they refer to it as the unconscious or subconscious mind—hidden memories. Likewise, in the human resources field, they refer to and measure an individual's spirit wisdom as EQ (emotional quotient), as opposed to IQ (intelligence quotient). They have come to realize in recent years that having a high IQ is not enough to choose potential leaders. However, ignorant of the spirit nature of a man they mistakenly accreted the emotions of the mind/soul for spirit feelings and the perception of its wisdom values as an emotional attribute of the mind. Acute wisdom values of the spirit and its perception is a far superior faculty than intelligence. A simple man with a limited vocabulary can shine and discern greater insight than one with lessor wisdom values but superior intelligence. However, they are both meant to work together in helping man perceive his world in a sound way.

Witchcraft: The practice of magic, especially for evil purposes, use of demonic spells and curses using the power of the devil, the power of the spirits of this world's current dark influences. Paul outlines: NIV *Eph 6:12* *For our struggle is not against flesh and blood, but against the rulers, against the authorities, against the powers of this dark world and against the spiritual forces of evil in the heavenly realms.* The power of witchcraft is a soulish, or emotional power by which one draws from to impose their will to achieve what they desire. The spiritual power they do tap into is from demonic spiritual forces independent and in rebellion to the Almighty as they are. That is because the individual in question, will not conform to the will of God but in every way impose their will to have what they want, drawing from spiritual beings who likewise are in stark rebellion to the will of God. Willful people out for number one are people who unwittingly tap into the powers of witchcraft just by the nature of what they will and how they impose it.

Woman Clothed with the Sun: The repentant Eve, the mother of all the living and all of her offspring that is created by God's plan to bring us salvation before the eventual destruction of the universe and the physical man. The 12 stars on her head is the crowning legacy and offspring of Israel (the 12 tribes) who usher in the Christ and His salvation by creating celestial humans from among fallen humanity, that when all is said and done excludes much of her offspring from eternal destruction. They are a people set apart for God's purposes to achieve God's salvation.

Bibliography

Abbott, S. (2015)Is there a hidden Message in Revelation 7? Why is Dan missing? Retrieved October 2017, from Reasons for Hope* Jesus:https://reasonsforhopejesus.com/is-there-a-hidden-message-in-revelation-7/

Amplified Bible. Scripture quotations marked (Amp) are taken from the Amplified Bible, Copyright © 1954, 1958, 1962, 1964, 1965, 1987 by The Lockman Foundation. Used by permission.

Good News Translation (Today's English Version, Second Edition). Scripture quotations marked (GNT) are from the Good News Translation in Today's English Version- Second Edition, Copyright © 1992 by American Bible Society. Used by Permission.

Malone, Dr. Henry (1999). *Shadow Boxing: The Dynamic 2-5-14 Strategy to Defeast the Darkness Within.* Vision Life Publications.

New American Standard. Scripture quotations marked (NAS) are taken from the NEW AMERICAN STANDARD BIBLE®, Copyright ©1960,1962,1963,1968,1971,1972,1973,1975,1977,1995 by The Lockman Foundation. Used by permission.

New International Version. Scriptures taken from the Holy Bible, New International Version®, NIV®. Copyright © 1973, 1978, 1984 by Biblica, Inc.™ Used by permission of Zondervan. All rights reserved worldwide. www.zondervan.com The "NIV" and "New International Version" are trademarks registered in the United States Patent and Trademark Office by Biblica, Inc.™

New Living Translation. Holy Bible, New Living Translation copyright © 1996, 2004, 2007 by Tyndale House Foundation. Used by permission of Tyndale House Publishers Inc., Carol Stream, Illinois 60188. All rights reserved. New Living, NLT, and the New Living Translation logo are registered` trademarks of Tyndale House Publishers.

New Revised Standard Version Bible (NRSV), copyright © 1989 National Councilof the Churches of Christ in the United States of America. Used by permission. All rights reserved worldwide.

The Holy Bible: King James Version. Scripture quotations marked (KJV) are taken from the King James Bible, which is in the public domain.

The Message Bible. Scripture quotations marked MSG are taken from *THE MESSAGE,* copyright © 1993, 1994, 1995, 1996, 2000, 2001, 2002 by Eugene H. Peterson. Used by permission of NavPress. All rights reserved. Represented by Tyndale House Publishers, Inc.

World English Bible. Scripture quotations marked (WEB) are taken from The World English Bible, which is in the public domain. Special thanks to Michael Paul Johnson and all who worked on the translation as a means to release a modern version of the Bible that is available for non-copyright use. A reminder that the Bible is not owned by man.

ABOUT THE AUTHORS

We are just a voice

^{WEB Jn 1:19} This is John's testimony (about himself), when the Jews sent priests and Levites from Jerusalem to ask him, "Who are you?"

^{WEB Jn 1:20} *He declared, and didn't deny, but he declared, "I am not the Christ."*

^{WEB Jn 1:21} *They asked him, "What then? Are you Elijah?"*

He said, "I am not."

"Are you the prophet?"

He answered, "No."

^{WEB Jn 1:22} *They said therefore to him, "Who are you? Give us an answer to take back to those who sent us. What do you say about yourself?"*

^{WEB Jn 1:23} *He said, "**I am the voice** of one crying in the wilderness, 'Make straight the way of the Lord . . ."*

True prophets in the Bible did not convince people who they were; in fact, they refused to talk about themselves. They refused to bring credibility to the words of God they spoke by trying to get people to believe who they were and trust them. They knew that it would be profaning the words of God to do so, and it would be elevating themselves above God's words. They knew that God's words have their own credibility because they are from God. And God will show them (His own words) as from Him.

God's prophets also knew that those who truly love God will, therefore, benefit from their words, and those who are lovers of themselves will not benefit from them, because they will be dismissive and not trust them. The time is over that we look at the person who speaks to decide if we believe. We must begin to discern if the words are from God and if they carry God's Spirit.

You might say to that, "but not everyone can discern God." If that is the case, then they indict themselves as not being "known" by Jesus. They unwittingly reveal about themselves that they desire to do their own will and not the Lord's, just as the religious leaders who wanted Jesus to prove His credibility so they could decide if His words were from God.

Amp Jn 7:16 Jesus answered them by saying, My teaching is not My own, but His Who sent Me.

Amp Jn 7:17 If any man desires to do His will (God's pleasure), he will know (have the needed illumination to recognize, and can tell for himself) whether the teaching is from God or whether I am speaking from Myself and of My own accord and on My own authority.

Many will think this is an oversimplified notion. However, it is so simple that it is not only true but reveals a simple but foundational truth about the person. What Jesus is saying is that if a man has a pure heart and wants to do the will of God above his own will, then what seems intuitively right (what sets well with that man) will be God's will and His words. However, even if you are a scholar, theologian, or work in the field of religion, and you desire to carry out your own will, having your own agendas and ambitions, well then, what seems right to that man is not God's will or His words, but that which lines up with his own will.

Generally speaking, the greatest religious minds in the world judge if something is from God by looking at the standing and qualifications of the man speaking them. In the above case, Jesus shows they may be smart in their own eyes, believing they know what is from God and therefore able to judge according to their knowledge of God. However, that would be saying in effect, we know everything about God because of our great knowledge. Therefore, if you say anything outside of our knowledge of God, or outside of the knowledge base of the accepted theological models, or if you are not a qualified student of those accepted models, then we must deduce your words are not from God.

To Jesus, they show about themselves that they don't recognize His words as from God because of their personal acquaintance with God. Instead, they have to judge by facts. They show themselves as having no real relationship with God; they would not recognize Him when He stands right before them. As a matter of fact, on another occasion when they showed contempt for Him, Jesus said of them:

NIV Jn 5:42 . . . *but I know you. I know that you do not have the love of God in your hearts.*

They were once again wanting Him to prove who He was, and what right He had to talk the way He did. Jesus, instead of being intimidated, marveled at how He spoke and acted out everything the Father willed, yet they did not recognize His words as His Father's. Furthermore, they were, by nature, hostile and offended towards those words.

Let's look at that closer through an illustration. For example, you have a woman who claims to be married to a man named Jim. Then, a man claiming to be Jim and her husband approaches her. The above case is like the wife doubting this man is her husband. So then, she begins to question him. For example, "If you're Jim, when were you born?" And, "What kind of car did you have when you first got your license?" If he doesn't answer to her satisfaction, she decides that he is not her husband Jim. This might seem reasonable, and if he got the answers incorrect or didn't remember, the people listening might believe her when she says, "this is not my husband."

If there was anybody in the crowd that had wisdom, they might say this begs another question, "Hey lady, are you really Jim's wife or are you an imposter?" The reasoning of the wise man is, do you really need factual evidence to know if he is your husband? Don't you know your husband when he is standing right in front of you? Jesus is marveling at the religious leaders who are supposed to know God and claim to be in union with Him. However, they don't recognize Him when He stands before them. They don't even recognize His words as from God. Do they really need factual evidence to know something that they are supposed to have intimate knowledge of? Next question, why does it not occur to anyone to question if these men of God, leaders of the Jewish faith, may be imposters because they don't judge if someone and their words are from God by their intimate knowledge of God? They need factual evidence?

What did that tell Jesus? It told Him that even the top religious leaders who know the written word by heart can't recognize God when they stand right in front of Him. It told Him that they were, in their inner man, hostile and threatened by God's words. It told Him that, in their inner selves, they really had no love or even any natural attraction towards God, His heart, and the Spirit of His words. They were obviously naturally repelled by them; they had no real love for God and their response showed it. However, to the religious leaders, they thought themselves wise and discerning to hold Jesus and His words suspect by judging Him with factual evidence. How disappointing it must have been to Jesus that the best of the best had no intimate knowledge of God and they were repulsed by Him when facing Him. Yes, Jesus' deduction was correct, there was no love of God in their hearts.

It is a Biblical fact that the major way we will be judged is it will be proven if we have a natural attraction to please God and do His will, therefore saying about us that we love Him more than ourselves. Learning by the folly of the leaders and the scholarly of Jesus' day, it is not by a knowledgeable and scholarly mind that one can successfully judge or discern what words coming from what person are from God or not. You can't judge superficially. No, it takes something much greater than to know every Bible verse by heart and to be able to have insightful knowledge of the person speaking them. It actually takes something much harder to attain than perfect scholarly knowledge of the written word. It takes a pure heart. Not meaning a sinless heart, but one which is single-minded, wanting to please God by serving Him and wanting to do His will at the expense of their own. This is what qualifies one to recognize if something is from God.

WEB Mt 5:8 *Blessed are the pure in heart, for they shall see God.*

It is true that as Colleen and I gain a larger following of our teachings and ministry, people will undoubtedly come to know us personally, and what kind of people we are. However, as teachers, we teach people how to live as spiritual men and women, discerning life in a spiritual way.

We have found the best way to teach discerning of spirit. It is not by knowing how to figure people out or to train them to have a spiritual power. No, we teach them to be single-minded when it comes to God, to be surrendered to His will in a pure or holistic way.

Having a still spirit which is not agitated with passions will create a huge contrast. The contrast of having the stillness of God's Spirit rule your heart coming in contact with the agitated spirit energies the people of this world operate out of makes one sensitive to discern spirit.

Jesus was right; wanting to do God's will with all your heart alone will cause you to recognize if one has God's Spirit in them and if they speak word's which are from God. As the saying goes, "You can't cheat an honest man."

NIV Jn 8:15 *You judge by human standards. . .*

NIV Jn 7:24 *Stop judging by mere appearances, and make a right judgment."*

As such, Colleen and I would like to be known first as a voice, just a voice. We want the words we speak from God to have more prominence and have their own credibility, than that of who we are. Therefore, we don't want to propagate people judging superficially if one is from God by giving our Bio. We want the words we speak to be more important than who we are. We want those who have a pure heart in wanting to serve God to check in their heart if we and the words we speak are from God.

We want those who don't have a pure heart to have a change of heart so they may know for themselves the voice and words of God when they hear them. However, we want to point people in the way to properly discern so they may know for themselves if we are from God and speak His words; in the same way John the Baptist tried to convey. You ask about us, and we will tell you about Him. You insist on wanting to know about us, and we will then tell you, we are just a voice making way for the One you should know and should be asking about. We are not a face or a name or people you should want to know, we are just a voice which gives voice to the One whose words you need to know.

OTHER BOOKS BY THE NAKED APOSTLES

The Christian Story
and its Message

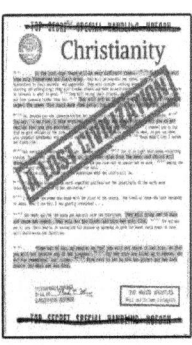

Christianity:
A Lost Civilization

For ordering information please visit our website at
www.nakedapostles.org

OTHER BOOKS BY THE NAKED APOSTLES

Understanding
the
New Covenant

revelation of Revelation:
An Urgent Message
for the Church

Volumes 1-6

For ordering information please visit our website at
www.nakedapostles.org

www.ingramcontent.com/pod-product-compliance
Lightning Source LLC
Chambersburg PA
CBHW071647160426
43195CB00012B/1385